HOW TO

Photograph

FOOD

Running Press
Hachette Book Group
1290 Avenue of the Americas, New York, NY 10104
www.runningpress.com
@Running_Press

Printed in China

Originally published in hardcover and ebook by ILEX, an imprint of Octopus Publishing Group Ltd
First U.S. Edition: October 2020

Published by Running Press, an imprint of Perseus Books, LLC, a subsidiary of Hachette Book Group, Inc.
The Running Press name and logo is a trademark of the Hachette Book Group.

The Hachette Speakers Bureau provides a wide range of authors for speaking events. To find out more, go to www.hachettespeakersbureau.com or call (866) 376-6591.

The publisher is not responsible for websites (or their content) that are not owned by the publisher.

With thanks to: Hallam Mill Studio, Manchester: pages 10, 34, 35, 56, 57, 62, and 124
The Flower Factory LDN, London: page 166
Topham Street Props: page 123

Additional photographs:© Claudia Goedke: pages 96–99, page 127 left; © Rachel Korinek: page 127 center, pages 164–167; © Eva Kosmas Flores: pages 184–187; © Linda Lomelino: pages 140–143

Print book cover by Susan Van Horn. Interior design by Hart Studio and Leonardo Collina.

Library of Congress Control Number: 2020933071

ISBNs: 978-0-7624-9962-5 (hardcover), 978-0-7624-9963-2 (ebook)

C & C

10 9 8 7 6 5 4 3 2 1

How to Photograph Food

COMPOSE, SHOOT, AND EDIT APPETIZING IMAGES

BEATA LUBAS

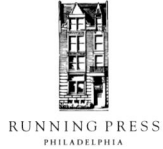

Running Press
PHILADELPHIA

Contents

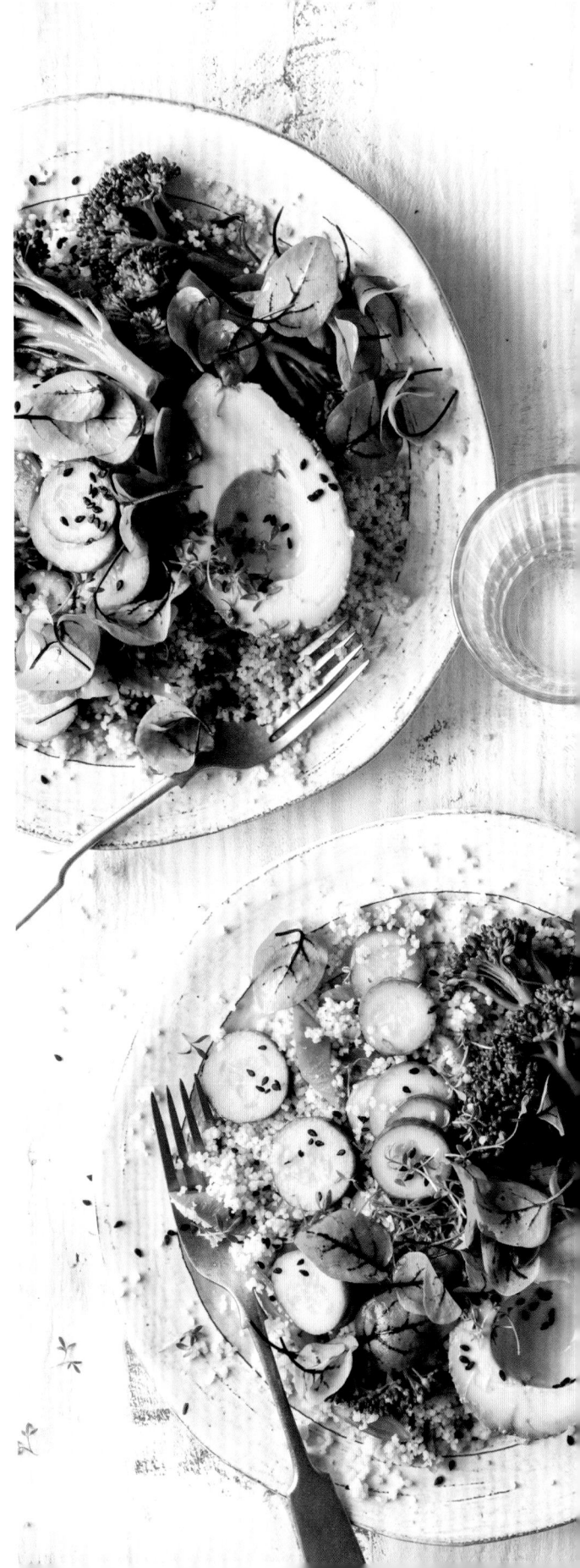

6—The Art of the Edit

7—Mindset & Growth

Plus plenty of beautiful food photos!

To you, dear photographer.
I hope this book will inspire you
on your journey and boost your
appetite to learn more.

—Bea x

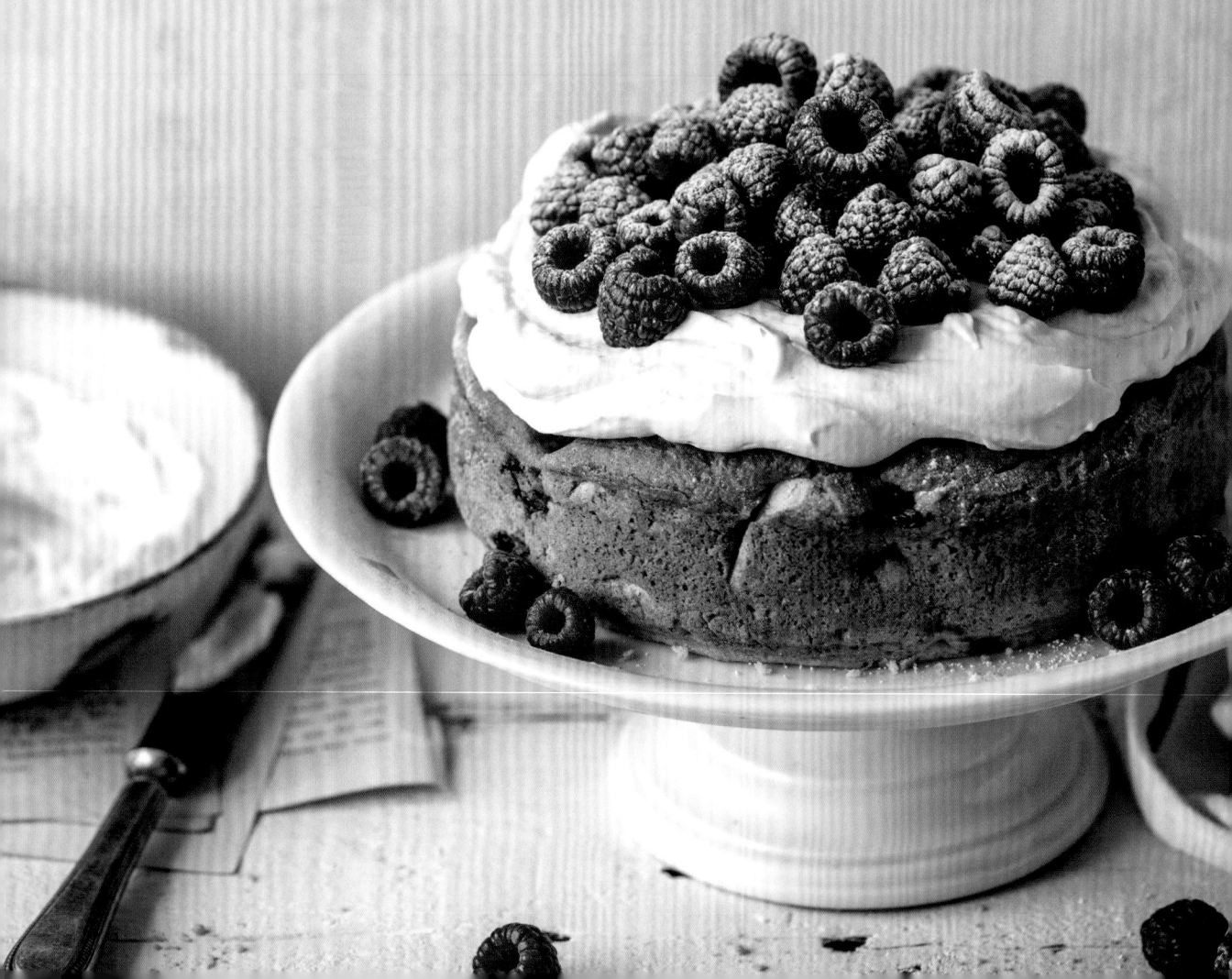

Introduction:
The Power of a Single Image

Picture this: You walk into your favorite bakery to buy a sandwich. Enticing scents fill the space. Your eyes move from one color and shape to another. You can hear the crunch of freshly baked bread being sliced, and as you take the sandwich in your hand, you feel its texture. And then there's the taste... that incredible taste!

Eating is a multisensory experience, and so is great food photography. But in photography there is no sound, smell, touch, or taste to support your message, so you need to get to your viewer's tastebuds through their eyes. You do this by drawing attention to visual details in your images to wake up their imagination. Your viewer is not there with you, so you've got to show them what you see, what you experience, what's important, and what they should know about the dish you are photographing.

Food photography is like taking your viewer by the hand and saying, "Here, look at this! This is what I love the most about this dish, what inspires me about this ingredient, what excites me about the preparation process."

A good photo makes you feel something. It brings back memories and puts a smile on your face. It makes you want to jump into the kitchen and cook. It awakens that "I want to eat it right now!" feeling. It tells a story.

A good photo inspires. It draws you in. It grabs your attention, it keeps you captivated, it leads your eye around the frame, and it encourages you to explore more.

A good photo surprises. It lets you see something in a way you've never seen before.

And the magic ingredient that adds something special to your images? That's you and the way you see.

Welcome note

I believe that creating beautiful images is a
skill everyone can master. Not convinced?
On the right, here, is one of my very first "artistic"
food photos. Oh—did you think I had a natural
knack for photography?

The truth is, photography didn't come easily to me, and
I took a lot of bad photos along the way. But I've always
been stubborn, and I believe that being stubborn in honing
your craft is far more important than "natural talent."
Sure, talent might help, but it won't take you as far as
your creative ambition will.

I want you to know that I am SO excited that you've
picked up this book and I can't wait for you to dive
deeper into it. You really don't need a massive studio,
a ton of expensive equipment, or to be an expert in
camera-club jargon to take appetizing pictures of
food. All you need is to let your imagination off the
leash, learn a few simple techniques, and take the
time to put them into practice.

If you are hungry to learn more about food
photography, then this book is for you.
Here, I spill my photography secrets—things that
I've learned from years of troubleshooting—so that
you can learn from my mistakes. If you feel that food
photography is complicated and overwhelming, that's
exactly how I felt when I first started out. There are
a lot of decisions to make when you create a food
image from scratch. Over the years, I've found my own
process and I want to share it with you in this book, so
that you can put my favorite tricks into practice too.

In the following chapters, I'll take you behind the
scenes and show you, step-by-step, how I compose
my images. And I wouldn't be me if I didn't invite
some of my favorite people to talk about their unique
approaches to food photography too; I am a huge
believer that learning from more than one person
makes you a better photographer.

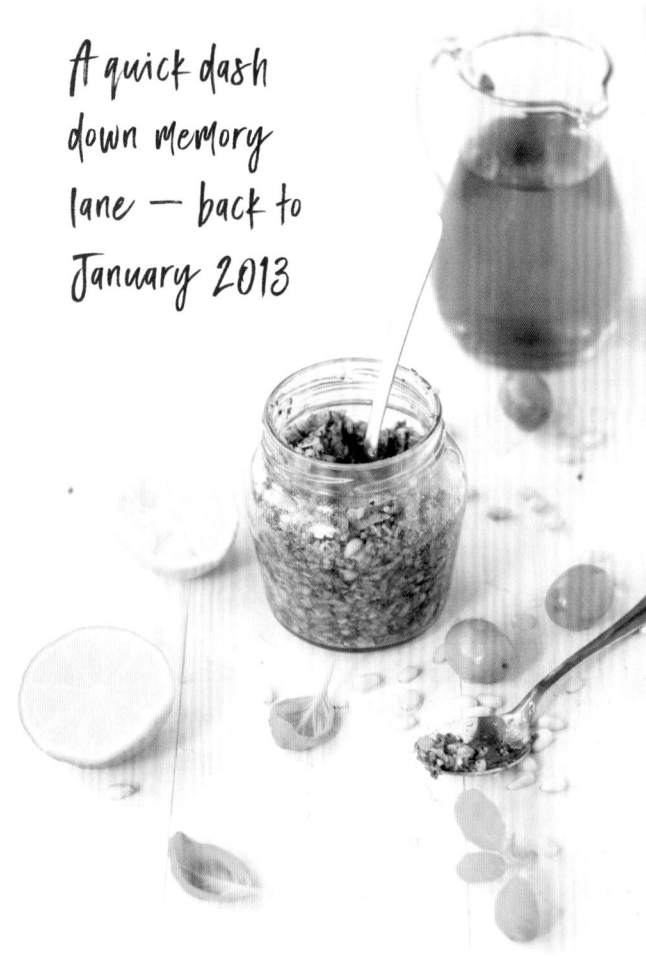

A quick dash down memory lane — back to January 2013

Your creativity is at the heart of this book, so you won't find any strict rules in here. You can dip in for ideas and tools that will strengthen your frame, take and try what you find inspiring and helpful, and leave what doesn't work for you. Follow your own path, at your own pace, and make your own discoveries along the way. We all work in different ways and that should be something we celebrate.

It all begins with the decision to show up, roll up your sleeves, and work on your craft. And don't forget to give your skills some space to grow. Taking great images doesn't happen overnight. It happens when every day you get a little bit better than the day before. It happens when you fail but don't lose your enthusiasm. It happens when you persist.

I believe that great photography involves a combination of technical knowledge and personal vision. Technical know-how is important to empower your creative vision: it adds quality to your work, gives you confidence, and speeds up your working process. Without vision, however, technical skills won't take you far. It's your imagination that makes your work stand out from the crowd.

But when I studied great photographers closely, I noticed there is one more thing they all have in common—something that often gets overlooked, and what I want to bring to the table in this book— a strong mindset.

The path to becoming a better photographer

The best photographers are those who never stop stretching their creative muscles; who always stay curious; who keep digging deeper; and who fall in love with the learning process more than the final destination. So become a student and never stop learning!

Take your creativity to the gym.
Creativity is like any other muscle. The more you train it, the stronger it gets. Our job as photographers is to take it to the gym. Every day.

Don't be afraid of what you can't do.
If there is a skill you think you'll never learn, don't keep putting it off, but *face it*. It's liberating and trust me, you can learn anything! It's just a matter of how much time you are willing to put into it.

Never become stale.
Every time you catch yourself becoming predictable, comfortable, and repeating the same old stuff over and over again, challenge yourself to get out of your comfort zone. Take a different tack and you'll start seeing photography from a whole new perspective.

Fail. Just don't ever lose your enthusiasm.
Don't give up when things get hard. Every mistake can become a learning lesson. And isn't learning the best part of this creative journey?

Creative technique + your vision + a strong, confident mindset = a great recipe for some breathtaking photos of food.

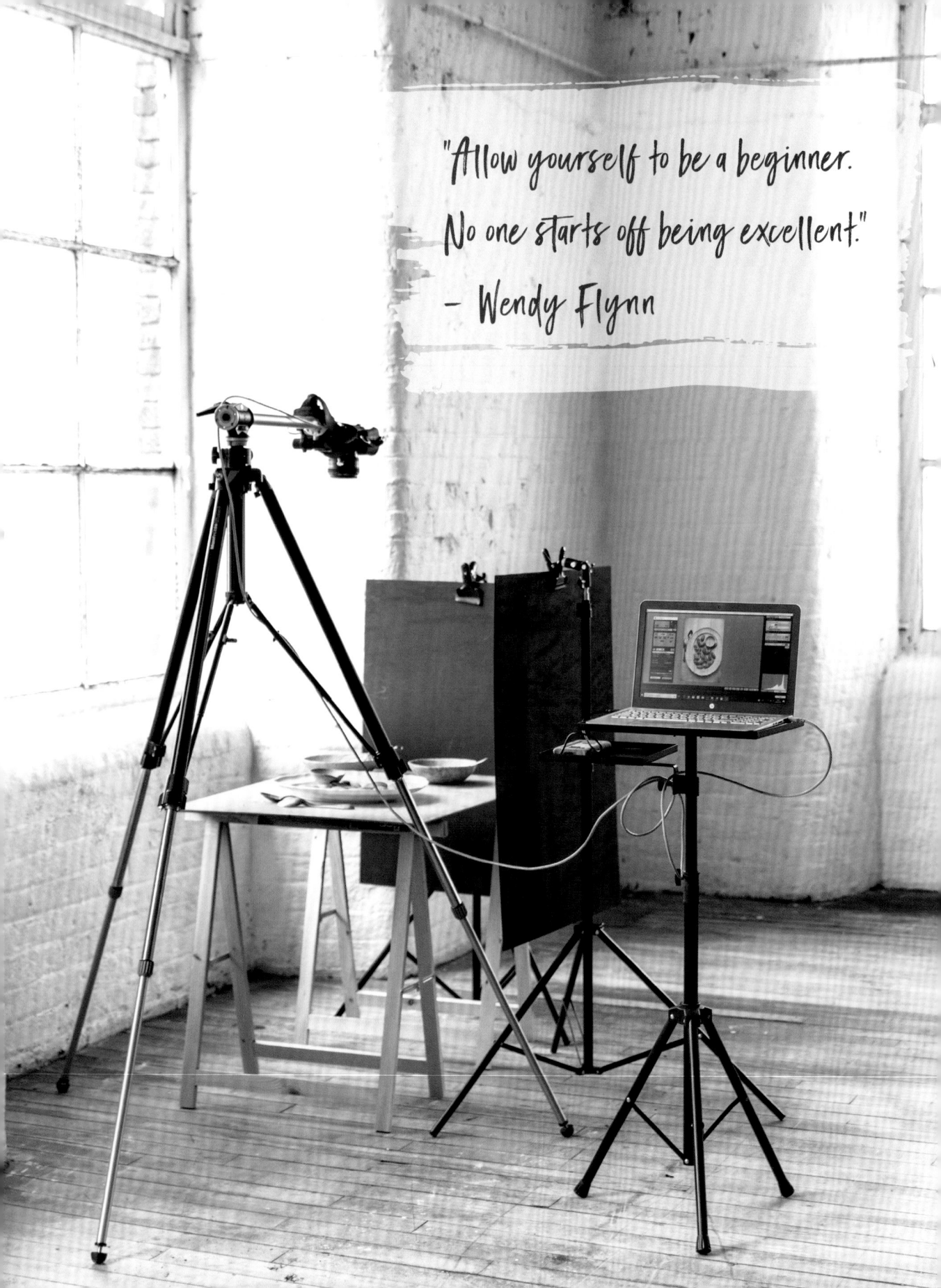

"Allow yourself to be a beginner.
No one starts off being excellent."
– Wendy Flynn

Tame Your Gear

Don't wait until you feel ready

A beginner's camera, a kit lens, a few old wooden pallet boards nailed together as a background, an untrained eye, and a heart full of passion— that's how I started. I didn't feel ready, but I also didn't wait until I had better equipment, a bigger space, more props, or I had learned every photography rule under the sun. The secret is just to start, and then figure things out along the way.

Start with what you have

I often hear from photographers that they don't have time, dedicated space to shoot, or good-enough gear. But guess what? No one does when they first start out. You've got to find time in the cracks of your busy life and work with what you've got. If Steve Jobs and Steve Wozniak started Apple in a garage, then you can start taking amazing food images in your kitchen.

There are a few behind-the-scenes images in this book, as well as food images, that were shot in a studio, but that doesn't mean a big studio space is necessary to take great food pictures. Some of my favorite images were taken in the corner of my living room in between a drying rack, a television stand, and a sleeping dog.

You also don't need to have a DSLR when you start your photography journey. In recent years, camera phones have revolutionized the photography world. They're small, fit in your pocket, take good-quality images, and are accessible with a swipe of a finger, making taking pictures easier than ever before. And why not take advantage of that? A DSLR will give you more creative freedom of course, but you can always upgrade when and if you want to. A lot of the tips and tricks you'll find in this book apply as much to camera phones as they do to DSLRs.

Your job as a photographer is to create a photograph. No matter where. No matter how. No matter what with.

All you need is a passion for creating.

Exercise your seeing skills

"You can't depend on your eyes when your imagination is out of focus."
—Mark Twain

Your eyes are your most powerful piece of photography equipment, so in order to be a better photographer, you need to master the art of observation. It might seem like a hard task at first, as it requires strong awareness, and we are usually too busy or deep in thoughts to notice what's around us. But slowing down, feeding your curiosity, and devoting a few minutes each day to just observing what's around you will help your photographic eye to develop. Seeing is a skill—the more you train it, the better it gets.

Switch on your imagination
(below left & right)

What do you see in the image below? An orange? If you look closer, you might unlock a world of possibilities. I'm talking about a world of highlights, shadows, colors, textures and shapes.

At first, I saw an orange too, but when I cut into it, it wasn't just a piece of fruit anymore. I saw circles and triangles, rich colors in different shades, and a shiny texture that was brought to life by the light. This was what I wanted to capture. The way we see is very personal—something ordinary to one person might be fascinating to someone else. This is part of what makes photography so exciting!

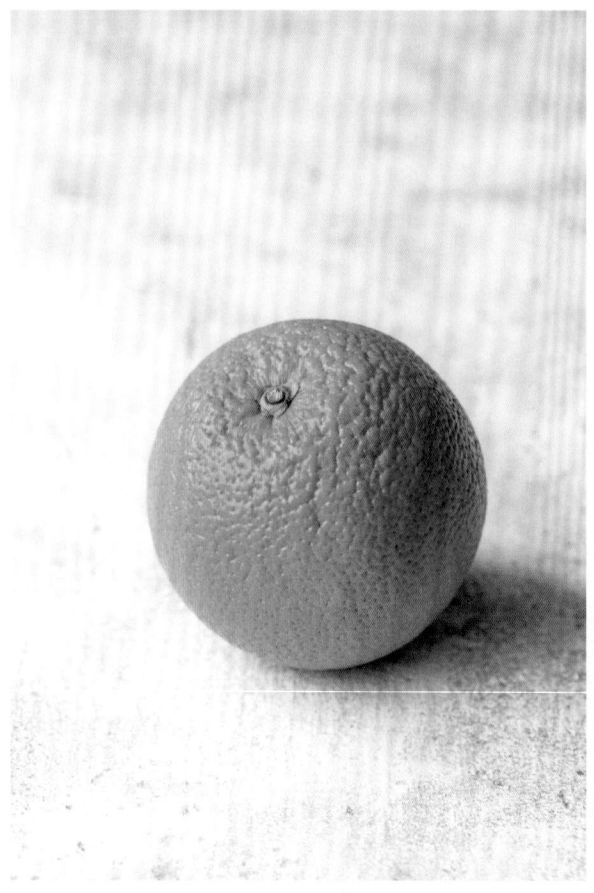

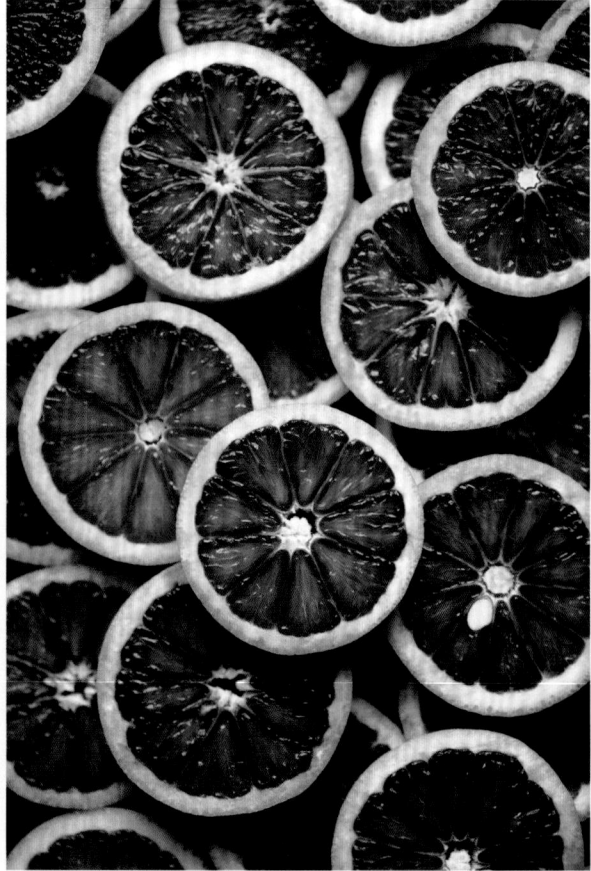

See past the plan (below)

This photo would have never existed if I hadn't had my seeing skills switched on. I was supposed to shoot these cookies baked for a client, but when I saw the pastry rolled out and the heart shapes cut out, inspiration hit me like a lightning bolt. The textures, colors, shapes, and the softness of light were all perfect. This became one of my favorite pictures before it was even taken.

We often get so caught up in the end result that we forget about the incredible moments in between. Pay attention to every step along the way. An opportunity for a great photo might be right there in front of you.

It's all in the details (below)

I had no prior plan on how to shoot this cake, decorated with white currants from the garden. When I picked the stems up, looked closer and put them against the window so that they gleamed in the light, I saw magic! Immediately, I knew that I had to use backlighting to replicate that amazing effect.

Switch off your thoughts and notice what's around you. Nothing is ordinary if you look closer. Learn to look for interesting qualities, not only in the dish or scene overall, but also in the details. "Details. Look for details," is what I constantly repeat to myself when I photograph.

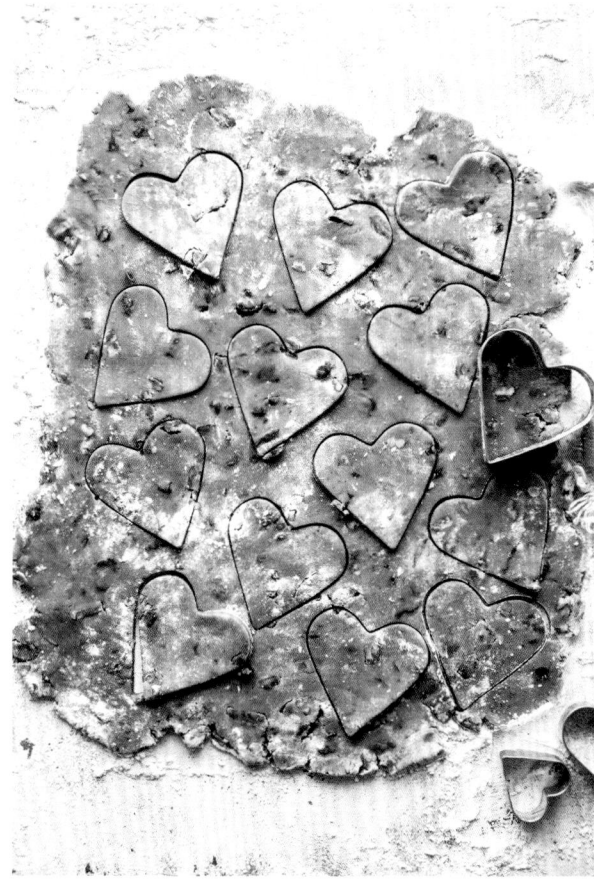

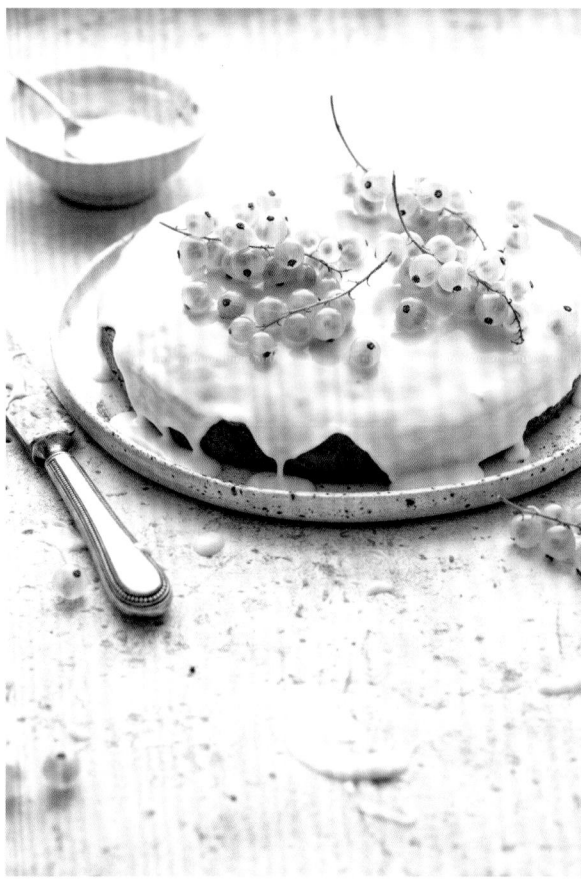

Your camera doesn't take pictures: you do

Don't shoot on autopilot

Sometimes when we grab a camera too quickly, we risk missing something. On my first visit to India a few years ago, the friends (also photographers) who picked me up from the airport couldn't believe that I didn't take a single picture on my 40-minute journey to the hotel. I didn't even take a camera out of my bag. "Don't you like India?" they asked. I replied, "Of course I do, and I am taking pictures, you know. But with my eyes."

India was so different from what I'd known and had ever seen. I was overwhelmed. It bombarded all of my senses and I wanted to get a feeling of what this place was like to me. I wanted to really see it. If I had put a camera in front of my face straight away, I might have missed something important.

Taking in my surroundings gave me a better understanding of what pictures I wanted to capture during my visit. When I went out with my camera later that day, rather than shooting on autopilot, I knew exactly what pictures I wanted to take. These pictures were all deeply intentional—and to this day, they remain very special to me.

I approach photographing still lifes of food in the same way. Having my subject in mind, or observing it, I spend some time thinking about what I see and how I want to capture it before I ever even look through the viewfinder.

Knowledge before gear

The desire to buy new gear is always strong, but taking great pictures is not about owning the most expensive equipment. It's about understanding your camera, knowing the fundamentals of photography, mastering your eyes, and stretching your imagination. If you don't believe me, take a look at the images on the facing page. The image on the right is much stronger than the one on the left, but I used exactly the same equipment for both. The difference between the photos comes down to nothing more than a few years of developing my photographic skills.

Invest in your skill set, not just your equipment! Learn everything you can about the camera and lens that you already have, research photography topics, go to photography events, read about techniques, sign up for online courses, shadow other photographers, experiment with editing, and hone your eye. And most importantly, just shoot as much as you can. We often blame our camera for not taking better pictures, when it's our skills that need to be improved.

Learn how your camera sees

The art of photography is a constant compromise between a photographer and their tool—the way you see and the way the camera translates your vision. It's important to learn what elements your camera picks up, what it finds attractive, and what looks good photographed and then edited. Think about what your dish or a food scene will look like within a rectangular frame. What about if you blurred some of the elements? Or if you moved a little closer? Or looked at it from a different angle?

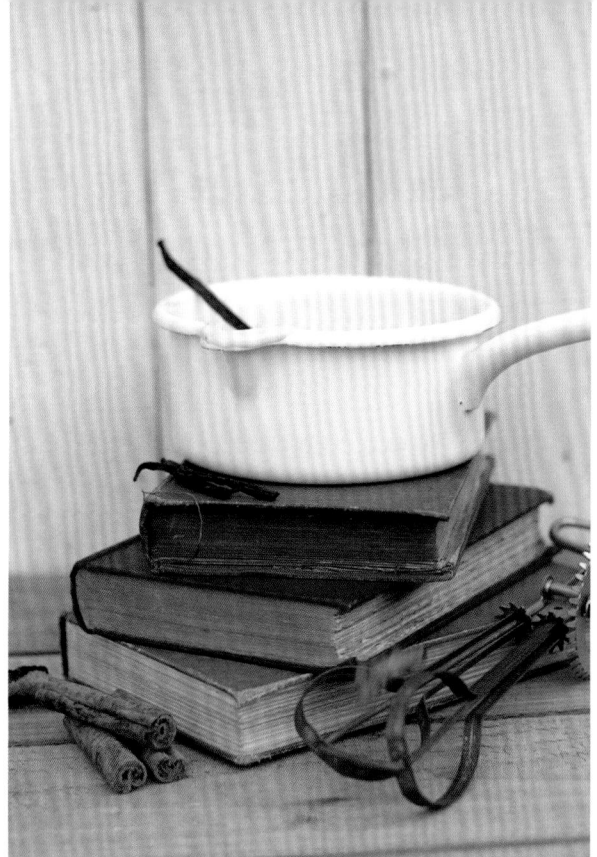

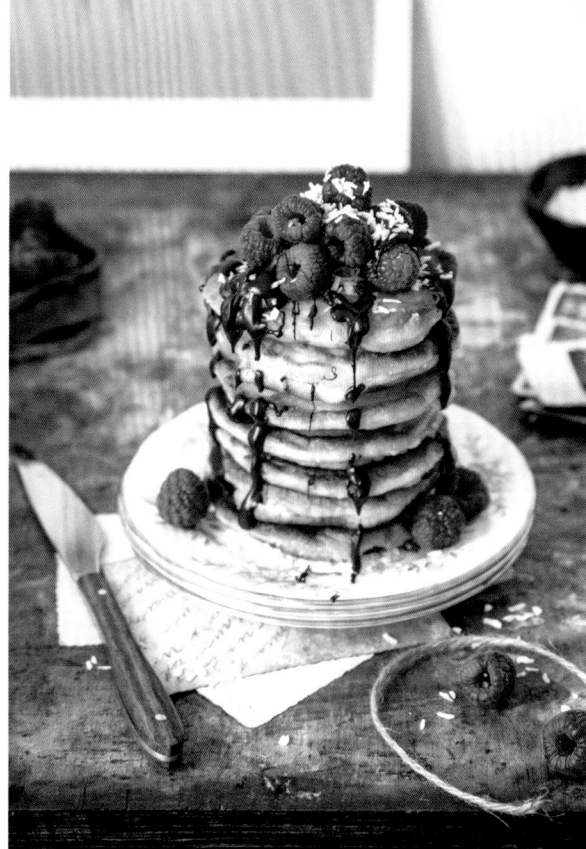

Who's the boss: you or your camera?

I am not completely against Auto mode. The truth is that there is a huge number of decisions to make when you take a picture. Shooting in Auto can take some of the pressure off while you are first learning to navigate the world of photography. And if you pay attention and study the settings your camera picks, Auto can teach you a thing or two.

However, there will be a moment in your photography journey when you will notice that when you shoot in Auto, it's not you but your camera that makes the decisions about what the image ends up looking like. And there will be a moment when you realize that the camera doesn't think the same way you do, and that to be creatively free, you need to come to grips with the settings and take the scary leap into Manual mode. It will be daunting and exciting, and I promise this moment will change everything for you.

Above: Same tool, improved skills. It's not the tool that makes you an artist. It's how you use your tool, combined with your own unique vision.

Challenge: An apple a day

The best way to learn how your camera works is by using it every day. Choose a simple subject—for example, an apple—and photograph it every day for a week, or even longer if you want. But try to create a different picture every time. Really switch on your imagination and try to think about the way your camera sees: think about light, shadows, textures, colors, shapes, and details. Spend some time studying the results, and think about what you're going to do differently tomorrow.

Master your manuals: exposure

Exposure is a term that you will be hearing a lot during your photography journey. When you begin to learn about Manual mode, it can seem like you have to memorize a daunting number of camera settings and strange-sounding numbers to get it right, but exposure is really nothing to be afraid of.

Light is everything in photography, and exposure is simply the amount of light that you let into your camera. Too much light and your photo will be too bright (overexposed). Not enough light and your photo will be too dark (underexposed). You have to find the right balance with the three tools your camera uses to control the exposure: aperture, shutter speed, and ISO. The aperture is an opening in the lens that can be made wider or narrower to let more or less light in. Slower shutter speeds allow more light in while faster shutter speeds let in less. ISO controls your

camera's sensitivity to light. A low ISO is used in bright conditions. A higher ISO can be helpful in low-light situations as it makes your image brighter, but it comes with "grain" or "noise" as a side effect.

Balancing these three elements takes some practice—so let's get to it. Switch on your camera, go to your Manual mode (M), and see where your aperture, shutter speed, and ISO are. Before you continue, make sure you know which buttons on your camera to press to change those settings (your camera manual or an internet search should help if you get stuck).

When viewing your aperture, shutter speed, and ISO settings, you will see numbers that are called "stops" appear on the screen. Move any of these settings by only one stop and this will double or halve the amount of light that enters your camera.

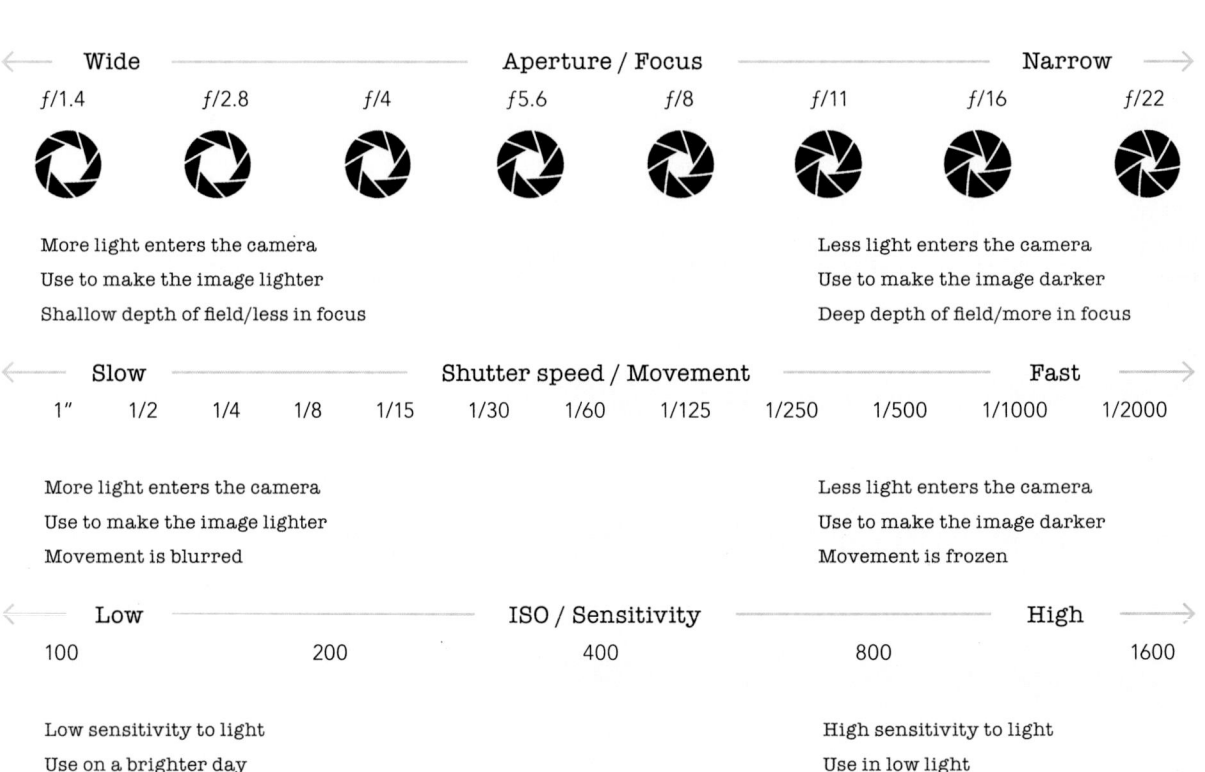

← Wide			Aperture / Focus			Narrow →	
ƒ/1.4	ƒ/2.8	ƒ/4	ƒ5.6	ƒ/8	ƒ/11	ƒ/16	ƒ/22

More light enters the camera
Use to make the image lighter
Shallow depth of field/less in focus

Less light enters the camera
Use to make the image darker
Deep depth of field/more in focus

← Slow					Shutter speed / Movement					Fast →	
1″	1/2	1/4	1/8	1/15	1/30	1/60	1/125	1/250	1/500	1/1000	1/2000

More light enters the camera
Use to make the image lighter
Movement is blurred

Less light enters the camera
Use to make the image darker
Movement is frozen

← Low		ISO / Sensitivity		High →
100	200	400	800	1600

Low sensitivity to light
Use on a brighter day
Less noise in image

High sensitivity to light
Use in low light
More noise in images

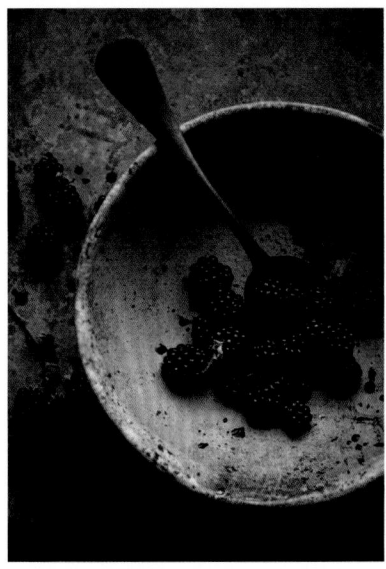

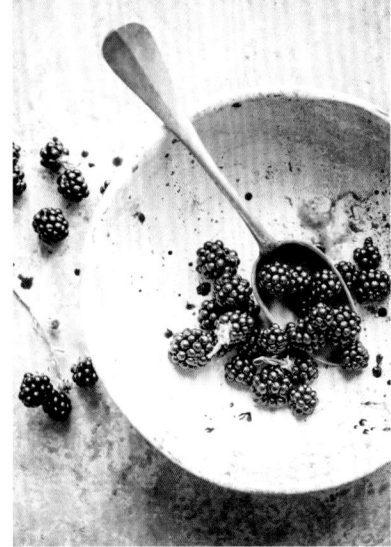

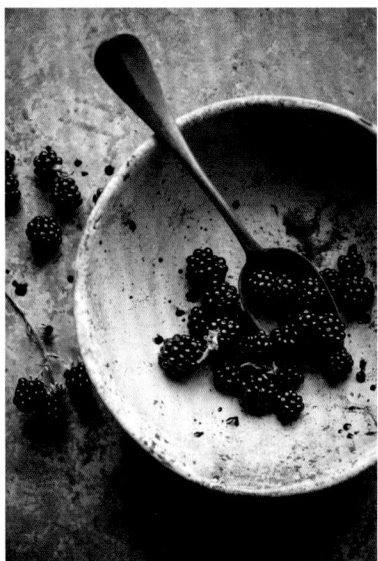

Light meter: -1   Light meter: +2   Light meter: 0

Measuring the light

Your camera's light meter is a tool you can use to
check if the light in your setup is correctly balanced.
Look through your viewfinder, press the shutter button
halfway and you will see it appear at the very bottom of
the frame. The light meter also shows up on your Live
View display. On my camera, it shows figures like this:

$$-3 \quad -2 \quad -1 \quad 0 \quad +1 \quad +2 \quad +3$$

The numbers here are also stops. You might see a little
triangle or a mark appearing on the top or bottom of
these numbers when you adjust your camera. When the
indicator is right in the middle (at 0), it shows that your
exposure is correct, according to your camera. This is
a good starting point.

It's all about finding the right balance (above)

In the first example (left), my light meter shows me that
my exposure is -1. In theory, that means my photo is
one stop underexposed, and if I want the exposure in
my photo to be correct, I need to increase it by one
stop. So to brighten my photo, I can make my aperture
one stop wider, my shutter speed one stop slower, or
increase the ISO by one stop.

In the second example (middle), my light meter shows
me that my exposure is +2. This means that my photo
is overexposed and I need to bring the light down by
two stops if I want to get the details in my photo back.
I could change one setting by two stops or I could
also choose to change two of the settings by one stop
each. So many possibilities!

Now, you might be wondering why on earth would
you learn Manual if Auto mode can choose the correct
exposure for you. That's because "correct" is a matter
of opinion. And apart from controlling the exposure,
aperture and shutter speed offer other interesting
effects of their own, and if you don't want to let your
camera make all the creative decisions for you, you
need to learn to control them yourself.

Aperture

Light control

The aperture is the round opening in your camera lens that you can make narrower or wider to control how much light you want to enter your camera. Make it wider and you'll let more light in, making your image brighter. Make it narrower and you'll let less light in, making your image darker.

The size of the aperture is measured with f-numbers (or f-stops); different lenses will have different ranges of f-numbers available. Confusingly, the higher the f-number, the narrower the opening in your lens, and the lower the f-number, the wider the opening of your lens.

Creative control

The aperture also affects how much of your image is in focus. This is known as depth of field. When photographers talk about a deep depth of field, it means that a greater amount of scene is in focus—things that are close to the camera as well as things that are farther away. Shallow depth of field, on the other hand, is when only part of your photograph is in focus—backgrounds and often foregrounds appear as a soft blur.

Knowing how different apertures affect the depth of field—or your area of focus—in your photo opens up a world of creative possibilities.

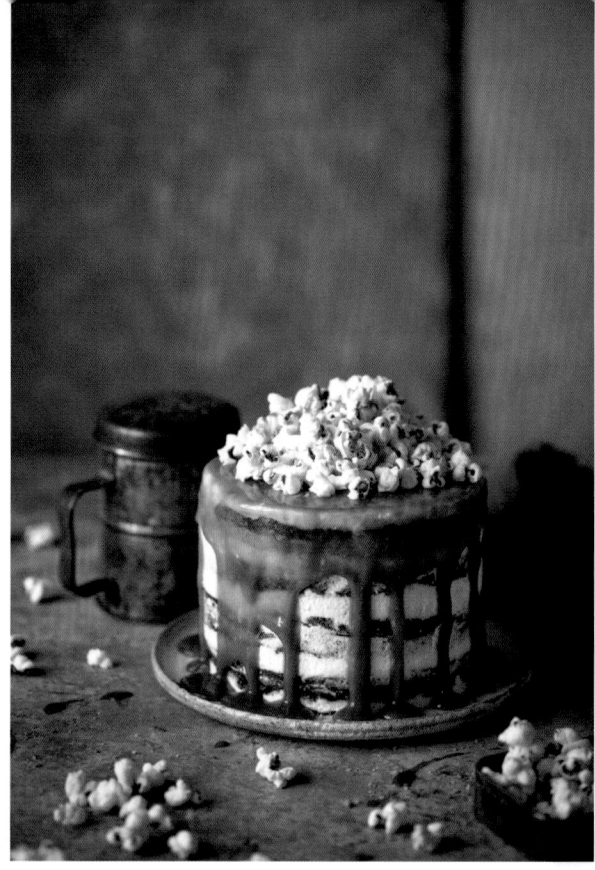

The beauty of blur (above)

Lens: 85mm, aperture: $f/3.2$

By choosing a low f-number (a wide aperture), you can focus on one element in your frame and creatively blur the rest. It's a powerful tool with which to separate your subject from the background and make it pop. Despite this being known as a "shallow" depth of field, using one actually creates a great sense of depth, bringing your images to life.

The blur that comes with using a wide aperture can create a beautifully soft and dreamy image. It also helps make the noise and clutter that might be around the frame less distracting, and draws your audience's attention straight to the area you want them to look at: your tasty dish.

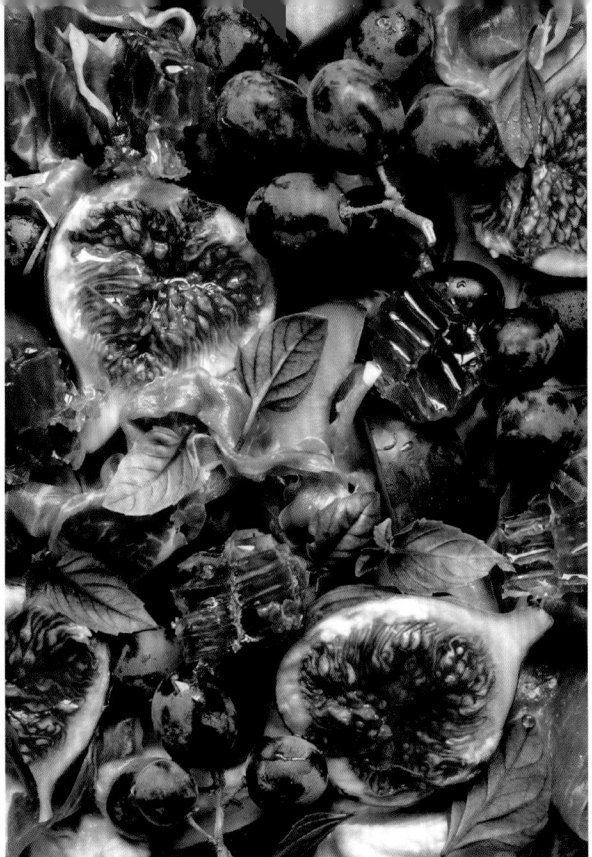

The power of detail (left)

Lens: 50mm, aperture: ƒ/11

By choosing a high f-number (a narrow aperture), you will keep more details in your image in focus, which is known as deep depth of field. This is very effective if every element in your frame has an important role, or if you want to put the focus on a whole scene, not just a singular subject or detail.

Blur for depth (below)

Lens: 50mm, aperture: ƒ/5.6

It's always worth experimenting with your aperture. You can create an image where a large part is in focus but there is still some blur to give depth. In this photo, all the props on the table are as important as the food, so everything is in focus, but by blurring the floor, I was still able to create depth in my image.

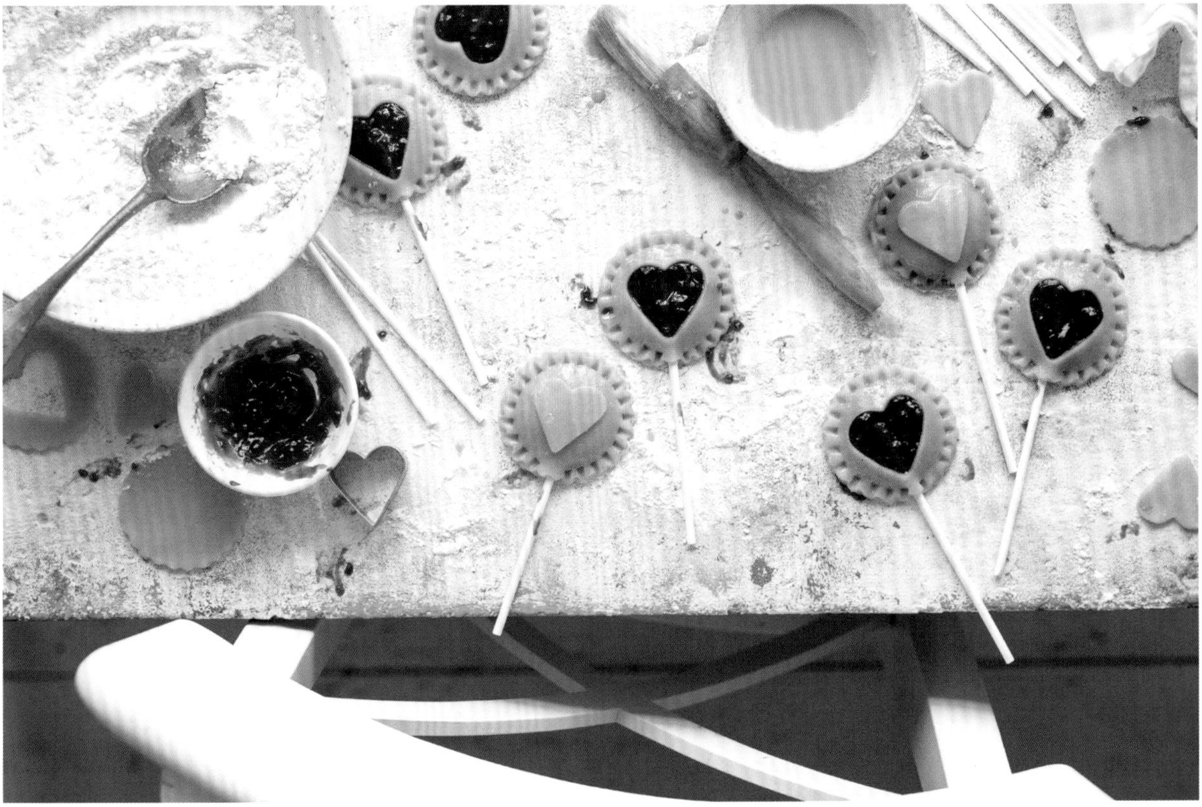

Depth of field & distance

We've seen how depth of field is affected by the size of the aperture, but it's also affected by distance. Photograph closer to your subject and more details in your scene will be out of focus; take a step back from your subject and photograph with the same aperture, and more details will be in focus.

Think about the distance between the elements in your frame too. How close or how far do you want supporting elements to be in relation to your subject? If you focus on your main dish, you can move other elements closer to it to make them a little less blurry, and by moving them away, you can make them more blurry. Think about how close or how far you are going to place your background too. Great photography is all in the details!

Creative depth of field

When you understand the different factors that affect depth of field, you can use it to make a stronger image, drawing attention to the important parts of the frame and making the supporting elements less distracting.

Choose your focus (right)

What's in focus is what draws the eye first, so make sure it's the most important part of the image. What's blurry directs your viewer's eye to the sharp area.

Below: Same aperture (*f*/5), different distance. See how the background is more blurred in the closer shot?

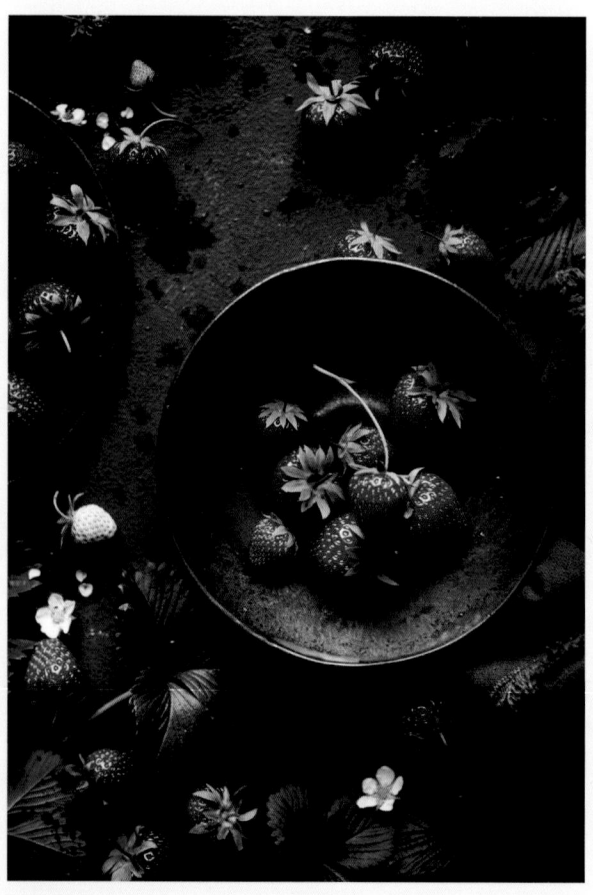

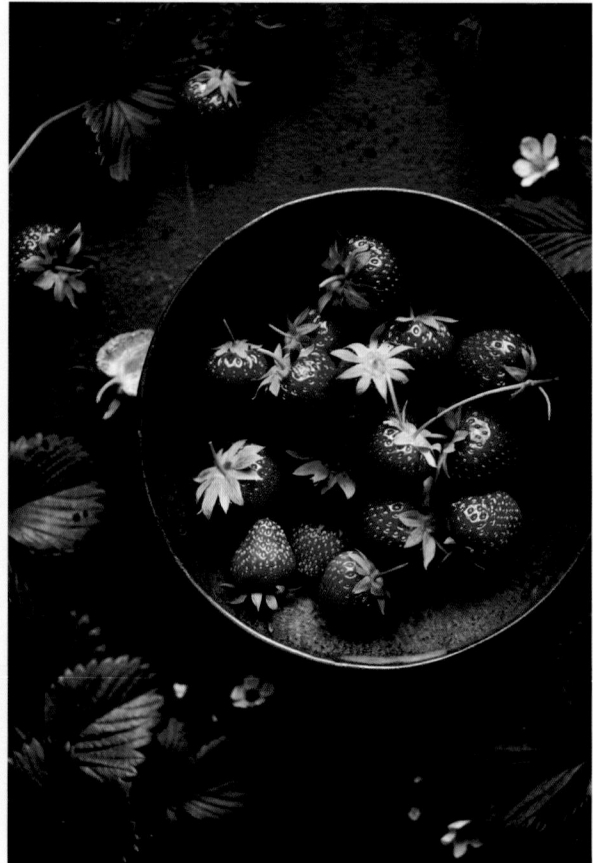

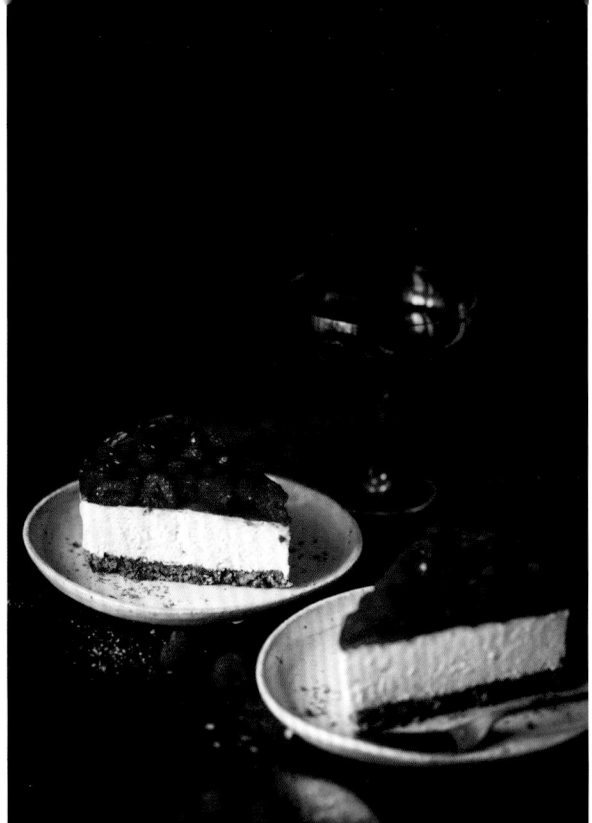
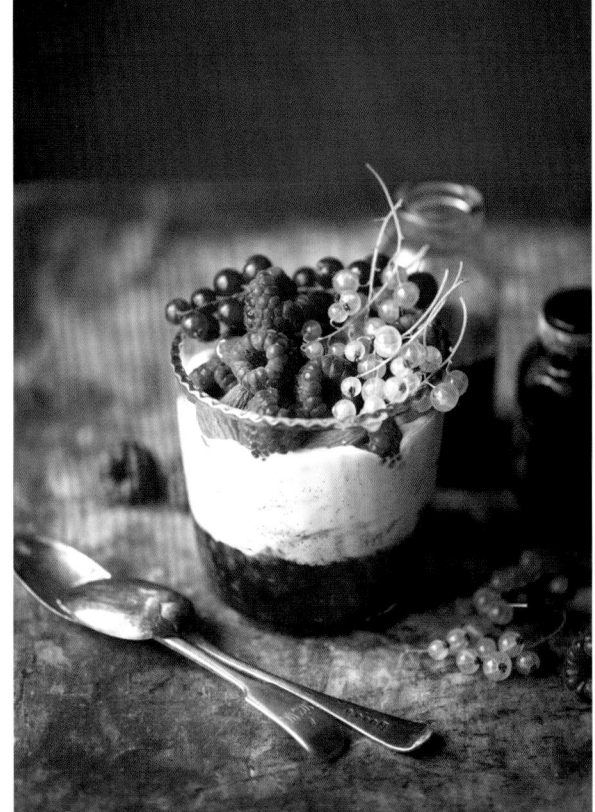

Hide & seek (above right)

A technique I often use is hiding elements behind the hero and blurring them out. This way, I can include supporting elements in the scene but the main subject is still the first thing you notice. Always make sure the hero is in sharp focus.

Challenge your favorite aperture settings

If a shallow depth of field makes you uncomfortable, great: make yourself uncomfortable and experiment with it. If you never shoot with a deep depth of field, try to use it creatively in your photos. Don't be afraid to break the rules and get out of your comfort zone—that's how you'll develop your skills and your confidence.

Depth of field is affected by:

F-stop

Lower f-number (e.g. $f/2.8$)=shallower depth of field. That's when you create a blurry background and have fewer details in focus.
Higher f-number (e.g. $f/22$)=deeper depth of field. That's when you have more details in focus.

Distance

Farther from your subject=deeper depth of field.
Closer to your subject=shallower depth of field.
If you move closer to your subject, consider shooting with a higher f-number in order to keep important details in focus.

Lens choice

Shorter focal length (e.g. 35mm)=deeper depth of field.
Longer focal length (e.g. 85mm)=shallower depth of field.
The rule of distance applies where lenses are concerned—longer focal lengths make your subject appear closer, so to get more details in focus try using a higher f-number.

Shutter speed

Light control

Directly in front of your camera's sensor is a small flap called the shutter. When you take a picture, the shutter opens, lets light in, and closes. The length of time the shutter is open for is called the shutter speed.

Shutter speed is measured in seconds or, more often, in fractions of a second. For example, when you see 1/400 or 400 in your settings bar, it means that the shutter is opened for a four-hundredth of a second. That's pretty fast. When you see a double quotation mark after the number—for example, 4"—this means that the shutter is open for a whole four seconds, which, in photography, is very slow.

When you open your shutter for a shorter period of time (a fast shutter speed), less light enters your camera. This is best for a bright day.

When you open your shutter for a longer period of time (a slow shutter speed), more light enters a camera. This is very handy in low-light situations, although you will require a tripod if you want your photos to come out sharp (see page 34).

Creative control

Now for the juicy part of shutter speed—the power to capture movement. Fast-enough shutter speeds can freeze movements and enable your viewer to see extraordinary details that the human eye wouldn't normally catch. A slow shutter speed, on the other hand, will create blur in a moving subject, giving a "living" sense to your images. The results can be extraordinary!

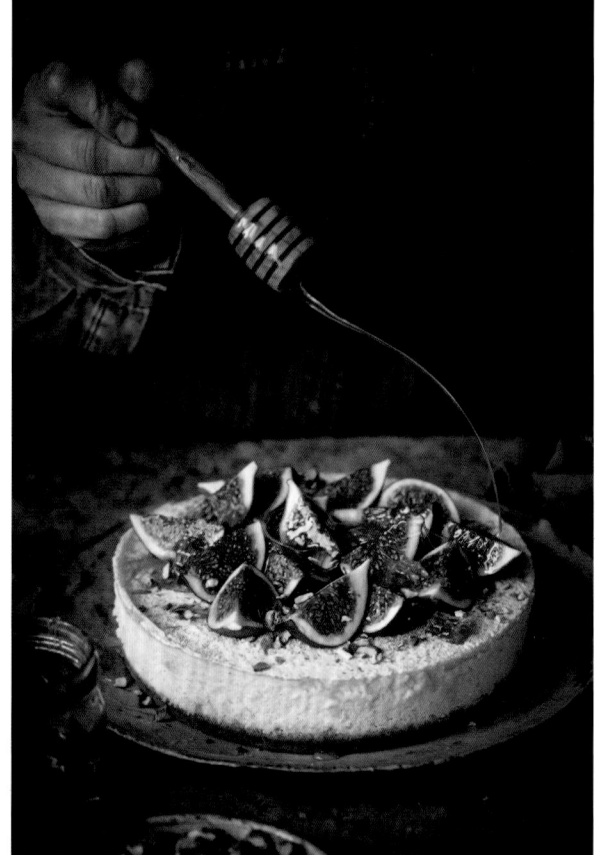

Freezing time (above)

Lens: 85mm, aperture: ƒ/4.5, 1/1000 second, ISO 2000

To freeze time, I like to set my camera on a tripod, choose a fast shutter speed and use manual focus to make sure my subject or the most important part of my subject is sharp. I also take into consideration where the movement is going to appear, as the aim is to catch it in focus (or as near as possible). In situations when I photograph and both of my hands appear in the photo, I use a 10-second timer to give myself a moment to get ready. If one of my hands can be outside of the frame, (and depending what I am capturing) I will photograph with a remote on a high-speed continuous-drive mode (or burst mode), when the camera captures several frames in quick succession.

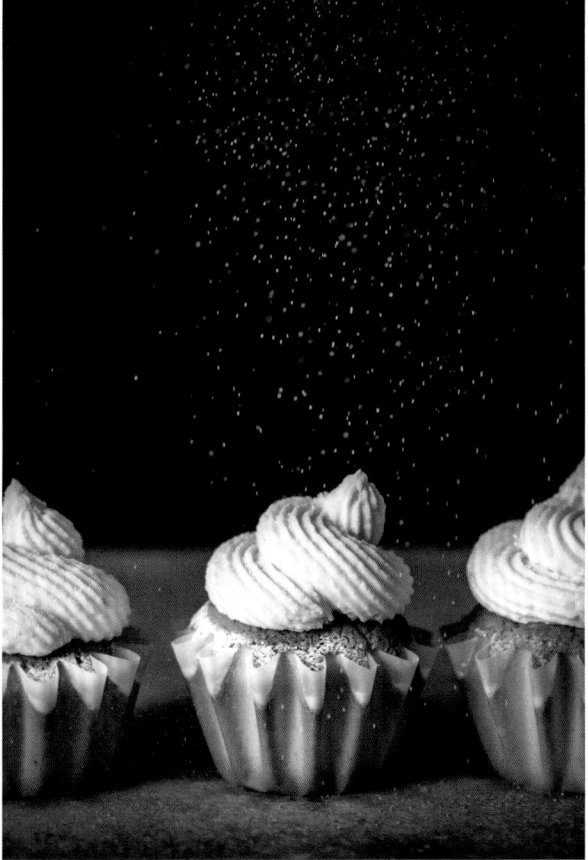

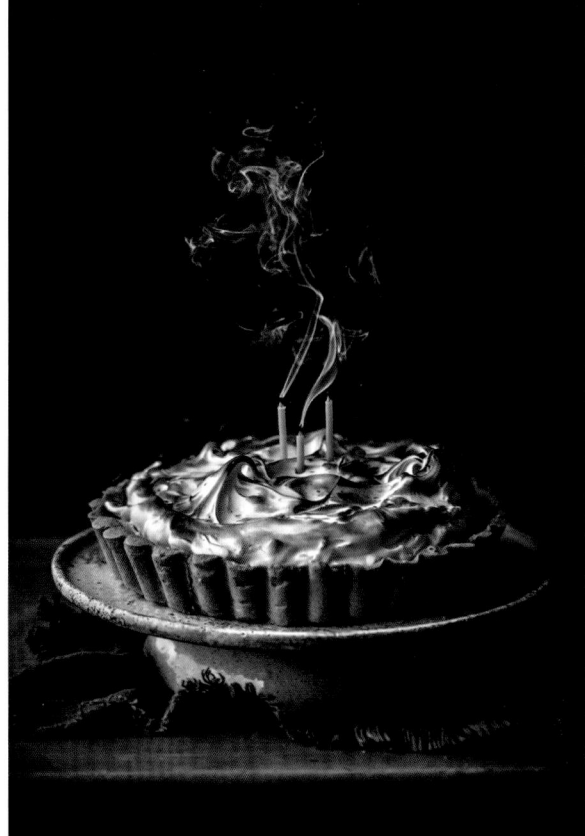

Interval shooting (above)

Lens: 100mm, aperture: ƒ/7.1, 1/800 second, ISO 6400

This is a little different to the continuous-drive mode I've just mentioned. You can find this option in the menu in most recently made DSLRs or you can get a separate intervalometer. With just one click of a button, your camera will take a number of shots one after the other while you are creating continuous movement. If I were photographing dusting powdered sugar, for example, I might set interval-shooting mode to take, say, 10 images at one-second intervals. This way, I'll have 10 pictures to choose from.

Tip

Consider choosing a background that contrasts with the moving element. For lighter things, such as smoke, powdered sugar, and grated cheese, try a dark background to ensure they are visible. For a darker element such as chocolate, contrast it with a lighter background.

Surprise your viewer's eye with all those frozen details (above)

Lens: 100mm, aperture: ƒ/5, 1/800 second, ISO 3200

Smoke, steam, powdered sugar, sprinkling salt, drizzling honey: there's no end to the interesting effects you can create. The shutter speed setting will always depend on the element you are catching and how fast it's moving. But you can start playing from around 1/250 second for pouring smooth chocolate or caramel; 1/400 second for catching the smoke; 1/800 second for falling icing sugar or grated cheese; and 1/1000 second for catching a honey swirl. Then look at your images and alter your settings if you need to.

Capturing movement is a combination of skill, patience, and luck, so don't feel discouraged if you haven't succeeded after a couple of attempts. It took 23 tries to capture that honey swirl, 41 photos to catch the perfect amount of icing sugar falling on the cupcakes, and over 100 photos to capture the smoke. And on many movement-catching occasions, it's taken even more attempts than that!

Blurring movement (right)

Lens: 100mm, aperture: ƒ/9, 1/80 second, ISO 640
Slower shutter speeds create motion blur, which can make an image look alive and visually interesting. Motion blur happens when, in between the time the shutter opens and closes, something in your frame moves.

To blur movement, a camera has to be perfectly still, so I always set it on a tripod and then choose a slow shutter speed. I also like to use a high f-number, as a deep depth of field (larger area in focus) contrasts well with a motion blur. If it's just me both creating the movement and photographing it, I focus manually on the element I want to be sharp (here I focused on the glass) and I either set the camera on a 10-second timer (when both of my hands are going to appear in the photograph), or photograph with a remote on continuous-drive mode (if one of my hands can be outside of the frame). Interval shooting is another option here too.

As with freezing movement, the shutter speed you require depends on the effect you want to achieve and how fast your element is moving. The shot on this page used a shutter speed of 1/80 second to achieve a subtle motion blur in the stream of wine. The slower you go the greater the blur.

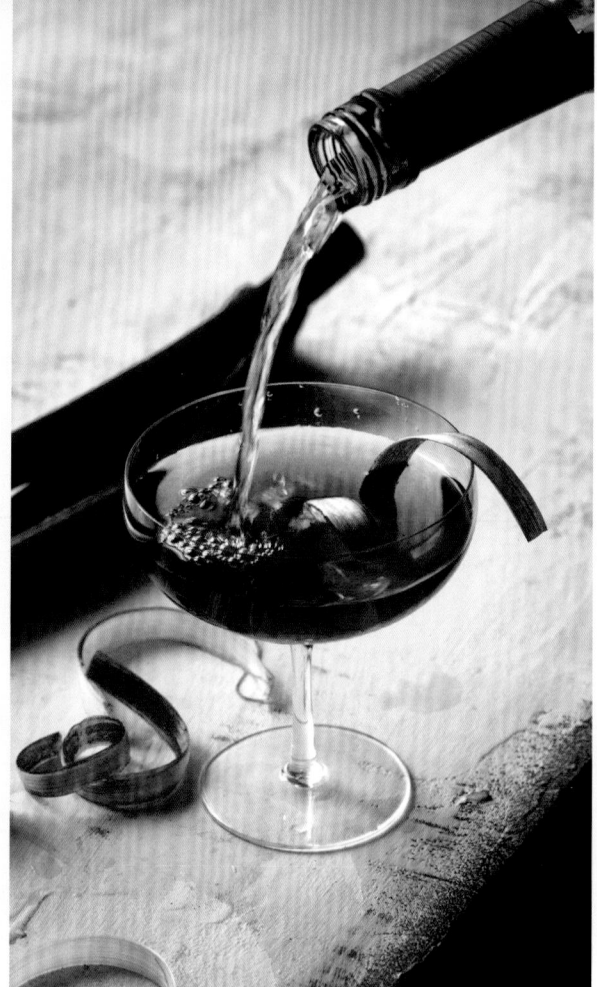

Motion blur is challenging, I have to admit! That's why many photographers avoid it. But it's something worth working on if you want your photographs to stand out. A great subject is important here: you need to think of movements that can be emphasized by this effect, such as the stream of liquid as it is poured from a bottle into a glass.

The risk of camera shake

When you photograph with a slower shutter speed while handholding your camera, you are risking camera shake ruining your images. No matter how steady you think you are, even the tiniest movement will make your photo blurry. I have seen some clever and creative ways to use camera shake in other genres of photography, but unless you want to intentionally create visually artistic and abstract images, it's something I would avoid in everyday food photography.

A rule of thumb for avoiding camera shake is to use a minimum shutter speed of 1/focal length when handholding. So for a 50mm lens, you should use a shutter speed at least as fast as 1/50 second. Unless you have weak hands like me—then you might want to give yourself some extra speed for safety. Otherwise, a tripod always saves the day!

ISO

ISO might seem to be the least exciting member of Team Exposure, but although it doesn't offer any creative visual effects itself, it will give you a helping hand on several occasions.

The higher the ISO, the more sensitive your camera's sensor is to light, and the more sensitive the sensor, the brighter your image. So if you want to add more light to your photo, you can increase your ISO. This is helpful in low-light situations and when you want to use high f-numbers and/or fast shutter speeds. But a high ISO also comes with a side effect: it can create "noise," which can reduce image quality and make your photograph look "grainy." Sometimes you will need (and you shouldn't be afraid) to use a high ISO, but when you can, try to keep it to a minimum. Always check your clients' requirements and those of any stock agencies you're intending to sell your images to.

Troubleshooting

Low light
To maintain quality in my still life images in low-light situations, I prefer to keep my ISO at 100–200, and use a very slow shutter speed instead, even if that means going as slow as a few seconds. When I choose slow shutter speeds, I always photograph with a tripod, use a remote, and avoid being too close to my camera to prevent even the tiniest camera shake. (You even need to be aware of not treading too heavily on the floor!)

Movement (above right)
Lens: 100mm, aperture: $f/4$, 1/250 second, ISO 8000
Catching and freezing movement always means I need to balance the fast shutter speed with a compromise somewhere else. I try to use lower f-numbers (wider apertures) when I can, but to keep the important details in focus, I might have no option but to use a higher ISO.

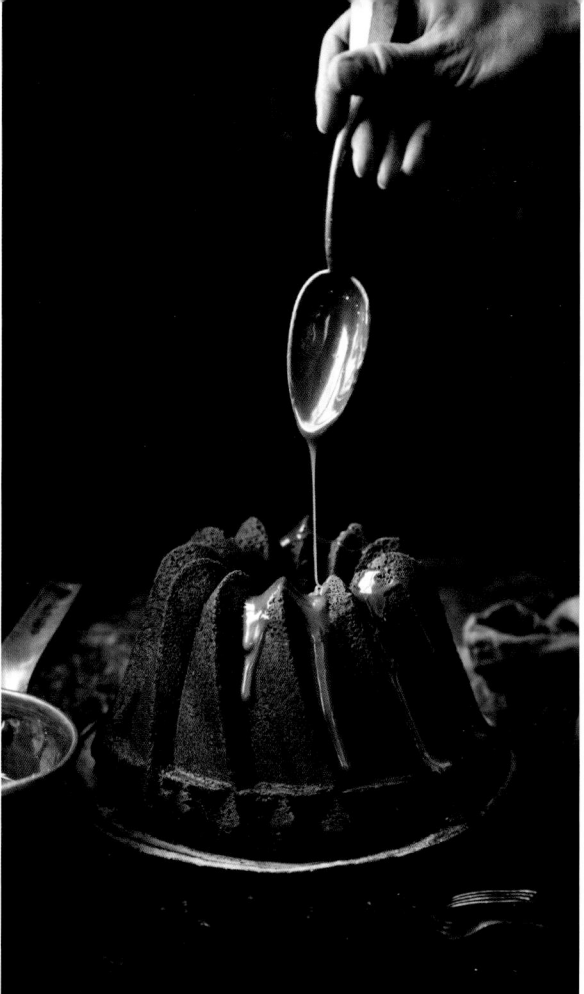

Get to know your ISO limits
Using a higher ISO makes most photographers anxious, as it might mean compromising on quality, but there will be situations when you have no choice but to increase it. Removing some of the grain in post-production (see page 155) will help to keep the quality, but it's also important to know your camera's ISO limits, as different cameras have varying tolerances.

Photograph in darker lighting situations with different ISO settings to see at what ISO your camera starts to produce a level of noise you don't feel comfortable with, and also see what you can do with it in post-production. This way you'll learn the limits of your camera and how far you can push it.

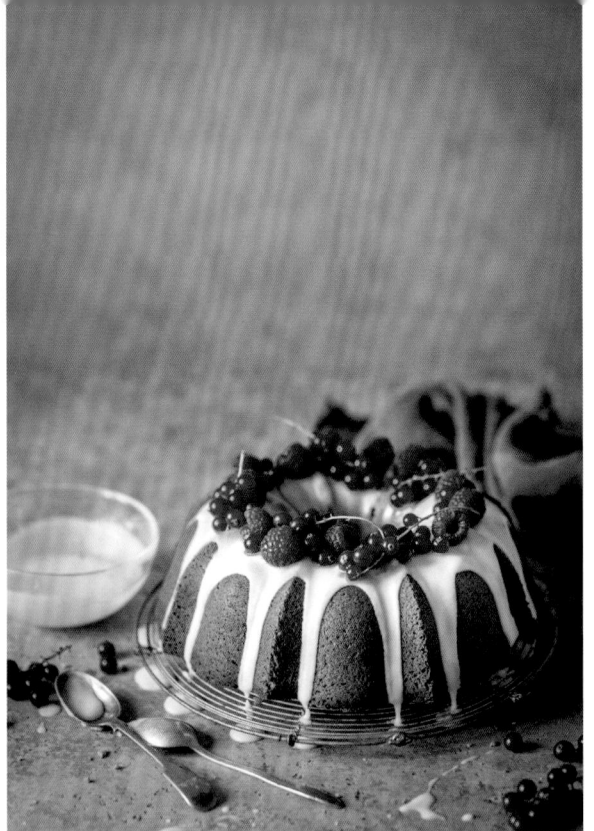

Learn one setting at a time

Although full Manual mode gives you the most creative control, it can also be overwhelming. I highly recommend choosing what your creative priority for the photograph is—depth of field or movement—and using one of the following modes. This way, you will ease into Manual mode by learning one setting at a time.

Aperture Priority mode

Flick your camera into Aperture Priority mode (AV or A). Your camera will calculate the shutter speed for you, and you can put your ISO setting to Auto, but you have control of the aperture so you can still enjoy all the creative effects of using different f-numbers. Study what shutter speed and ISO your camera picks for each image.

Shutter Priority mode

Flick your camera to Shutter Priority mode (TV or S) and set your ISO to Auto when you want to experiment with the shutter speed without having to worry about the other settings. Try capturing different types of movement, using a tripod with slower shutter speeds to avoid camera shake. Again, study the aperture and ISO adjustments for each shot.

Once you feel confident enough, switch to full Manual mode.

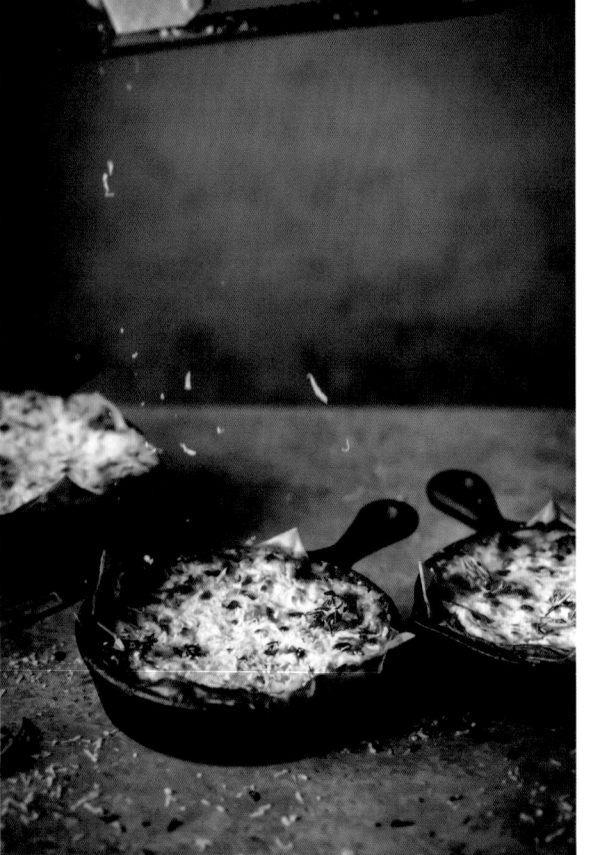

Top left: Experiment with depth of field while using Aperture Priority mode. See how changing the f-number and focal length, and shooting at different distances from the subject affects how much of the frame is in focus.

Left: Switch your camera to Shutter Priority mode and try freezing and blurring moving subjects without worrying about all the other settings.

Tools of the trade: lenses

Choosing a lens can be one of the most confusing tasks a photographer has to face, but it's also an important investment.

Get to know each lens's hidden talent

Lenses don't just make your subject look closer or farther away. Each lens has its own unique personality and the power to change our relationship with the subject, how we compose our frame and how the viewer connects with our image.

What lens we choose alters the way we photograph and has a huge influence on our style. Explore the character of each one, learn its strengths and weaknesses, and think about how it fits with your personal style and what you want to achieve.

Is your camera a cropped sensor? (below)

The shorter the focal length, the more of a scene that fits into the frame: that's the basic rule. However, some cameras have a cropped sensor, which means that the frame that is actually captured will be smaller than what you would expect from the focal length. Whereas on a full-frame sensor, a 50mm lens gives you a 50mm focal length frame, a cropped sensor makes it look as if it has been shot on a focal length of around 75mm, while a 35mm lens will give you the effect of around a 50mm focal length. As you can see from the image below, the difference of a few millimeters makes quite a big difference to your shot!

Before you buy a lens, you should find out your camera's crop factor first (if it has one; the internet will assist you here) and use it to calculate the effect the lens will give you.

Full-frame sensor   Cropped sensor

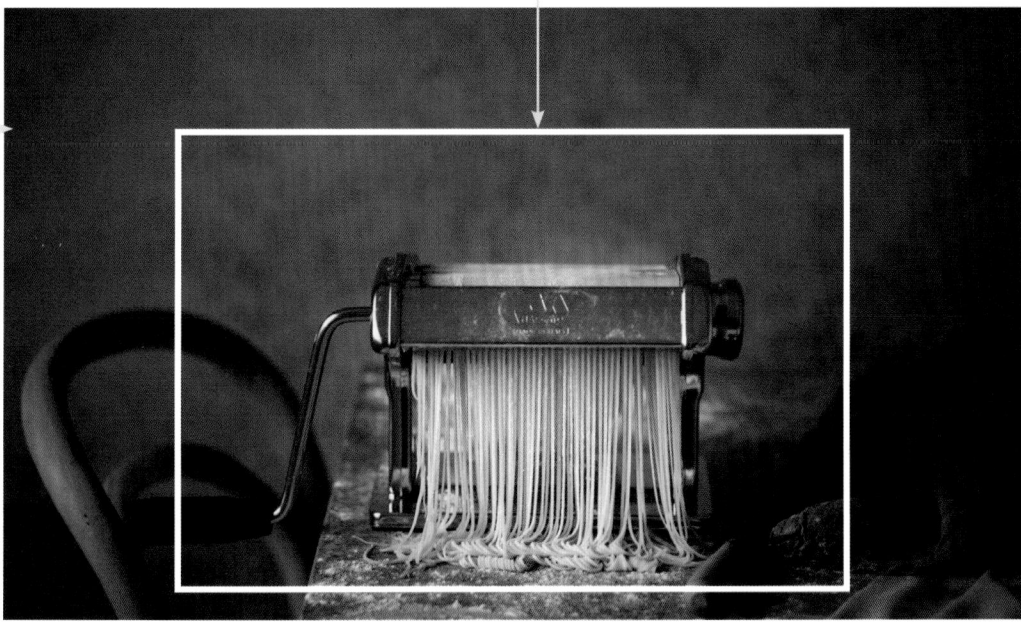

Focal length

That number you see by every lens description (such as 35mm, 50mm, and 85mm) is its focal length. The focal length will change how you see a scene when looking through the viewfinder, which in turn will change how you compose the frame.

Lenses with short focal lengths (e.g. 35mm) are called wide-angle lenses. Lenses with longer focal lengths (e.g. 85mm) are called telephoto lenses. 50mm is a standard lens.

The shorter the focal length, the wider your field of view (which means everything appears farther away and you have more space in your frame). The longer the focal length, the narrower your field of view will be (which means everything appears closer and you have less space in your frame).

Compression (below left)
Compression makes our food portraits more proportional. Telephoto lenses create an illusion of compressing depth, giving the impression that background elements are closer to your subject or larger than they really are.

Distortion (below)
Some lenses (especially those with shorter focal lengths) will make your food scene look distorted and your food look out of proportion, sometimes even a little bit weird and deformed when shooting close up. Distortion stretches the components in your scene too, giving an illusion that your background elements are farther away or smaller than in reality. I personally try to avoid using shorter focal lengths for close-up food shots for this reason.

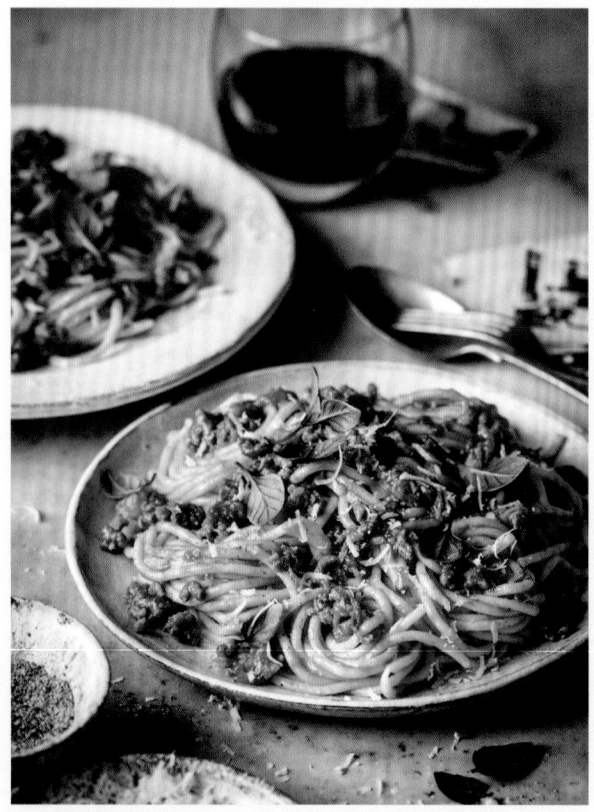

Compression

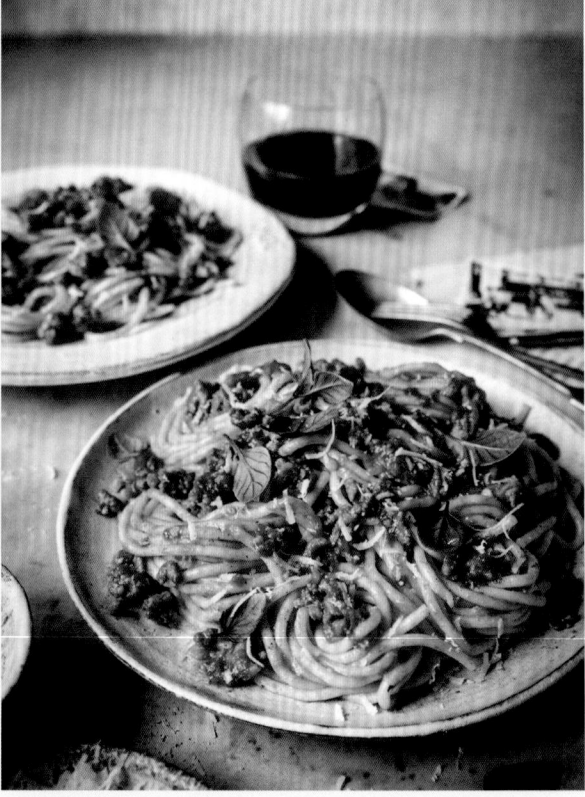

Distortion

Types of lenses

Primes

Prime lenses have a single focal length, and since you can't just zoom in or out to frame your subject, primes make you move and maybe even experiment more, as you have to use your feet to come closer or move away from your subject. With fewer elements inside them, prime lenses tend to produce sharper images than zoom lenses (although it might not always be the case) and they often come with wider maximum apertures, which is useful for shooting in low-light situations as well as for creating a shallow depth of field.

Zooms

A zoom lens offers a range of focal lengths in a single lens, which makes it more flexible than a prime lens. It's perfect for situations when you have to think and photograph fast, as there is no need to swap lenses. With a 24–70mm zoom lens, for example, you can use its shorter focal length for wide overhead shots and a longer focal length for closer straight-on and three-quarter-angle shots. All available with a flick of the wrist. However, this benefit can make you a bit too comfortable, so always remember to not just move your lens, but move yourself too!

Tilt-shift lens

If you want to challenge your photography skills, rent this lens, even if just for a day or two: it will change the way you see photography. Play with its tilt, shift, and rotate functions and see how flexible the plane of focus can be: you can create interesting effects that are impossible to achieve with other lenses. Using this lens will help you to grow your skills and add something fresh and interesting to your portfolio.

Which lens should I get?

Although a photographer's wish list is long and wide, it's best to buy with intention! You don't want to end up with a collection of lenses getting dusty on your shelf. Think about:

* Why do you need a new lens? Have you exhausted all of your current lens's possibilities? What are you trying to create that your current lens is not able to offer you?
* How much space do you like to have in your frame for a specific subject? Lenses and composition are very much connected, and your choice of lens will influence the sense of space in your photographs.
* What aperture to consider? Keep in mind that low f-numbers come handy in low-light situations and help you to create blurry backgrounds.

Start with one lens and push it to its limits. It will help to stretch your creativity, as you'll have to find ways to make it work for different situations. Borrow or rent a lens, if you can, before you commit to buying it.

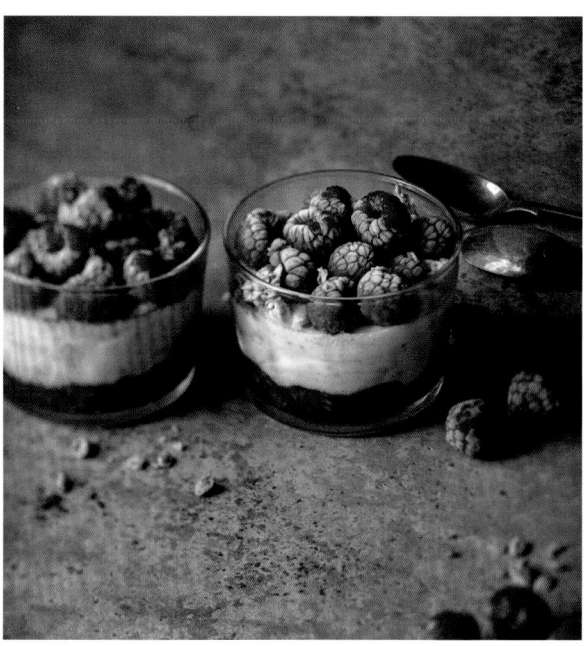

Right: This photo was taken with a tilt-shift lens. See how the dessert on the right is in focus and the one on the left is not? That wouldn't be possible with any other lens.

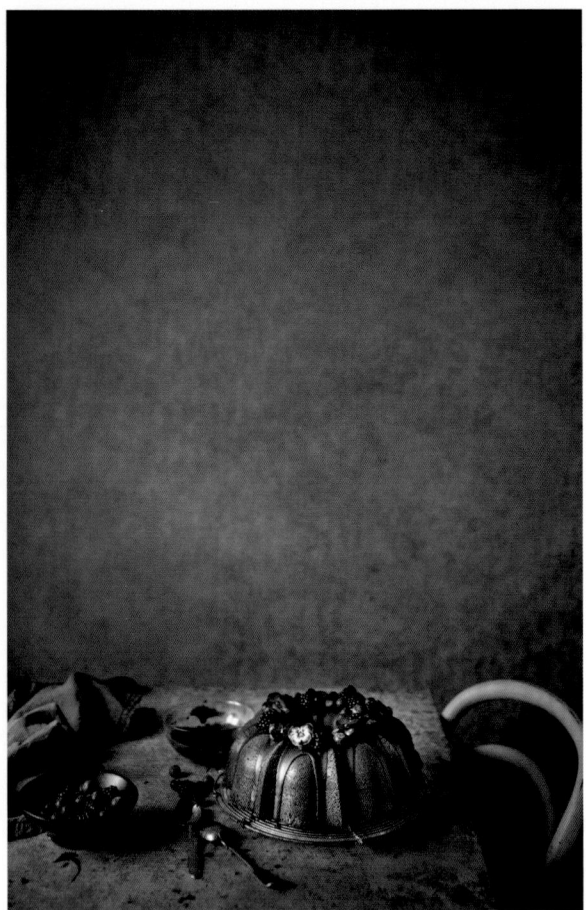

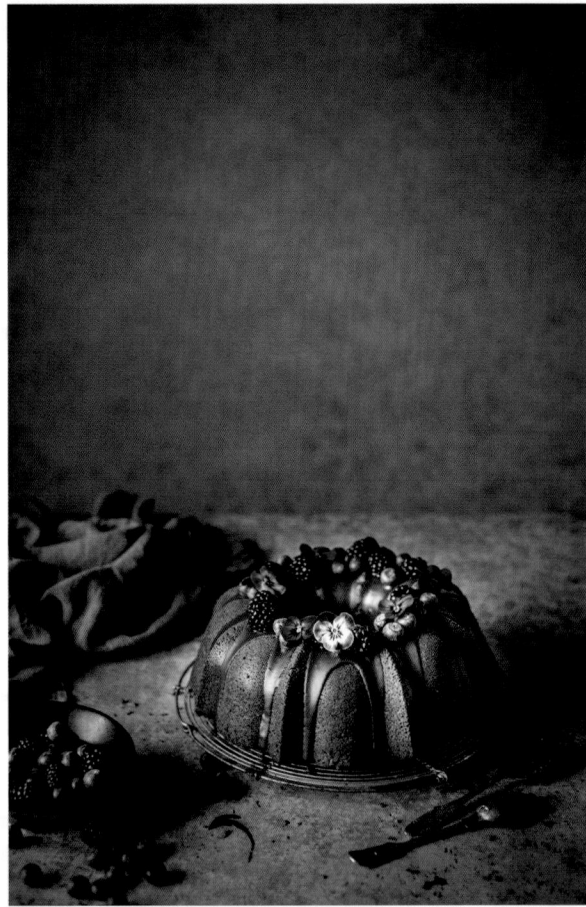

35mm (above)

This lens offers lots of room for contextual details and storytelling elements. You will appreciate it especially for wide overhead scenes—although with the extra space it offers, you need to pay more attention so that the hero of the shot doesn't get lost in the composition.

Its biggest downfall is the distortion it creates in food scenes. The closer you get to your subject, the more out of proportion and unnatural it will look.

50mm (above)

The 50mm lens is a great choice for overhead images, but you can also use it for straight-on and all the in-between angles. It gives you room to include more elements or negative space in your frame, which can be useful if you need to include room for text or want to explore various crops in post-production. Great for soft, blurry backgrounds and for low-light situations, as it's available to buy with wide maximum apertures. It's a perfect option if you don't have much space in your shooting area.

Though it's known for its diversity, it is not a great candidate for close-up shots. It introduces distortion as you get closer to your subject and it will have a hard time focusing at a short distance.

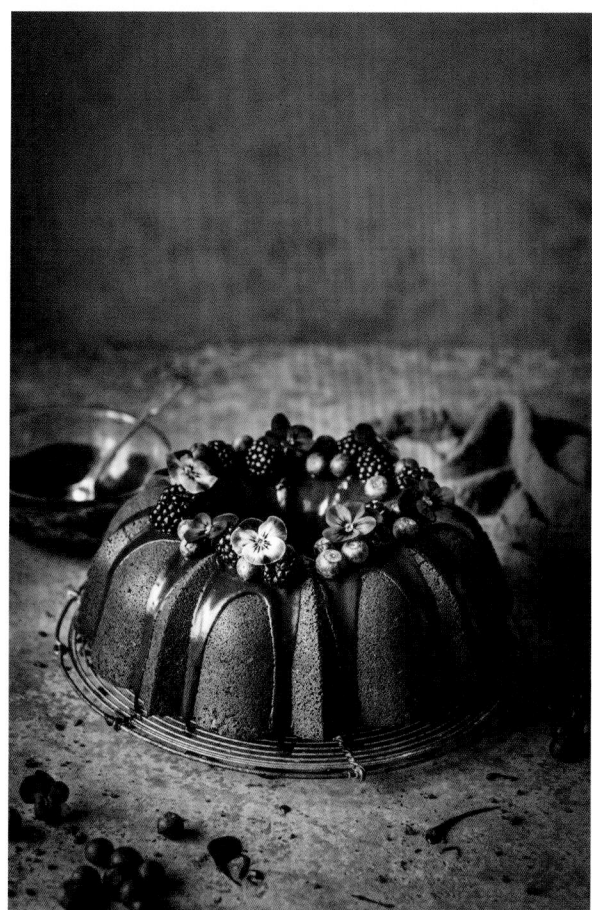

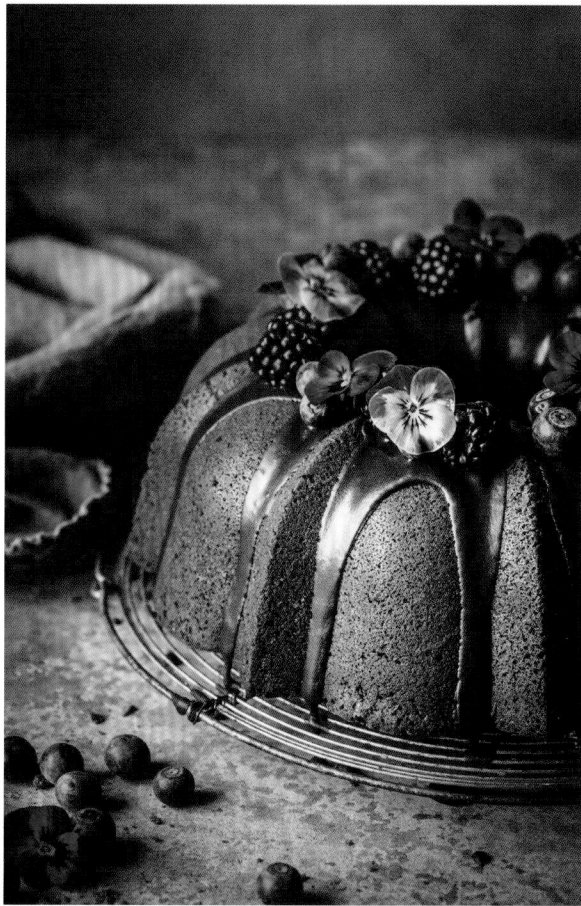

85mm (above)

This lens brings your subject forward and it's great for capturing closer details and for creating a soft background. This lens is perfect for tight compositions; making our food scenes more proportional thanks to the compression effect it offers. It can work well at all angles, although if you want to use it for overheads, a tall sturdy tripod will be necessary. Its minimum focusing distance might be its only flaw, as it means you have to stand back a bit from your subject.

100mm (macro)

A macro lens will wake up your curiosity as it allows you to notice more. It is a great lens for close-up food-portraiture shots and capturing fine, eye-catching details. It will emphasize a blurred background and make elements look more proportional with its compression.

Remember that distance and focal length influence the depth of field. As this lens allows you to get closer to your subject, you'll need to use a high f-number (narrow aperture) to get some of the details in focus. Having space to shoot is important in exploring this lens. Your styling and details have to be spot-on too, as the closer you get, the harder it is to hide mistakes.

The technical side of photography

Creating a food image from scratch takes time and involves making a lot of decisions. You don't want to put in all that time and effort only to find that your images are blurry, not properly focused or exposed, or marred by dirt on your lens.

Manual or autofocus?

On the side of your lens you'll find an AF (autofocus) and MF (manual focus) switch. Each mode has its own benefits and drawbacks according to the kind of shooting you're doing.

Manual
The manual focus is regulated by a movable ring on your lens (separate from the zoom ring, if you have one). Manual focus allows you to set the focus to exactly where you want it to be, giving you total control.

One-shot/single-servo autofocus
When you half press the shutter button, the camera will focus on the subject you are pointing it at and lock it there. This is great for shooting a still subject.

Continuous/ai-servo autofocus
With this option, when you half press the shutter button, the focus will keep tracking a moving subject.

Tip

The LCD screen on our cameras are quite small, so it's worth using the magnification button on your camera, or looking at the images on the laptop when tethering, to check that what you want in focus is beautifully sharp. If it's not, troubleshoot and eliminate what might be causing the problem.

Maximize the sharpness

Making sure your images are tack-sharp adds quality to your work. Achieving this can be as simple as cleaning your lens before you shoot and holding your camera steadily, but there are a few extra things to think about:

* Lower your ISO when possible to avoid any "grain."
* Use fast shutter speeds when handholding.
* When using slow shutter speeds, shoot on a sturdy tripod with a remote or timer to avoid camera shake.
* Pay attention to how the depth of field, distance and focal length are affecting your focus.
* Find out your lens's sweet spot: it is said that the sharpest aperture is typically two to three stops down from the widest aperture of your lens.
* Watch out for your lens creating diffraction when photographing with a very high f-number, as this can cause a photograph to lose its sharpness.
* When photographing handheld, keep your lens vibration reduction (VR) on. When you are using a tripod, turn it off: by looking for vibrations to fix when there are none, the VR function may actually cause some!
* If you can't get details to be in focus and as sharp as you want, it might be because of the way the plane of focus (which is parallel to the camera sensor) falls on your subject. Play with your shooting angle to change the plane of focus and see if that helps.
* Try using the lock-up mirror feature with slow shutter speeds. This doesn't apply to all cameras, but if you're noticing camera shake that you can't find a reason for, it might be the motion of your camera's mirror flipping up for the exposure.

Metering

The camera's built-in light meter measures the intensity and amount of light in the frame to assess whether the scene is correctly exposed. There are different metering modes that measure the light in different ways.

Evaluative (Canon) or matrix (Nikon)
This mode divides the frame into zones, measures the light from each of them and ensures that there is an overall balance between dark and bright tones. It's the default option on most cameras and it does a great job!

Center-weighted
This mode concentrates on evaluating the light in the center of the frame. It's useful for when your subject is in the middle of the picture.

Spot
This metering measures light in just a small spot of the frame. It can be useful when your subject is small and/or has a contrasting exposure to the rest of the image.

Histograms

A histogram is a representation of the tones in your image. You can find this tool on the LCD screen on your camera, or in most post-processing software. It takes the form of a pixel graph that maps the tonal range in the image: from the blacks (on the far left), through shadows, mid-tones, highlights and whites (on the right). Pay attention to your histogram—it can tell you a lot about your image:

* If the image is overexposed—with too many pure whites—you will see a spike touching the right edge. This means you lose detail in this part of the photo, which is known as "clipping."
* If the image is underexposed—with too many pure blacks—you will see a spike touching the left edge. This means you lose detail in this part of the photo, which is known as "clipping."
* Which tones are predominant in your image.
* How much contrast your image has.
* If your image has a variety of tones: that's when tones will be spread across the graph.

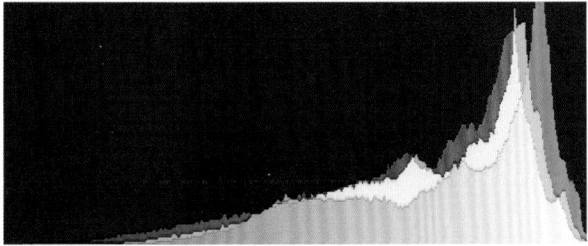

Above: A spike toward the right shows that there are a lot of highlights and whites in the image: this represents a bright-toned photo.

Above: A spike towards the left shows that there are a lot of shadows and blacks in the image: this is representative of a dark-toned photo.

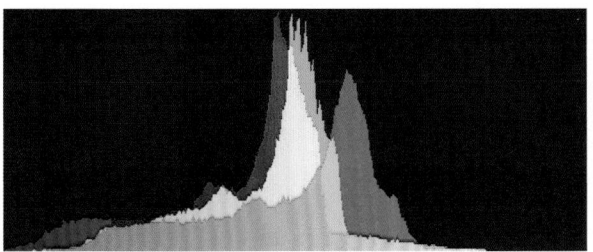

The spikes concentrated in the middle indicate that this image is heavy on midtones and low in contrast.

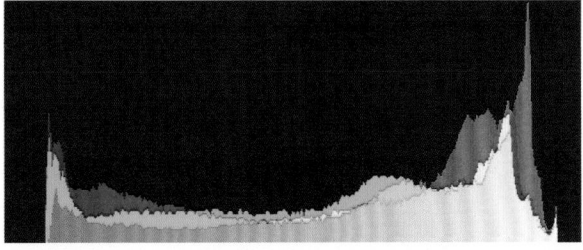

Above: The spikes show that the largest number of tones are in the highlights and the shadows, so the image is high in contrast.

Studio essentials

Although my approach to photography has always been about the vision, over the years I have learned to appreciate the kit too. Fancy gear won't take pictures for you, but being curious about the industry and keeping up with the ever-evolving technology can be a great support for your vision. It can help speed up your creative process too. Here are a few things I could not live without.

Lighting & accessories

To be able to control and shape natural light to create different moods in your images, a diffuser and a selection of different sizes of white and black boards/reflectors will come in handy (see pages 54–57).

Tripods (right)

A sturdy tripod is a lifesaver in low-light situations, when you need to use a slower shutter speed and your camera has to be perfectly still to prevent any shake that might result in a blurry image. I use my tripod even on bright days because I just love the control it gives me. It allows me to tweak my food scene while keeping the camera at the same position. Once the camera is set up on a tripod, I use electronic levelling to make sure it's perfectly straight.

An overhead arm will give you the ability to shoot flatlays (overhead shots), and although some tripods come with an extendible arm, it's usually very short. I highly recommend getting a separate arm instead (e.g. Manfrotto 121 D), that you can attach to most tripods.

Heavy, tall and reliable equipment is worth investing in, especially for overhead shots, so that you don't have to worry about it tilting over and dropping your camera in a bowl of soup!

For straight-on and up to 70-degree angle shots, a light tripod might often be a faster option. If you use it for overheads, remember to weigh it down with something.

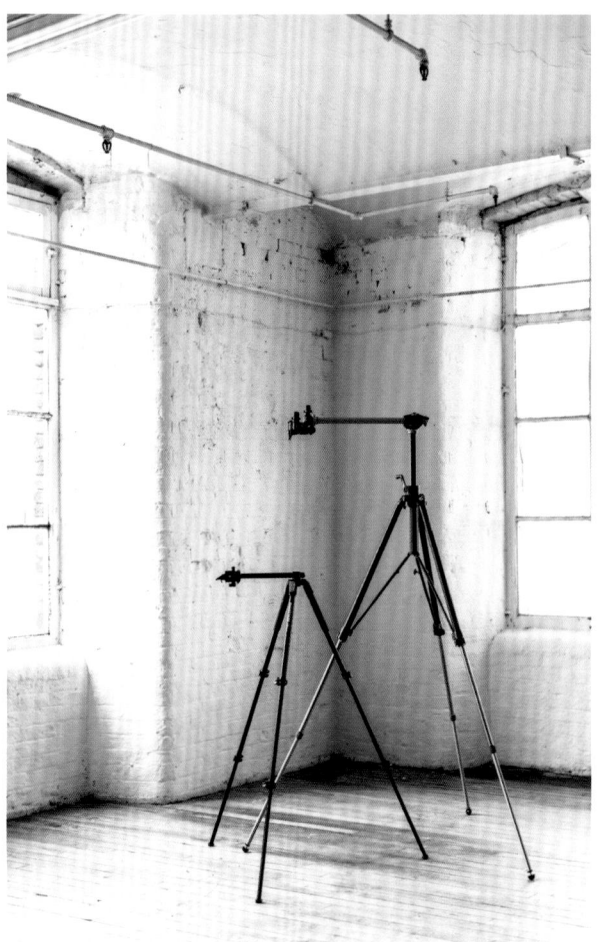

Above: It can be useful to have a strong, tall and heavy tripod in the studio and a light, portable one for taking out and about. In the studio, I use a Manfrotto 058B tripod with Manfrotto 131D arm and Manfrotto 410 junior gear head—nicknamed the "Beast" (shown here on the right). For shooting on the go I use a Manfrotto 190/ or 055 tripod with X pro 3 head or ball head—nicknamed "Littlen" (shown here on the left).

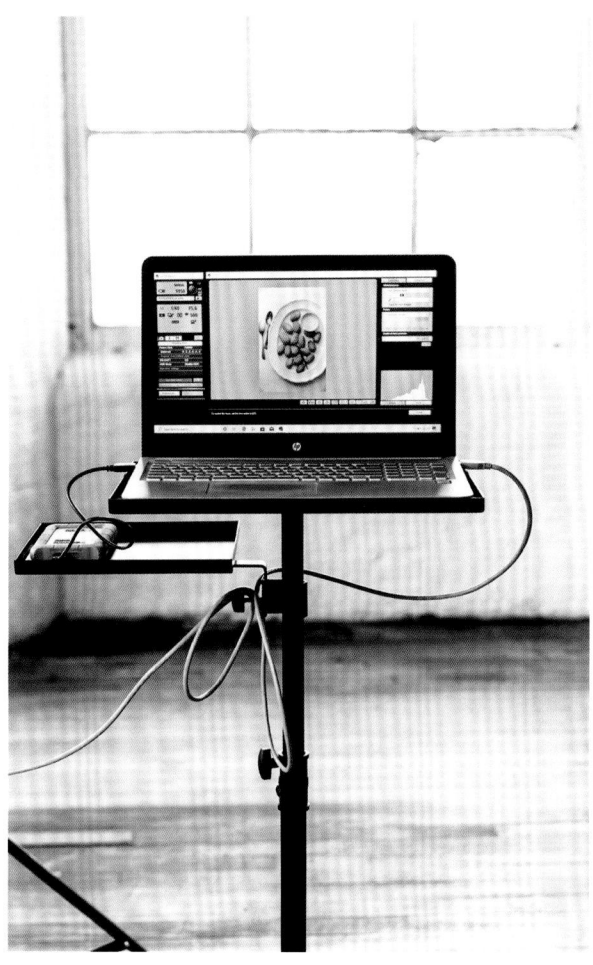

Batteries, cards & hard drives

An organized space saves you time and makes you feel like you are in control of your photography process, so keep spare batteries charged and memory cards ready to use. Have a dedicated space to keep these essentials, and find a system of storing them so that you will know immediately if they are ready to use or need charging or emptying. With batteries, you can turn them upside down to indicate that they need charging. You can keep your memory cards in a dedicated card wallet and turn the full ones upside down and sticker them to know what's on them. Then transfer to a hard drive as soon as you can and format the card to get it ready for the next shoot.

Tethering (above)

Tethering allows you to connect your camera to your laptop, either through a tethering cable or through Wi-Fi (if your camera has this option). Tethering software is necessary, and it will enable you to change settings and take pictures from your laptop as well as view your images larger. Camera brands also offer mobile apps that allow you to control your camera and view pictures on your mobile phone via a Wi-Fi connection.

I tether 95 percent of the time. Although it takes a few moments to set it all up, it always saves me a lot of time in the long run. I can see details in live view on the laptop that I might not notice on my small camera screen, which is especially helpful when my camera is high up on a tripod. It also allows me to save my photos exactly where I want them to be straight away and to edit on the go.

Essentials

* Fast cards
* Spare batteries
* Remote release
* Tethering cable, tethering software, cable connector/port protector (a tool that prevents your tethering cable from disconnecting)
* Comfy bag for transporting kit
* Reflectors
* Diffusers
* Black boards
* Photography stands and clamps to hold backgrounds and reflectors in place
* Camera cleaning kit
* Hard drives
* Post-production software (see Chapter 6)

Backgrounds

The background is the foundation of your photograph, so don't underestimate its importance. A great background will complement your dish and add texture and depth to your scene. A bad background choice, on the other hand, can weaken your composition or even distract from the main subject.

When it comes to backgrounds and props, the biggest thing for me was realizing that the camera sees things differently than I do. Not every item I personally liked looked good photographed and edited, so I had to learn what did.

Always make sure that any props, backgrounds, and surfaces (especially if painted) are safe if you are putting food products directly on them.

What makes a good background
* Lightweight and portable.
* Doesn't take up too much space (double-sided backgrounds are a great idea) and is easy to store and clean.
* A size that will fit a bigger scene if needed (I like mine to be 28 × 35in/72 × 90cm).
* Matte/non-reflective.
* Not distracting (try to avoid colors, patterns, and textures that will compete with your hero subject).

Color choices
Having a few different colors in your collection will be useful for creating various food stories and will add diversity to your portfolio.

Colors that will work with most foods are white, black, grey, blue (preferably cooler tones), and less saturated brown tones for wood.

Colors to explore include cream, peach, blush, deep pink, purple, pastel yellow, and green. These are slightly braver choices that won't work with every dish, but will add something interesting and fresh to your work.

Background materials
* **Vinyl**—Available in many different colors and looks, these are lightweight and can be rolled up, so they are a great choice for taking on a shoot.
* **Wood**—It's a heavier option, but a good-looking wooden background will age gracefully and stay with you for years.
* **Stone**—Very photogenic, but also very heavy and not practical. Bear in mind that certain foods might leave stains and marks (e.g. lemon on marble).
* **Hand-painted**—Available in lovely colors and textures, they are usually made of thin but steady wooden board. Their slim size and manageable weight make them easy to store and work with.
* **Canvas**—These are hand-painted fabrics that come in various colors and effects. You can fold or roll them easily to take them on a shoot with you.
* **Fabric**—A good-quality linen tablecloth or a cut-to-measure fabric will make a perfect background too.

Look for unexpected background ideas
Look around. Potential backgrounds are everywhere. Often a background might look like nothing special until you see it in a photograph, so don't write something off until you've taken a shot. Some ideas include:

* Walls
* Floors
* Tiles
* Furniture
* Newspaper/music sheets/books/notebooks
* Shirts/jackets
* People/hands
* Plates
* Chopping boards
* Curtains
* Parchment paper
* Wicker baskets/boxes/trays

Learn what looks good

Changing your aperture setting, the distance you shoot from, or the white balance will affect the way a background looks in your images. Light and shadows will have a huge effect on the background, and you can enhance this in post-production.

Texture also makes a huge difference to the look of a photo, so it's important to learn what textures look good photographed. A slightly uneven texture will play beautifully with light, adding depth and dimension; backgrounds with a mix of lighter and darker shades of the same color have a similar effect. Smooth textures add lightness to images and will contrast beautifully with more textured food (pasta, I am looking at you!). Keep in mind that smooth textures are considered "flatter," so you might need to add that depth in a different way. Fabrics offer another kind of texture, and can be patterned too, if you are after a different style. I personally love the way flowery and lace patterns add romantic vibe to any photo.

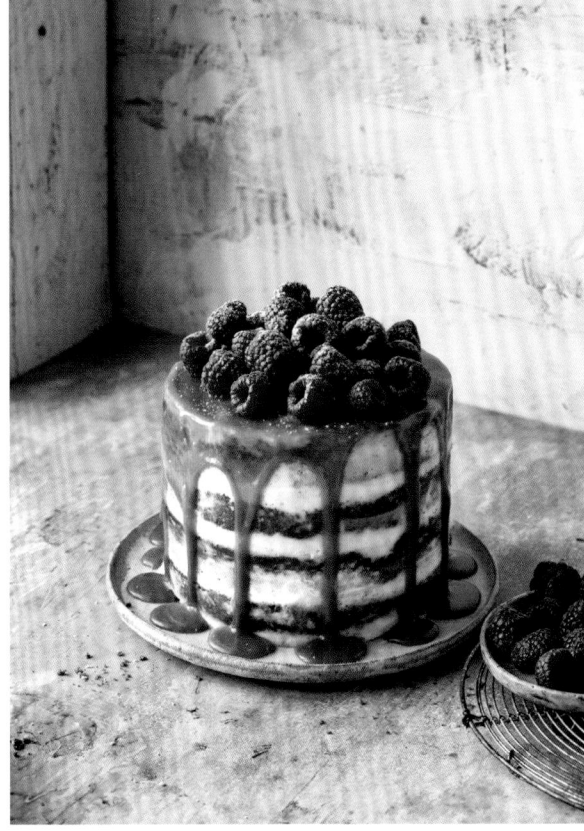

Above & below: Think about interesting ways to place your backgrounds. Not only do the backgrounds here add an interesting texture and a contrasting color, but the way they are placed and shot also adds depth and dimension

Tips

* Always be conscious about your background. Does it add to the whole story? Does it distract from the main subject?
* If your background is too busy, you can blur it by photographing with a shallow depth of field—this will also add depth to your image.
* Experiment with the distance between your subject and the background to see what works best.
* A tighter crop can hide any distractions.
* Take pictures of interesting surfaces wherever you find them, both as a reference for inspiration and to learn to see what works when photographed, and what doesn't.

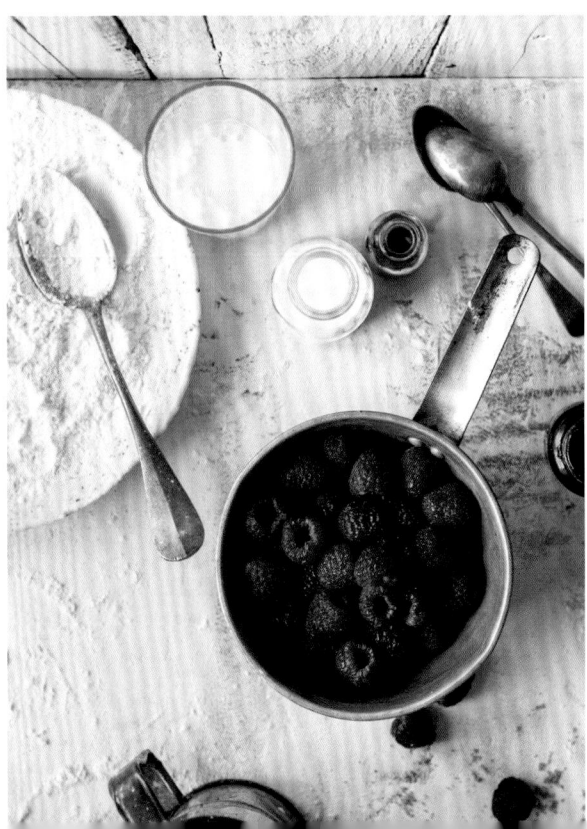

Props: not just a supporting cast

Although the food should always be the star of our photographs, props can help to add details and interest to our compositions and create a beautiful frame for the dish we are presenting.

When choosing props to buy and use, always take your personal style and the message you want to convey into account: is it modern and minimal, classic and traditional, rustic or maybe romantic? Match the props to the message to craft a meaningful story.

Choosing your props

Color
Neutral hues like whites, off-whites, beiges, browns, grays, and blacks are all-around choices that can be used with many dishes. These colors make up about 80 percent of my own prop collection. The other 20 percent is reserved for a pop of color—and here I can be a little bit more adventurous with my prop choices, but I always make sure the style mixes and matches well with my neutral pieces.

Size, height & weight
Props should always be proportional to your dish so it's good to have a variety of sizes and heights to go with different recipes. If it's too big or too small in relation to the food, the viewer will spot right away that something is off. When it comes to the weight, I often reserve chunkier pieces for hearty dishes and delicate items for lighter recipes.

Shape
I always look for pieces in simple shapes and soft lines as they are gentle, pleasing for the eye, and match every food story. Bold shapes, on the other hand, can add an element of surprise to a specific photo, but be mindful that they don't distract from the food itself.

Texture
The camera loves matte, hand-made, and rustic pieces with texture: in the right lighting, it's what adds life and interest to our images. But it's also worth investing in smooth (but not too shiny) props: they are timeless and classy. Wooden textures can add diversity to your collection too.

Patterns
Subtle lines, dots, or floral patterns can add interest to your images. More understated designs are a safer option as they don't compete with the food for attention. But as with shape and color, it's good to have one or two bolder pieces in your collection too—just bear in mind that they will be too memorable for regular use and need a strong subject to balance them out.

A capsule collection
Creativity needs a space to breathe and I truly believe that having fewer props can be good for our imagination. Too much choice often makes us feel overwhelmed and confused. Plus, if we have too many props to use, we will likely forget what props we have anyway! It's therefore helpful to build a collection of essential, classic items that never go out of fashion, mix and match well, and work with every food. These are the pieces worth investing in.

What makes a timeless prop?
* Not too memorable or distracting in color, shape, size, or pattern.
* Something universal that you can use over and over again with many different dishes.
* Not too shiny or reflective.
* Something that will look as (or more) beautiful with time and use.

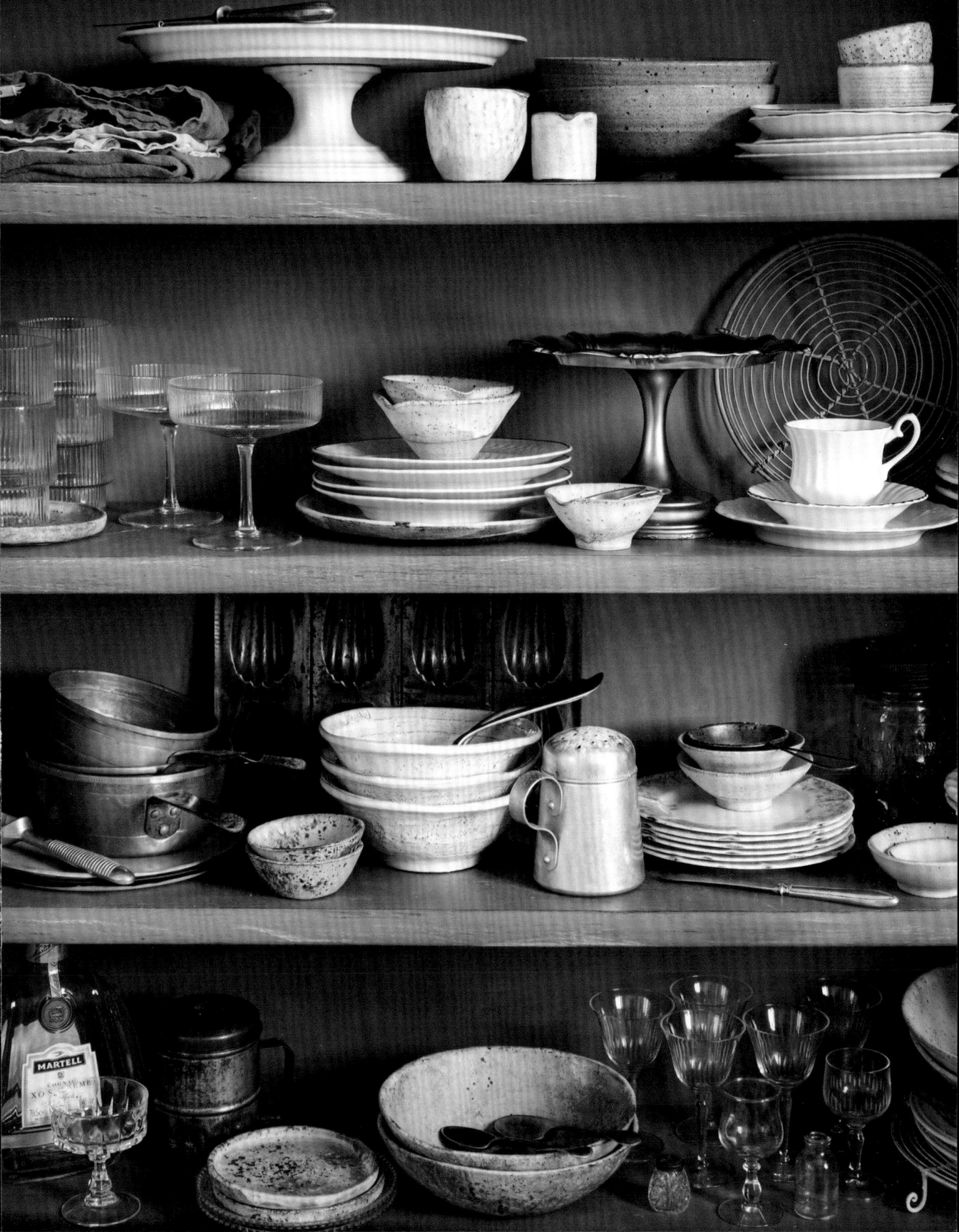

What to look for in your props

Before you buy anything, ask yourself the following questions to make better prop choices:

* Is it just me who likes it, or will my camera find it attractive too?
* Will I use it often? Can I use it with different dishes?
* Do I already have something like this?
* Does it go with the rest of my collection and my style?
* Where will I store it?

Crockery

Invest in items that work with many different recipes: for example, a large oval platter, a few dinner and side plates, shallow bowls that can be filled with salads, soups, and pastas (but not only these!), a selection of small/tiny plates, condiment and pinch bowls that you can fill to support your narrative. A small/tiny jug will always come in handy, as will a couple of small tea/coffee cups. Handmade ceramics look especially attractive, but I am also a huge fan of fine china pieces with subtle patterns that have a romantic charm. These can be very affordable and often look best when pre-loved and even slightly faded. I never buy full sets (unless for a specific job): having a range of pieces that work well individually and can be mixed and matched for different food stories gives you more interesting options.

Glasswear

In most cases, smaller-sized glassware is easier to photograph. Try to find pieces that work with light beautifully. Rippled (my favorite for flatlays) or crystal-cut glasses will look impressive, but plain pieces are a staple in every collection. Items that work with drinks as well as desserts will be the best investment.

Small/tiny glass bottles and jars that you can fill with a variety of things will be useful for supporting your story.

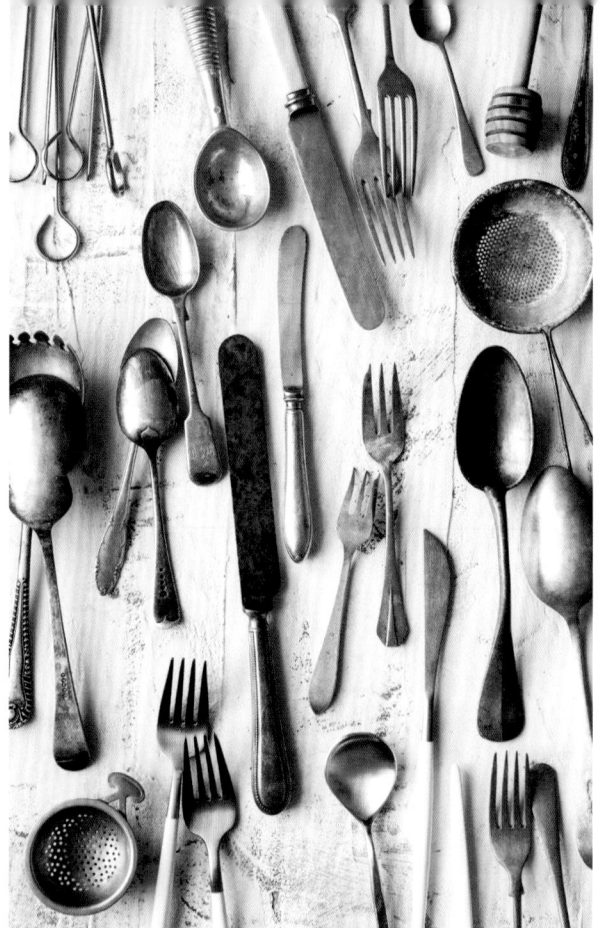

Cutlery (above)

Apart from standard table cutlery, salad servers, dessert spoons and forks, and cake, butter and paring knives are items you will need often. It's good to have a variety of styles in your collection too: vintage items, modern pieces, a selection of silver and gold, white enamel cutlery and those with wooden handles will all photograph beautifully. You don't want distracting reflections, so avoid anything too shiny.

Bakeware, cookware & accessories

Cookware and bakeware looks its best when it has a few signs of wear and tear: visibly aged pieces tell a better story. Look for items that you can use over and over again with both sweet and savoury dishes: cooling racks, cutting boards, iron skillets, metal tins, pots, and measuring cups are always useful. When it comes to these pieces it's best to stick to "safe" colors as described on page 38.

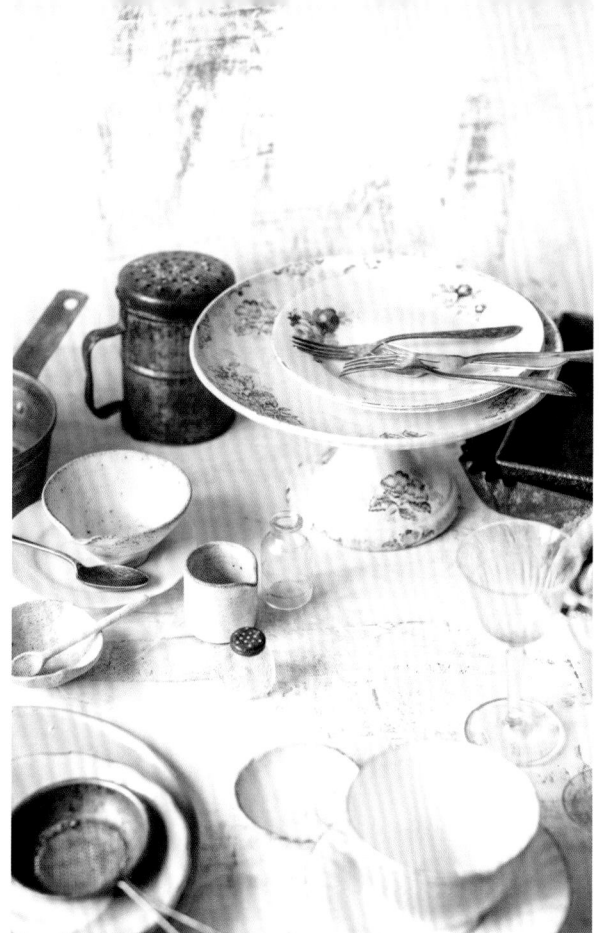

Creative ways to use props

Repurpose

A baking tin doesn't only have to be used for baking and roasting; it can work as a serving tray too, beautifully framing the food presented in it. A salad can be layered in a jar or a glass, or spread across a chopping board. Lasagne can be presented in small, individual skillets. And if you don't have a cake stand that will fit your cake, you can create one by putting a bowl upside down and placing a plate on top of it.

Layer (right)

Layer some of your props on top of each other to add depth and interest to your frame. You wouldn't serve a slice of cake on two stacked plates in real life, but it's something that can add visual interest to your photos.

Think outside the box

Use ingredients as props, or bring everyday items into the frame for storytelling (e.g. chairs, old photographs, spectacles). Look around the house for items that will add extra charm.

Fabrics

The softer the better! You need something flexible that will flow beautifully in your images. If your linens are a bit stiff, mist them with a tiny bit of water to soften them before placing them in a scene. I like having a few napkins with frayed edges and some with floral patterns for variety.

Storytellers

These are one-of-a-kind items with character that helps to tell the story of your hero dish. Good things to have are a sugar sifter, a cake server, an ice cream scoop, salt and pepper grinders, and a cheese grater, just to name a few. You only need one or two of each, so look for something charming (and matte) that will work with multiple styles. These items take the longest to source, so make a wish list and don't rush it, as they will stay with you for years.

Tips

* If possible, display your props in a visible place so that you can see each item's full potential before a shoot.
* Rent props if you can.
* It's better to use no props than ones that distract from your main subject.
* I usually photograph a prop with my phone before I buy it (always asking permission), then quickly edit it in Lightroom Mobile App. This gives me a good idea of whether it's worth buying.

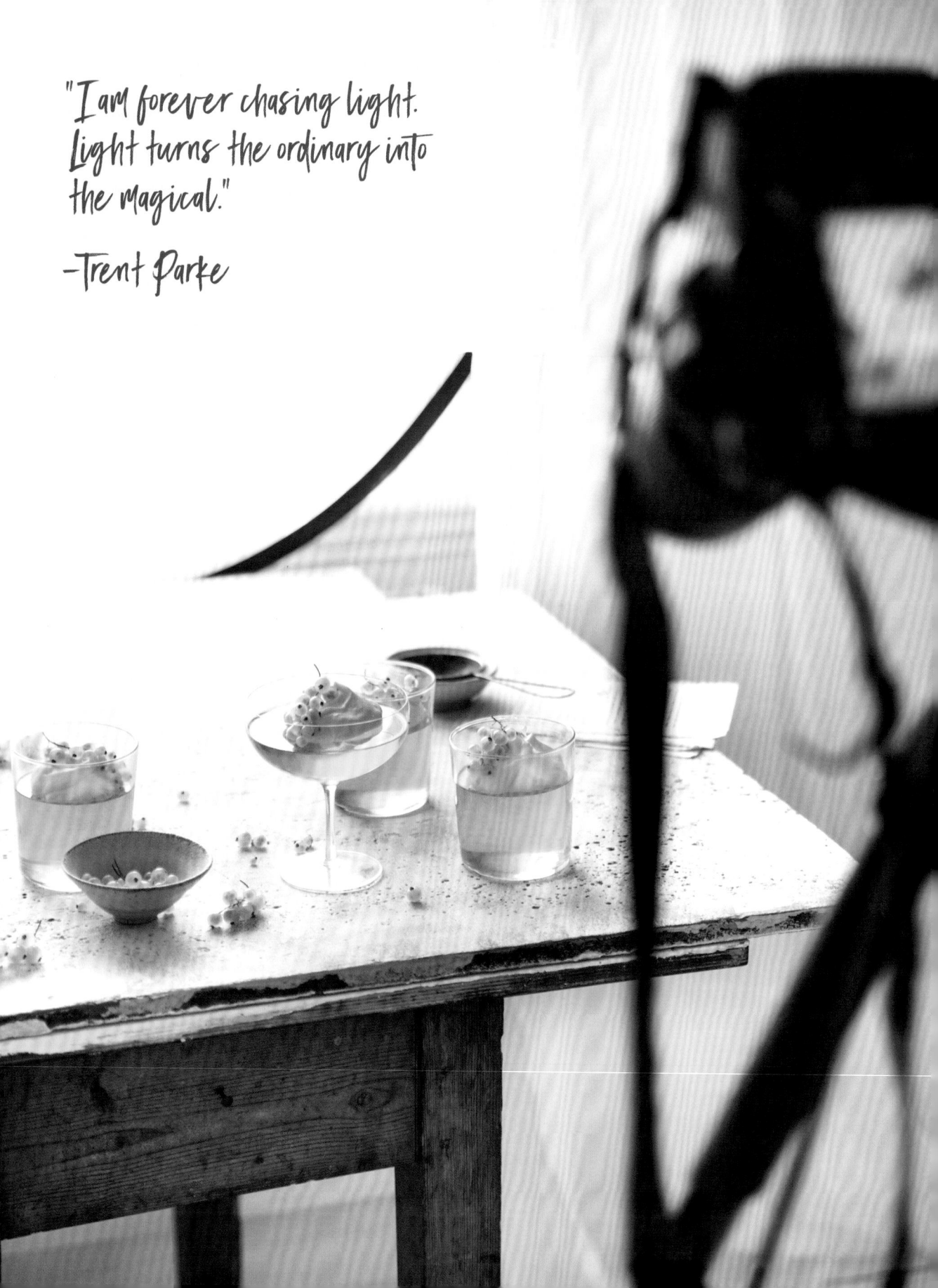

"I am forever chasing light.
Light turns the ordinary into
the magical."

—Trent Parke

Become a Student of Natural Light

Light is the beating heart of every image

There are no great photos without highlights and shadows interacting playfully together around the subject. It's the highlights that our eyes are drawn to first, but it's the shadows that shape the light and direct our attention to the brighter parts. It's this play of light and shadow that adds depth and dimension to an image, without which even the most beautiful food will appear flat and lifeless.

Light first!

It isn't easy to constantly pay attention to something that is intangible, and I myself was guilty of focusing too much on composition and fancy props in the early days, while forgetting about this—the most crucial ingredient. No wonder my photos were boring! If you want your images to have that special something, you have to start thinking of highlights and shadows as characters in your food story. They have the power to bring your compositions to life, and how you use them influences the whole mood and atmosphere of your work.

Become a student of light and stay a student forever

Many photographers don't like how changeable natural light is. Sure, it can be frustrating at times, but natural light can also be the best teacher and spark inspiration for a shoot. It's also free! Observe it closely, stay curious, challenge yourself, and never get too comfortable with one lighting setup. Photograph at different locations and at different times of day. See its magic and your photos will never be dull. Get into a habit of paying attention to light even for as little as one minute a day (but every day!). I promise that this will soon change how you see light in your photography.

Whether you are an aspiring or seasoned photographer, there will always be new and challenging lighting situations you'll have to face. Knowing what influences the look of natural light can take some of the pressure off and will help you create arresting photos in any environment, whether it's in a corner of your home, a restaurant, or a studio you've never shot in before.

Get to know your shooting environment

When I'm photographing in a new space, the first thing I always do is take a few minutes to look around the space, assessing all the windows and doors I have available, and paying attention to how the natural light is shaped by that space.

The size of the windows in your shooting area can have a huge impact on how your images look. Wide and tall windows let plenty of light in, producing a brighter and softer scene with minimal shadows. Small windows allow less light in, creating deep shadows and giving your scene more contrast.

If you have a big window and you would like to create more shadows to add drama to your scene, you can decrease the size of the light source with the use of blackout curtains or by partially covering windows and doors. Of course, it's much harder (if not impossible) to increase the size of your light source if you want to minimize the shadows to get that bright and airy look. Make sure any window coverings are completely pulled back, or try to find a bigger light source if you can.

When too much light becomes a problem

While we photographers obsess about light, more light is not always better. A bright interior doesn't always equal great food photography. It's an important lesson that too much light in food photography can wash out all of your shadows and kill dimension in your images. If you have big windows on multiple walls, you might actually have too much light in your space, and covering and blocking some of the windows might be necessary to achieve depth in your image. If you shoot in a room with skylight windows, the light coming in from above may be the reason your photos have no shadows and look flat—easily solved by closing the blind. Don't forget that food subjects are relatively small and don't really need as much light as we would if we were photographing interiors or people.

Below: The size of the light source makes all the difference here. The image on the left was shot with a large window; the middle image was shot with a small/medium window; and the image on the right was shot with a thin strip of light coming through drawn curtains.

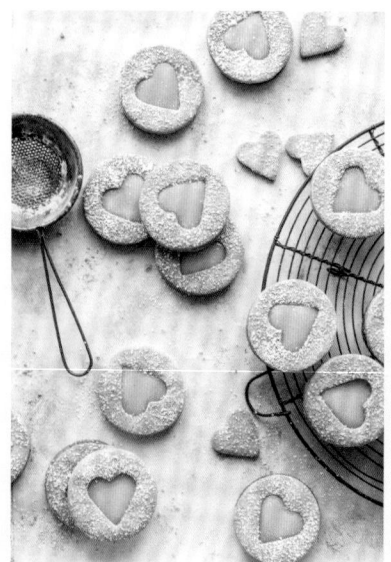
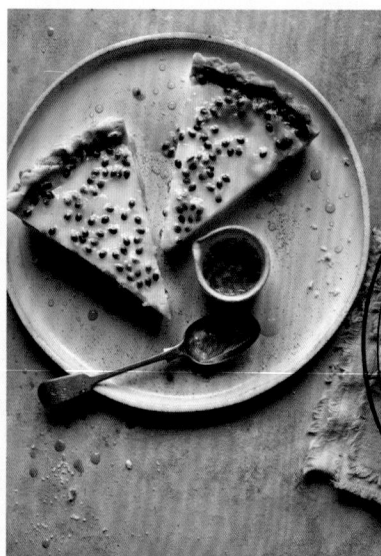
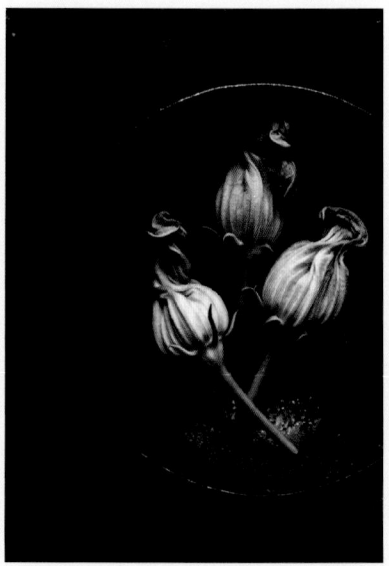

Let natural light be your teacher

You might think that there is no good light where you live, but magical light really can be discovered everywhere. Studying changing light in your home will open your eyes to the possibilities natural light has to offer. Pick one window and place a simple subject nearby, then photograph it a few times throughout the day, paying close attention to what the shadows and highlights look like. You will notice that there are a few factors that influence the look of natural light.

The direction your window is facing

The direction of your window will influence the intensity and color of the light in your photos, depending on the time of day as well as which hemisphere you live in. Keep an eye on what time the sun comes and goes in the room, how this affects contrast and colors, and when light feels the most attractive to you.

The time of day/year

The lower the angle of the sun, the longer the shadows. You can observe this in the morning and from the late afternoon until the sun sets. The higher the sun is in the sky—for example at noon—the shorter your shadows will be. The sun appears differently throughout the seasons, too. The angle is higher in the summer and lower in the winter.

The weather

Light is hard and intense on a sunny day and soft on an overcast day. This will completely change the atmosphere in your photographs and what your subject looks like.

How your walls affect your light

The color and surface of the walls will influence how the light is reflected in your images. White walls brighten your scene, open the shadows, and reduce the contrast. Dark, especially black walls, on the other hand, absorb the light, adding contrast and shadow to your scene. Be aware of vibrant colors, as they can create an unwanted color cast in your images.

Let yourself be challenged

Knowing the light in your main shooting space inside out is important, but the best way to grow your lighting skills is to photograph at different locations. I've shot in many challenging spaces over the years, from a large and bright London studio to a tiny and dark kitchen on a Croatian hill, and it was all these out-of-my-comfort-zone experiences that shaped me into a better photographer.

Tip

Remember to turn off any artificial lights you might have on in your shooting environment. Natural light doesn't often mix well with artificial household lighting.

Assessing a shooting space

* How many windows are there? Are they big or small? Are there windows on more than one wall, providing light from different directions? Which direction are they facing? Are there any skylight windows?
* What is the weather like outside? Is it sunny or overcast?
* What is the angle of the light? How do the shadows look? Are they long and deep, minimal and soft, or washed out completely?
* What color are the walls, and how does that affect shadows and color cast in your images?
* Is anything obstructing the window?

Hard & soft light

When talking about natural light, the light of a sunny day hitting your window directly is called "hard light." Light shining through clouds on an overcast day or indirect light (shade) is called "soft light."

You can recognize hard light by well-defined shadows with razor-sharp edges, and soft light by its soft, transitioned shadow edges. The difference between hard and soft light lies not only in the appearance of highlights and shadows, but also in the mood, atmosphere, and story they create.

Hard light (right)

Hard light is punchy, dramatic, and high in contrast. It draws out textures and emphasizes dimension. Its intensity gives you a green light to use faster shutter speeds and higher f-numbers, which in turn helps make every detail in your image sharp and visible. Powerful shadows themselves become a subject in your composition, attracting your audience's attention as light becomes almost tangible. Hard light will help you add energy to your images and catch your viewer's eye with something unexpected.

Because of its unevenness, direct sunlight can be challenging and it might not be effective in every situation. But that doesn't mean you should avoid it.

If you have never photographed with hard light before, don't be afraid of it. Study, explore, and experiment with it. Think about the shape of the food, as this will be echoed in the shape of its shadow. When picking your subject, take into consideration that hard light intensifies texture, and not every texture handles it well. Subjects with strong uneven surfaces can be tricky to work with. Hard light will expose every imperfection too. Anything smooth, on the other hand, will photograph beautifully.

When working with hard light, leave enough room in between the subjects for the shadows to play, and take into consideration that the lower the angle of the sun (like in the morning for example), the longer the shadows will be. Drinks in crystal cut glasses will create impressive shadows but round smooth fruit is also a great subject for first-time hard-light explorations. Since hard light adds a lot of depth to the composition, it can also be a clever way to bring flat food to life.

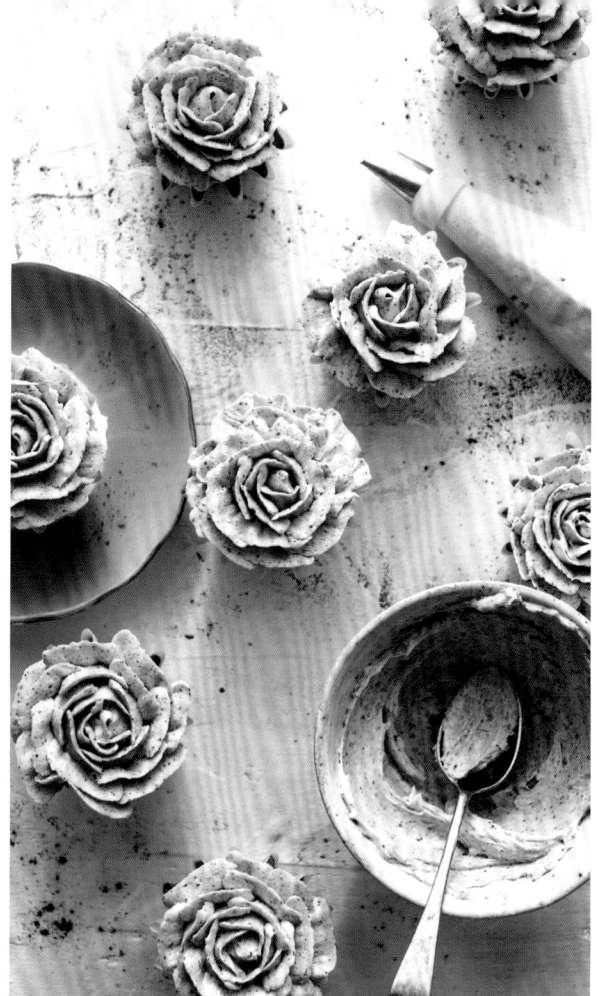

Tip

Use hard and soft lighting to evoke certain emotions around your recipe. If there is a recipe for which you'd like to conjure a sense of vibrancy, energy, or fun, hard light can help you tell that story. Soft light, on the other hand, is perfect for creating a gentler atmosphere and suggesting a feeling of calm or even nostalgia.

Soft light (above)

Soft light is gentle and imbues photographs with a sense of calm. The transition between highlights and shadows is subtle, making soft light easy to work with. This type of light wraps delicately around the subject, smoothing uneven surfaces, which in food photography can be a very useful thing! The flattering quality of this light might well make it your new best friend.

Clouds work as a natural diffuser for hard light, and you will notice that, depending on their formation, they filter light differently. A thin layer of cloud will create a beautifully soft light, whereas thick and heavy clouds can create very little contrast and make everything look flat. When you combine clouds with rain, fog, or snow, it creates yet another completely different experience of soft light.

When there are no clouds in the sky, you can still turn hard light into soft light with the use of a diffuser. Sadly, we can't turn natural soft light into hard light—but we can create it with artificial lighting.

Working with hard & soft light

The images below demonstrate a typical setup for working with (natural) hard and soft light: the major difference you'll notice is that hard light is direct, while soft light is diffused (in this case by using a professional diffuser). However, it's important to know that hard and soft light are about more than just sun and clouds.

To create hard light you need a small light source. Distance plays an important part here too—for example, in nature, direct sunlight produces hard light. The sun is pretty big, but because it's so far away, the distance makes it relatively small in comparison to our subject.

To create soft light, you need a bigger light source, and/or place it closer to your food scene (so that a smaller light source appears relatively larger).

Why not see for yourself? You will get the best results from this exercise during the evening, in a dim room and away from any light sources.

Hold a small object such as a coin in your fingertips against the wall (around 30cm away from it), shine a small flashlight on it and move the flashlight away from the coin. Can you see how defined the edge of the coin's shadow is when the light source is farther away (and relatively smaller)? It should have a sharp and defined edge. That's hard light.

If you move the flashlight very close to the subject, you will see that the edges of the coin's shadow start to become softer and more blurry around the edges. That's because the light source is now closer to the subject and relatively larger in size—which is how you get soft light. This will prove especially useful if you ever want to experiment with artificial light.

Hard light setup

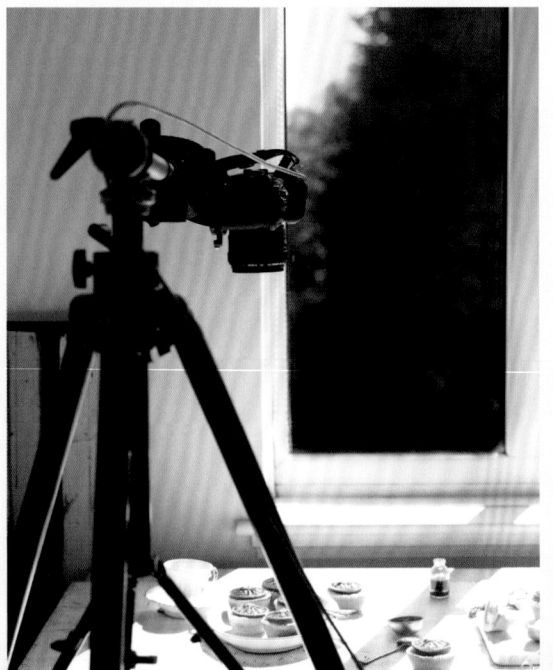

Soft light setup

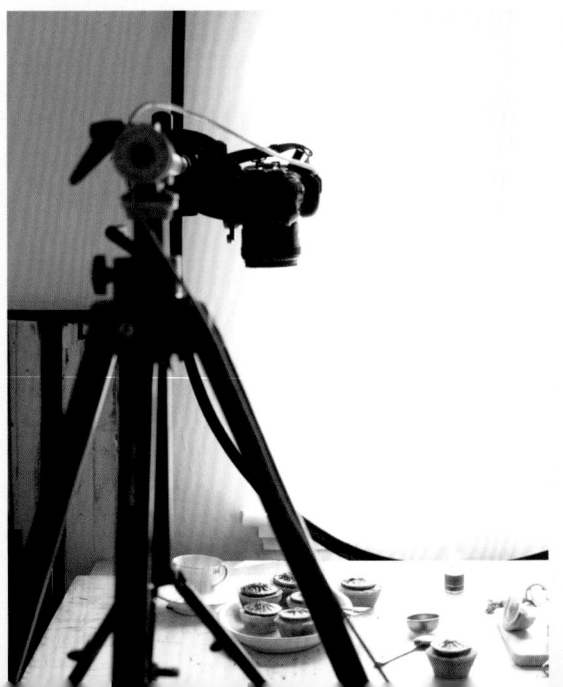

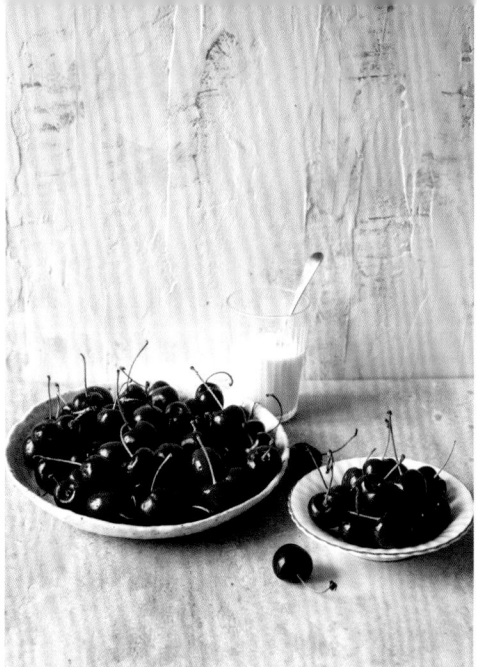

Above: Next to a window, the highlights and shadows are well defined and high in contrast.

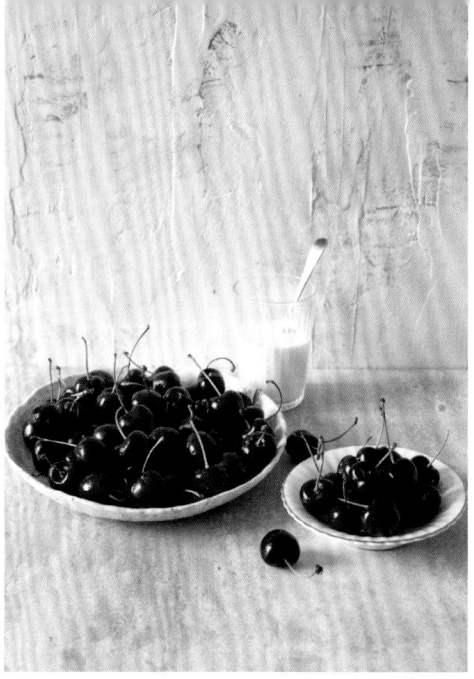

Above: Two meters from the window, the scene looks more evenly lit. The shadows are longer, but also less punchy and the image starts looking flat.

Intensity of light

The farther away you are from your light source, the less light reaches your subject. Logic would suggest that if you doubled the distance from the window or light source, you would halve the intensity of the light, right? In fact, this is not the case. A rule known as the inverse square law says that when you double the distance from your light source, you are actually left not with half the intensity as expected, but only a quarter. As the distance increases, the drop-off slows.

This means that you have a lot of light intensity when you photograph close to a light source and very little in other parts of the space. So, do I measure the distance every time I move my setup? No, I don't. But understanding how this law works on a practical level is really useful and worth trying out for yourself.

In daylight, pick a room with a small, single window that provides soft light, and stand in front of it, side on. Take your phone out and take a selfie (trust me, this is for science!). Half of your face will be bright and the other half will be covered in shadow. There will be a noticeable contrast.

Now walk to the other side of the room and take another selfie, again facing the same direction. The light on your face will look much more even. The highlights will have lost their punch, the shadows won't look as dark, and there will not be much contrast in between the two. You can see how distance from the window affects the intensity of light and contrast.

You can play with distance to manipulate contrast and the way your shadows and highlights appear. When your food scene feels too dark or too flat, moving it closer to the window can be a great solution. When the light is too intense and your food scene has too much contrast, you can move your scene slightly away from your window. Find distance that works best for your subject and the mood of your story. You will see the biggest difference within the first two meters from the light source.

Always remember to tweak your exposure settings when needed.

Direction of light

If you want to uncover natural light's full potential, don't photograph on auto-pilot with the same lighting setup over and over again. Table at the usual position, camera where it always is, light coming from the same direction. Every. Single. Time. It might feel comfortable, but you will never discover anything new and potentially more exciting.

Your lighting setup really doesn't have to be complicated to be successful. Something as simple as moving your camera can change the look of the light in your photographs for the better. Every angle and position has its strengths and enhances different types of dishes. Most of the time photographers will talk about three types of lighting—side, front, and back—but challenge yourself to find more!

Try not to always position your camera bang on the side; travel all around your subject, tilting your table towards the window or away from the window if you need to. See how the direction of light changes when you move your setup slightly below the window sill. There are so many angles in between the front, side and back. You don't want to miss any of them.

Front lighting

Illuminating your subject from the front can be quite tricky for food photography. Front light means placing the camera (and quite possibly yourself) between the light source and the subject, which means that you will be obstructing the light and creating a shadow that falls on your food scene. At the same time, the subject's shadows will fall behind it, making it look flatter and darkening other elements and the background too.

It's said that this type of light is "not suitable" for food, and personally, I haven't yet created any food images to be proud of with this type of lighting. But maybe you can be the one to prove everybody wrong!

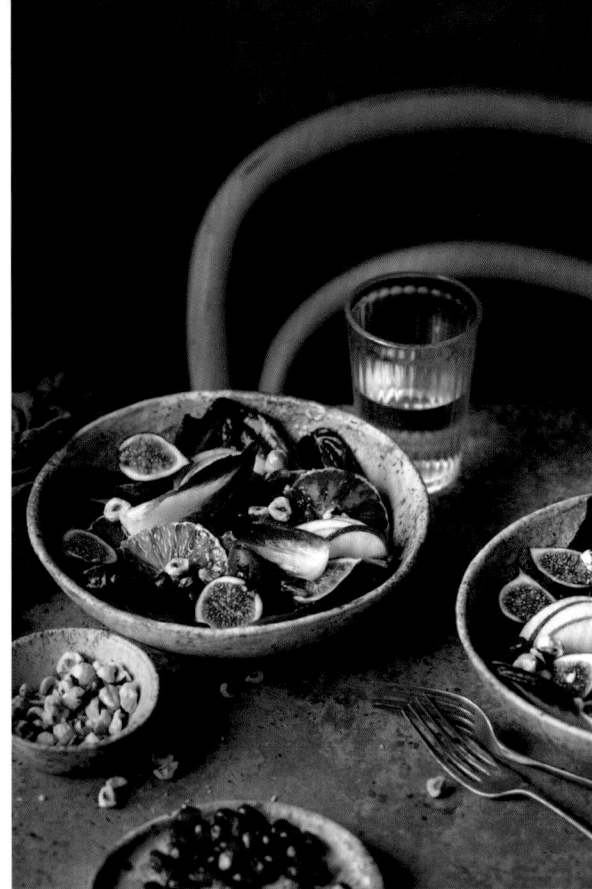

Side lighting (above)

We are talking about side light when the light comes from the side of your subject. The direction you choose to photograph from will affect where highlights and shadows appear in your photograph. Be intentional about where you arrange supporting elements too, as, for example, a large prop placed near the window can cast a shadow on your hero dish and dull its potential.

This is the most popular lighting direction in food photography and it's no surprise really, as it is flattering for food and easy to work with. It's perfect for adding balanced contrast, creating tonal depth and softening textures—exactly what most of us are aiming for in our food photos. Its biggest downfall is making food photographers too comfortable, so if you only photograph with side light, always relying on the same setup, it's time to stir things up.

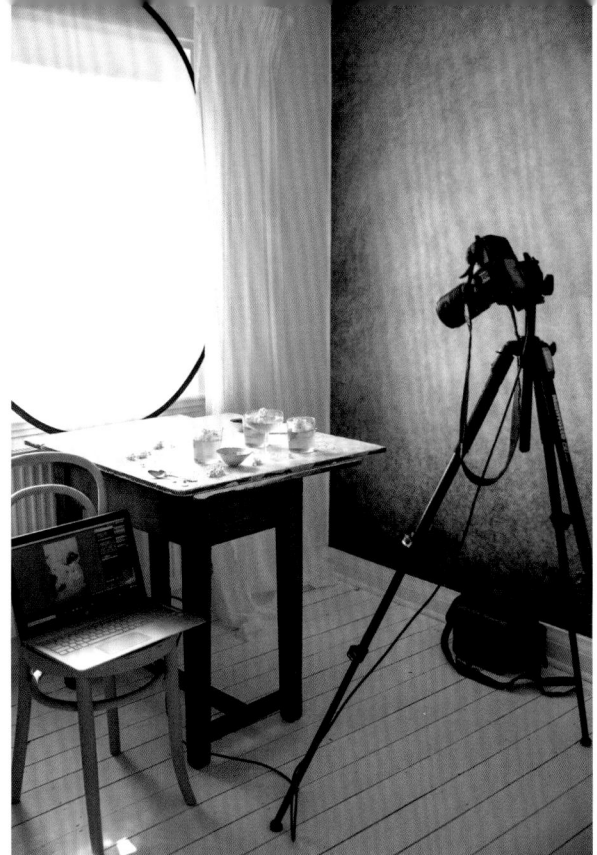

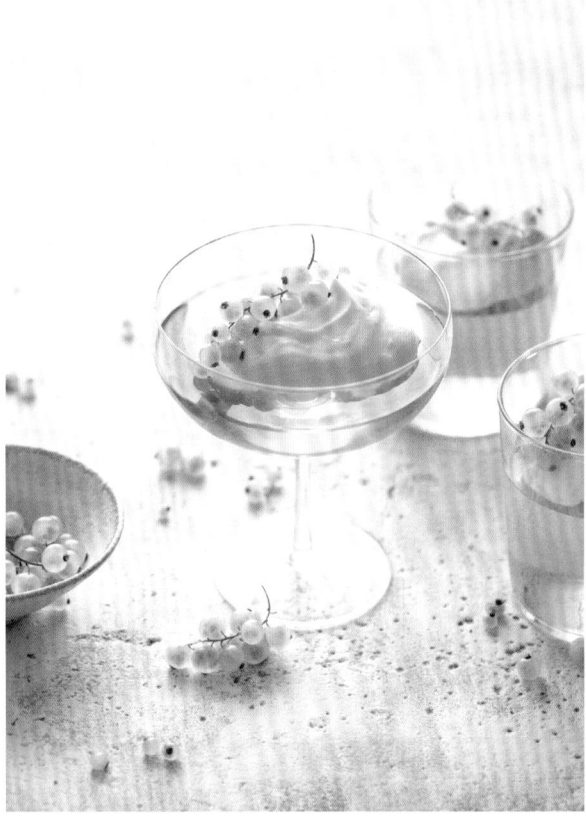

Backlight magic (above, left & right)

Side light may take all the fame when it comes to photographing food, but don't overlook the power of backlight, because it can create a *wow!* effect in your images.

Backlighting is the process of illuminating the subject from the back, so that your main light source is behind the subject and you are shooting towards the light. This can create spectacular highlights that give your images a glowing effect, really bringing the scene to life when done well.

When you experiment with backlighting, explore various angles to see where your camera's position meets the light to capture a brilliant shine. Not every angle will capture these incredible highlights, but I find that angles between 20 and 80 degrees work best for most images, depending on the subject I am photographing. As you can see from my setup (above), the key to backlighting is keeping your subject between the camera and the light source.

What to take into account when using backlighting

Backlight loves texture

Smooth shimmering caramel, soft and shiny chocolate frosting, glistening fruit: when light meets that texture, something magical happens!

Think about what kind of food could be captured with this glowing effect. This will be something with a shine: chocolate ganache, icing, soft ice cream, and beverages all make perfect subjects for backlighting. I also love how it highlights the glisten of various fruit and vegetables (although sometimes you might need to help them shine with a spritz of water).

A little warning here: backlight picks up every imperfection. If your ganache doesn't look smooth, this light will intensify the flaw.

Backlight brings the little details to life

Droplets of water on freshly washed cherries, sprinkles of sugar on pie pastry, sparkling bubbles in a glass of Champagne—details that might have been lost with the use of side lighting are beautifully enhanced and highlighted with the use of backlighting.

Backlight can be reflected

Backlighting creates a lot of shadows, which can add dynamism to your images, but sometimes too much of a good thing becomes a problem. To balance the image and make the lighting look more even, you can reflect some light back by placing a reflector or something with a white surface in front of your frame, making sure it's not obstructing your camera.

Backlight can also be blocked

You can also block the light to create a shadow in the top part of the frame, which is what I do in most of my images (and not only the backlit ones). With this little trick, you can add dimension and prevent a background from looking washed out.

Backlight keeps you on your toes

Backlighting is not effective in every situation! You have to pick the right subject and focus on the texture here. This type of light can be challenging. But it also forces you to train your seeing skills and pay attention to the details. Good subjects to start with are beverages and dewy, glistening fruit.

Tips

* Diffusing might help make the shadows softer. Just be careful that too much diffusion doesn't leave your images looking flat and lifeless.
* Spot metering is helpful for accurately measuring exposure when shooting with backlight.
* Make your backlit images extra eye-catching by choosing brave colors or combining backlighting with creative movement.
* Backlight will be a great choice when you are trying to capture steam in your photographs.
* You can balance out those more problematic, unevenly lit areas in your photos in post-production if you need to.
* Backlight should always enhance your food subject and never overpower it.
* Just play! Backlit photos might not always be "perfect" in terms of exposure, but that's okay. It's all about having fun and trying to create something different.

Opposite: There are many ways of using backlight and many subjects to explore: see how inventive you can be.

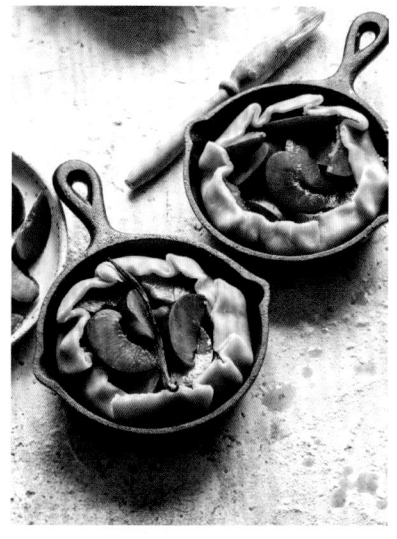

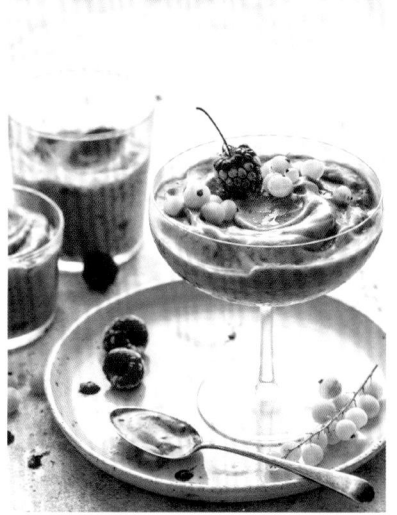

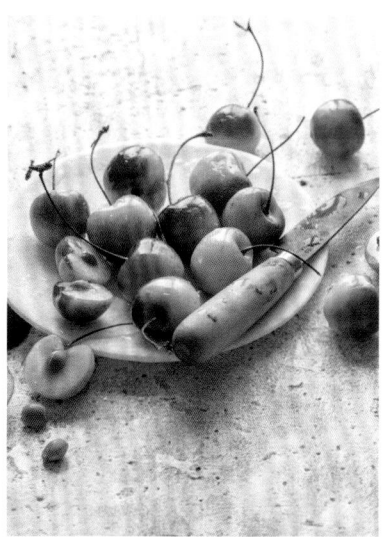

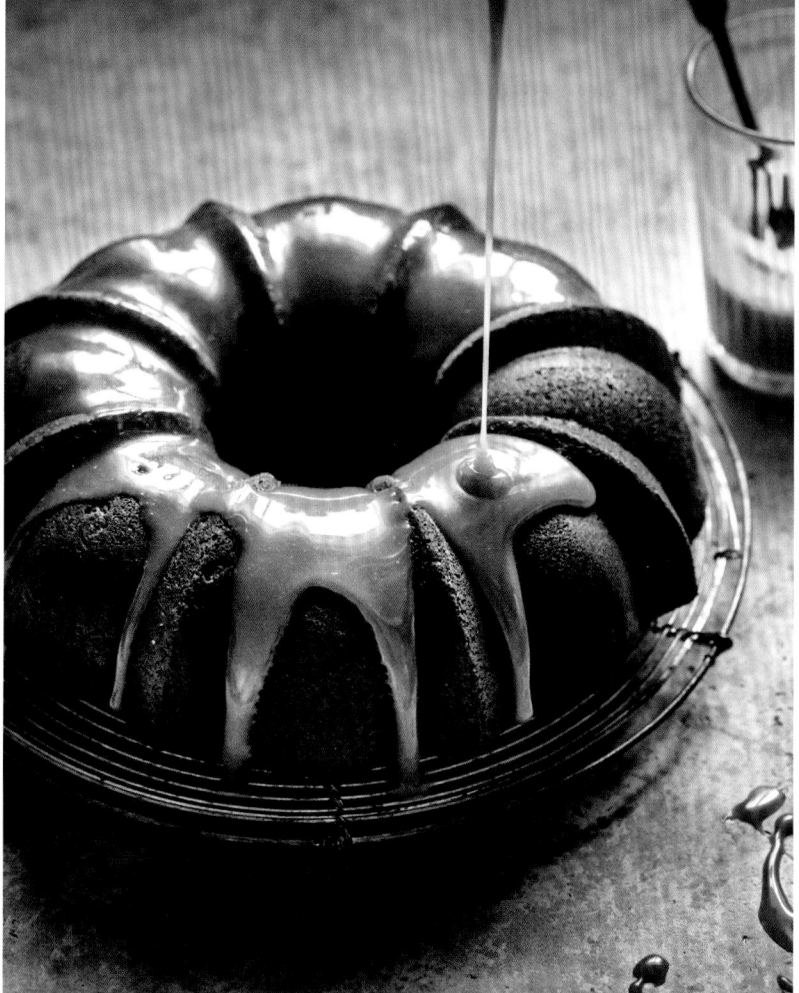

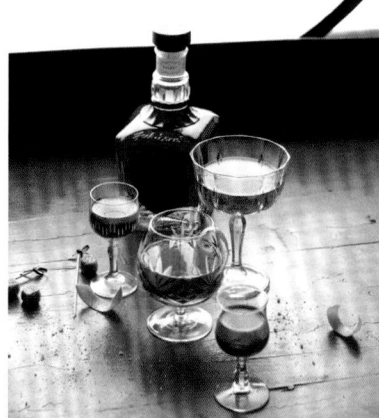

Above: Blocking backlight (setup)

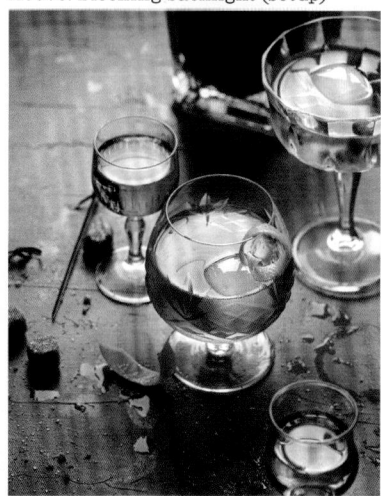

Above: Blocking backlight (result)

Shaping the light

Natural light can be capricious, but when you study it carefully, you'll find that it is full of potential too. Although we can't control natural light's behaviour, we can creatively shape it. By knowing what light you want to create in your images, you can stop being controlled by what's available and start shaping it into what's possible. And the best part? It's easy!

Diffusers

Diffusion is a method of filtering hard light through a semi-transparent material to create softer light. Diffusers are used to tame punchy highlights and shadows when you want to create evenly balanced and calm-inducing light. Professional diffusers are very affordable but a thin white sheet or window voile will do a great job too.

To use this technique, place your diffuser in between the subject and the light source. This will disperse the light, creating a bigger area of softer illumination.

The size of your diffuser and how close you place it to the subject will change the look of the shadows. The bigger the diffuser or the closer it is to your food scene, the softer the light will be.

Depending on the subject I work with and intensity of the light, I might choose to diffuse the light even on an overcast day, when it's already soft, to achieve that extra-soft look—always being mindful of how this affects my image. Too much diffusion can reduce the contrast between highlights and shadows to the point that the light loses all its character. Always try to find the perfect level of diffusion for the mood of your story.

Below left & right: A diffuser is placed between the light source and the subject to create a balanced tone: ideally without destroying all the highlights and shadows.

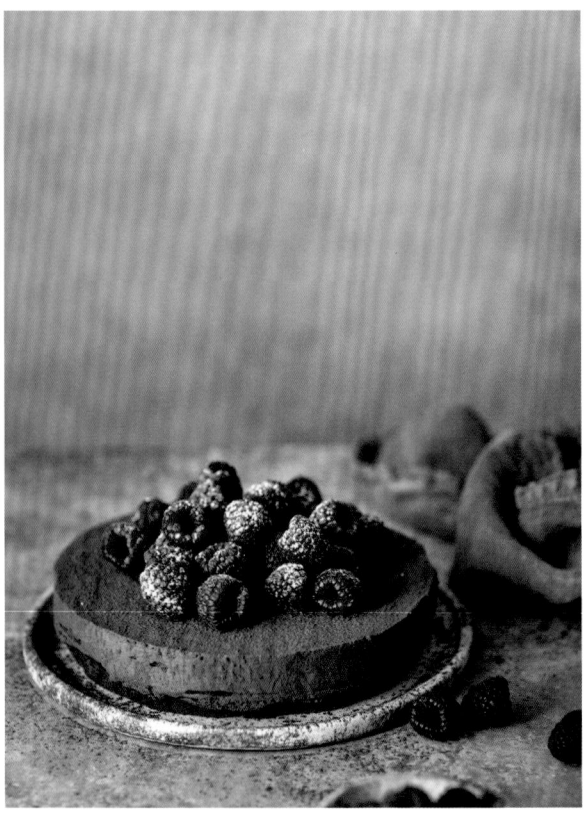
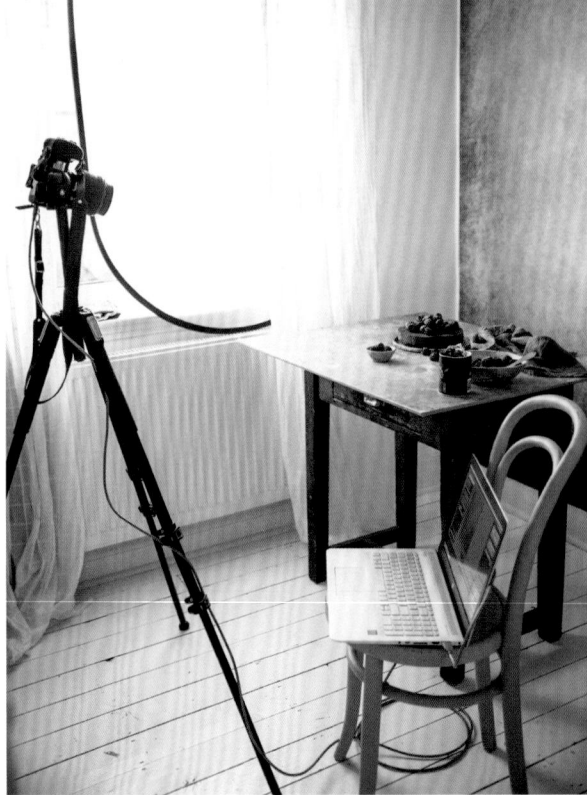

Reflectors

White (or silver or gold) reflectors are used to bounce light back onto your subject, to brighten the shadows and create even light. Reflectors can be placed opposite the light source and/or on different sides of your food setup. All types of white or shiny surfaces will work as a reflector, although for my own work, I like to stick to matte white boards. Gold and silver reflectors will give your images a warmer or cooler tone, respectively. Shiny surfaces will bounce light back more intensely than matte surfaces.

You will often hear photographers using the term "fill light." This refers to light coming from other directions than the main light source and "filling in" the shadows, for example, the light that the reflector bounces onto a scene. It's worth remembering that, as well as dedicated reflectors, bright walls, floors, and ceilings will also reflect light back onto your subject; even what you wear. That's right: you are a walking reflector!

As with diffusers, the size of the reflector and its distance from your subject will influence the light in your images. A closer and/or bigger reflector will bounce more light back onto your food scene. You can use a smaller reflector (such as a small piece of thick paper or white cardboard) to target a small or specific area of your food scene effectively.

Use reflectors with some caution: too much reflected light will get rid of all the shadows in your scene, leaving you with flat light and no sense of dimension or texture in your subject.

Below left & right: Reflectors are placed around the dish to brighten dark shadows and balance the light.

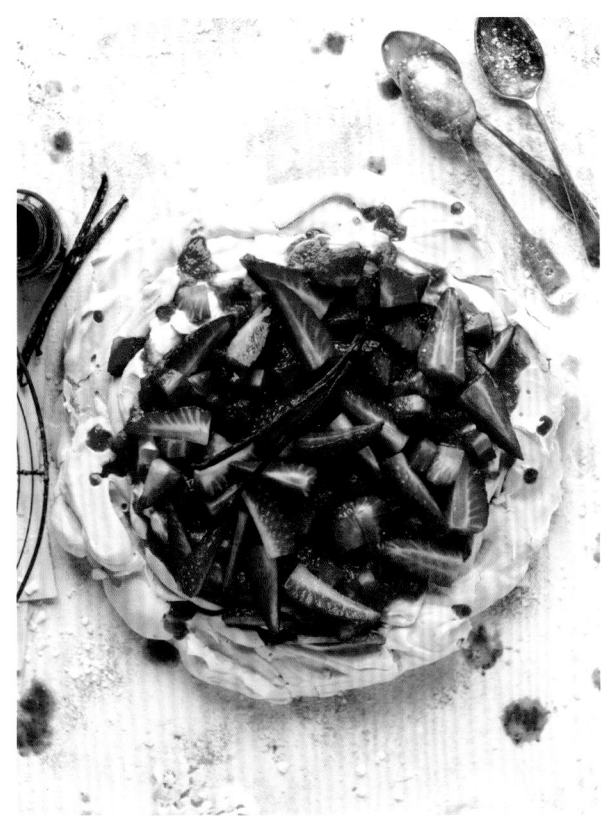

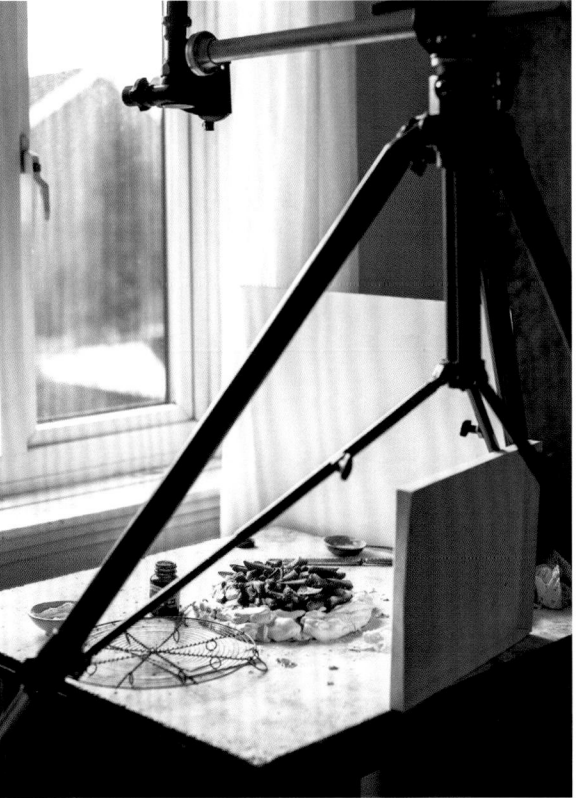

Black boards/cards

Any type of dark surface can be used to reduce the light that is reflected back onto the food scene; you will often hear photographers referring to this as a "negative fill." This method helps to emphasize shadows and adds contrast and energy to your images. Just like a white reflector, a black surface can also be placed opposite the light source as well as on other sides of your food scene to get different effects.

If you have white walls in your shooting space, they will bounce light back onto your subject. If you want to prevent that and create a darker scene with deeper shadows, you can absorb the light by placing black boards or cards all around your subject. Painting one wall dark in my studio was a game changer—it immediately added more dimension to all my images.

Again, the size of your black board and how close it is to your subject will influence the light in your images. Closer and/or bigger, it will absorb more light, so more shadows will be brought out and they will also be darker.

Below left & right: Black boards can be used to prevent ambient light washing out all the shadows in your subject. You can still achieve a bright image, but it will now have depth.

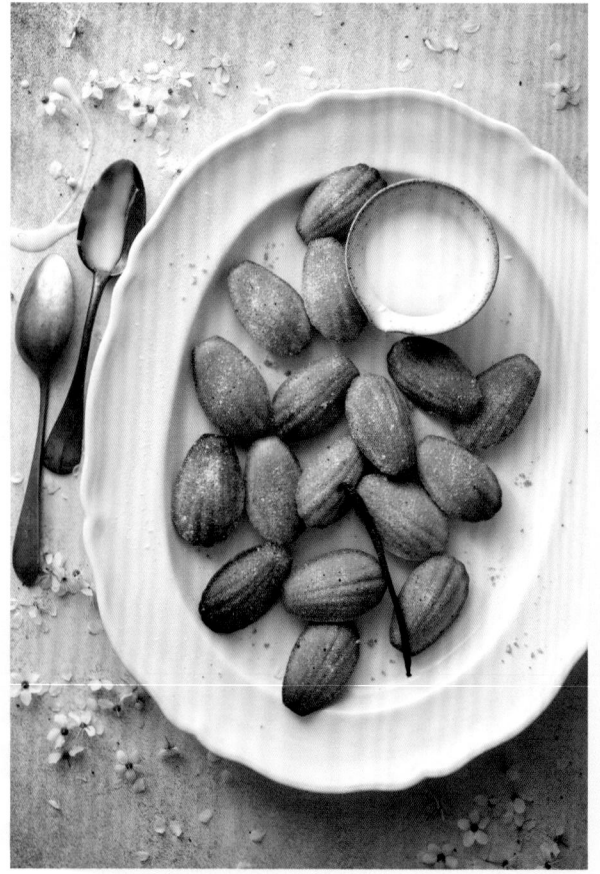

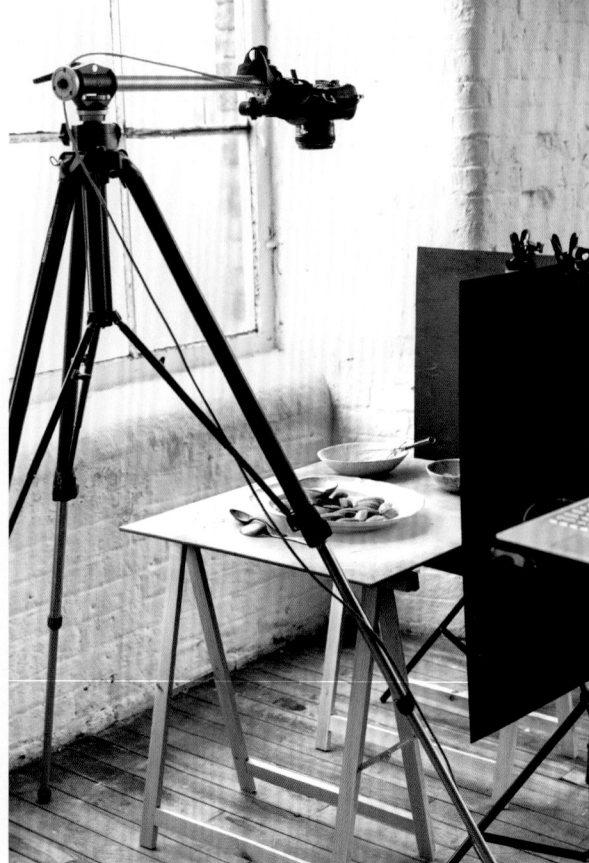

Blocking tools

Photographers use blocking tools to add more contrast, enhance the shadows and create an evocative atmosphere. Most of the time, you will find me subtracting the available light by drawing the blinds and blocking the windows, rather than adding light.

Blocking the light is a way to add drama and depth to your images. Anything with a black matte surface will work like a charm. You can use the same surfaces you would use for negative fill to absorb light, but in this case, you use them to block the light. A blocking tool can be any solid surface that you put in between your subject and your light source.

The larger and/or closer the blocking aid is to the subject, the longer and more intense the shadows will be.

Using light shapers

Always use shaping tools with purpose. Before you do anything else, assess the space where you photograph by looking around and taking a few test shots. Once you've done this, select your shaping tools based on the light you have available and the mood you want to achieve.

Safety always comes first, so make sure your light shapers are safely positioned. I recommend investing in some simple (and inexpensive) stands and rotating clamps to hold your tools.

Below left & right: Blocking tools do pretty much exactly what you'd expect: you use them to block out light in order to improve the contrast and create deeper shadows.

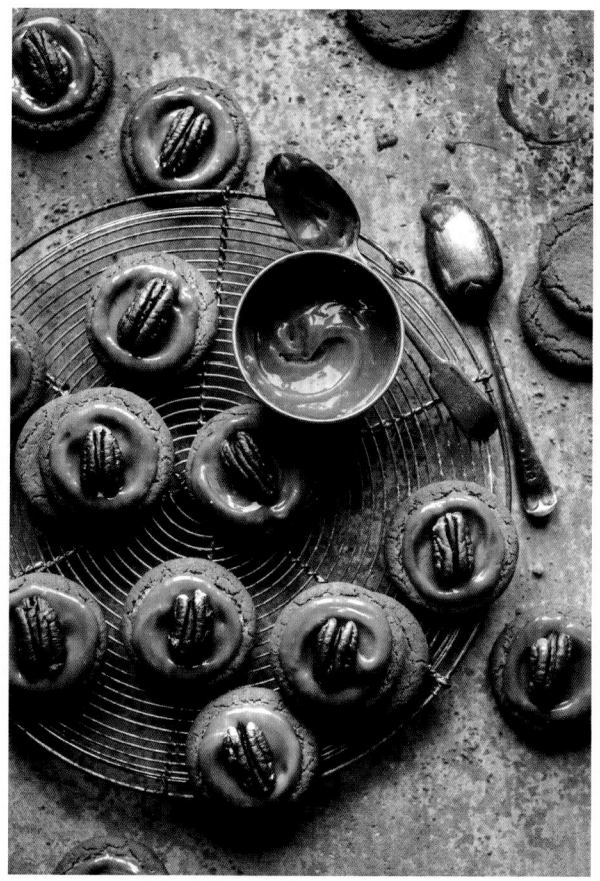

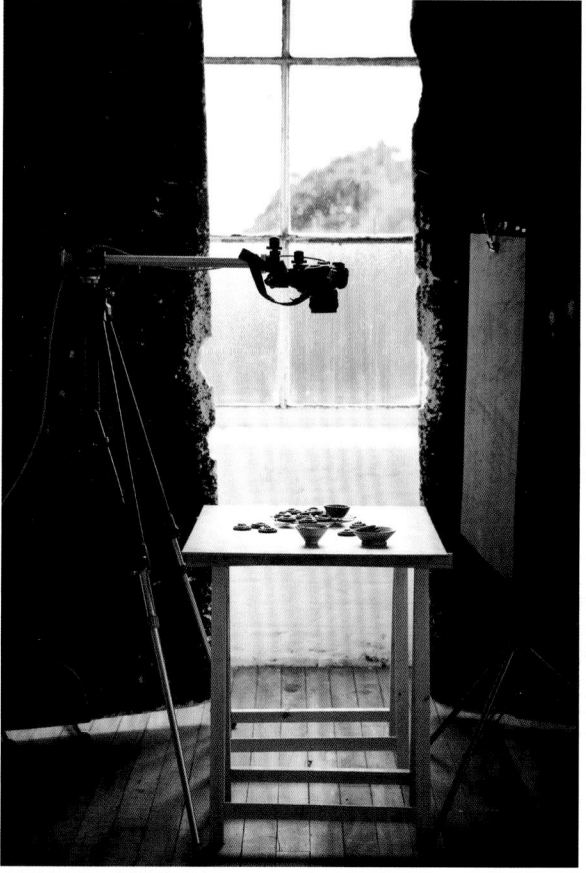

Color temperature

When you walk into a white room early in the morning or in the late afternoon on a sunny day, you might notice that instead of being pure white, the walls have a warm cream or even orange color to them. Walk into the same room on an overcast day and it might look different: grey or even blueish. At night, when the room is lit by artificial lights, it will look different again.

As you study light more, you will notice that every type of light has a different color. This is to do with the color temperature of the light, which is measured in Kelvin (K).

White balance

Our eyes are clever devices and they adjust and balance the color of light incredibly well. Our camera, however, sometimes needs a helping hand. The camera's Auto White Balance (AWB) setting will aim to make our whites appear white, but this works by essentially neutralizing the warmer and cooler hues in an image and it doesn't always produce the results we are hoping for.

To achieve more accurate results, turn off the AWB and explore the white balance presets that your camera comes with. These presets come in handy for making the colors look natural to the eye in common lighting situations; for example, in direct sunlight, on an overcast day, with artificial lighting and so on. If the presets don't do a great job with a specific scene, you can also set white balance by using the K setting, which allows you to adjust and control color temperature.

When you feel your image is too warm (with an overall yellow or orange tone), turn the color temperature (K value) down. If it feels too cool (blueish), turn the color temperature (K value) up. It's pretty much that simple.

I like to set the white balance manually in the camera, always trusting my eyes as to what looks and feels good for the mood I want to create. But I also never get too stressed out about it. As we'll see later, this is something you can also change in post-production.

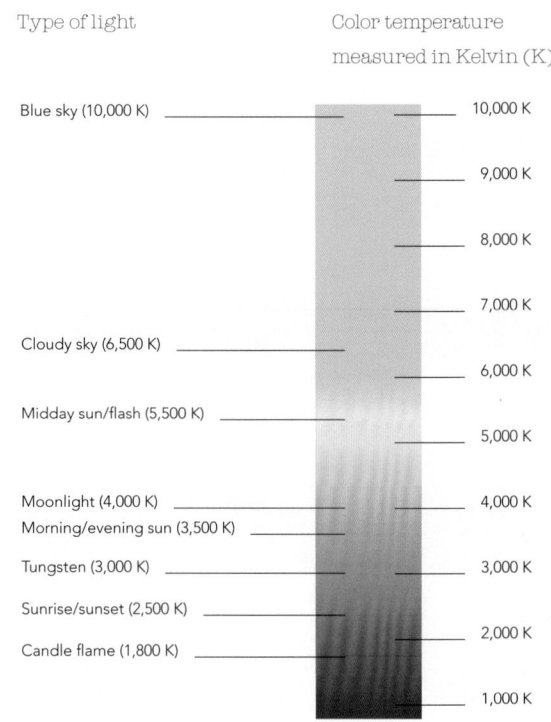

Above: As you can see, warmer-colored light (red/orange) actually has a lower K value, while cooler-colored light (bluer) has a higher K value. When aiming for a "neutral" white balance, the Kelvin setting on your camera should correspond to the lighting situation you are in. For a warmer white balance, set your camera to a higher K value, and for a cooler white balance, choose a lower K value.

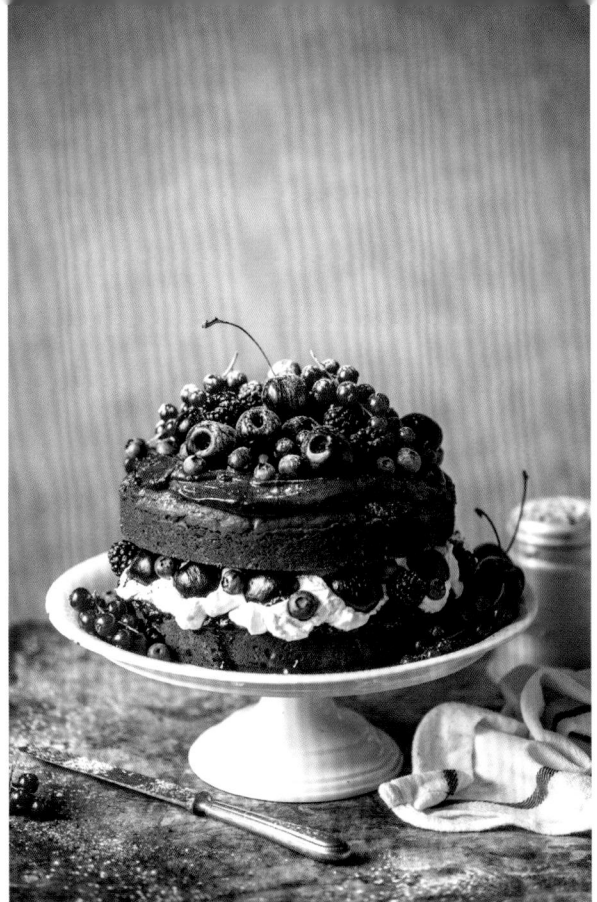
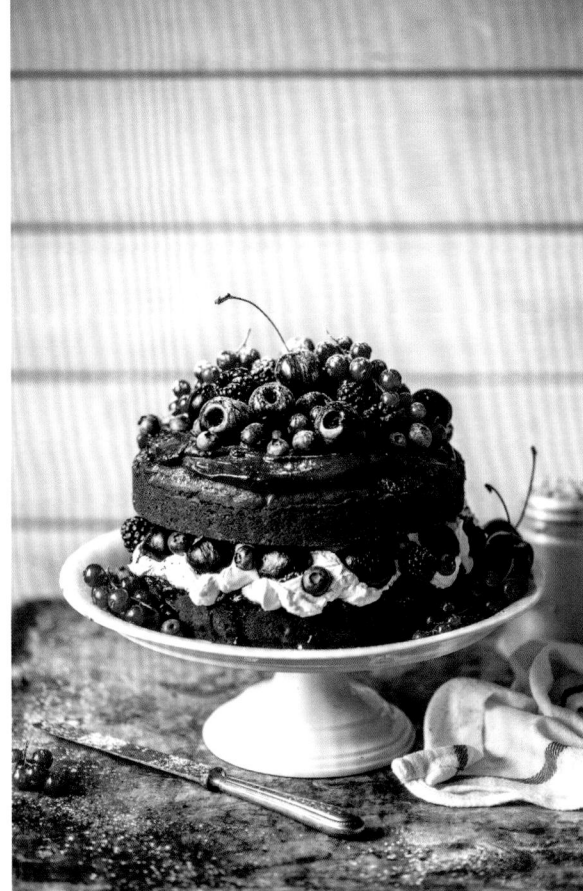

Color considerations

You will notice that adjusting white balance changes how certain colors appear. Colors that are already on the warm side—reds, oranges, creams and yellows—often look even richer when shot on the warmer side of the white balance. Conversely, when a food scene has predominantly cool colors (such as blues, purples, or pale pinks), you might want to consider moving the white balance to the cooler side to make them look even crisper. This is absolutely not a rule in my photography, though, and it's important to find out your own preferences.

Above left & right: Notice how the different white balance affects the colors of the berries, the icing, everything. Notice how the blueberries look more vibrant and the silver props look more accurate in the image on the left. On the other hand, the warm white balance accentuates the creams, browns and reds in the picture on the right, making them look even warmer. Neither of these images is *right* or *wrong*—it all depends on the effect you are going for and your personal taste. Which one do you like better?

Tip

When there is a human element in your food pictures—such as hands holding a bowl—always make sure the skin tone looks natural.

White balance & storytelling

"You've got to know the rules to break them."
—Alexander McQueen

Color temperature doesn't only change the appearance of hues in our images. It alters our perception and the overall mood of the photograph. We experience color on a subconscious level, without giving it much thought. But it's a powerful tool that artists have used for centuries to influence how viewers experience and react to their work. The ability to control color temperature gives you a great advantage: you can create more than one interpretation of the same scene.

An "inaccurate" white balance is not necessarily a bad thing as long as you use it intentionally and it doesn't make your food look unappetizing. A blue color cast can give your food scene a beautiful crisp feel and, add freshness to the colors of the food. An orange color cast, on the other hand, makes a scene feel warmer, radiating cosiness and a feeling of comfort.

How we use white balance artistically is of course subjective: there are no hard and fast rules. Try to pay attention to how certain images make you feel and what the predominant color temperature is in those images. Then connect the dots and use these observations to craft food stories that have impact.

How I like to use white balance artistically

1. To represent the weather
I photographed this beautiful scene (1a; styled by Eva Kosmas Flores) on a warm, summer afternoon. The sun was lovely and although I usually like to photograph lilac and green colors on a cooler side (it makes them look beautifully crisp), I really wanted to make my viewer experience what I felt—warm, golden sunshine.

Even though I wouldn't normally choose such a cool white balance for this subject (1b), I wanted this image to reflect the true weather outside.

2. To evoke emotions about the food
There are some dishes that inspire emotional responses on their own—the way comfort food might make you feel cosy in winter (2a), or ice creams and smoothie bowls make you feel refreshed in the summer (2b)—but as a photographer, you can give them a helping hand. Try matching the color temperature to the emotion you feel about the dish.

3. To create an atmosphere in a scene
Warmer light radiates comfort and positive energy (3a), whereas cool images feel slower, have a calming and soothing effect and make us feel reflective (3b).

Tip

As Michael Freeman says in *50 Paths to Creative Photography*, technically wrong can of course be artistically right. Although it's important to know how to set your white balance "correctly", don't always aim for neutral.

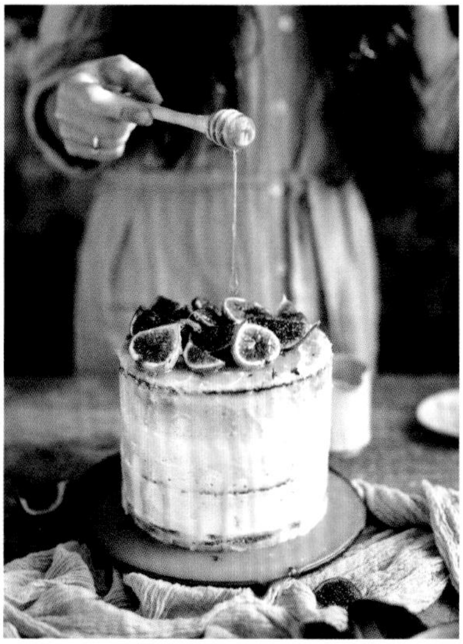

1a

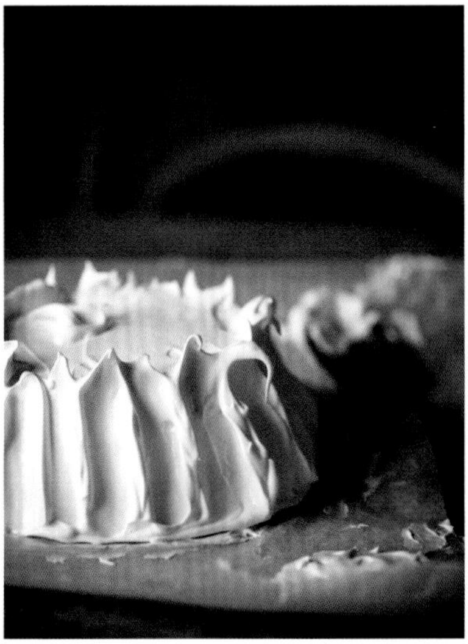

1b

2a

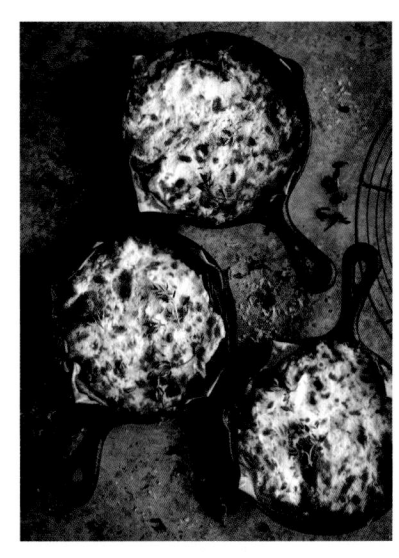
2b

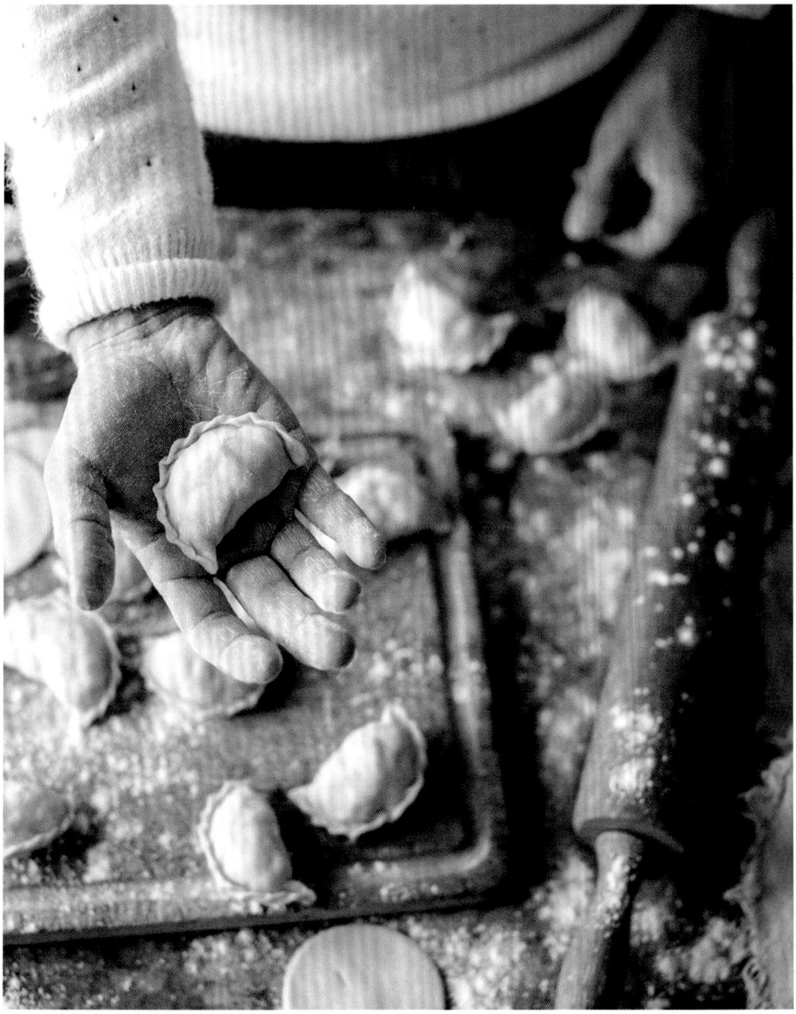

3b

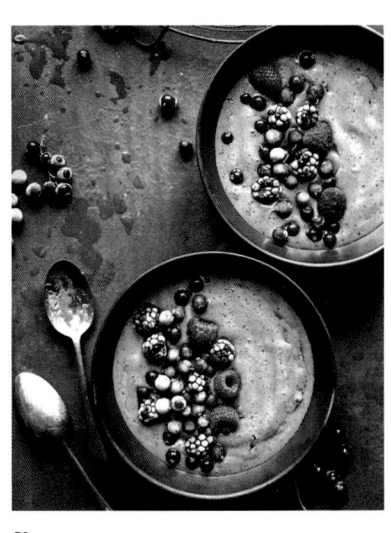

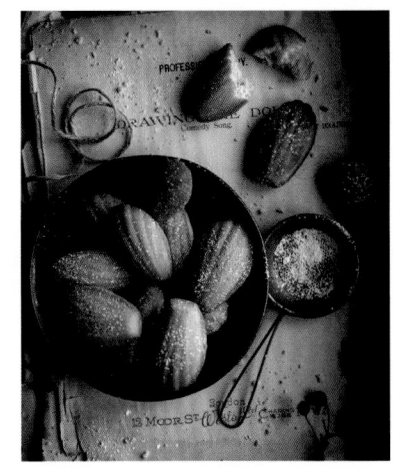
3a

Using light creatively

Putting the time into understanding light and how shaping it will influence your images is the biggest time investment you can make if you want to craft better photographs. Even if you find a light that works for all your images, never stop exploring. Look for something unexpected and try to weave the light into your food story. From time to time, push light to the front of your shooting method and make it the subject of your photograph.

There is no one perfect setup because there is no single lighting situation and no single way to portray a subject. Think of the lighting setups you've seen in this chapter just as inspiration, and go and play with your own light.

Food in the spotlight

When I visited the Prado Museum in Madrid, I couldn't get over how Rubens and Caravaggio skilfully crafted light and shadows in their paintings to lead your eye to the most important element in the frame. They knew exactly where they wanted you to look and they used light to direct your attention there. There is so much we can learn from the Old Masters of art. They knew what an important part contrast plays in good lighting: it's what makes you see depth in a two-dimensional image.

When you study Dutch and Italian Masters' paintings, take inspiration from the dramatic lighting technique they favoured. This technique, called "chiaroscuro," uses very strong contrasts between light and dark to heighten emotion and focus attention.

For some modern-day inspiration, be sure to check out the work of Valentina Solfrini and Zaira Zarotti. These photographers are masters at using the chiaroscuro technique in food still lifes!

Below left & right: By reducing the size of the light source to a narrow strip, and photographing in the box, I added a lot of deep shadows to the scene. The bright subject is not an accident: it provides contrast and stands out even more.

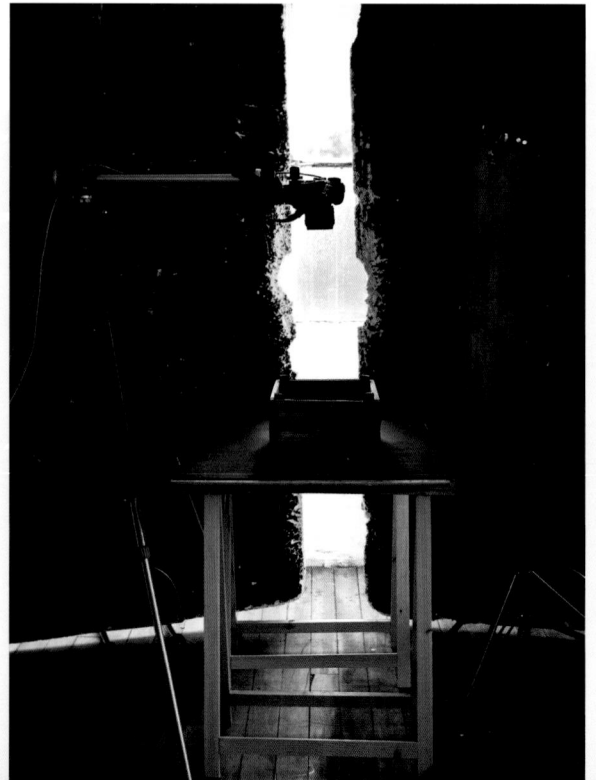

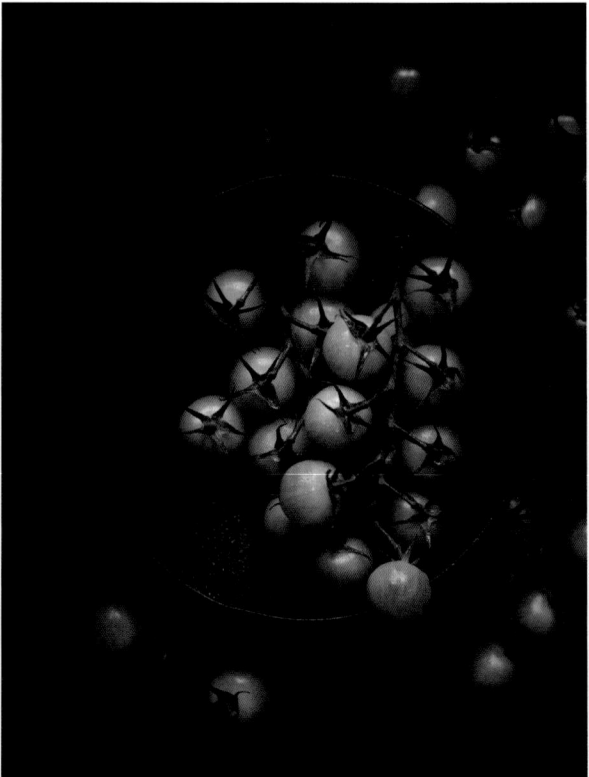

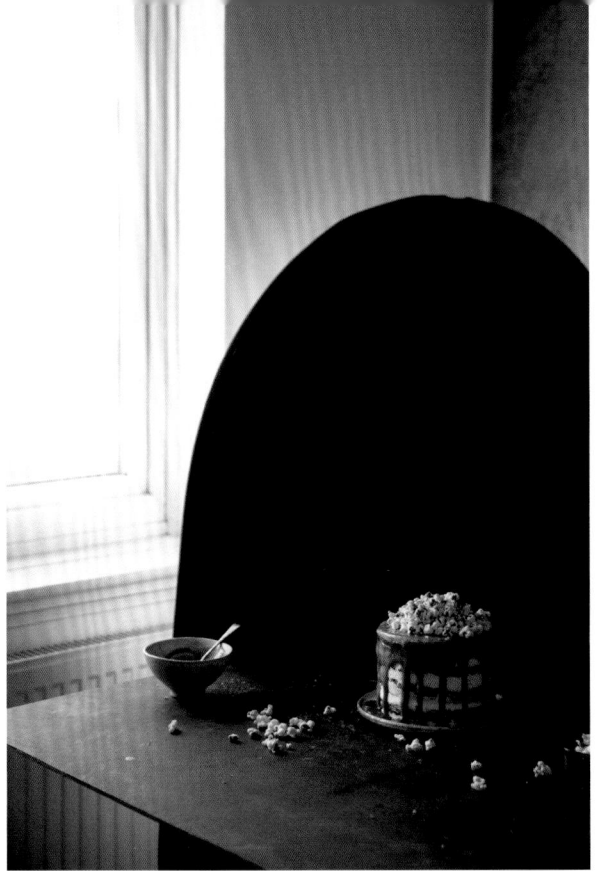
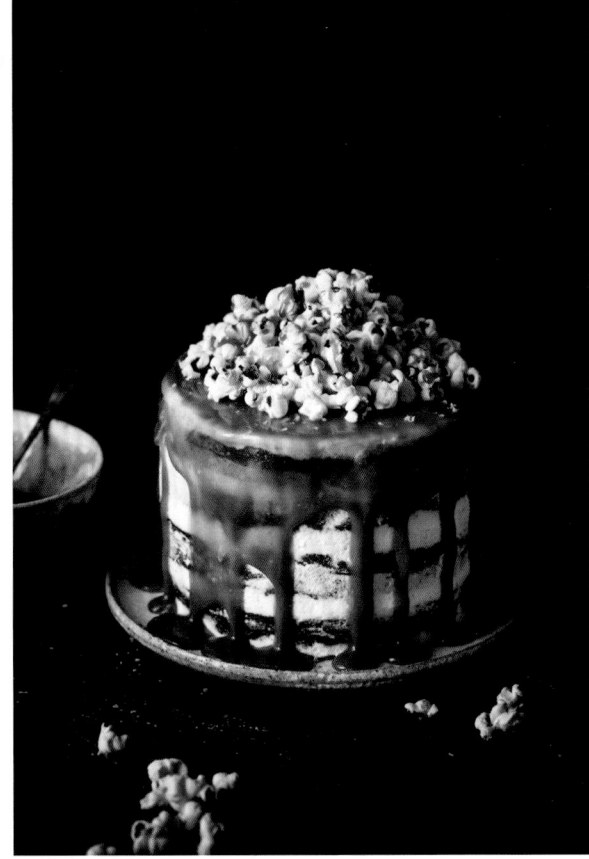

Above right & left: When blocking the light, the background should be in shadow but light should still reach your subject.

The art of shadows

Dark, cocooning shadows are a powerful way to draw the viewer's attention straight to the hero subject, but the image should be bright enough to reveal what's important. Think about where you want your viewer's eye to land, then craft the shadows to lead it there.

You might be surprised how little light you actually need to create an arresting image. I remember walking in to one particular house to do a photoshoot, thinking, "How will I take pictures in here?" It was so dark! But when I looked through the viewfinder, I couldn't believe my eyes: the play of highlights and shadows was mesmerizing. When working in darker spaces, I try standing closer to the window, and I shoot with a tripod and slow shutter speed (unless freezing movement: then I'll bump up my ISO). I very rarely underexpose my photos: making sure I don't lose details in my darks gives me more freedom in post-production.

What influences the look of shadows

Shadows add dynamism and atmosphere to a composition; learn how to work with them and you'll be halfway to achieving a strong image.

* **Size of window:** big = shorter; small = longer.
* **Type of light:** hard = well-defined edges; soft = blurred edges.
* **Position of the sun:** high = shorter; low = longer.
* **Position of camera:** determines where shadows appear (in front, behind, to the side).
* **Distance from the window:** close = darker/shorter; far = paler/longer.
* **Light shapers (which are influenced by their size and distance):** reflecting/fill light = brighter; absorbing/negative fill = darker; diffusing = paler, softer edges.

How is light playing with your subject?

Great light makes us stop in our tracks. When you focus on the way it falls, how it's reflected, and how it interacts with your subject, you can create something magical. Be sure to take your camera off the tripod and walk around your scene, scanning and looking for the perfect angle where the light picks up the texture beautifully. This is what breathes life into your photographs, so it's worth spending the time to make sure light is interacting with your subject in the best possible way. Sometimes you might want to move or tilt your subject just a little bit, or play with cuts of fruit and veg so that they catch the streams of light in different ways. Simply misting your subject with water droplets can transform it into something much more interesting.

Same subject, different light

You will often find me exploring the same subject in different types of light: I can't recommend enough how useful (and fascinating!) these experiments are. You can create a completely different story by simply changing the way you shape the light, tweaking the white balance, switching the angle to backlight, or placing your subject in hard light.

The best subjects for these kinds of explorations are things that stay fresh for longer, such as baked goods and certain fresh produce.

There are so many ways you can use light creatively, and to me, this is the most exciting thing about photography. Next time you grab a camera, think about light first, before anything else, and use it to bring your food images to life. The magic of photography happens the minute you stop taking pictures of food and start taking pictures of light.

And finally, remember that we are not finished with light until we have interpreted the final image in post-production: that's when you can add even more emphasis. We'll explore this in Chapter 6.

Below: Precious stones are shaped and cut in certain ways for a reason: to catch and reflect light. Think about this when you cut the food you're photographing.

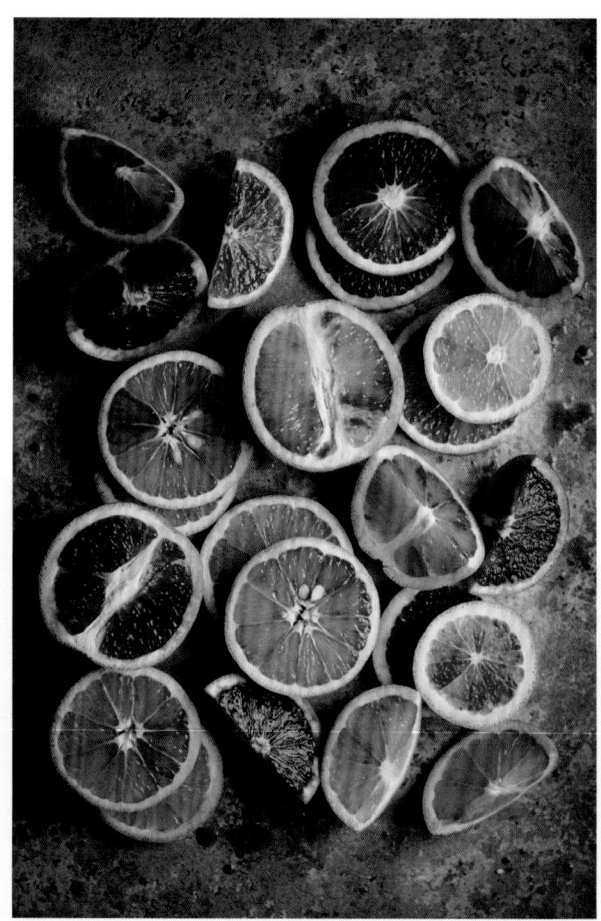

Tip

Don't forget that you don't necessarily need dedicated equipment to play with light—you can experiment with the curtains or blinds you have on your windows at home.

Tips for shooting light & dark

You probably won't need to put all of these tips into action at once: assess your light first, then troubleshoot.

Bright & soft images (below)
* Pick light-colored surfaces and props.
* Photograph in soft light by a large window.
* Bright walls will bounce light back and open up the shadows; alternatively, use a reflector to even out darker areas in your scene.
* If there is too much contrast, try using a diffuser.
* Choose a cool white balance for a crisp look and a warmer white balance for a cosy vibe.
* Bright doesn't mean shadowless: keep some shadows so that the image doesn't look flat.

Dark & dramatic images (below)
* Choose darker backgrounds and props.
* Photograph with soft light by a small window, or block some of the light from a larger window.
* Place black boards/cards around your setup to reduce the light reflecting from walls.
* For more contrast, try moving closer to the window.
* Pick a bright subject and contrast it with a dark background and shadows for a chiaroscuro effect.
* Experiment with white balance to change the atmosphere of the scene.

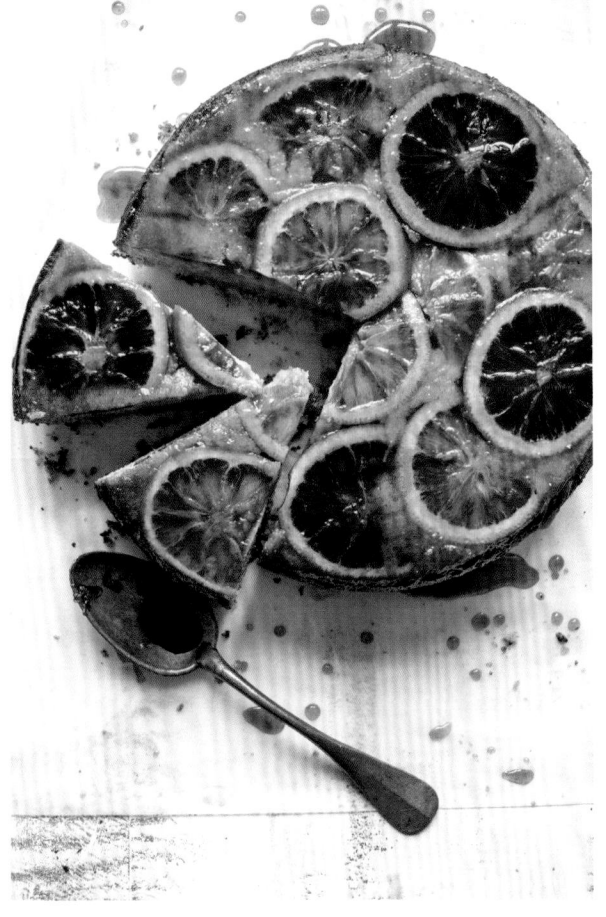

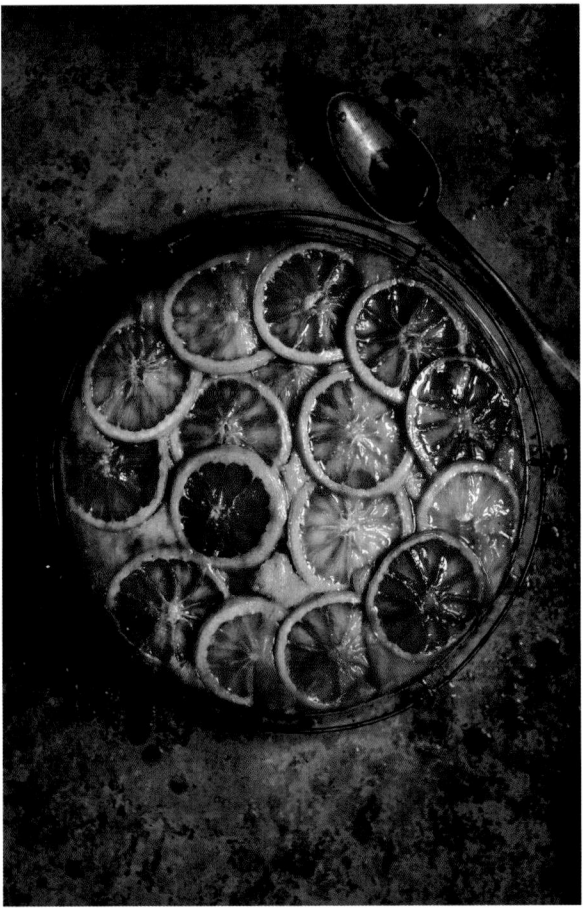

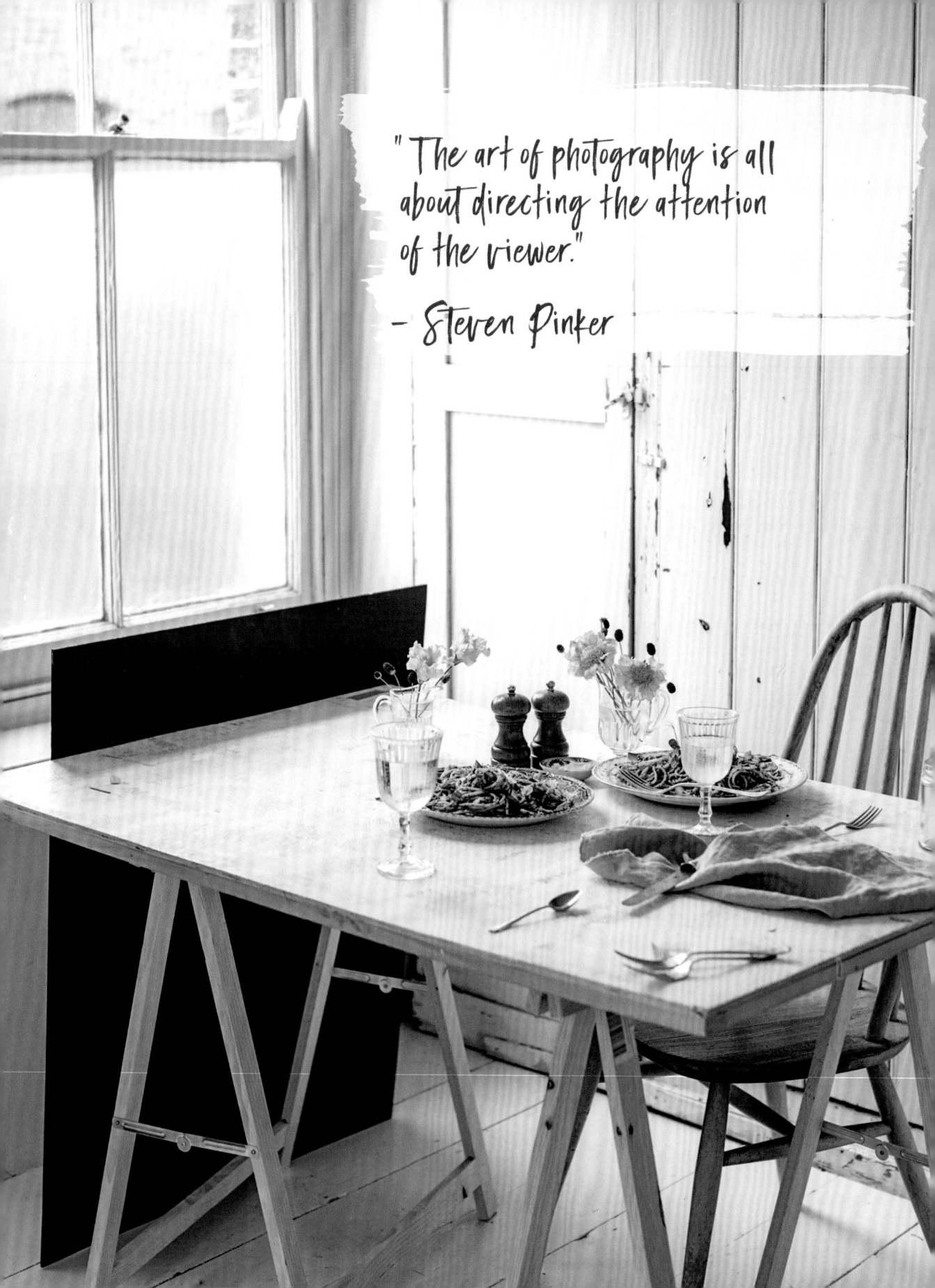

" The art of photography is all about directing the attention of the viewer."

– Steven Pinker

Work the Frame

A great composition takes your audience on a journey, drawing them in and guiding their eyes around the frame, pointing out the most important elements. It's saying, "Here, this is what I love about this dish; this is what I want to show you."

Make every inch count

Composition is all about how you organize the space and elements in your photo. It's you, the photographer, who is responsible for creating the whole scene from scratch, making decisions about what enters the frame and what doesn't. Often, what you leave out is as important as what you include. Everything in your photo should be carefully thought through and everything should be there for a reason.

Trust your instincts

Composition is about creating a photograph that feels right, and that is very subjective. As you develop as a photographer, you have to learn to trust your own taste and intuition, and have the confidence to show what's the most important aspect to YOU about the dishes and scenes that you photograph. Then, convince people with your frame!

Bring your images to life

Adding depth, movement, balance, strong visual interest, and color that helps to tell the story are all ways to inject that special something into your composition, elevating boring, flat stills into art that pops out of the page and excites your viewers' eyes. At the same time, you should keep in mind that compositional techniques are here to help you or inspire you when you get stuck, but they should never control you. The secret to making successful images doesn't lie in knowing every compositional trick under the sun. It's finding the ideas that have the biggest impact on your own work and executing them well.

Don't get too caught up in following the "rules." Ultimately, what will bring your images to life are the stories you tell and the surprise and delight you can offer your viewer with them. And sometimes, to tell a good story or to do something truly new, you need to break the rules.

Left: Food and prop styling by Amy Kinnear.

First things first

"Where do I start with my composition?" I hear you ask. You are not alone. It's something I asked myself over and over again when I first started, and it's the question that always pops up any time I have a conversation with aspiring photographers.

Personally, I like to have a flexible plan for my photoshoots. If I don't already have a strong vision for the image, I think about a few compositional ideas that might work for the dish and keep these in mind (or on paper). This helps me to focus, especially when it's a busy day and there are several dishes to photograph. On days like that, having a structure helps me to work faster and be more efficient. The plan is never too strict, though, because new ideas could be born at any point. Either way, there are a few basic decisions that always come into play.

Start with the story

The story is the message you want to send out to the world. It's something you want your audience to know about the recipe, ingredients, or the process of making the dish as soon as they look at the photograph. The story is also the emotions and associations you want to evoke about the dish or scene. As with any story, you need to know who the main character is and make sure that the supporting cast isn't stealing the focus! Planning what you want to draw attention to can make all the other decisions—like picking the angle, lens, and supporting elements—much easier.

When it comes to what elements to include in your composition, there is no right or wrong, really, as it is your story. I like to think about props that will complement the food and what help me to illustrate my message. I often think about what the dish might be served with and what techniques or ingredients have gone into making the dish, which may not be obvious to the viewer, but that I would like them to know about. I often gather all the props on the background to see how everything works together as a whole. If something sticks out right away, I remove it.

The number of components you put into the frame depends on the recipe, the style of your photograph, and also your approach. Some photographers choose to keep things simple; others love a full and busy scene.

What story do you want to tell? (right)
Everything about this image says "baking time!" The messy details—flour on the surface, a little berry juice and the pastry brush—all help build the story of a freshly prepared pie about to go in the oven. Fresh blackberries around the frame tell the viewer the flavor of the pie, and draw the eye to the hero subject. The strongest part of the image is the lattice, so this is the biggest thing in the frame, while the other elements are subtle enough not to distract from it. A sprinkling of sugar adds to the texture and makes this pie even more tempting. It's a very simple message—but the best stories are never overcomplicated.

Where to position the subject

* Try placing it right in the middle.
* Try using the rule of thirds.
* Place it at the periphery—on the edge of your frame. Be bold and even let some of your subject be cut off, out of the frame.
* When organizing multiple subjects, experiment with placing them along different kinds of curved and flowing lines.
* Explore different grids, such as the Fibonacci spiral, Phi, and the golden triangle.

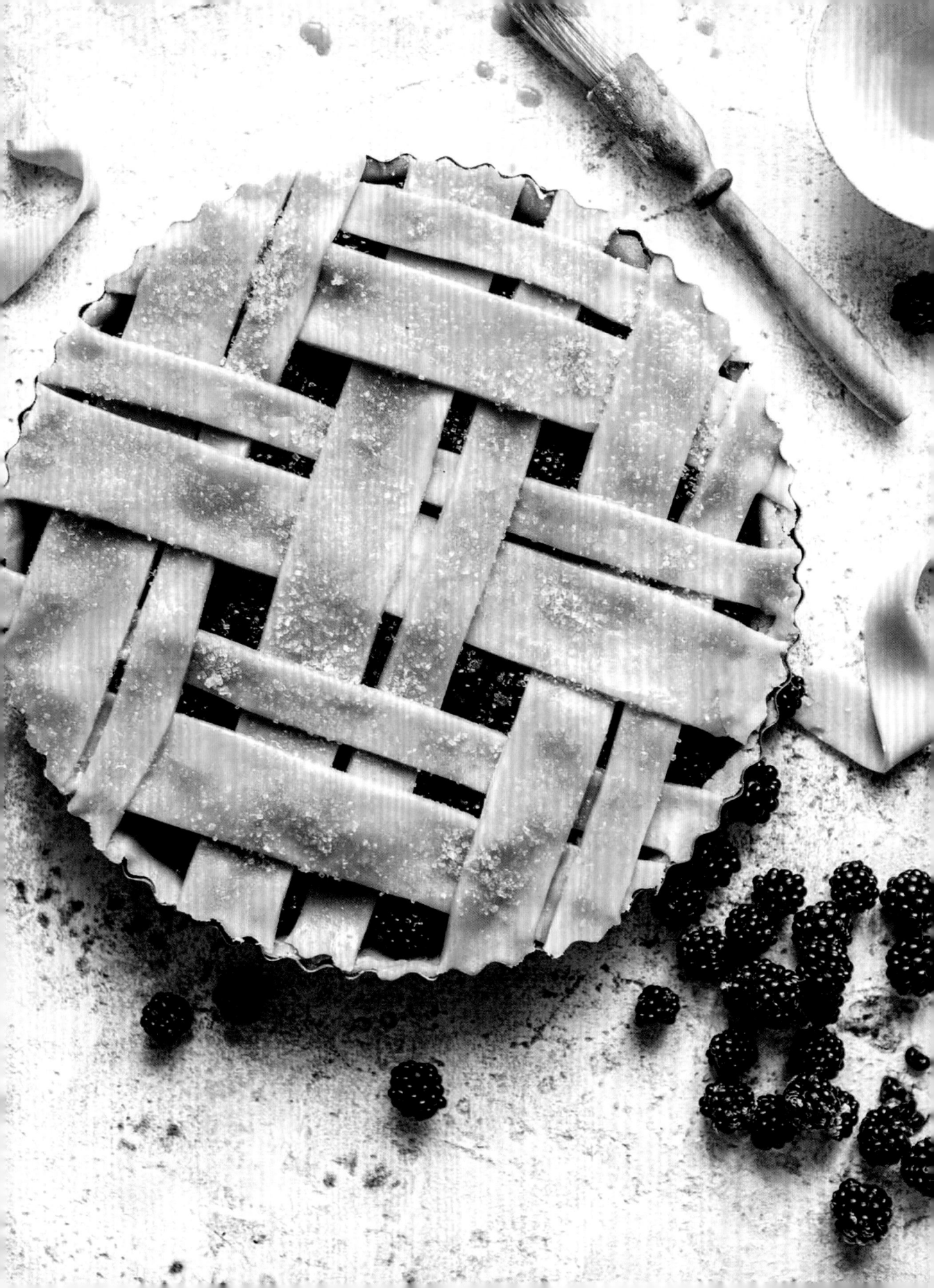

The best orientation

Before you start shooting, it's important to know how you (or your client) are going to use your images; where they are going to appear and what aspect ratio you need to ensure that an important element is not cropped out of the frame. It's a good time to think about whether you need to leave space for text too. So one of the first decisions you have to make is whether to frame your subject in a landscape or portrait orientation.

Landscape images are great for a header on a website, but as much as I would love to see them used more often on social media, they are not very Pinterest- or Instagram-friendly. When you work with a client, the intended use is something that should be indicated in the brief or during the conversations about the projects. Portrait images are definitely more popular, and it's a format widely used across social media. When you shoot overhead shots, why not challenge yourself and come up with a composition that can work both ways?

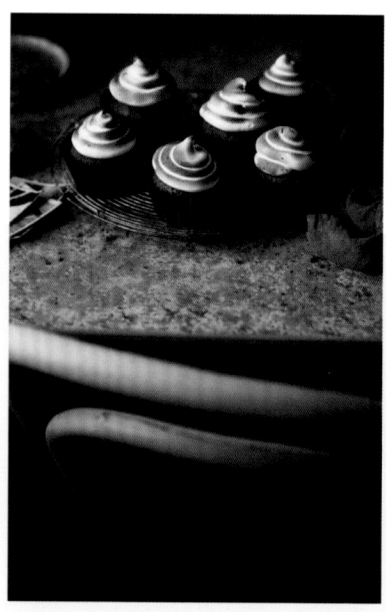

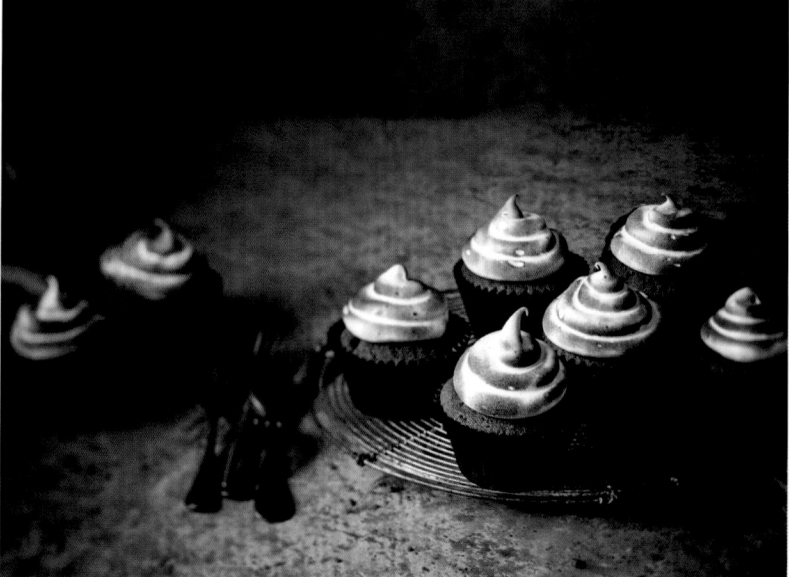

Portrait (above)
* Naturally moves your eyes up and down.
* Widely used in magazines and cookbooks, and is social media-friendly.
* Complements taller subjects and conveys a sense of height.
* Great to use for vertical movement (for example, maple syrup being poured on pancakes).

Landscape (above)
* Encourages the eye to move from side to side.
* Can be used in magazines and books as a double-page spread.
* Often considered as having a calming effect, because it reflects how our eyes see the world.
* Complements wider and shorter subjects, and conveys a sense of space.
* Great for horizontal movement (for example, pastry being rolled out).

The hero angle

Some food looks attractive from every angle. Others have one better-looking side. When deciding where to position your camera, it's worth thinking about what makes your dish special and what angle is best to shows that off.

A simple guide (not a rule!) is to think about the height of your dish (is it tall or flat?), whether it has interesting layers that can't go unnoticed and what its strongest side is (or maybe it has two?).

Show off layers & height with a straight-on angle (0–20 degrees) (right, top)

A straight-on angle emphasizes the height of a dish and it's an excellent way to highlight all the tasty layers that might not be visible from a different position.

When the camera is parallel with one side of the dish, this whole side will be in the plane of focus. This means that with a straight-on angle, every detail of the side you show will be sharp and visible in the image, which is great when your subject is beautifully layered like this stack of pancakes. What I love about this angle is that it beautifully blurs the foreground, which additionally directs the eye straight to the sharp subject.

Show dimension with a three-quarter angle (20–80 degrees) (right, bottom)

This angle highlights the three-dimensional qualities of your subject. The more sides you capture, the greater the sense of form and depth. It's ideal for those dishes with more than one interesting side that you want to tempt your viewer with.

In this example, the caramel is an important flavor to highlight, and shooting from an angle that shows off both the gooey top and the tasty drips is the best way to spark the imagination.

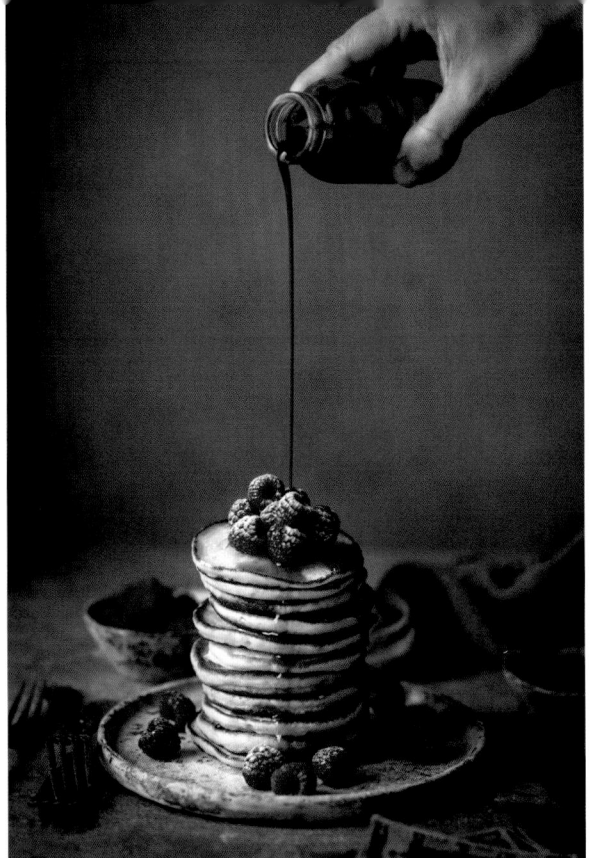

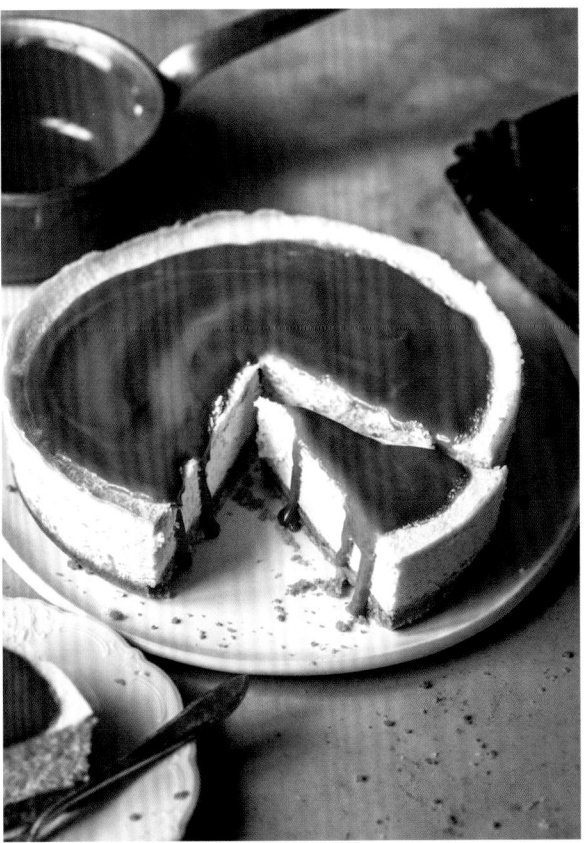

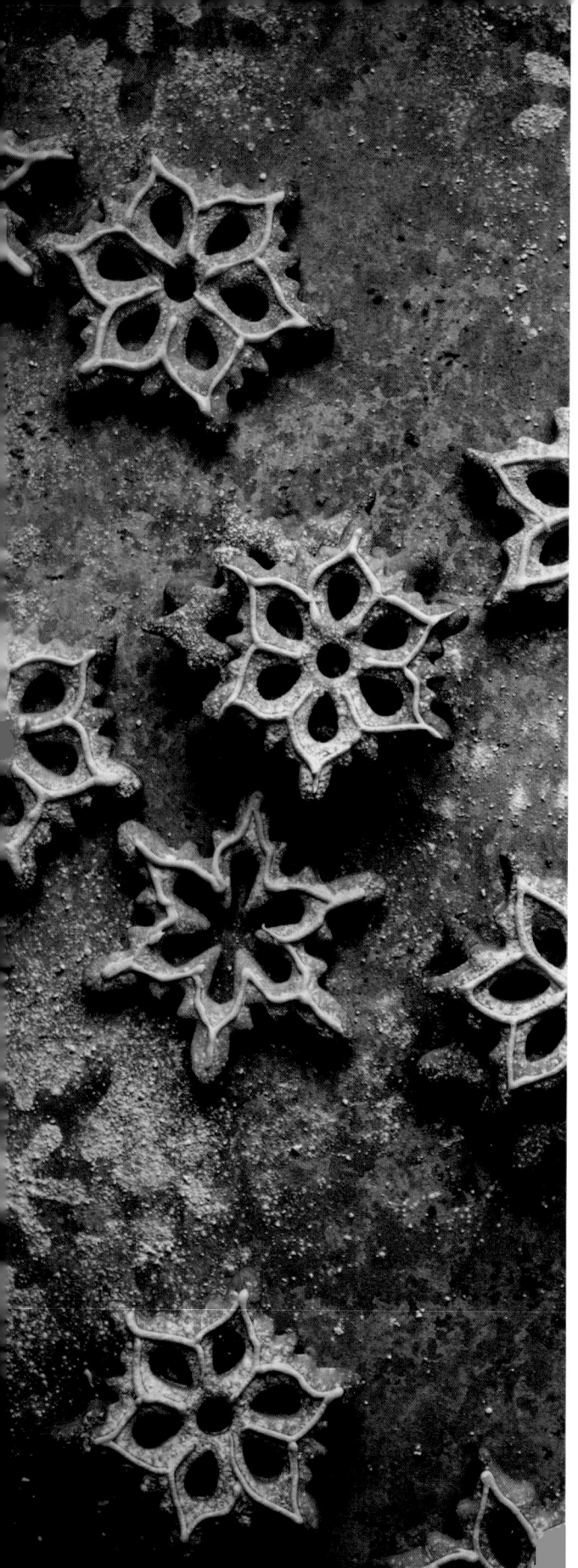

Show off the shapes with an overhead angle (80–90 degrees) (left)

This angle (also known as a flat lay) shows a scene in a graphic way, and I often use it when I want to show off many components and have them all in focus. Using a tripod and tethering gives you more control to compose overhead photographs exactly how you want to.

An overhead angle is a great choice for flat foods that have an interesting shape, like the cookies in this image. Keep in mind that by only showing the top side, the overhead angle emphasizes the flatness of your subject, so you'll need to think of other ways to add depth to your frame, for example, by stacking some cookies on top of each other.

Turning some of the ingredients on their side (where possible) is a great way to show a detail that is not visible from the bird's-eye view. You can see how I used this technique to make a more interesting flat lay scene in the photograph of microherbs on page 119, where I show the tops of some and the colorful sides of others.

Note that if you shoot hot food from this angle, your lens is liable to steam up! In some cases, you can let it cool down before you shoot it, but be mindful that certain foods lose their shape, texture, and color when left out for a while.

Keep on moving

Even when I have my hero angle in mind already, I always take my camera in hand to scan the scene and search for something interesting, then reset my tripod if I find a new angle that is worth a try. Photographers do all sorts of gymnastics around their setups—squatting, bending, down and up—everything they can think of to find a fresh perspective and get the best shot.

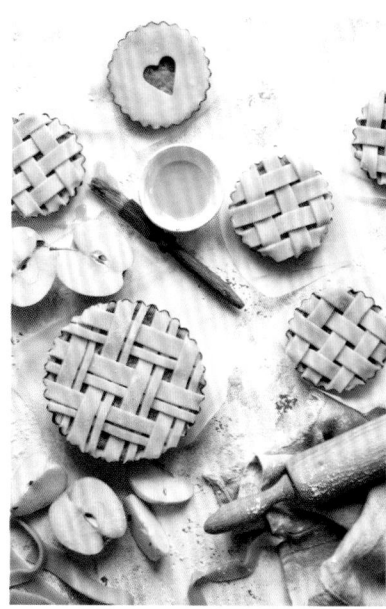

Far

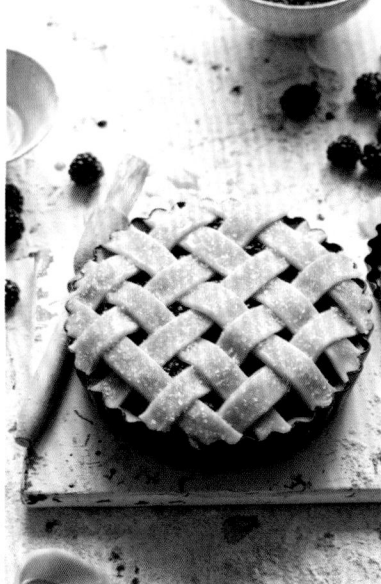

Closer

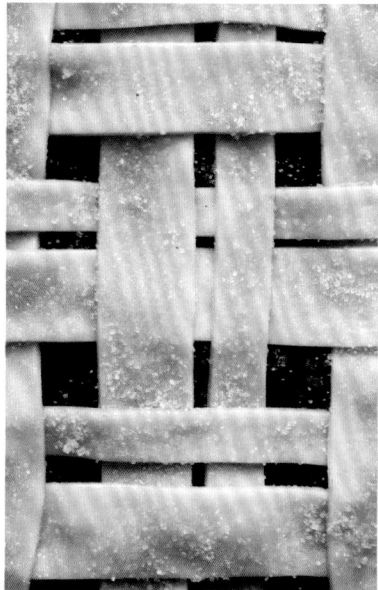

Close

Distance

As we saw on pages 30–31, your lens choice will have a huge impact on your composition: shorter focal lengths can capture a much wider scene, while longer focal lengths offer a narrower field of view, allowing you to focus on a detail. If you have a few different lenses, you will want to consider which one to use before the photoshoot. If you have only one lens, the decision will be about how near or far to position yourself from the subject—although keep in mind that not all lenses focus well at close range, and some will introduce distortion.

The question to ask yourself when deciding on distance is, "What do I want to show?"

Far

Step back from your scene to show your viewer more context. Here, your scene and setting become the subject of your story. If there is an element in your frame that is more important that others, make sure it remains as the focal point. Standing away helps to give your subject some context, but it also means there is more to control, as every single element in the frame has an impact on the final image.

Closer

Sometimes, showing too much can be distracting. That's when you want to move closer to capture the beauty of your dish. Tighter framing draws you in without distraction, making an image that's all about the food or ingredient.

Close

Focusing on the details speaks to our curiosity. It makes us notice something we might not have seen before. It draws attention to the small-but-telling details that would be lost in a wider composition.

Tip

Remember to be flexible with your first decisions. It's okay to change your mind if things are not working out. The most powerful compositions are born when you allow yourself to play.

 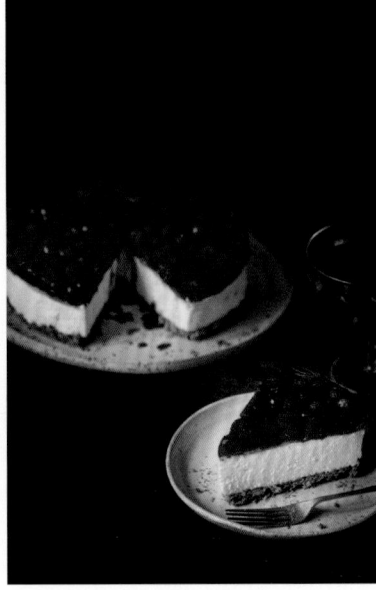 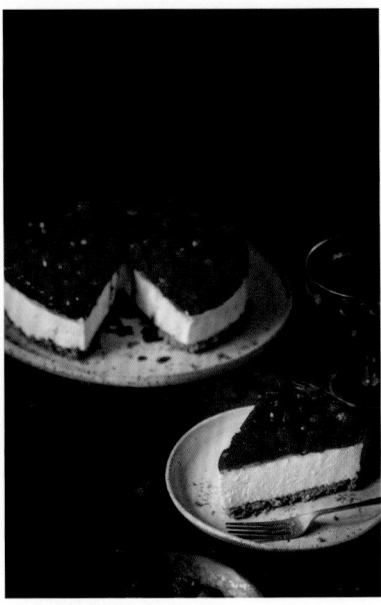

Bring your images to life

Add depth

If you study great images closely, you'll notice they all have one thing that sets them apart from the rest: a great sense of depth. It's what gives your audience the feeling that they are part of the scene, like they can almost reach into the photograph and grab the food. There are a few useful tricks you can use to add this desired dimension into your frame.

Foreground, mid-ground, background (above)

This simple trick works best from a three-quarter angle. Place a few supporting elements in the foreground and a couple more in the background, and you will instantly draw your viewer deep into your composition. This creates an especially strong effect when supporting details in the foreground and the background are out of focus. Your viewer's eye will naturally travel to the sharp spot: where your hero subject is.

Always keep one eye on the subject and one on what's going on in the scene. Make sure your foreground, mid-ground and background elements work together well. Try to keep an organic and laid-back vibe in your composition, layering and overlapping components to make it look less staged.

Take scale and proportion into consideration when crafting your image. If the props in the foreground are too big, they might take attention away from your hero subject. I try to find smaller elements that can support my food story, such as a small bowl with a selection of ingredients, or a pinch dish with spices.

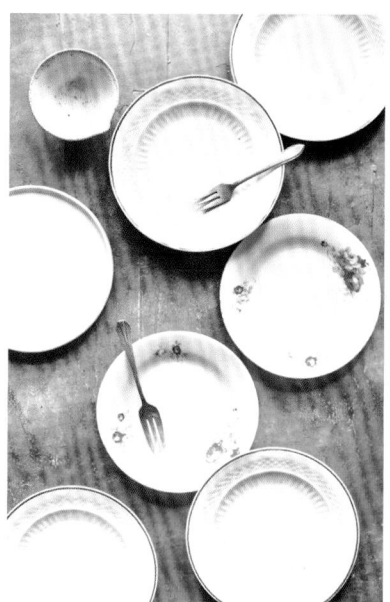 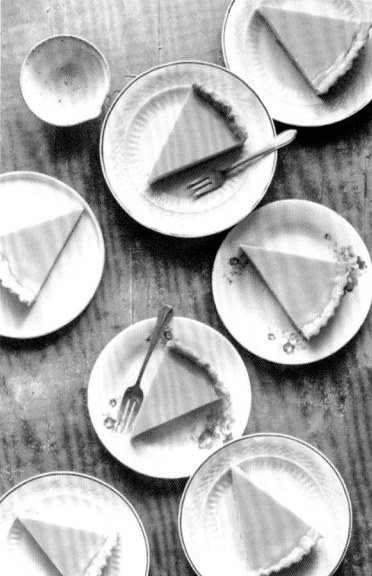 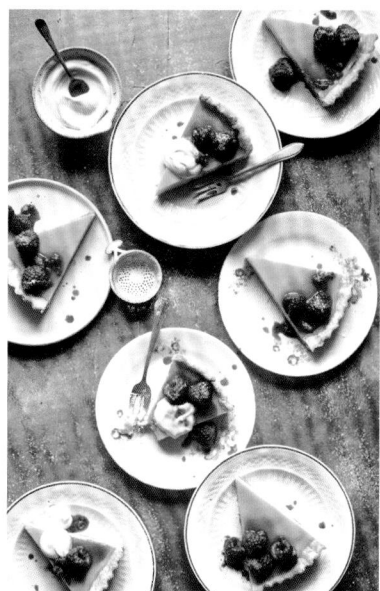

Rule of heights (above)

Here is a sure-fire way to add depth to overhead shots. As you can only see the top side of your subject from this angle, it's harder to draw out its dimensions, but through clever layering and by including elements that have different heights, you can still create an impression of depth.

There doesn't need to be a huge height difference between the components in your frame, maybe only an inch, but that's enough to heighten the sense of depth. Even a simple trick like placing one plate slightly higher than the others can make your image look less flat, which is simply achieved by placing a stack of coasters underneath to balance it.

If you would like to use taller props, for example a vase with flowers or large wine glasses, always make sure that they don't look distorted.

Don't forget these two powerful tools for adding depth

On page 18 we looked at using a shallow depth of field to blur out the background (and often the foreground too), which never fails to add a sense of depth to the frame.

The other important tool at your disposal is of course creative use of light. Images with less tonal contrast will always look flatter than those that harness the sculptural power of highlights and shadows, so remember to work your lighting setup to get the best effect.

Framing

Framing works as you'd expect: it involves using other elements in the scene to create a frame within the image frame. Not only does this technique add depth to your food portrait, but it's also a clever way of drawing attention to the main subject, which can be very handy when you're shooting a busy scene. It gives an especially strong effect when your framing is quite obvious, and the texture, tone and/or depth of field provides your viewer with a distinction between your subject and the frame itself.

In food photography, props offer endless possibilities for perfect framing. I particularly like using baking pans with high sides that I can blur for depth, but plates, chopping boards and parchment paper are other go-to framing tools.

Try also to think outside the box when it comes to framing—it doesn't have to be a literal frame. You could frame your image by shooting your scene behind someone's arm or shooting through flowers. A good use of this technique can elevate your image into something much more captivating.

Below left: Not only is the baking pan an effective way to arrange these garlic cloves in a strong composition, but it also adds to the story, letting the viewer know that they are soft and caramelized from roasting.

Below right: Here, a dynamic use of lines beautifully draws the attention straight to the sage leaves, framed by the hands, right in the center of the frame.

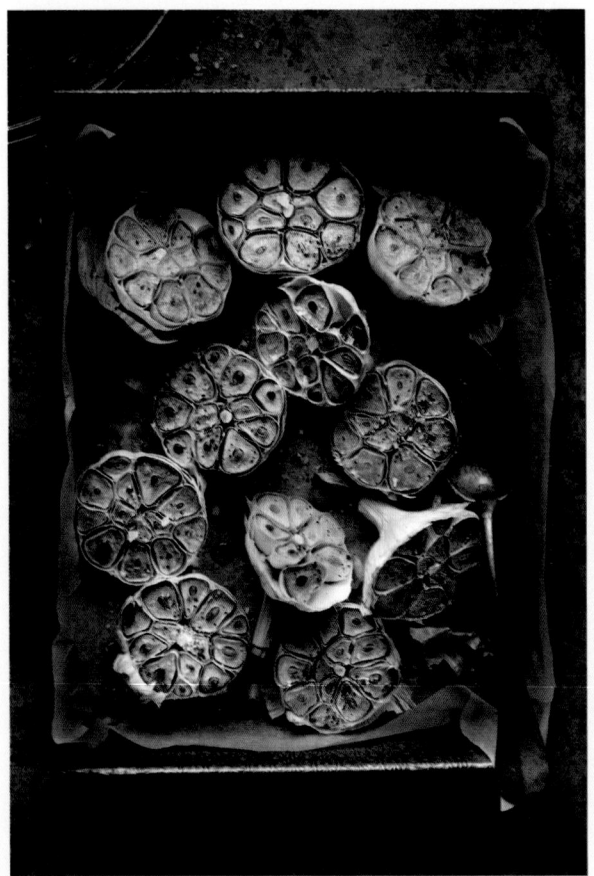

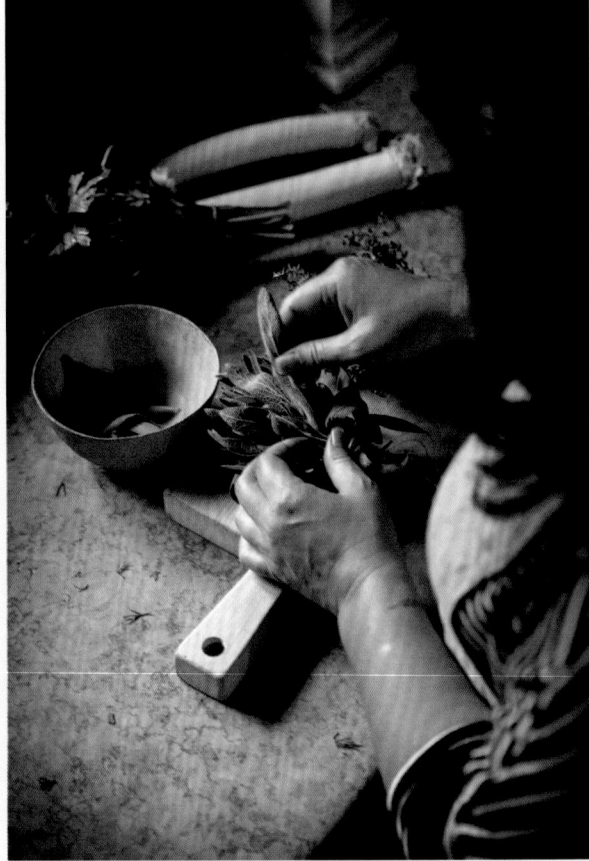

How to make it feel natural

Still life images might be carefully arranged, but that doesn't mean they have to feel unnatural. The aim is to create images that are easy on the eye and don't look too staged. These methods will help you inject a more organic vibe into your food portraits, and make them much more interesting to look at, too.

Don't show everything
A natural photograph is a small slice of a bigger picture, and by cropping the edges, you can suggest this in your created scenes. Of course, placing everything in the center of the frame might work for some images, but by cropping some of the elements, you leave space for the imagination to wander. Our eyes still recognize what is cropped out, and it helps give the illusion that the image is part of a real scene.

Keep the items at different distances
Experiment with moving your elements closer and farther apart, and don't be afraid to have some objects touching. By introducing different proximities, you make the scene look more organic.

Overlap
If you look at what's around you at this moment, everything is likely at different planes and overlapping. That's what our eyes are used to seeing, and that's why when everything is evenly spaced out, it might not be perceived as a naturally occurring scene. The eye can separate the overlapping elements, even if one is hidden behind another and/or blurred out.

Group
Having elements placed in one or a few groups is an easy way to add a natural "flow" to any composition. You will often find me grouping items in threes and placing them around the frame in the shape of an irregular triangle. It's important that each group has a good mix of sizes, shapes and/or styles.

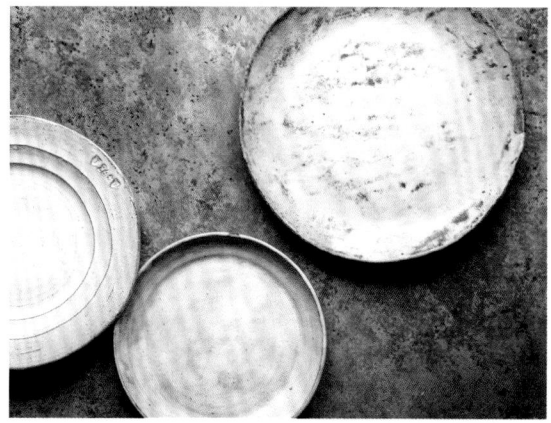

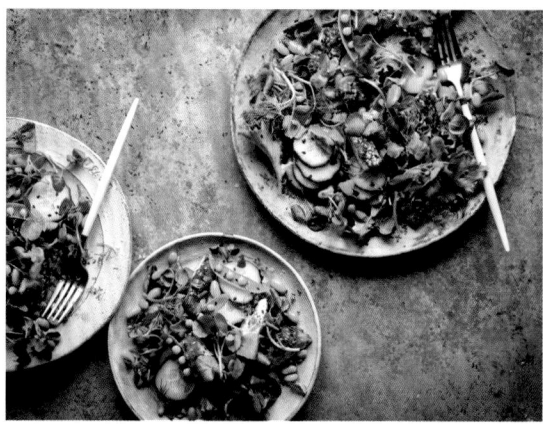

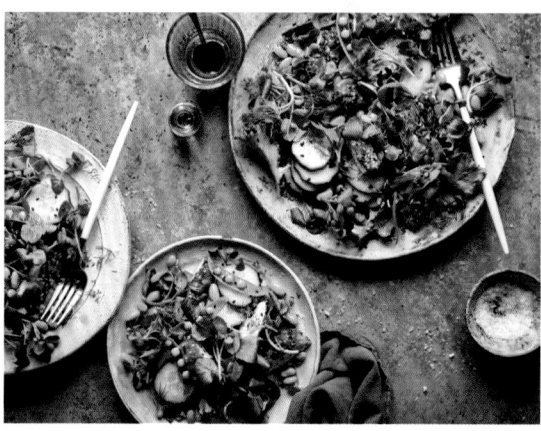

Above: A combination of cropped edges, varying distances between and overlapping of the components, and grouping makes this scene easy on the eye.

Layers, layers, layers

Layering involves placing elements in your frame, one on top of another or one behind another. Using this technique allows you to place items at different planes within the same photograph, making it look more dimensional and balanced. Layering is easy to do, but hard to do well. The trick here is not about just adding the layers: that's easy. The trick is *how* you place these layers in your image to make your composition look natural. The layers should be subtle, cohesive and proportional: everything in your photo should feel like it belongs there.

Layering is effective when there is a notable contrast in the shade, size, height and texture of overlapping objects. This way, you will make it easier for your viewer's eye to separate these items. But remember, it's all about balance—make sure that the supporting layers don't overpower your subject. They should never distract or look forced.

If you make sure your image has many beautiful layers, the eye will be irresistibly drawn in.

Layering to add height & depth

If we study this image from the bottom to the top, we can see how the various layers create a sense of height in the image. The cake stand raises the pavlova up off of the surface and then the dark-colored cooling rack

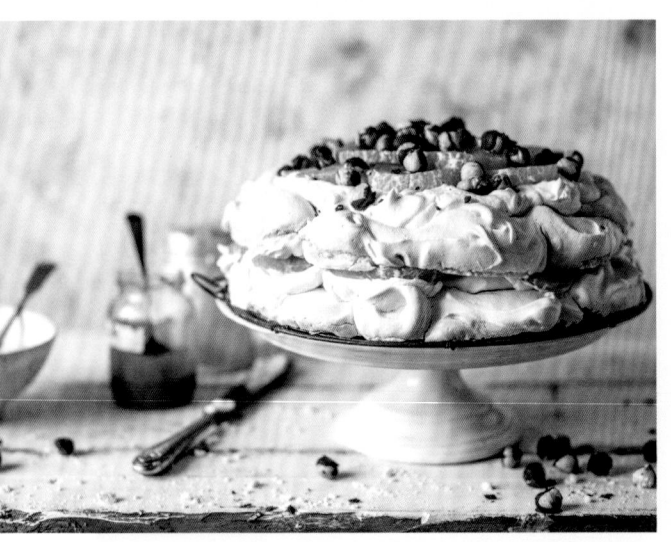

subtly separates the pavlova from the prop. Then we have the first layer of pavlova, cream, slices of mandarins, the second meringue, cream, mandarins and hazelnuts. That's a lot of layers that all help our subject to stand tall—and all emphasized by shooting from a straight-on angle.

When we view the image from the front to the back, we can see how props are placed over different planes within the image to divide our image into foreground, mid-ground and background. We have our layers of nuts spread in the foreground, our pavlova, and then props of different sizes, shapes, colors and textures spread across the scene, overlapping one another and receding into the blurry background. Despite all the variation, the layers all work together as a whole to direct your eyes to our star.

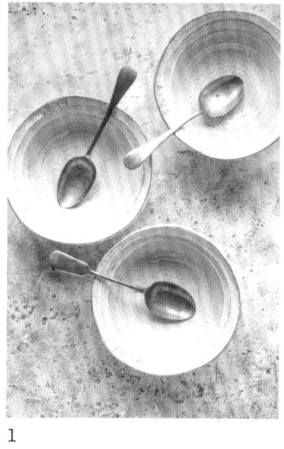

1

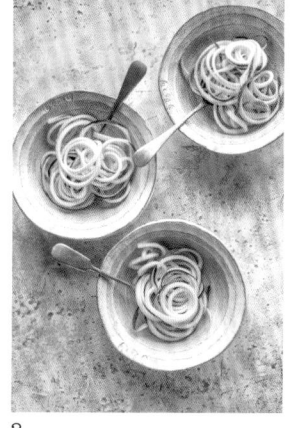

2

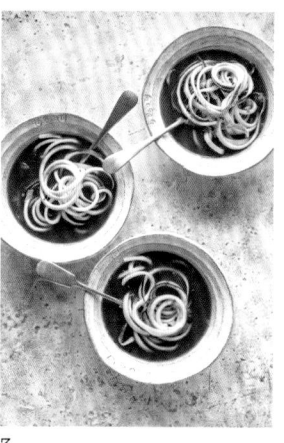

3

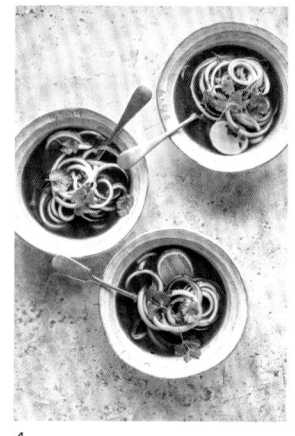

4

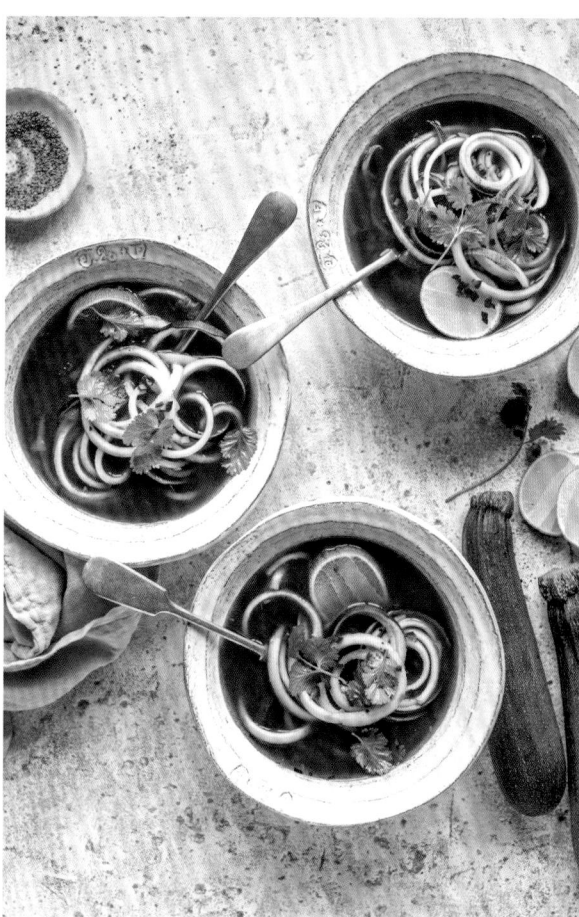

Final image

Let's have a look at how layering works, step by step (above)

The props here work as **layer 1**. What I love about these bowls is that their circular lines are already creating a sense of depth, before the food is even added. Then we have **layer 2**—our zucchini noodles, which again, thanks to their shape, create a layer with more than one dimension. **Layer 3** is the broth, into which you can see the noodles disappearing. **Layer 4** is really four mini-layers of garnish: the lime slices, chopped chile flakes, cilantro leaves, and freshly ground black pepper, each bringing a different texture and shape to enliven the dish, but harmonizing with the colors of what's already in the bowl.

In the final image, additional elements were spread across the scene to complete the frame. The last step is not necessary if you prefer a minimal look, because our bowls already have enough layers to create depth in the image. You need to trust your gut and decide for yourself what you like.

Just play

Look at your favorite images and count how many layers you can see in the dish itself and how many layers there are around the scene. When you compose your own images, pay attention to that number, trusting your instincts to tell you how much is enough and how much is too much.

Visual flow: using lines

Compositions that use lines in a smart way make you experience movement, even when nothing is actually moving. Find and use lines intentionally—in your food, props or background—and your viewer won't be able to take their eyes off your images.

Leading the eye (below)

Lines are dynamic and rhythmic, and they playfully invite you to look at a photograph for a little bit longer. Some lines act like a pointing finger, while other gently guide you through the frame. The shape of our subject, the way we cut it and which direction it faces, as well as how we place the cutlery, napkins and other props, all create lines that encourage the eye to travel within your composition.

When using lines, think about the feeling you want to create within your image. Curvilinear lines are extremely pleasing to the eye and add softness and harmonious flow to your scene, while diagonals can be exciting and stimulating.

One of my favorite tricks to inject more movement into the composition is to create a soft, curvilinear flow towards the hero using a folded napkin (below right).

How lines add emotion to your images

* Horizontal lines have a calming effect and indicate stability, rest, and a slow pace.
* Vertical lines are full of strength. They reflect the sense of growth and emphasize height.
* Diagonal lines (below left) add a sense of action. They add a feeling of movement and energy.
* Curved lines (below center) are experienced as soft, gentle, and organic.

Cutlery acts a bit like arrows: I like to place spoons, knives, and forks to face in different directions, sending the eye zipping around the frame. And a circular cooling rack may be one of the easiest and the most charming ways to add some gentle movement to an image—even if it's just peeking in.

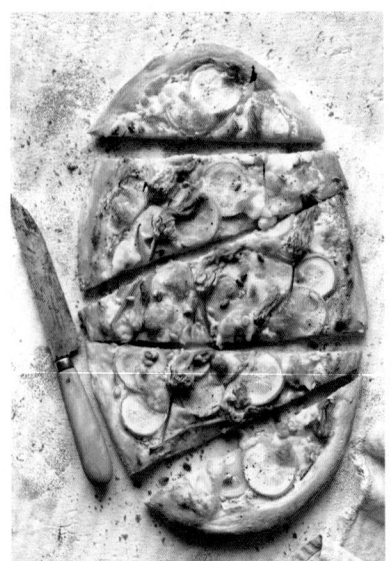
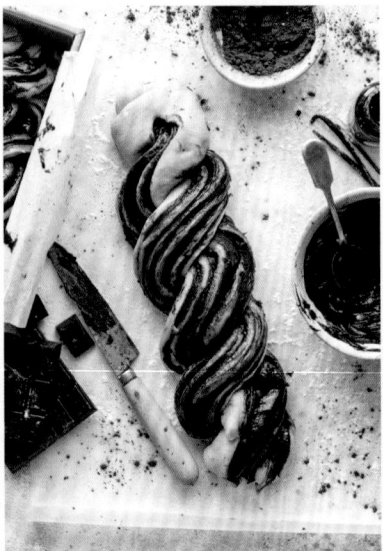
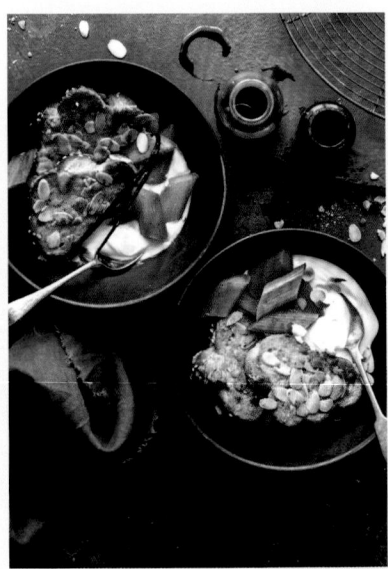

Actual & implied lines (below)

We experience two types of lines when we look at a photograph: actual lines and implied lines (also called optical). Actual lines are clear and visible, whereas implied lines have a more subtle role, and they hide within the composition.

We can create implied lines with the way we place our subjects. They should be incorporated well enough so that your viewer doesn't see them as lines. Implied lines can be straight, diagonal, and curvilinear too.

Try doodling various shapes on paper—soft, curved ones, or sharp, straight and diagonal ones—and arranging the elements of a composition around these shapes. Then photograph your composition and study the image to see what the effect is.

Find the lines

One of the tasks I was given in a photography evening class that I used to go to was to leave the classroom for an hour and look for lines to photograph. It was such an eye opener and made me realize that lines are everywhere, if we only make a conscious decision to look for them. Study your older work and notice how you might have used lines before (maybe even unintentionally). Which lines worked well and which could be improved?

Next time you shoot, pause for a minute, have a glance at your composition, find the lines, and think how they encourage the eye to move.

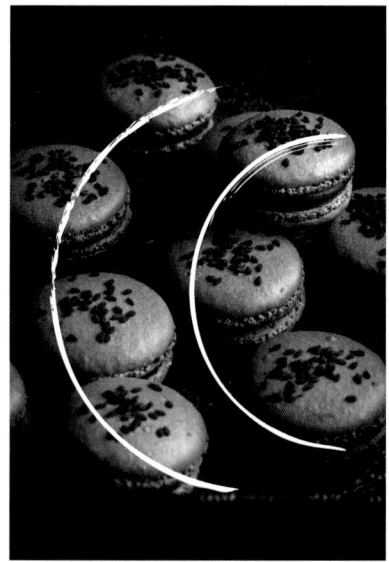
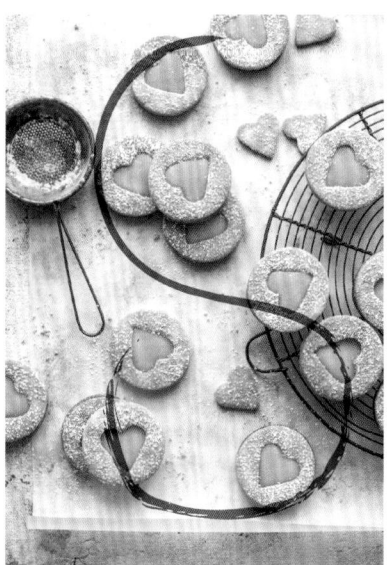
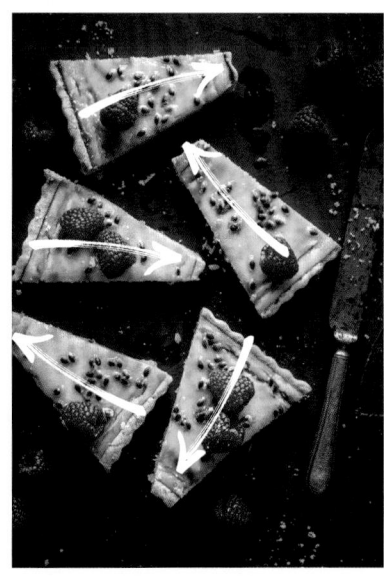

Dive into the world of color

We eat with our eyes. I am sure you've heard this saying before, but in food photography it's especially important. Color gives our audience a clue about what the dish tastes like and how fresh it is. It enlivens our recipe, makes it visually pleasing, and it's often what first catches our viewer's attention. But not only that, color is also a great storyteller and it is the voice of our images. It plays on our emotions and perceptions, and if you learn how to use it well, you will help people to connect with your food stories. In my opinion, it's one of the most powerful tools in food photography.

Nothing has a "true" color. As we saw in the section on white balance (page 58), light affects and influences how we see different hues. But how we pair colors together also alters the way we perceive them. Some colors intensify one another, while others calm each other down. Color theory is like learning a new language. And it's fascinating!

Colors that look good together

Sometimes color combinations will just feel right; at other times, it might seem like things are not falling into place. That's when the color wheel comes in handy—there are a few theories for achieving harmonious color combinations, and you can use the wheel to find them if you get stuck.

1. Monochromatic
These are various shades, tones, or tints of one color; for instance, a range of oranges varying from light to dark. Monochromatic schemes are easy on the eye, producing subtle, delicate, and soothing effects.

2. Diadic
A diadic color scheme takes two colors separated by one color on the color wheel, to give a softer contrast than a complementary pair.

3. Analogous
These colors sit one next to one another on the color wheel, for example red, orange, and pink. Use them to make your image feel more harmonious.

4. Complementary
The page poppers! These colors are opposite each other on the color wheel, for example, blue and orange. When paired together, they make each other more pronounced, adding contrast and energy to your work.

5. Split-complementary
Instead of a pair of opposites, it uses one base color (e.g. orange) and the two colors that flank its opposite on the color wheel (e.g. purple and blue). It still has a strong visual contrast, but with less tension.

6. Triadic
This scheme uses three colors that are evenly spaced around the color wheel. It has a similar effect to split-complementary colors.

7. Rectangle/double-complementary
This scheme uses two complementary pairs. It makes for colorful, eye-catching images, but it also creates competition between colors so proportions should be used carefully. It often works best if one color is just an accent. It can be a great tool to use for styling colorful dishes such as salads.

8. Square
Very similar to the rectangle, but with all four colors spaced evenly around the color wheel.

...And don't forget black & white
In my opinion, black and white pair well with every color, but find which combinations you like best.

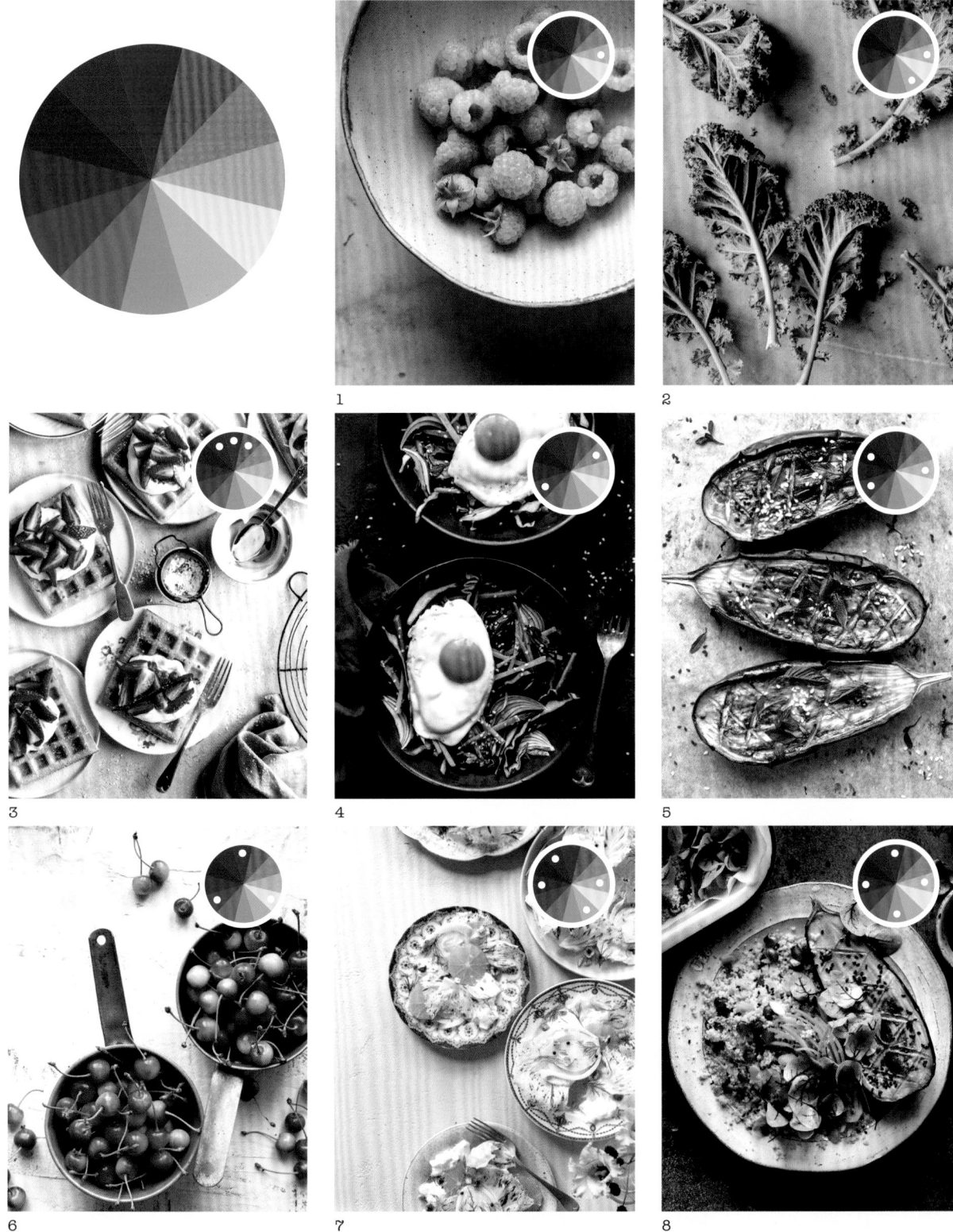

1

2

3

4

5

6

7

8

Work the Frame 83

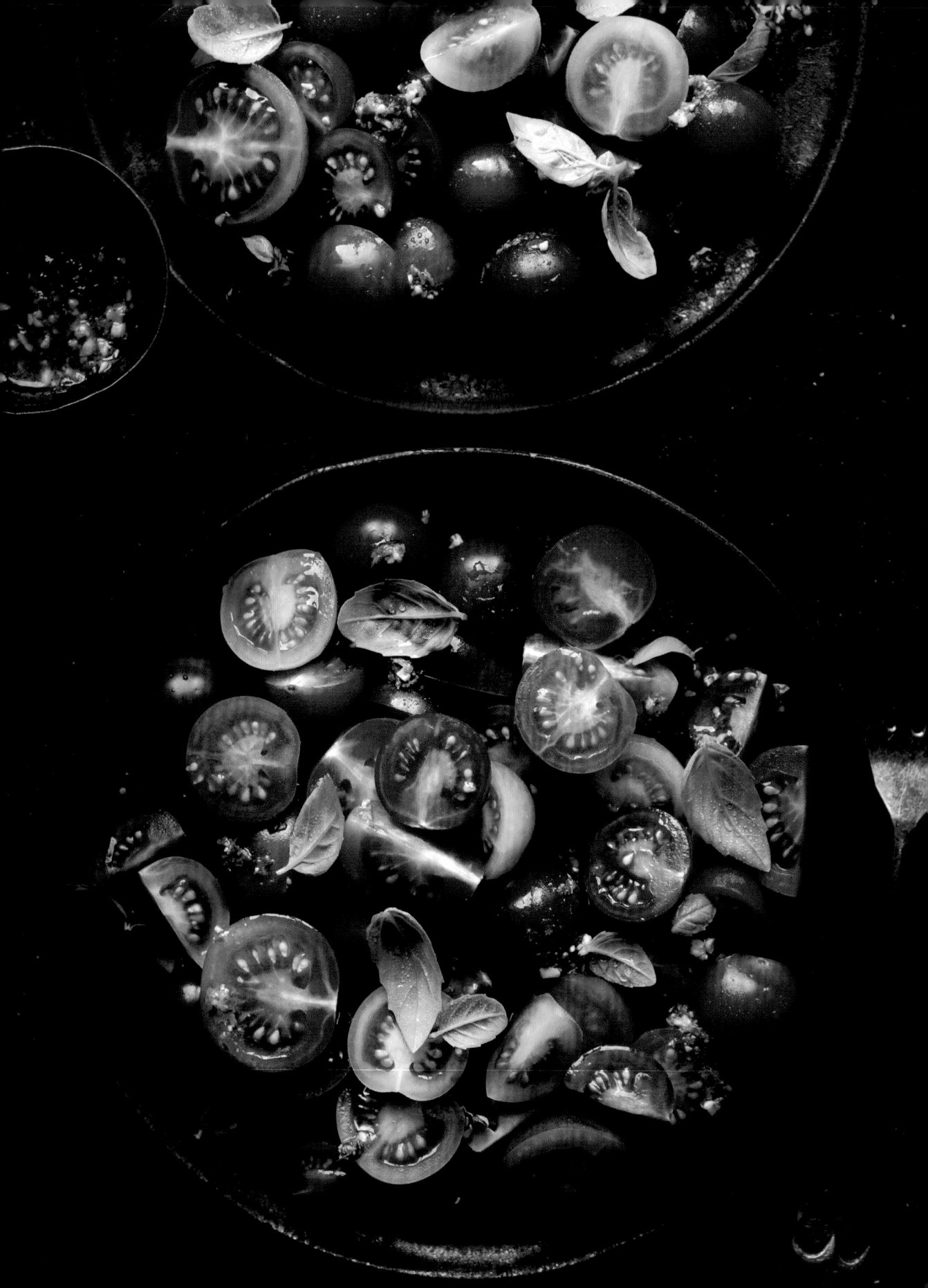

Color choices

Light or dark

Light colors are lightweight and delicate: they add freshness and a sense of space to an image. Dark colors feel heavier and will make a photo feel more intimate. Both are equally interesting, but both create a different feeling.

When combined together in one image, they can create contrast, and I will often photograph light subject on a dark background or dark subject on a light background for an extra pop.

Warm or cold

Warm colors project energy, comfort, and coziness. Cool colors, on the other hand, have a calming, soothing or even refreshing effect, just like a breath of fresh air. Warm colors advance: they seem to come towards us, feel closer, and they usually catch our attention first. Cool colors recede: they feel more distant, creating a sense of space.

When combined together in one image, warm and cool colors will create contrast, a sense of depth and more visual engagement. Warm colors will also feel even warmer when paired with cool tones, and vice versa.

Saturation

Saturation describes the intensity of a color. Highly saturated colors are vivid and deep. They excite the eye and are full of energy. Less saturated colors are softer and much more gentle.

Highly saturated hues stimulate the eye and grab our attention faster than those that are less saturated. Keep in mind, though, that too much saturation and too many vibrant colors in one composition can strain the eye and have a jarring effect. A proportional use of more and less saturated hues is very important to create balance here. I like to make sure that my subject is vibrant and eye-catching; but to make it stand out even more, I either pick props and backgrounds that are less saturated or I will desaturate them later in post-production.

Active colors

Colors that are "active" always grab our attention first in a composition, while less active colors take a supporting role. Warmth, vibrancy, intensity, and often quantity are factors that play a role in making a color more active. When choosing your palette, always think about which colors grab the attention first. Are any colors in competition with each other? Most importantly, ensure that your background and supporting elements aren't too active and don't distract from your hero subject.

Left: Here is a perfect example of how using a combination of light and dark and cool and warm colors adds high contrast and visual engagement to the image, and make the subject pop. Using saturated colors grabs the attention even more!

This all adds up to a dramatic treatment that might not be right for every subject, but when you understand the effect each of these factors has on a composition, you can use them to create the food stories you want to tell.

Tip

The best way to master color is to take a moment every day to notice it and to recognize how it makes you feel. When you are out and about, pay attention to the colors that catch your eye more than others, and think about why that is. Then use that knowledge creatively in your work.

Color in practice

"Color in a picture is like enthusiasm
in life."
—Vincent van Gogh

Color is so subjective. When I posted these three
photos (right) of the same soup in three different color
palettes on my Instagram, asking everyone which colors
they liked the most, it started a debate that generated
over 500 comments! Everyone had an opinion based
on their personal taste, and every opinion was different.

Our tastes and perceptions about color are personal,
influenced by where we live and what we like. For me,
this is just another reason why we should always go with
our gut when we create and do what feels right for us.
However, there are a few ideas that I like to think about
when I put color into practice.

Less is more
When the photograph is filled with too many colors, it
can look cluttered and distracting. Limiting the number
of hues in your frame can not only give your subject
more impact but your composition will also feel more
balanced and harmonious.

One of my favorite and most-used methods to draw
attention to the food is to pick props and backgrounds
in different shades of the same color, so they blend
nicely together, and I make sure the color of my food
pops against it.

Keep it in proportion
60-30-10 is a "rule" for color proportion often adhered
to by interior designers and florists. I also love using it
in my food photography when I'm working with three
colors (which happens very often).I might not stick
to exactly 60-30-10, but I do like to keep in mind the
principle of one color dominating, a second playing a
supporting role and a third color being just an accent.

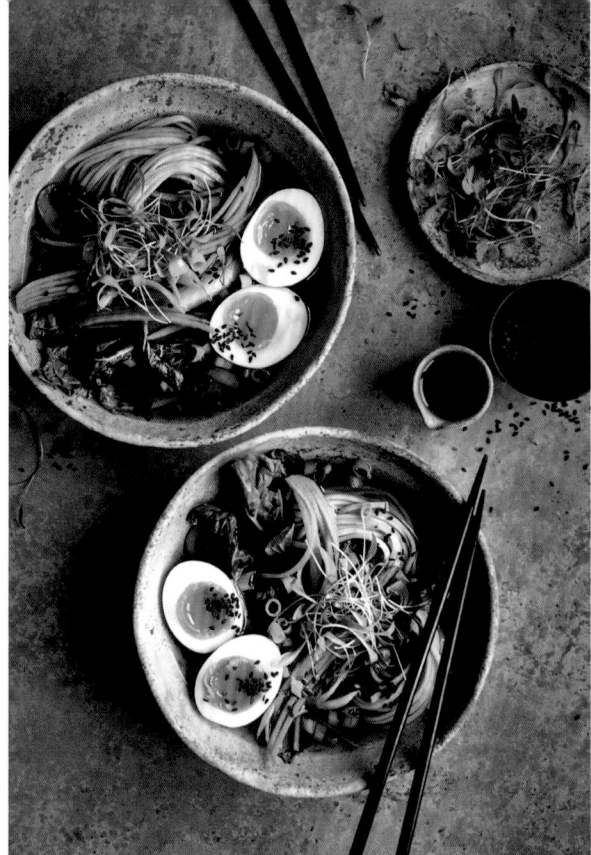

Color repetition
Repeating the same color across different elements is
an easy way to achieve rhythm and harmony in your
frame. Anytime I get stuck with what colors to pick for
my backgrounds, supporting elements or garnish, this
simple yet powerful trick saves the day. I have a quick
glance at what colors are already in the dish, and then
think about which of them I could possibly repeat. You
can see this in action on page 75 where I echo the color
of raspberries in the floral pattern on the plate and the
background.

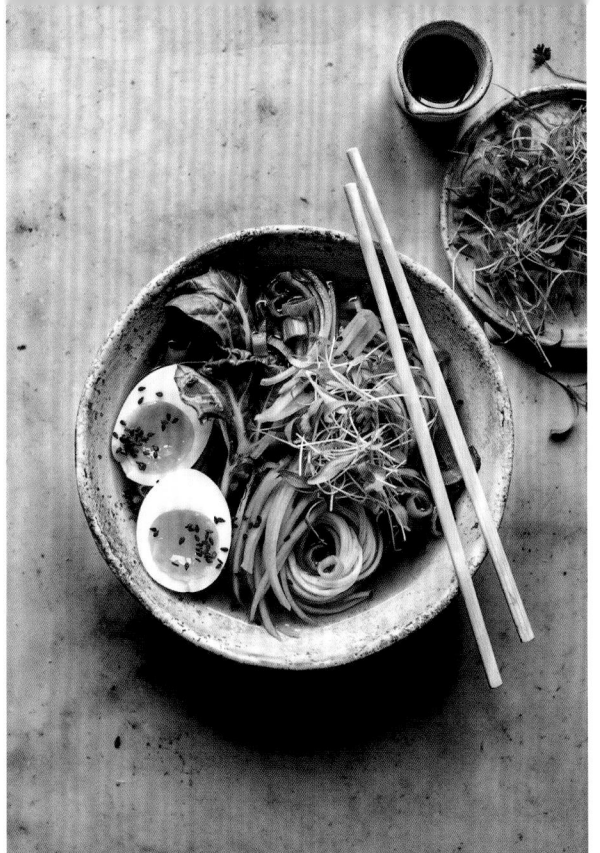

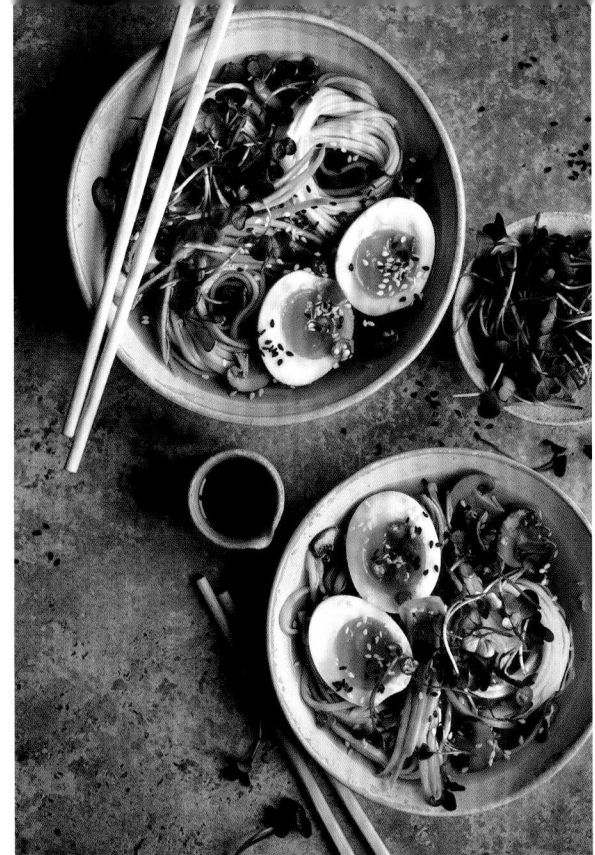

Let the world inspire your color choices

A red and green poppy field on the journey home, a white and pink shop window in London, a green and brown café in New York—these are just a few real places that sparked the color choices for my food stories. When you take a little extra time to stop and look at what's around you, you will never run out of inspiration for your color palettes. Have eyes wide open. Find colors that make you feel something. Think about what food would work for that color palette and create a food story around it.

Color psychology

Some colors can make us feel energetic, while others have a calming effect. Some project warmth and coziness, while others add a sense of freshness. Every color has a personality—consider how you can use this in your compositions.

* **Yellow** is warm, joyful, and positive.
* **Orange** is energetic and warm.
* **Red** is connected with love, passion, energy, heat, and excitement.
* **Purple** is luxurious, exotic, and feminine, and is connected with wisdom and spirituality.
* **Pink** is sweet and romantic.
* **Blue** is cool, calm, and contemplative, but is also connected with melancholy.
* **Green** is organic, natural, and healthy.
* **White** is minimal, pure, and simple.
* **Black** is bold, sophisticated, and mysterious.

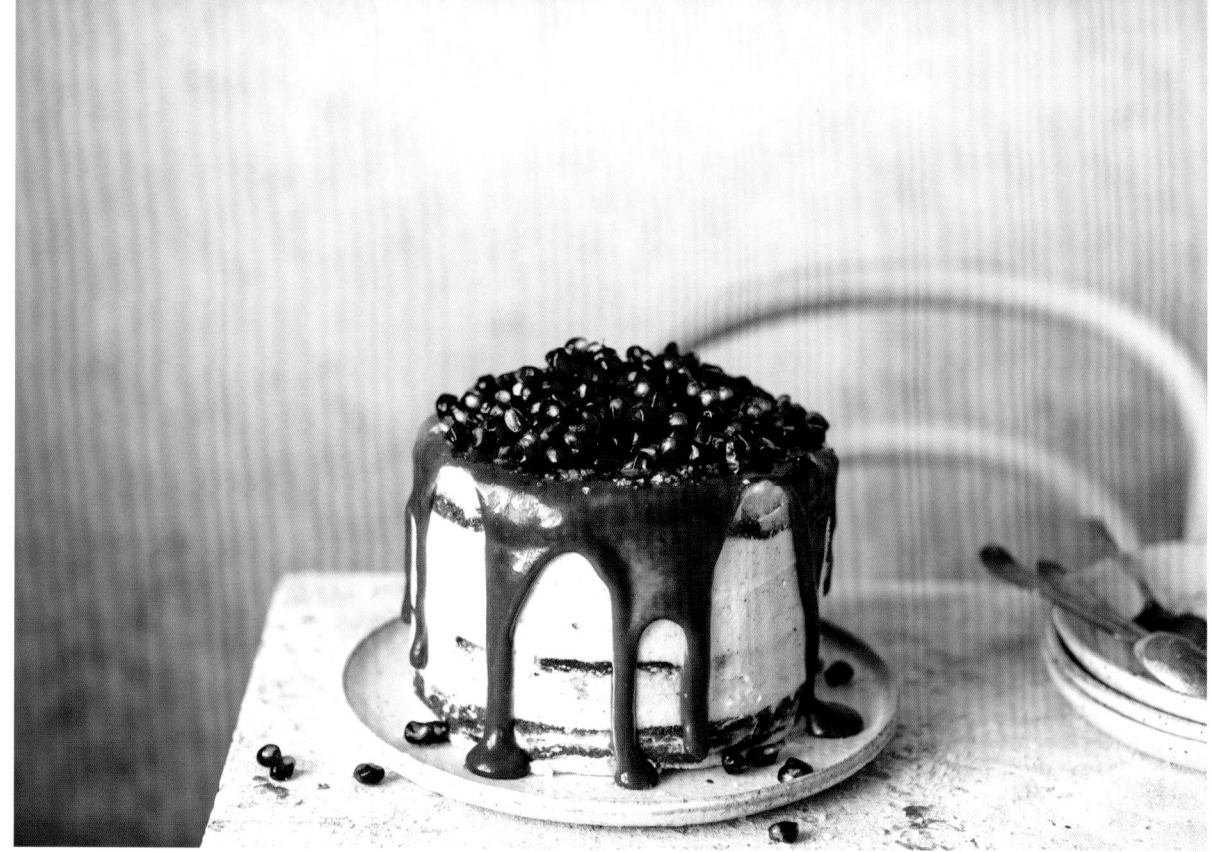

Creating a sense of balance

Understanding what makes a balanced composition is important if you want to achieve photos that "feel right." When the elements in the frame feel natural and their arrangement is harmonious, the photo will be engaging and pleasant to look at. Here are a few ways to make sure your food stories are appealing to the eye.

Negative space (above)
Negative space is the empty area that surrounds the components in an image. Leaving large amount of negative space adds lightness, opens up your photograph, and makes it feel more spacious, as though everything has a little room to breathe.

I used to be afraid of leaving any negative space and would just keep on cramming stuff into my photographs without much thought. Later I realized that by taking things out of the frame, I was actually making my images feel more balanced and enjoyable.

When a frame is filled with too many patterns, colors, and shapes, the eye can be easily distracted. Giving the hero subject a little breathing space means that the viewer can identify the main character of your food story right away. Negative space can also be a clever method to strengthen emotions about the recipes that carry a message of simplicity, or any dish that you would like to evoke feelings of calmness and balance.

Negative space is a great tool but that's not to say that filling your frame to the rim is always bad. The trick is to always think about what works for the specific subject or story. Sometimes a subject looks better when left alone or without much company; other times it might be stronger in a group. There is never just one correct treatment that applies to all the photos we create.

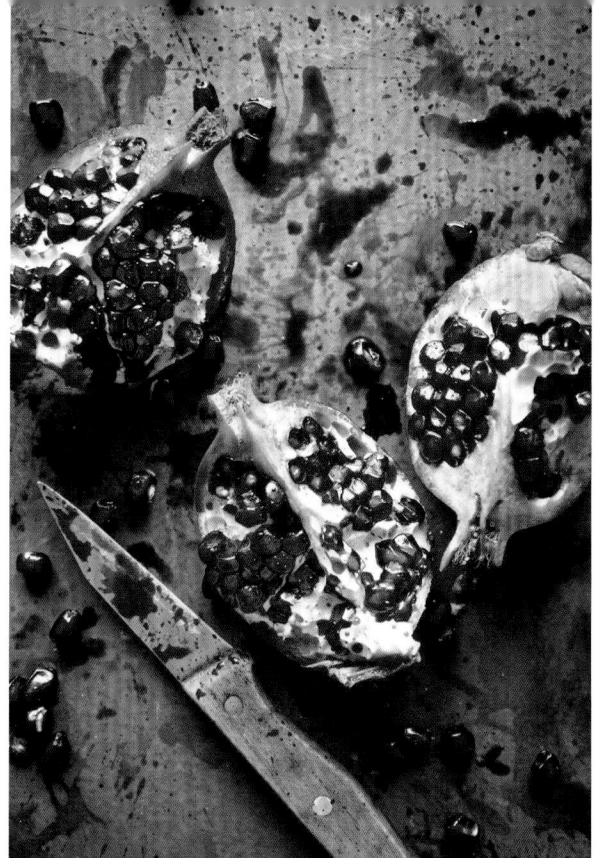

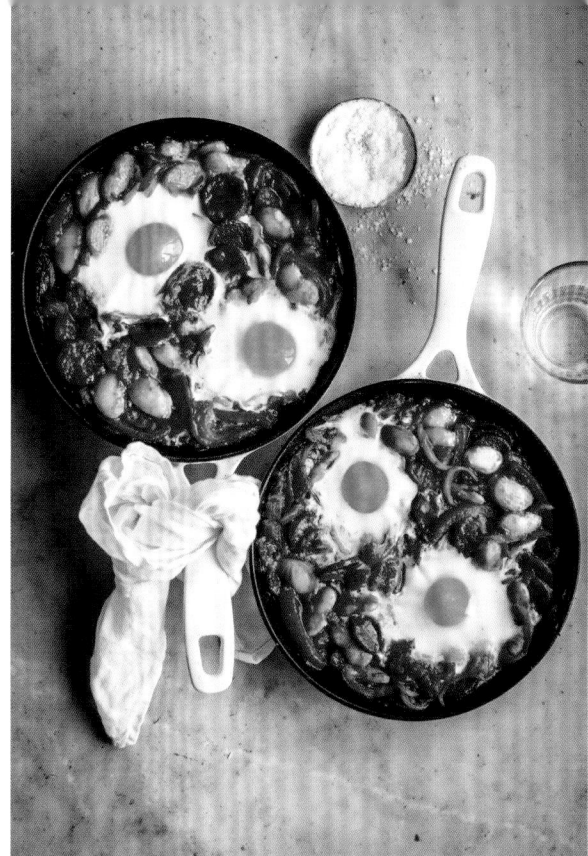

Creative rule of odds (above)

It is said that an odd number of elements in a frame is more visually pleasing for the eye than an even number and that a group of three creates harmony and balance. Although it works pretty well, if my compositions always featured three of the same subject, my images might start to look a bit predictable. So I like to use odd numbers in a more creative way; for instance, I might frame one large subject and put three plates next to it or choose three (very different) props for the story; I might pick three colors for my compositions, or I might try grouping many elements into three irregular clusters, and so on.

Remember that the rule of odds only applies until the number is so great that it just looks like a lot of elements in the frame. For me, five is probably the maximum number of elements the eye can easily identify, and I will often choose five elements over four or six.

Keep it asymmetrical (above)

The simple beauty of symmetry is something the eye can never resist. We are naturally drawn to the harmony it creates. But although perfect symmetry works well for some subjects in food photography, I personally feel the "rule" works even better when slightly bent. When everything is flawlessly mirrored, an image might feel too unnatural or even a little bit boring. I like to bring some additional elements to the frame, to create a more organic and dynamic scene—without upsetting the balance.

For instance, you will often see me placing my main subject right in the center of the frame. In my opinion, it's a powerful method to signal the importance of the hero. But to avoid making the food portrait too symmetrical, I will also add a couple of carefully chosen elements on either side of my subject.

Create visual interest: what catches the eye?

Some things hold our eyes more than others, and in a great food story, there is always a hierarchy of elements: main subject and supporting cast. What we look at first in a photograph is what interests us the most: these things are often described as having more "visual weight." That's why if you want to draw the eye to your hero subject, you've got to make it the most interesting part of the photograph, so that your viewer has no choice but to notice it straight away.

A strong focal point is what will set your photo apart. It's what shouts "Hey, look at me!"

Contrast (right, top)

Photography is a play of contrasts, and a strong contrast always draws the eye. One of the most effective ways of putting all eyes on the hero is by focussing the light only on it and contrasting it with beautiful, deep shadows. A prominent color contrast (such as bright subjects on a dark background or other way around) as well as a striking difference between the texture of the food and that of the background will make your subject pop too.

The sharp spot (right, bottom)

The sharpest part of your image will almost always catch the viewer's attention first, whereas what's out of focus serves to direct the eye to the sharpest area. This is a great tool when there are a few items in your frame but you don't want them to distract from your hero subject. Using a shallow depth of field will separate your dish from the background, which helps it to stand out even when there aren't many competing elements.

When we decide to have everything in focus, we put emphasis on the scene, rather than on a single element, which can work well for many images. Just make sure your most interesting subject has enough visual weight in another way (such as color or size), so that it's the first thing your viewer will spot.

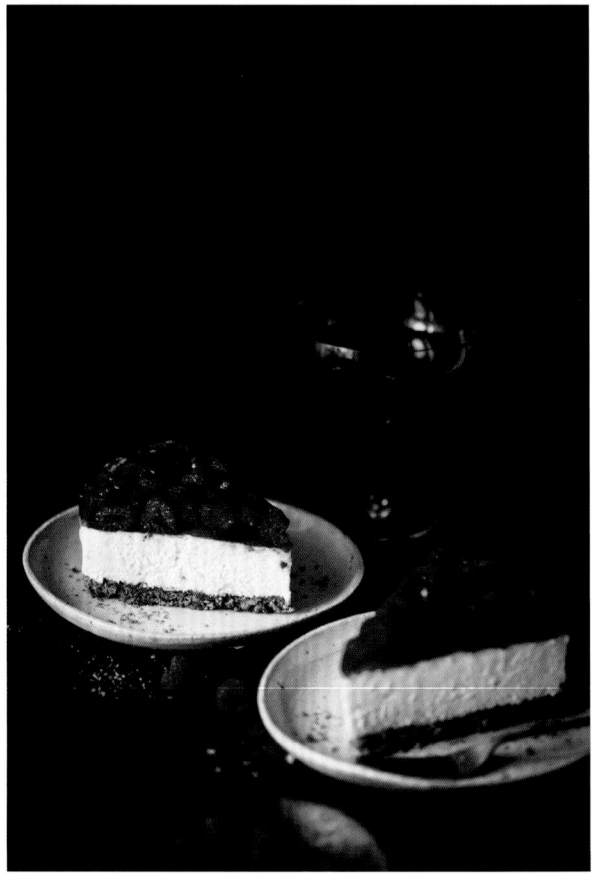

Blurred movement

Isn't this contradicting the previous point? Of course it is, because in photography, there is an exception to everything, and keep in mind that the eye is always attracted to contrast. In this case, if we have a sharp image, but we have a moving subject that is blurred because we used a slow shutter speed to capture it, that blur is where the eye will go.

Surprise

If you show your viewer something they've never seen before—a "flying" detail captured with a fast shutter speed, for example—you'll be sure to catch their eye. People will look twice at something that surprises them.

Size (right, top)

Bigger (or heavier) objects carry more visual weight than smaller ones, and making sure your hero is the largest item in the frame will leave the viewer with no doubt to where to look first. On the other hand, not only can a too-large prop look out of proportion and make our photograph unbalanced, it can also compete with your intended focal point. In this image, if the plate with raspberries was bigger and I included more of it, for example, it might have pulled the eye away from the trifle. Always pay attention to the size and weight of your supporting elements, and be aware that a small item is still likely to distract from your dish if it has a more vibrant color or eye-catching pattern.

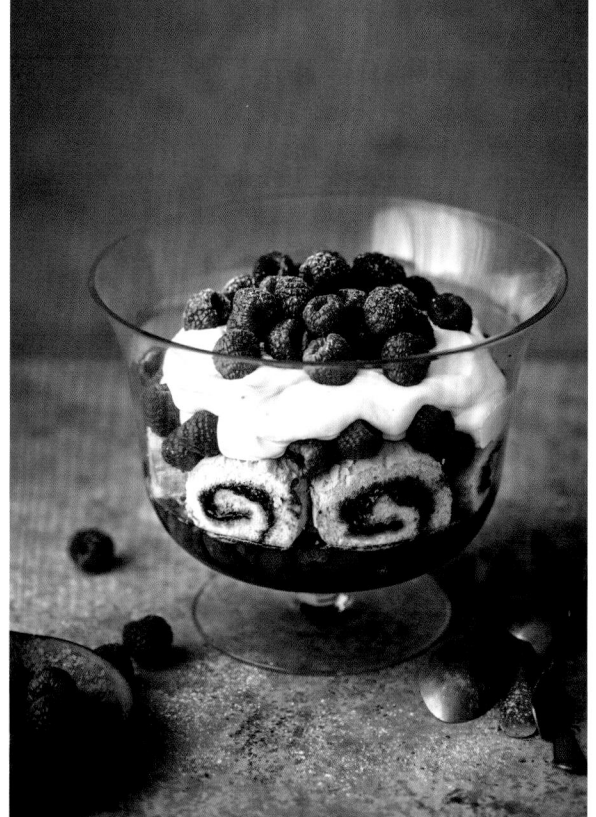

Color (right, bottom)

Highly saturated and intense colors stand out more than gentle and neutral shades. A burst of contrasting colors against a more subtle background can provide a strong focal point in your photo, and make the hero subject stand out. On the other hand, if a supporting element has a more active hue (see page 85) than your subject, it will draw attention away from it.

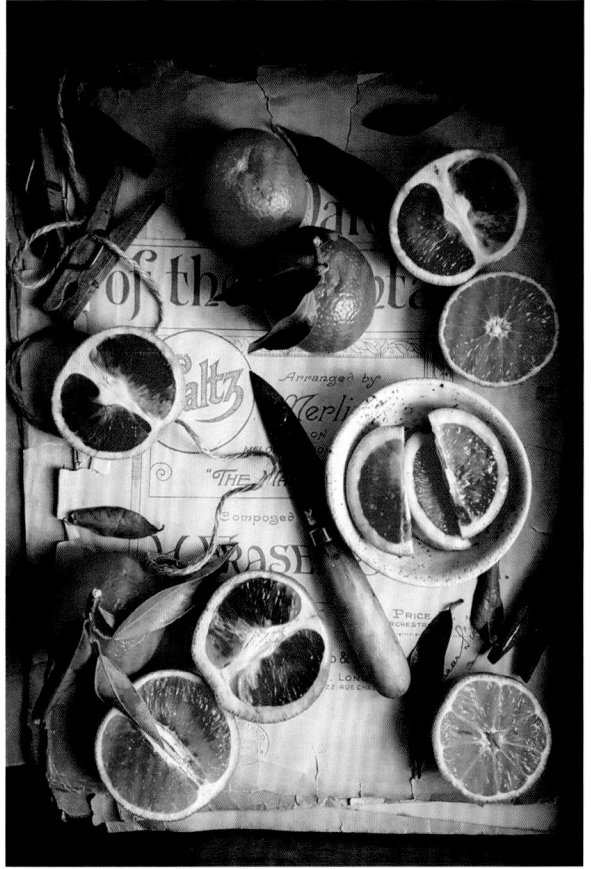

Shape

Shapes can be a great way to add visual interest to your image when you focus on them in your composition. Think about this next time you pick or prepare your subject, when you slice it or when you decide on what props to include within the frame.

Repetition (right, top)

Repeating a subject several times emphasizes its importance within the image. Partly, this relates to the principle of size, in which what has the greatest quantity draws the eye, and partly, it's because repeated elements create an eye-pleasing visual echo.

It doesn't just have to be the subject that's repeated. A good way to create a unified, harmonious image is by repeating a color or a shape, etc. This image is appealing because the eye enjoys sorting through the similar shapes, sizes, textures, and colors it sees to group those that it recognizes as being the same.

Pattern (right, bottom)

Pattern is created by the regular repetition of a subject, color, or shape, similar to what we talked about in the previous point. But pattern can be added in other ways, too, such as on our props or in the way we decorate our food. Bear in mind that a strong pattern can be hard to tear our eyes away from, so if a design on a supporting element is too powerful, it might steal all of the attention.

Faces, eyes & hands

Our brains are wired to see humans first, which can be both a good and bad thing. If you can see someone's face in your photo, it will likely have more visual weight than other components. However, if this person is looking at the food, then you will follow their gaze. We're also attracted to hands, and if we show these hands in contact with our food, it can be a great way of adding to our food stories while simultaneously leading the eye to the most important thing in the frame.

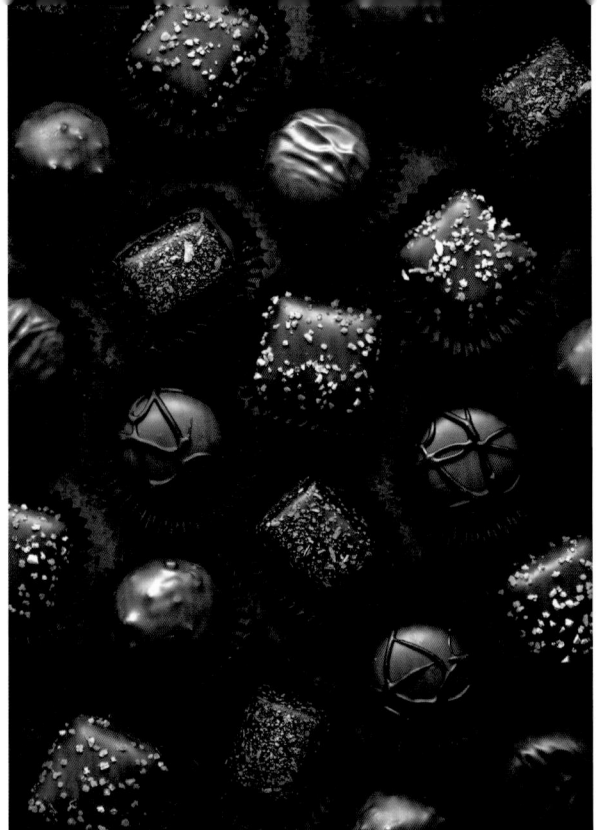

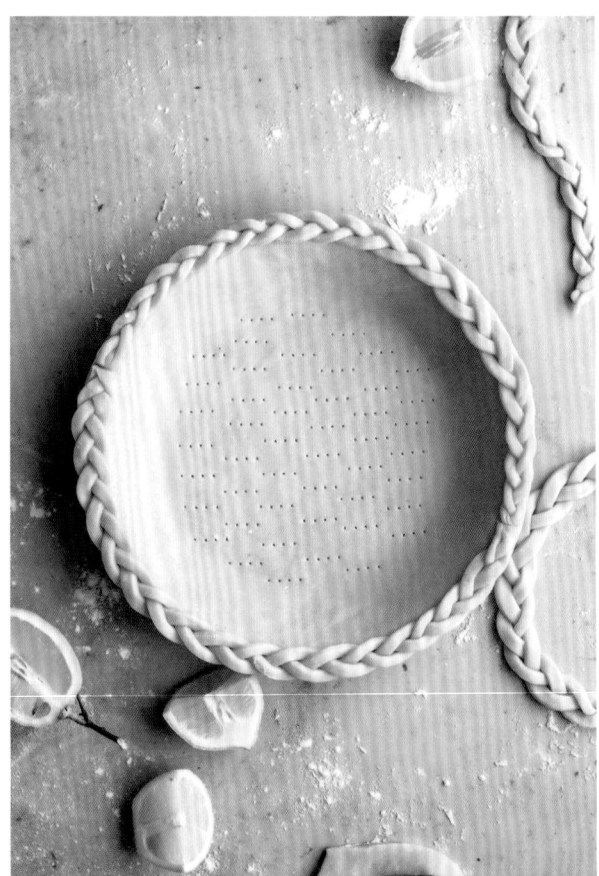

Text

Our eyes are always drawn to any type of text, so if there is an important message you want to make sure the reader will get, it might be a good idea to literally spell it out, with alphabet-shaped cookies, pastry, or in flour, for example.

Be aware that text will be a bad thing if your viewer is trying to read it rather than looking at the food! Try to use some creative blurring to hide any writing that appears on your props. If you're using newspaper, a recipe, or any other written material in your image, avoid showing too much legible writing, and take care that nothing you can read is inappropriate to your food story.

Texture (right, top)

Texture holds a lot of interest and our eyes are drawn to it naturally. For instance, there is no color contrast in this photograph, so the texture plays an important role here. The background is smooth so it doesn't hold too much visual weight, leaving the full attention free to go to the most textured part of our photo: the pasta. Always keep an eye on props and backgrounds that have a strong texture and make sure they are not too distracting.

Closeup (right, bottom)

By getting really close to your subject, you get rid of all the distractions, and there is no doubt as to what's important in the frame. It can also be a way to surprise your viewer, by showing them a detail they might not have seen before.

Make sure that the viewer can still recognize what the closeup is and that important details (in texture or shape, for example) are sharp and visible.

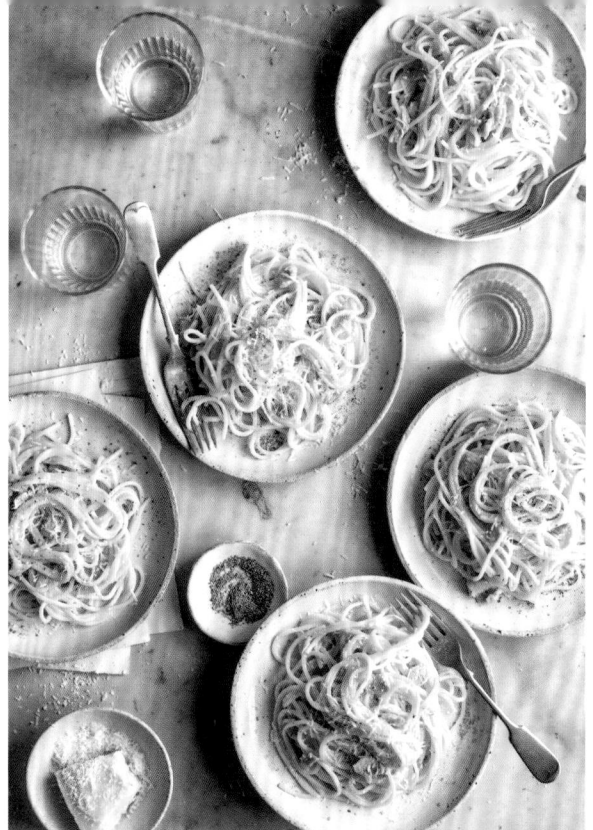

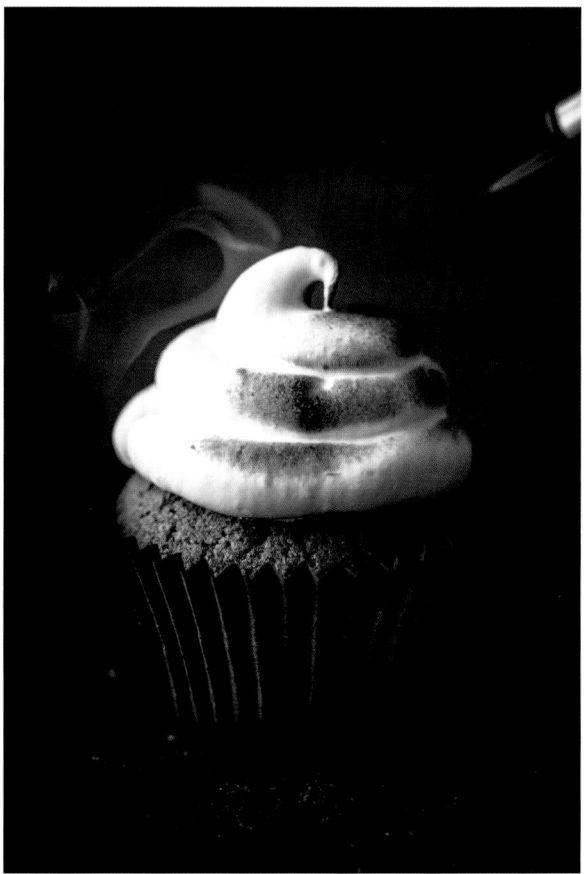

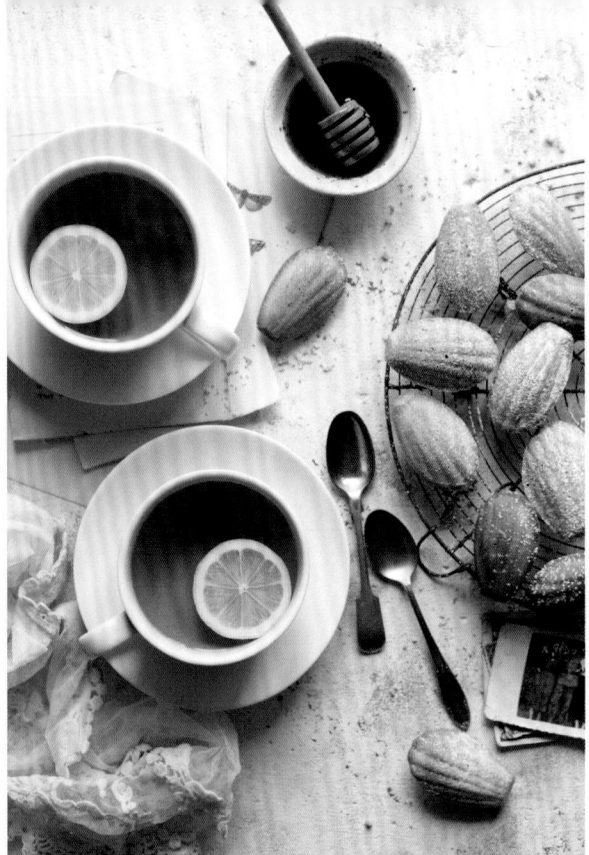

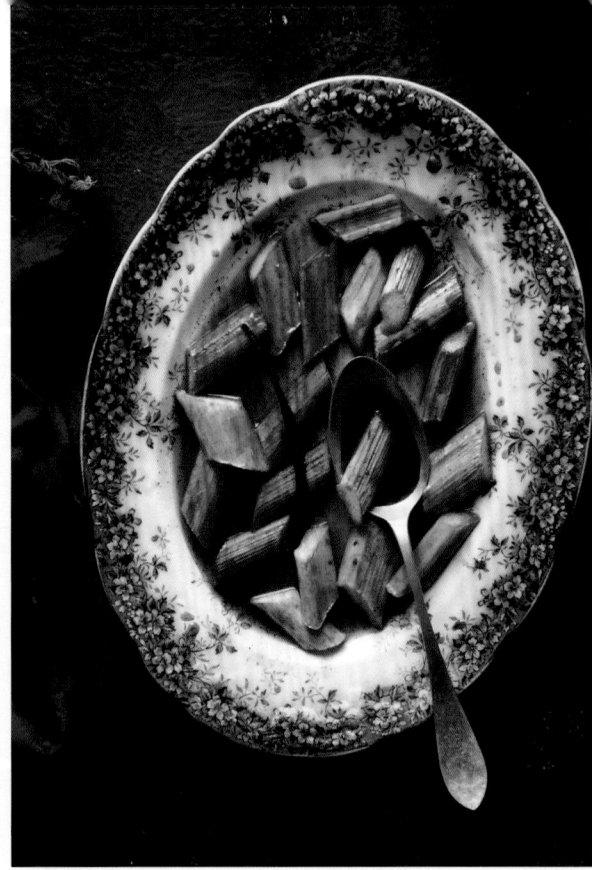

Troubleshooting

When you want to include a lot of different elements in your food stories, that can mean many parts of a photograph vying for the viewer's attention. This can make it hard to know where to look first, and if we are not careful, interesting props and supporting elements can distract from our dish.

Photographing eye-catching subjects on a plain background, with few props, is a sure-fire way to keep all eyes on the hero, but I want to show you that the scene doesn't always have to be minimal to keep the viewer's attention where it should be. There are other methods you can use to make sure your main subject stands out.

What's the story? (above, left)

This photograph could succeed or fail depending on the interpretation. If I was aiming to make an image about tea time, then it's a winner. But if it's about a recipe for madeleines, then it would fail. If I wanted the madeleines to be the main point of interest I would make them a bigger part of the image by including more of the cooling rack with our subjects in the frame. I would also pick smaller cups for the tea, or at least push these big ones to the edge of the frame and crop them so they don't take all the attention.

A distracting prop (above)

There's a very heavy pattern on this plate and there is always a risk that the prop might be more interesting than the subject itself. If you decide to go for patterns, you've got to make sure to always choose a subject that is visually stronger than any pattern it might have to compete with. In this example, the color of the food outweighs the floral design, and by blending the color

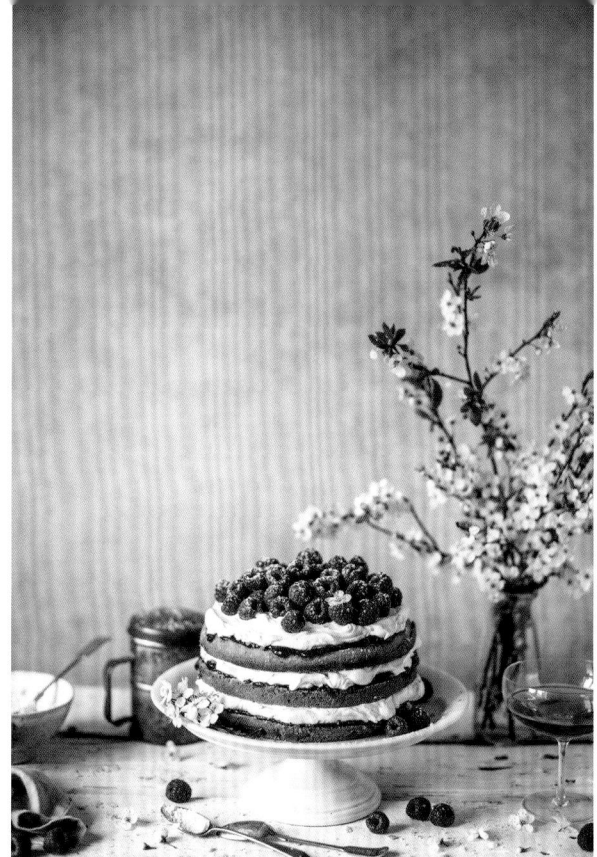

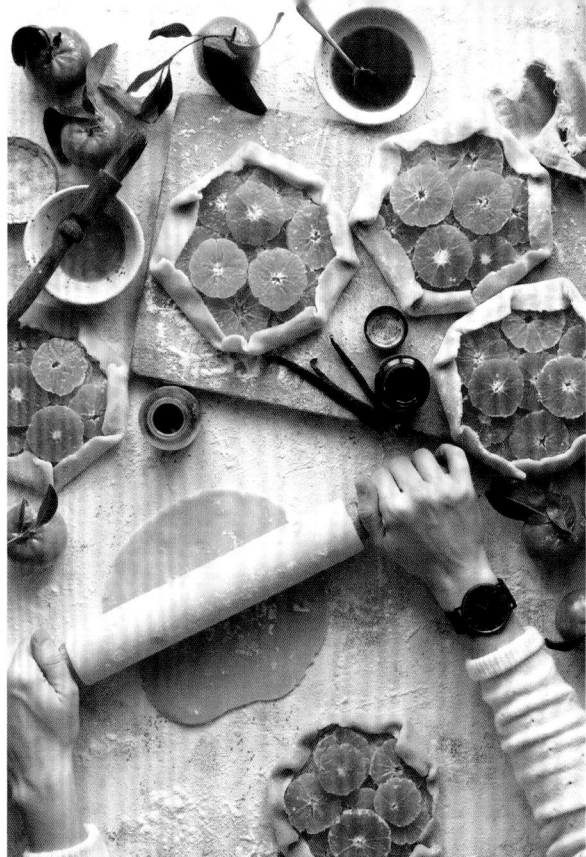

of the plate into the background, the contrast makes the rhubarb pop. I also desaturated the blues in post-production, which makes the vivid pink even more powerful.

Competing size (above)

The flowers in this picture are the tallest, but by keeping them out of focus and behind the main subject, they lose their significance. They would be much more distracting if they were next to the cake and in focus. Using a glass vase was a great move too, as the material makes the prop feel lighter, making the cake the heaviest—therefore the most important—part of the image. Additionally, its warm colors contrast with the rest of the scene, ensuring that the viewer will notice it right away.

Busy scene (above)

There is a lot going on in this image and I had to be very careful if I wanted the mandarin galettes to remain the focal point of the frame. In order to do that, I decided to keep the colors to a minimum. I made sure that all the supporting elements had a neutral color so that the vibrant galette filling was the first thing that caught the eye.

The supporting elements are also smaller in size in comparison to our heroes, so they don't carry as much visual weight. I also included not one, but five galettes to strengthen their importance through repetition. The human element doesn't fill much of the frame and it looks proportional; it adds to the whole story rather than distracts.

Interview:
Claudia Goedke

I've been following Claudia since I started out as a photographer, and she has always been a huge source of inspiration to me. The way she sees the world and captures her unique perspective is incredible. She always has creative ideas and solutions up her sleeve, not to mention that her photos look so natural, as though they have never been arranged.

I have seen you in action a few times and the way you work is fascinating to me. You have such a great eye for details and you seem to see things other people don't notice. Is this something you have mastered over the years, or does it just come naturally to you? Are there any tips you could share on how to train the eye?
I'd say it's a combination of both: 30 percent my own creativity and 70 percent influenced by studying photography, looking at and analyzing countless images each week. In retrospect, I'd say that training my eye has helped in ways that I would have never expected and that I benefit from it every day when I'm working.

This would be my advice: Look at as many photos and images as you can and analyze them. Find out what you like about a certain photo and what you don't like. Don't just limit yourself to the photographers you already know, but rather look at photographers throughout history such as Dorothea Lange, Diane Arbus, Ansel Adams, Henri Cartier-Bresson, Nan Goldin, Stephen Shore, and so on. Studying the work of photographers who didn't focus on food photography shaped the way I see a composition much more than looking at what other food photographers do.

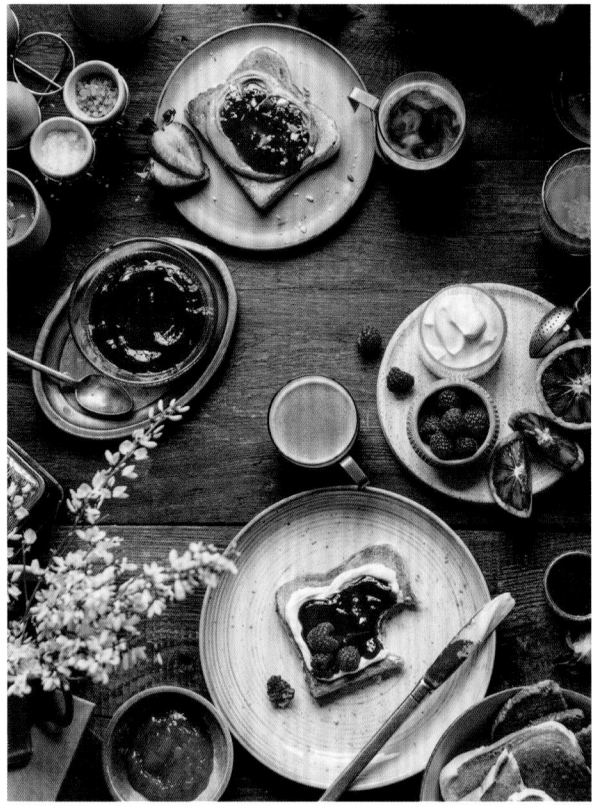

It feels like none of your images are ever the same. How do you keep compositions in your photographs fresh and exciting?
For all my shoots for clients, I try to work with either a stylist, a food stylist, or even better: both! Working with talented people who focus on one job in particular allows me to focus on the photography. While a stylist sets up a set, I have enough time to walk around it, getting a feeling for different angles and possible close-ups. Most times, I also take images of the props laid out before the styling or after the food was taken off the plates. Of course, I do have my own comfort zone and a few angles that always work. But if I see a beautiful setting, it would be a waste not to photograph it from every possible angle, if I have the time. I just really like to play and always try to get the best out of it.

Do you ever plan your shots beforehand? What goes on inside your head before you start composing your image?

I typically think through every possible scenario before I even begin to shoot. Once, I was teaching a workshop, styling a set, and one of the other photographers asked, "But when will you look through the camera?" The question totally surprised me, but in hindsight, I get it. I'm a meticulous planner.

Here's a rough description of my workflow: As soon as I have a theme for a photoshoot, I start by making notes and thinking about possible color schemes and motives. After some research, I like to put together a mood board to combine different shooting angles, ideas, colors, and textures into one PDF. If I'm working alone, I will try to sketch my ideas for the images, to have some kind of guide for the shooting day. The drawings also help me to think of the additional decoration and props that will be needed for each shot.

I then try to think of as many shots as I can—not just of the final dish, but also the ingredients, a step-by-step image, or something similar. Don't just think of the end result, but also pay attention to what could be interesting while you're preparing the dish.

On the day of the shoot, the mood board and sketches help me to pick out the props and start the actual work of photographing! I start by arranging the first image exactly how I imagined it, and when everything I thought about beforehand is in the set, I will get my camera and take a first look. Personally, I also like to tether my camera and then look at the computer screen while I'm arranging the props.

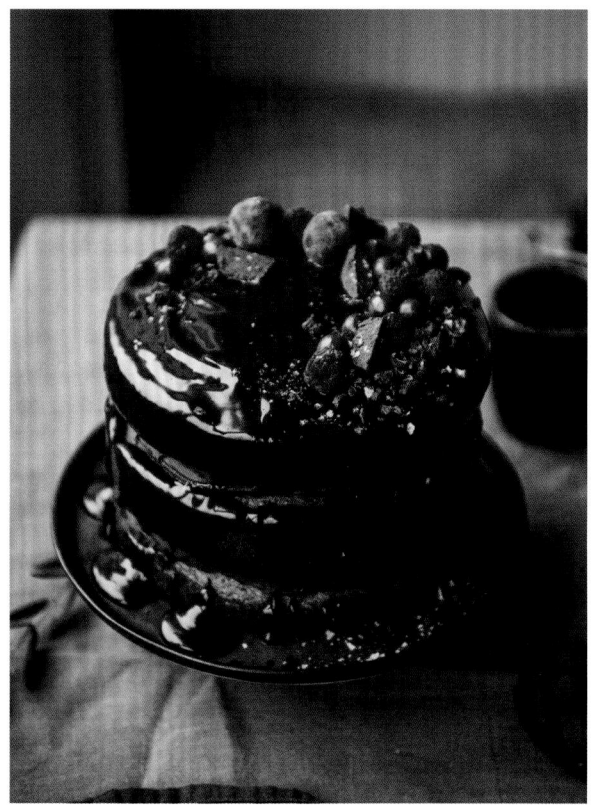

How long does it take you to compose an image? And what do you do when you get stuck?

When I'm not working with a stylist, I like to put all my props on the background and just play around. This gives me a rough sense of the textures, height, and size of the props. It's usually the first photo I take. When working alone, it might take me between an hour and an hour and a half to be happy with my set and to put the food in. When working with a stylist, it depends on the size of the set, but can also range from half an hour for a small set to two hours for a perfectly decorated table for six.

I used to be very hard on myself when I would get stuck and couldn't figure out how to make a certain angle or type of food work in the frame (any type of rolled cakes or éclairs are my kryptonite!). I would tell myself, "But you are a creative person! You should be able to solve this!" Turns out, that sometimes it just won't work. Maybe the backdrop is not right, maybe the food doesn't look good, maybe you're just having an off day. Instead of forcing something that might not work anyway, I like to dismantle the set and turn on some good music. I will then go ahead and put all the props away and start on a new backdrop with a few new props. Remember being a kid and building a huge tower with building blocks, only to tear it down and build something new? Just like that! And if it really won't work, just leave it and go back to it the next day. Chances are, you've got a lot of other things to do anyway and can tend to them instead of despairing over a few plates and bowls.

Any favorite tips on how to keep your compositions looking natural?

This is a thin line to navigate and is always based on the taste of the person who is creating an image or looking at a photo. Once I worked for a client who was never happy with the photograph, unless we had a lot of spilled ingredients on the backdrop, salad falling out of its bowl, sauce dripping from the jar or a lot of flower petals scattered around. It seriously stressed me out, as it was just too much and unnatural. Who would want to sit down to eat at a table like this, with a perfectly styled plate of pasta in front of them and the rest of the table looking like it was attacked with a leaf blower? Eventually, I understood why they had requested this, so I was fine styling the table the way they preferred it. This is just a personal pet peeve of mine—I do like a bit of salt and a crunched up napkin here and there—but when I take a photo, I want to evoke a good feeling, not one that has me reaching for a dishcloth. Think about what you'd do in real life and you'll be fine.

Are there any foolproof compositional tools or techniques that you rely on when arranging your food stories?

I don't have any specific rules I follow but rather do what feels right, but there are a few things I always pay attention to. When I work with a lot of different-sized bowls in one shot, I like to arrange them randomly, so that one touches another but then a third one stands a bit farther away. When shooting overhead, I also like to incorporate flowers in a vase, a plant, or anything else that sticks up a bit to add some height. I also like to cut

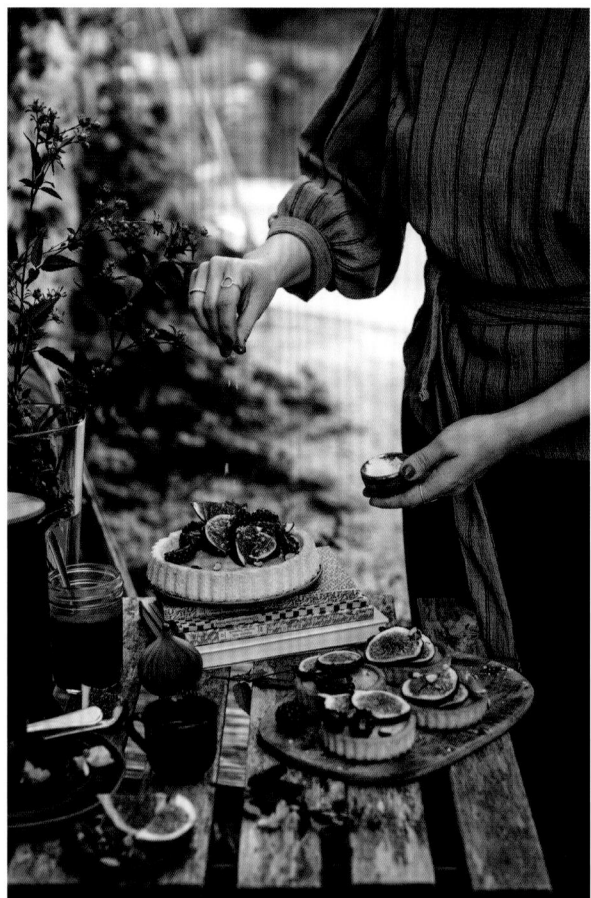

off certain elements in the frame and just have them peeking in or cast a shadow from outside the frame. I feel like it comes down to practice. Practice as much as you can and you'll develop a sense for compositions.

There have been a lot of conversations about arranged images being fake and unauthentic: how do you feel about that?

The moment you open up a fashion magazine and see the newest summer clothing or beauty trends, you will always see staged photoshoots and series to show the products in the best way possible. Why should it be different with food photography? Creating worlds, scenarios, and moments is an essential part of our job. We won't save the world with our work, but making just one person look at an arranged photo and think "Wow, I'd love to sit down at that table and enjoy a nice meal with my friends!" makes me happy.

What was the biggest "aha" moment for you that influenced the way you photograph today?

This might sound a bit stupid, but when I was studying photography, I despised shooting still lifes because it meant working in a studio with artificial lighting, which was no fun for me at all. However, after I graduated, I fell in love with Linda Lomelino's photos. Was this real life? Was it okay to shoot still lifes using only natural light? This was my "aha" moment, which got me started on my journey to learn everything I could about natural light and daylight photography. So if you're reading this: thanks, Linda!

What are some of the biggest lessons you've learned from running a photography business?

If it's not a YES, it's a no. Don't take criticism personally, but professionally. Don't be afraid to say no. Try to find and offer solutions the client hasn't thought about, instead of saying you can't do it, say "I can't do that, but here's what I can offer you!" Know the worth of your work and don't sell yourself short.

I love that you keep educating yourself, learning from others, and participating in workshops even though you are an established photographer. That's very inspiring!

Life would be boring if you stopped learning, right? Times change, technologies change, styles change. For me, it's fun to learn new things and stay on top of my game or improve certain techniques. Seeing other people's workflows and how someone approaches a photoshoot is so interesting to me. These are the things you don't learn when studying photography. So venturing out and learning new stuff is crucial for me.

And the last one! What's your favorite lens, and why?

I have just two lenses: a 24–70mm and a 100mm macro lens. The first I use about 80 percent of the time, but the 100mm is a game-changer when shooting close ups or table scenes.

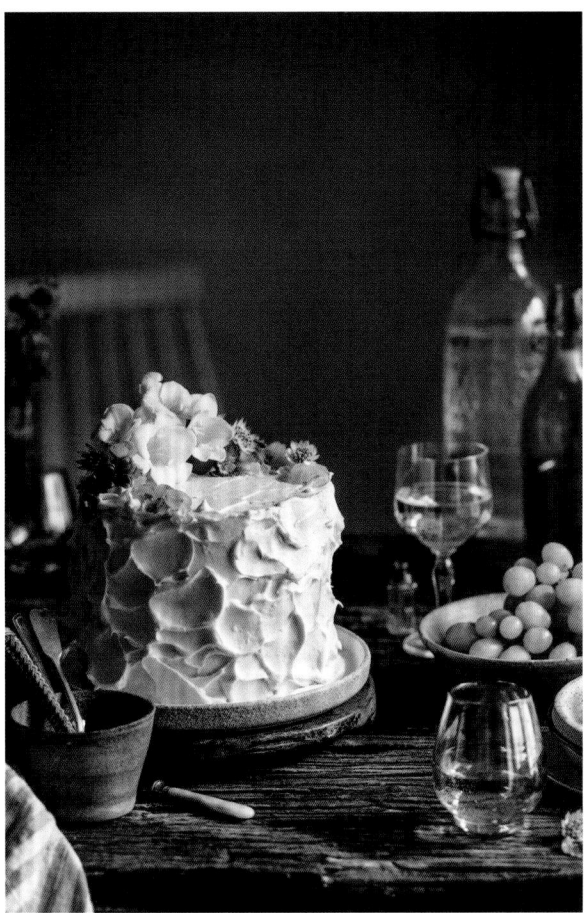

To get more inspired by Claudia, check out her work at:

www.claudiagoedke.com
@claudiagoedke

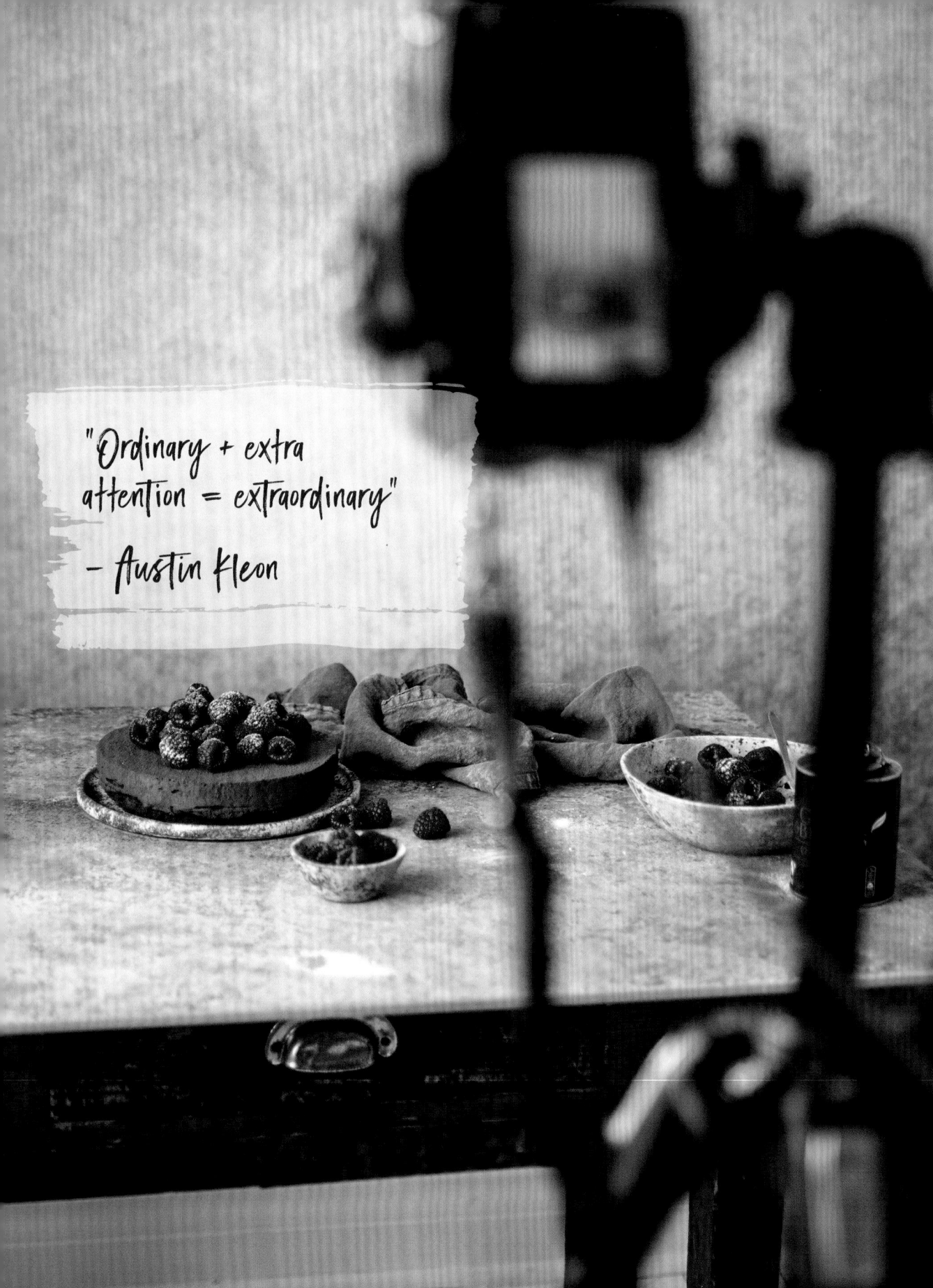

"Ordinary + extra
attention = extraordinary"

– Austin Kleon

Styling Made Easy

If you want your food images to tease all the senses, a beautiful subject is essential. You can be a master of lighting, composing, and editing your scenes, but if the food doesn't look delicious, your photographs will always lack that special something. That's where the crucial skill of food styling comes in.

Food styling is the art of making food look as tempting as possible and contrary to popular belief, it doesn't have to involve sneaking petroleum jelly, shaving cream, or glue into your dish. I personally feel huge satisfaction when I can make real food look irresistible, and in my opinion, with a little bit of imagination, a few simple techniques, and some basic food science, it's possible.

The food styling process begins long before plating up the dish in front of the camera; it all starts with sourcing the best-looking produce. That is non-negotiable. Once you've got your ingredients, it's all about keeping them as fresh as possible, knowing how to prepare each one so it doesn't lose its vigor during the cooking process, and then putting it all together on the plate, using some styling know-how to help it look picture perfect.

Some of the tips shared in this chapter will be useful if you create your own recipes. Often, the best ideas for presentation are born during the recipe development stage: that's when you can really get creative to combine flavors with colors, textures, and shapes to create something spectacular. However, on many occasions, you won't be able to change the recipe you work with. That's when you have to nail it at the preparation stage, often thinking outside the box, since food for the camera requires a different approach than dishes served at home.

This doesn't mean that it's necessary for a food photographer to have impressive kitchen skills and chef's knowledge. It isn't. If you prefer to focus on the photography, you can team up with a chef or a food stylist (or both!) to work with on all of your exciting projects. I still think, though, that even in those circumstances, having some basic food styling knowledge will make you a better photographer.

Beautiful food=beautiful photos

Fresh, local, and seasonal produce is the key element to good-looking dishes, and going the extra mile to get your hands on the choicest ingredients will always pay off. Keep in mind that average food will often mean average-looking photos. So if you want to get the taste buds going, your food needs to tempt with its color, texture, and shape.

Always get more, just in case
It's always worth getting more ingredients than you need, just to be safe. On many occasions, I have cut into a beautiful-looking avocado only to discover it has dark spots on the flesh. Getting a bit more gives you the opportunity to pick the best-looking ingredients and experiment with the presentation if you need to. It doesn't have to mean wasting food, either: you could freeze the leftovers, gift them to friends, or try creating a brand new recipe out of them.

Keep your ingredients fresh
Knowing how to store your ingredients is essential for preserving their freshness. Keep things in airtight containers and learn which food should be kept in the fridge, which prefers room temperature, and which might benefit from being kept in water. Some products will be fine in the fridge for a few days, but perishable foods such as lettuce, delicate herbs, meat, and fish look their best when bought fresh, so don't be tempted to purchase them too early. I like to buy herbs in the pots (if I can) as they will stay fresh for longer. I always have a spray bottle and a bowl of icy cold water on set too, just in case any fruit or vegetables need a little pick-me-up mist or bath.

Prepare with care
To turn your dishes into showstoppers, you've got to know how to prepare every single ingredient correctly. It's probably not a big deal if you slightly overcook your dinner, but when it comes to food photography, little slips like that have a huge visual impact and can be a deciding factor as to whether your photo will leave a great or bad impression.

Hurry up
Most baked goods will give you plenty of time to play around with light, composition, and settings, but many dishes need to be shot straight away. The first thing I do before a photoshoot is think about how much time I actually have to photograph each dish. For the more urgent shots, I set everything up with empty dishes and once I am happy with the frame, I'll fill the plates and bowls with food and shoot quickly before the food goes dry, changes color or texture, and starts to look unappetizing.

Add a wow factor
Blush oranges and buttonhole kale in winter; pink rhubarb and wild garlic in spring; white currants, zucchini flowers, and yellow raspberries in the summer; and pumpkins, squashes, and interesting varieties of mushrooms in the autumn: search for something different, unexpected, and rare to add an element of surprise and intrigue to your images. It could even be something as simple as edible flowers, microgreens or black sea salt—it's the little details that give your images a wow factor. At the same time, don't limit yourself to photographing superstar ingredients only: they stand out even more when they're mixed with more ordinary products.

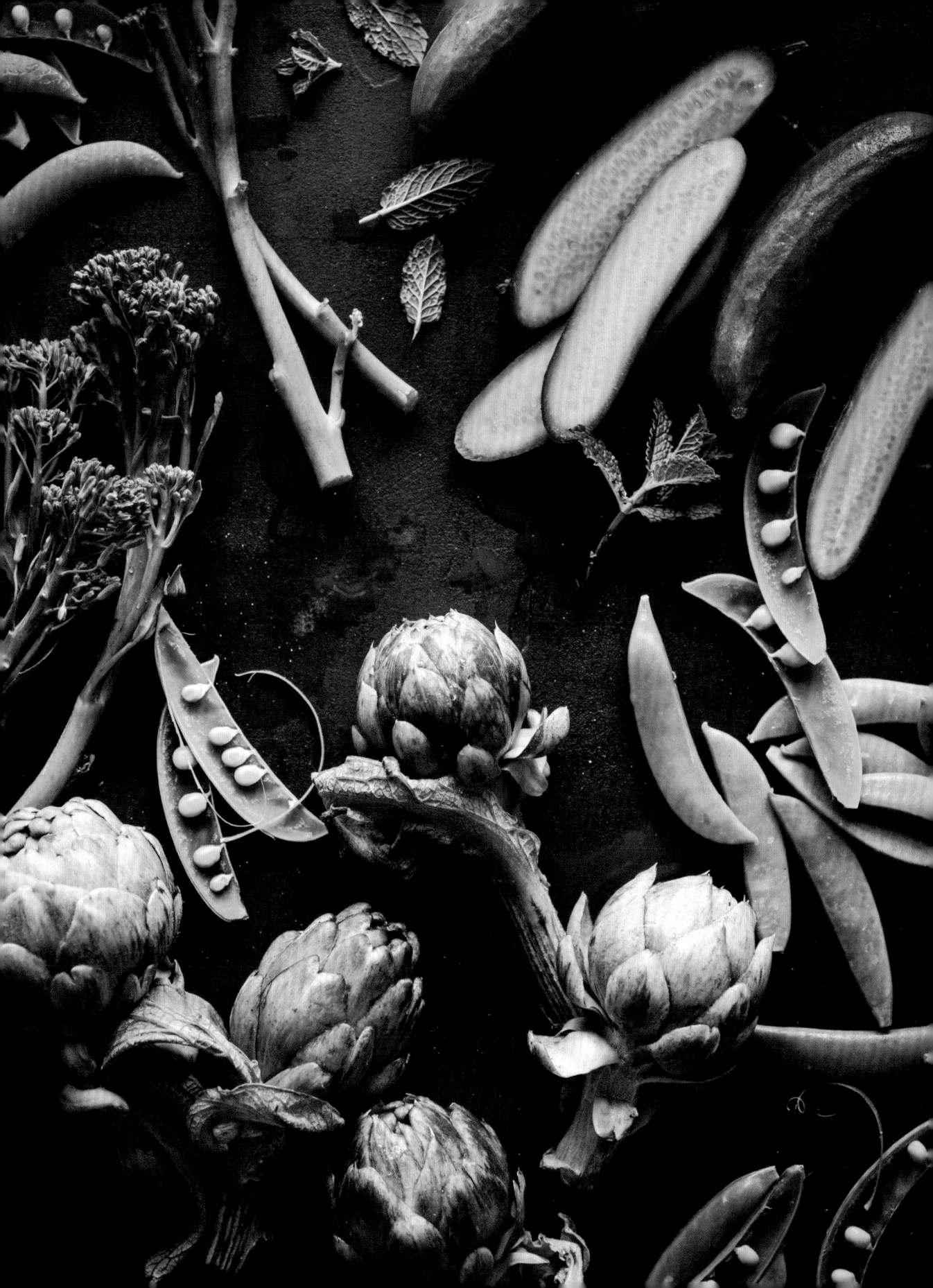

Tempt the eye

In food photography, we can only grab our viewer's attention through their eyes. We can't capture the smell, flavor, or sound of biting into food. That means we have to get a little bit more creative with the visual side of our dish to give our viewer the best sensory experience possible. Focusing on the small but mighty details and showing off the texture, color, and shape is how you make mouths water.

The power of texture

The texture of food not only indicates the ripeness of our ingredients or freshness of our dish, but also how someone will enjoy the recipe—or if they will enjoy it at all!

Texture can make or break a photograph. I learned this the hard way when I was working on my first magazine cover and it took three days to nail the texture of the chocolate sauce that the hero cake was covered in. No matter how beautiful the light was, the texture of that chocolate sauce was ruining the image. It meant baking and putting this cake together three times, but the commitment to excellence and patience paid off in the end.

Think about your recipe and what its most interesting or important texture is. Consider how you can style and photograph your dish to highlight that texture to make it impossible to resist.

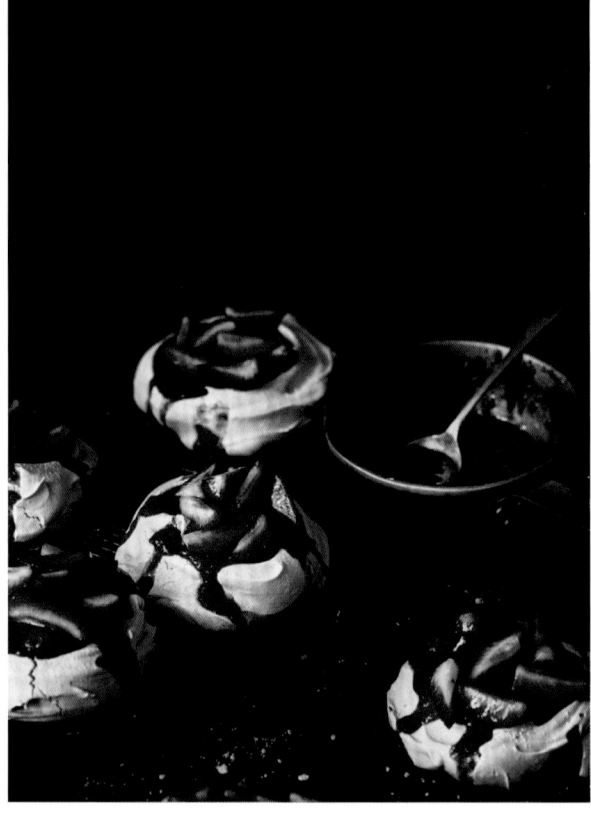

Juicy (above)

Let's be honest: dry food rarely looks attractive. When preparing and photographing recipes, I always think about what I can do to add that extra juicy-and-succulent factor to my dish, as well as how much time I have to photograph it before it starts to dry out.

When I photograph cut-up fruit, I toss them in a little bit of sugar and leave them for 10–15 minutes so that they start releasing their juices and become even shinier. This trick works whether I'm topping a pavlova, cake, or yogurt. Meat also dries out rapidly after preparation, so you have to work quickly to get the shot. You can liven meat up by brushing it with some leftover juice from the pan: be careful not to make it look greasy though.

Consider drizzling your dish with a sauce, syrup, or dressing, and don't forget to show drips and droplets: they fuel the imagination, making your dish even more tempting.

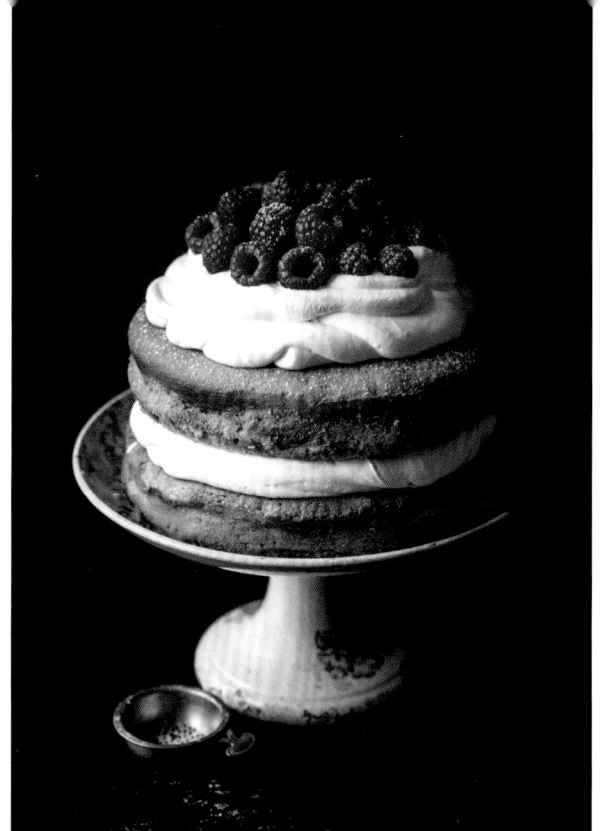

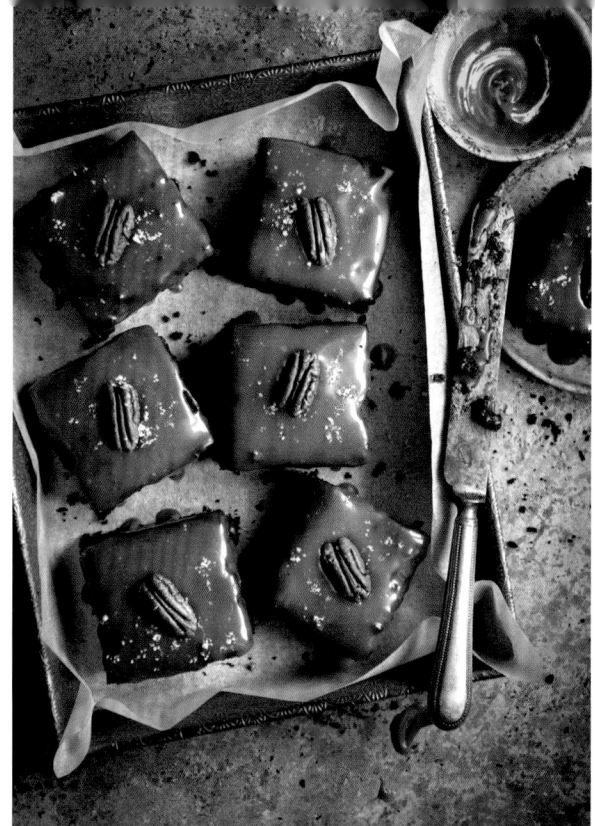

Creamy and smooth (above)

Any food that looks creamy, pillowy, and smooth is impossible to resist. With only a glance, we know exactly how it's going to feel: light, fluffy, and melting in the mouth.

Whipped cream is one of those things I often see going wrong in photographs because when the cream is overworked, it looks heavy and this spoils the charm of the images. The trick is to stop the mixer in the right moment. If you have missed that moment, you can add a few splashes of cold cream or milk and mix it in with a spoon. How you spoon the cream is important too, as you want it to be soft. I spoon it on quickly, let it overflow and either leave it as it is or lightly touch it with the back of the spoon to form swirls. Perfection comes with practice.

Whether you are photographing a creamy soup or any other recipe that you'd expect to have that beautiful smooth texture, focus on the consistency and thickness, and show off some swirls.

Gooey (above)

I think we can all agree that it's hard to resist the smooth, shimmering, and gooey texture of caramel. Highlight this beautiful texture by playing with lighting and angles of shooting until you find that magical gleam, and show off some drips or a thick swirl in the bottom of a bowl to emphasize the sticky consistency.

If you are photographing any cheese-heavy recipe, you can also highlight its delicious cheesiness, by focusing on its gooey texture—pulling one piece out from a pizza while it's still warm and photographing the strings of cheese is a good way to make anyone hungry.

Tip

The texture of your food, its shape, and how it is angled all affect how light can bring it to life.

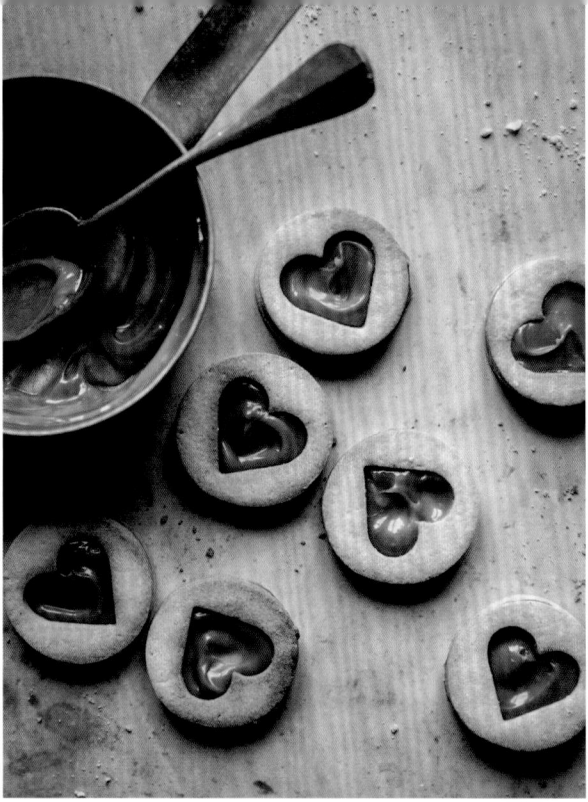

Crumbly

Show off the crumbly nature of the food you are photographing by breaking off a piece of it rather than cutting it neatly with a knife. For instance, breaking off a chunk of cheese instead of cutting it will reveal a texture that you might not even have known was there.

Crunchy & crispy (right)

These are qualities that are definitely best recognized with our sense of hearing, but there are a few visual clues we can give our viewer to help them imagine the crunchy or crispy nature of the dish. For example, you could show some cracks on your cookies and scatter some crumbs around the scene. Or you could make sure that meat or roasted vegetables have browned or caramelized edges (in these particular examples, you would need to photograph them quickly after preparation so that they don't become soggy and soft as they release steam).

Final details

Little burn marks on the cheese topping of a lasagne; grill marks on meat and grilled fruit and vegetables; blistered tomatoes still on the vine; toasted bread with a scattering of crumbs; a layer of dusted powdered sugar—all these little details add another layer of texture that makes our photographs more tantalizing. Something as simple as sea salt flakes on smooth caramel or a generous pinch of cracked black pepper on a pasta dish can elevate an image from "that looks nice" to "I have to try that".

Tips

* Get a good, fine sifter that will give you control and precision.
* Use a power blender or a food processor for smooth, creamy soups and sauces.
* Use a spatula to spread cake frosting smoothly.
* Have a selection of different-sized brushes to apply juicy sauces or to remove something you don't want to be on a plate.
* Have a stash of cotton balls or pads to remove any unwanted splashes or marks.
* Use a dripping bottle for more control over those artistic drips.
* Use a chef's blow torch to turn any meringue topping into a golden textural landscape.

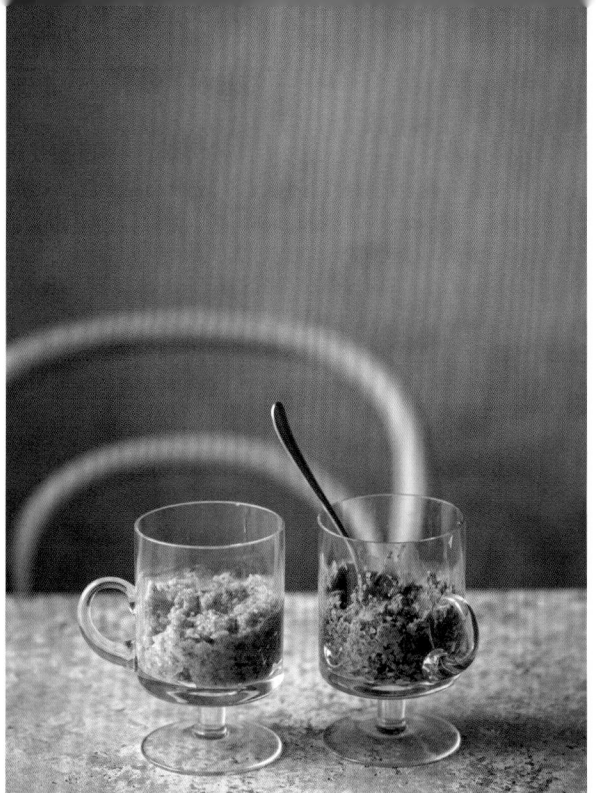

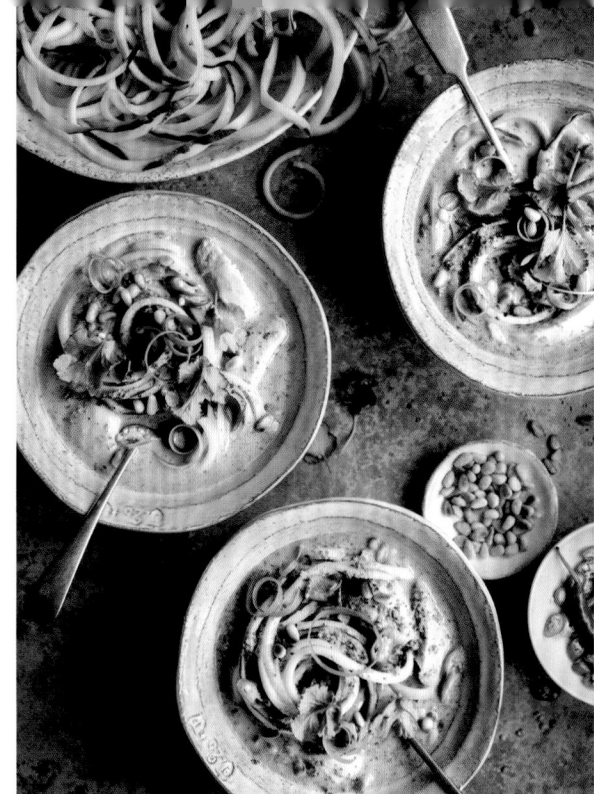

Impress with color

What would food be without color? It's one of the very first things our eyes notice and what sets our expectations for what something will taste like. It's a visual clue that helps us identify the flavor, quality, and freshness of the ingredients. Some colors stimulate the taste buds, while others can effectively kill our appetite: it's further proof that we don't just eat with our mouths, we eat with our eyes, too; so it's something that food photographers and food stylists should consider very carefully.

Our eyes are tempted by deep, rich colors; they suggest to our brain that the food is full of flavor. For instance, we all assume that deep red strawberries are the sweetest. So if the food you photograph is vibrant, it will look more appetizing.

When pairing ingredients and assembling your dish, keep in mind the things you've learned about color theory (see page 82). It applies as much to putting your dish together as it does to composing colors in your food scene.

Above left & right: What you see in the image on the left is not some kind of exercise in Photoshop manipulation. The soup I was photographing (above right) required a jar of Thai green curry paste, so I ordered it online. I was disappointed when it arrived because, as you can see (above left), the paste which arrived (in the glass on the left) was more yellow than green. Comparing the two pastes in the image, which do your eyes tell you is tastier? The most important part of the photograph was the vibrant green color, so there was no other option but to make the paste from scratch to control the vibrancy of the green. The outcome was the paste in the glass on the right.

Show off the shapes

Good shapes can make any dish a little bit more exciting for the eye: they are the secret ingredient that will help to set your images apart.

Choosing your ingredients

When picking my ingredients, I always pay attention to the interest and movement they are going to bring to my frame. Remember that curved and straight lines bring different energy to an image (see page 80), and this definitely applies to the shape of your food.

When it comes to vegetables like carrots, beets, and radishes, think about leaving a couple of inches of their leafy ends on them. This applies to the stems and leaves of fruit, too: how much less attractive would the bowls of cherries on page 49 be without their stems left on to lead the eye?

It's always worth considering how you might combine different sizes and shapes of the same ingredient, for example, mixed lettuce leaves, heirloom tomatoes, or mushrooms. Variety is often more engaging than a group of identical ingredients.

Below: How many ways can you slice a carrot? Not only do different cuts add movement and variety to our dishes, but they also catch and reflect the light in different ways.

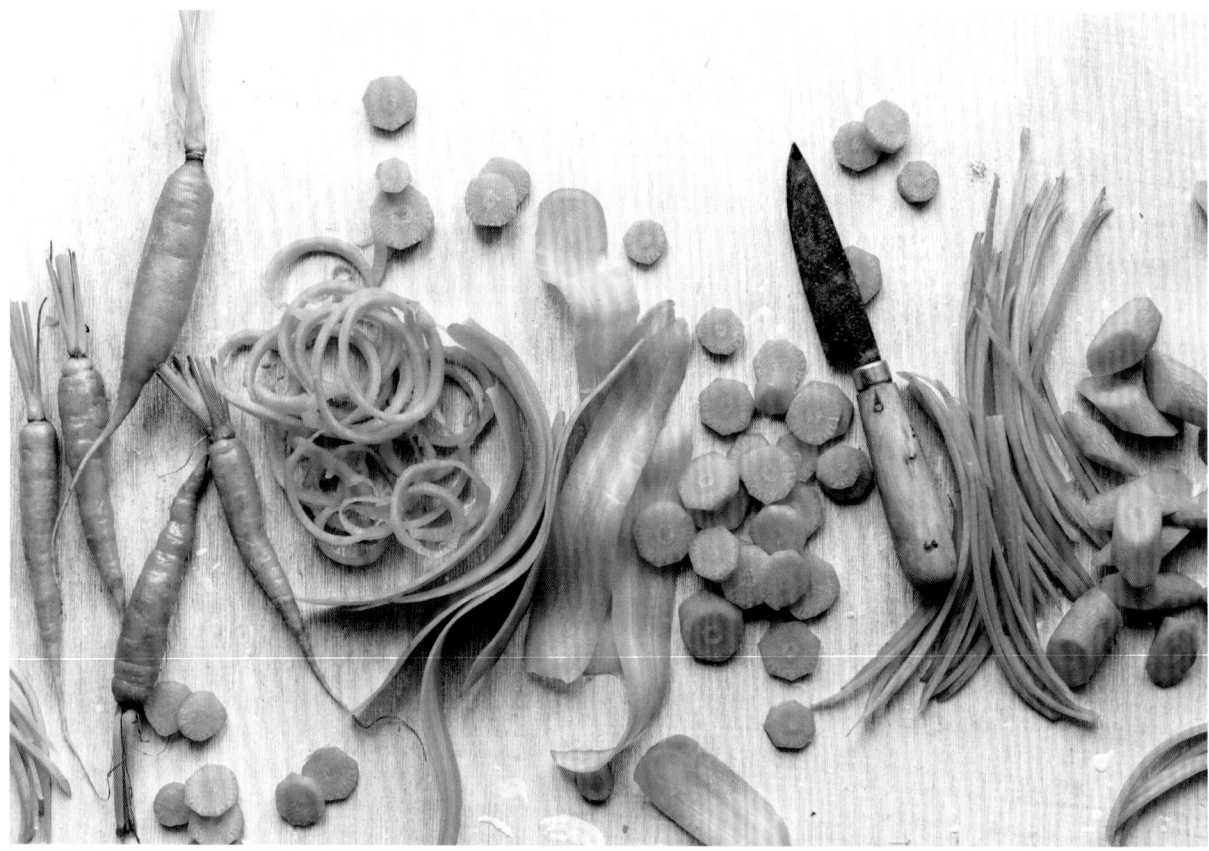

Shaping skills

Always question whether there is a better way to present your food than the obvious, from the way the vegetables are cut to what you do with the little pieces of chocolate decorating a cake: do you want to shave them, curl them, or break them roughly? With a few inexpensive tools and a little bit of imagination, you can create culinary magic. Think about how all the components will work together, as well as what kind of story you want to tell—some stories call for precision and uniformity, while others need something a bit more rough and ready.

Also consider whether you can slice into your ingredients, revealing a different texture and tempting your viewer by showing what they will be biting into. I like to show contrast by slicing some things and leaving others untouched.

For shaping, a good, sharp knife is a kitchen essential. Spiralizers, Y-peelers, and julienne peelers can all help turn your vegetables into something extra special.

Use your hands

Some foods, such as figs, look beautiful when sliced or cut in half, but they also look gorgeous when they are torn. You can also give bread a rustic, homemade feel by tearing it rather than slicing it.

Shaping the dish (below)

If you have control over what your dish looks like before it's ready, think about what shape will enhance it best, and how it will be presented.

Some dishes will rely on the props you will be cooking and serving them in, so investing in beautiful items is essential. I would highly recommend getting few different shapes of baking tins and baking dishes (round, rectangular, and square); I also love bundt pans for their elegance and extraordinary shapes.

Always think outside the box to make your food more eye-catching. How can you present your dish in a different, better way? How can you shape it or slice it to make it look even more impressive?

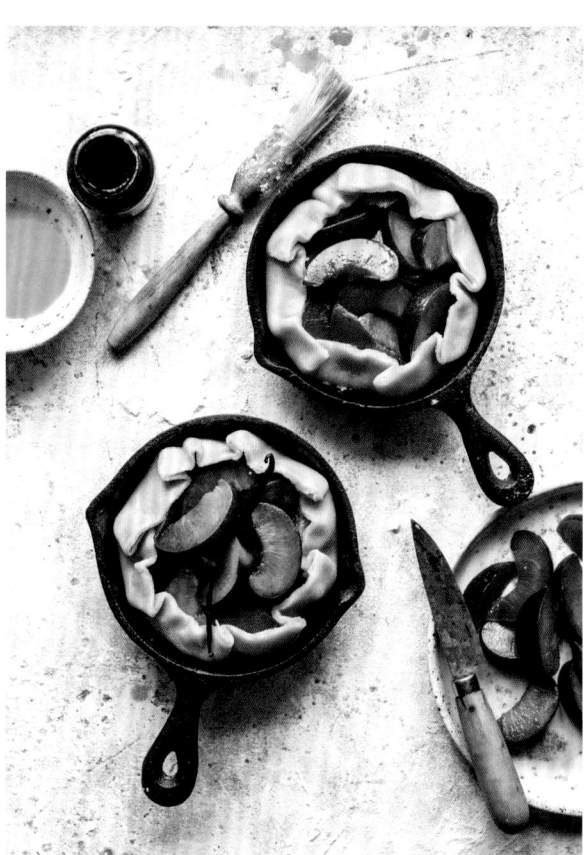

Build it all up

The secret to effortless-looking food is always making an effort. By effort, I mean taking the time to plan how you are going to approach the dish, meticulously preparing it and putting it all together with care. Your attention to detail is priceless here, and you will only get better with practice. The more you look, the more you'll notice. Here are some things you should think about when building a dish.

Consider the props

Color, texture, and size all come into consideration and if I can, I'll put the food on a few different dishes to test out the ideas before making the final decision.

Style it for the angle

Some dishes might work really well from several angles, but many will need to be restyled or at least tweaked to show off important components each time you move the camera.

Identify the biggest strength of the dish

What is it that makes your dish extraordinary? Is it the color, the shape, layers, or a certain ingredient that is playing a starring role? It might be more than one thing. The biggest strength of the ramen soup (opposite) is the beautiful layers it has in it, so I focused on nailing them here and making sure the viewer can see every ingredient clearly.

Not too hot

Not only can hot food steam up your camera, but in many cases, room-temperature food is much easier to style and manage. A cooler dish also won't make vegetables cook any further or make the garnish wither too quickly.

However, in cases when the food completely changes shape, texture, or color when it cools down, such as cheese, make sure you capture it while it's still warm.

Layer, overlap & create height

This will add volume to your dish and make the presentation more organic and easy on the eye.

Which way is it turned?

Sometimes, I might line up the ingredients all facing the same direction. Most of the time, however, I prefer to have the components scattered around, facing different directions to create more dynamic movement and to show multiple angles.

Group some of the ingredients

A few clustered ingredients adds interest to a dish. Make some clusters tighter and leave others looser for variation. When you position the groups around the plate, make sure you leave irregular gaps in between them too.

Don't overwork it

Arranging a beautiful plate of food for the camera will always take more time than serving it at home for dinner, but try to keep styling as natural as possible, otherwise the dish will look too forced. Perfect styling lies in imperfections: your dish should look effortless.

Keep it fresh and alive

Once the dish has been assembled, your job is to keep it alive. Ensure that nothing looks dry and unappetizing and retouch it or replace ingredients if they start looking sad.

Don't give up—and keep playing

If the styling doesn't work out, don't settle: try again. And again. And again until you get it right. Success often means being stubborn.

Right: Building a dish to photograph takes time. Assemble it with care, and with consideration for every detail.

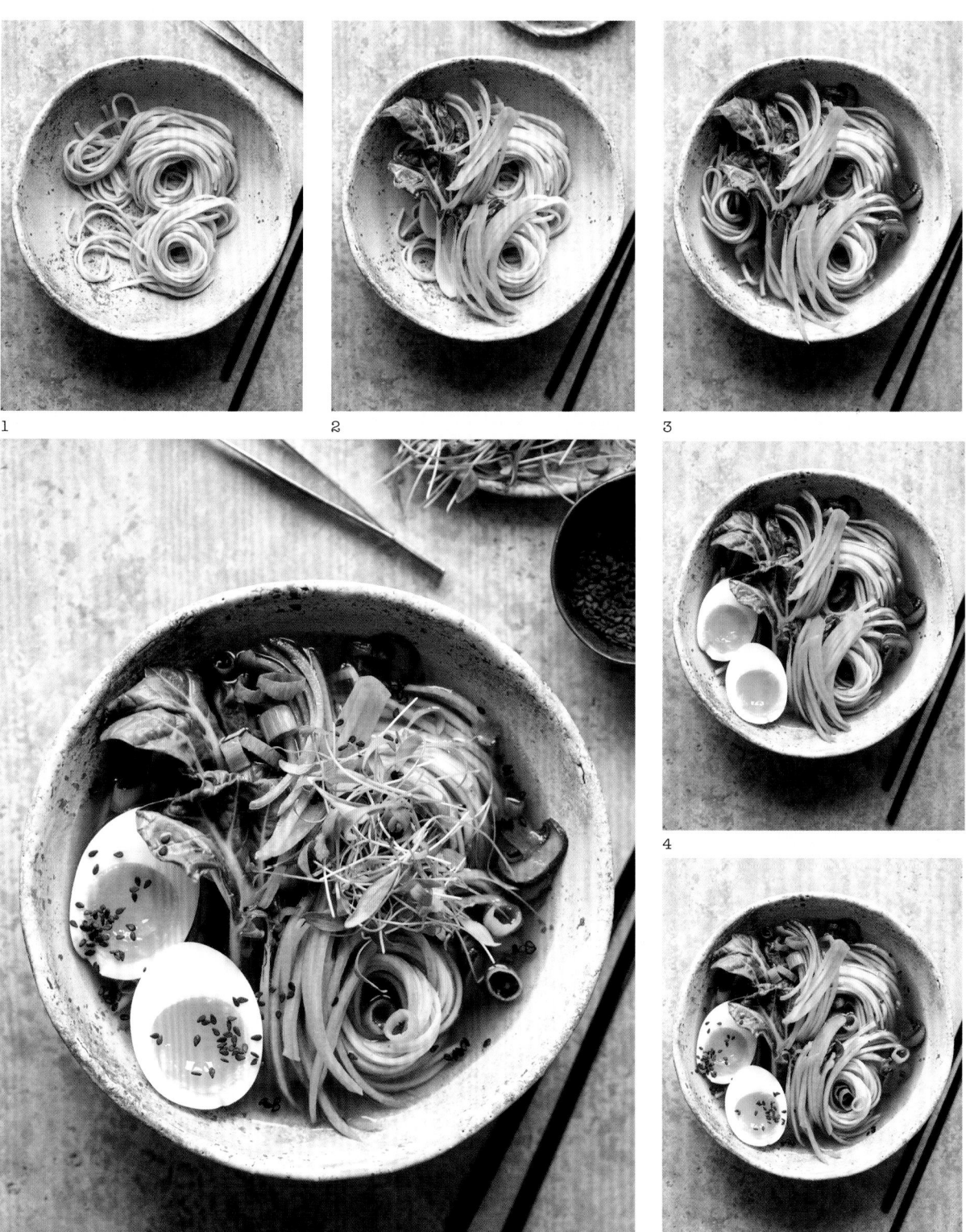

1

2

3

Final styled dish

4

5

Tricks of the trade

Preparing food for drool-worthy photographs isn't the same as creating delicious dishes to serve and eat at home. Although I personally like the food in my images to always be edible, sometimes I might need to "cheat" a little to make my still visuals look extra tasty. Food photographers and food stylists have a lot of tricks up their sleeves to ensure the food looks as scrumptious and impressive as possible.

Take control (below left)
In this image, the aim of the story is to make the viewer imagine that the galette has just came out of the oven and it's still warm, which is why the ice cream is melting. In reality, the galette was room temperature so that the ice cream didn't melt before I'd even got behind my camera—I just heated a couple of tablespoons of ice cream in a pot over a very low heat, let it cool down and poured it carefully under the still-cold scoops, controlling exactly how I wanted the melt to look.

Visualize the taste (below center)
It's your job as a food photographer to show your viewer what important flavors or ingredients they can expect from the recipe—especially if it's not obvious. Something as simple as placing a few whole apples in the frame helps the viewer immediately identify the flavor.

Focus on a recognizable shape (below right)
When you work with a dish that is all cooked together, like a curry, stew, or pasta bake, include some shapes that your eye can recognize and focus on. For example, when I was photographing this pasta bake, I didn't use much mozzarella cheese so that the tomatoes, sauce and pasta shells were readily identifiable and could tempt with their rich layers.

Prepare separately
When you make one-pot dishes such as risottos, everything ends us jumbled together in a pot, which might not be the prettiest idea for food photography.

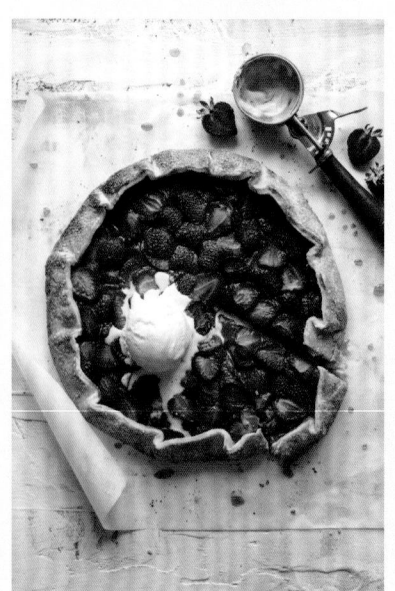
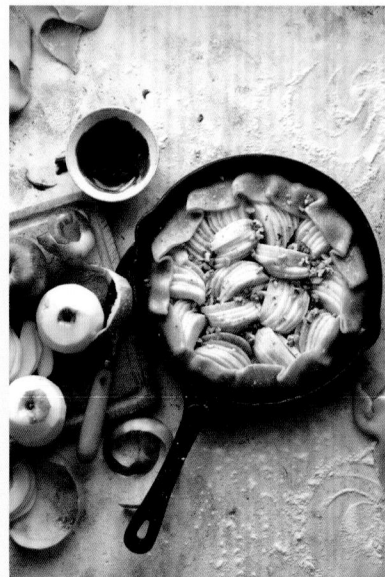
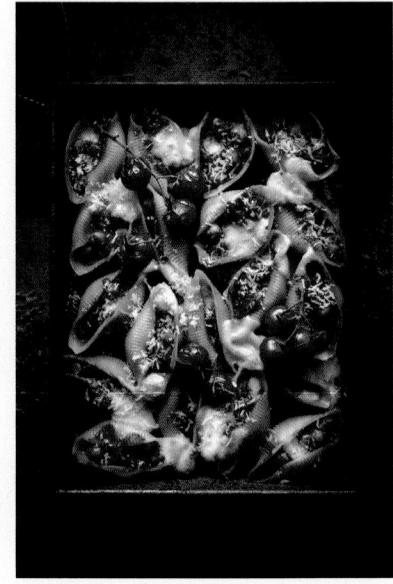

To make the dish look more appetizing, think outside the box and prepare the ingredients separately. In a risotto, for example, the rice can be cooked the traditional way on its own and the other ingredients can be cooked in a separate pan then put together at the very end.

Hide imperfections

When the dish doesn't look picture perfect, all is not always lost. Think of ways to camouflage imperfections with another texture if you can; for example, the cake shown on page 54 didn't come out with the smoothest surface, so I dusted on some extra cocoa powder.

Natural mess (below left)

A little crumb here and there makes your food look more realistic, and including a few drips and droplets suggests that the food has just been made, giving it that extra oh-so-delicious factor!

Keep it straight (below center)

Sometimes you have to help your subject stand tall to make it more impressive. This could be by cutting the bottoms of the pears slightly to ensure they are not losing their balance, putting a skewer into a layered sandwich to prevent slices from sliding off or placing a tiny bit of cardboard under a pancake stack to ensure it doesn't look like the tower of Pisa!

Dig in (below right)

Take a slice out, scoop up a spoonful, dig a fork in, break a piece off or even take a bite—it will make your viewer want to do the same! This can be a great way to show off a different texture, teasing your audience with all the other flavors hidden in that dish.

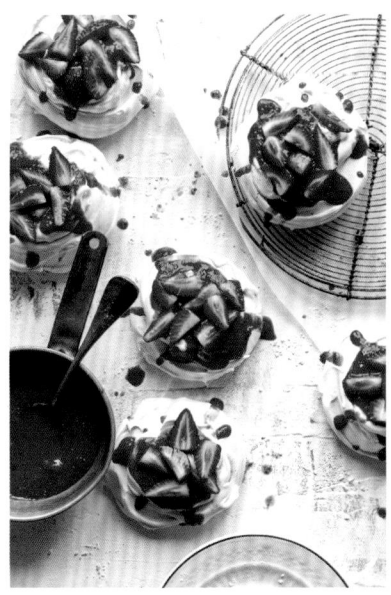
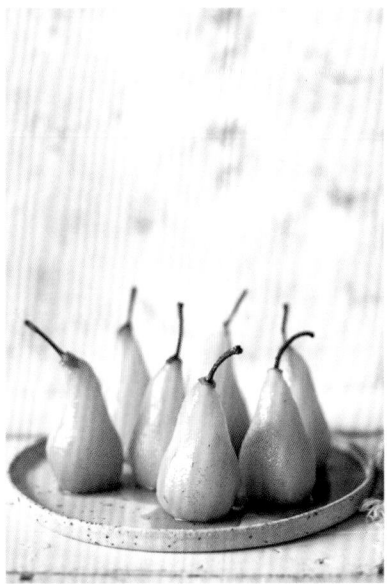
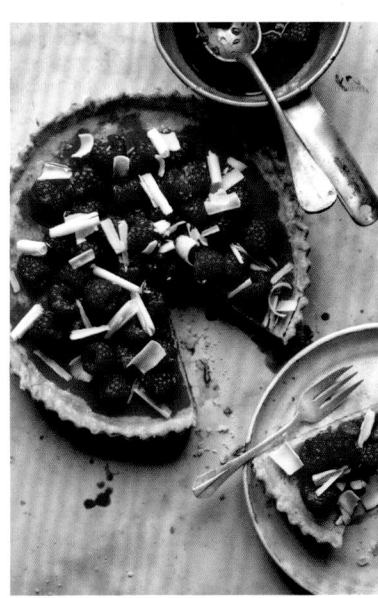

A bit of food science

If you want your food portraits to be as good as they can be, you need to learn how to store and prepare food so it still tempts with its texture, color, and shape.

Fruit & vegetables
* Blanch-and-shock is a great method for keeping your greens extra-green—it preserves the color (and nutrients) of the vegetables. Place your green vegetables in boiling water, simmer until crisp but cooked, then carefully remove them from the pan with a slotted spoon and plunge into ice-cold water to halt the cooking process.
* You can plunge some green vegetables such as asparagus, broccoli, runner beans, and sugar snaps into cold water right after sautéing or steaming to stop the cooking process and prevent them from losing their attractive texture, shape, and color.
* Prevent cut-up fruits and vegetables from browning by spraying them with lemon juice or by dipping in salted water (1/4 tsp of sea salt in 1 cup of water).
* To enliven vegetables such as carrots, radishes, and beets when they start to look tired, submerge them in cold water, leave for a while, and they will soon have their vigour back.
* To cheer up sad-looking lettuce, let it sit in cold/icy water for a while. This works for a lot of herbs, too.
* Storing bananas with other fruits and vegetables will make them ripen more quickly.

Meat
The advice below also applies to just about anything you fry, including mushrooms and vegetables.

* Moisture is the enemy of browning and of crisp skin. If you want a crisp skin on your chicken (for example), wash it, pat it with a paper towel and place it in the fridge for a few hours to ensure it dries completely. This way, prepared chicken will roast to a deliciously golden color.
* Overcrowding your pan will create moisture, so if you want your meat or vegetables to get crispy,

don't put too many on the frying pan or baking tray. Ideally, they should not be touching.
* When browning meat, leave it out of the fridge before frying to bring it to room temperature. When you put cold food on a scorching hot pan, it reduces the temperature of the oil, which prevents it from getting that beautiful brown color.

Eggs
* To soft boil eggs to perfection, lower two to three medium-sized eggs carefully with a spoon into boiling water, then cook for six minutes over a medium heat. If you add more eggs to the pan, they will need to cook a little longer. Once they are cooked, place them in cold water.
* To peel eggs smoothly, I like to either peel them in a bowl filled with cold water or while running them under cold water—this helps to loosen the shell.
* Wait for soft-boiled eggs to completely cool down before cutting them in half. This way, the runny center won't develop a film so quickly, which will give you more time to photograph.

Tip

When food is cooked, it loses some of its color, shape, and texture along the way. This is natural: these visual changes are part of how we know something is cooked. However, the finished dish should still have an appealing presentation, even after preparation.

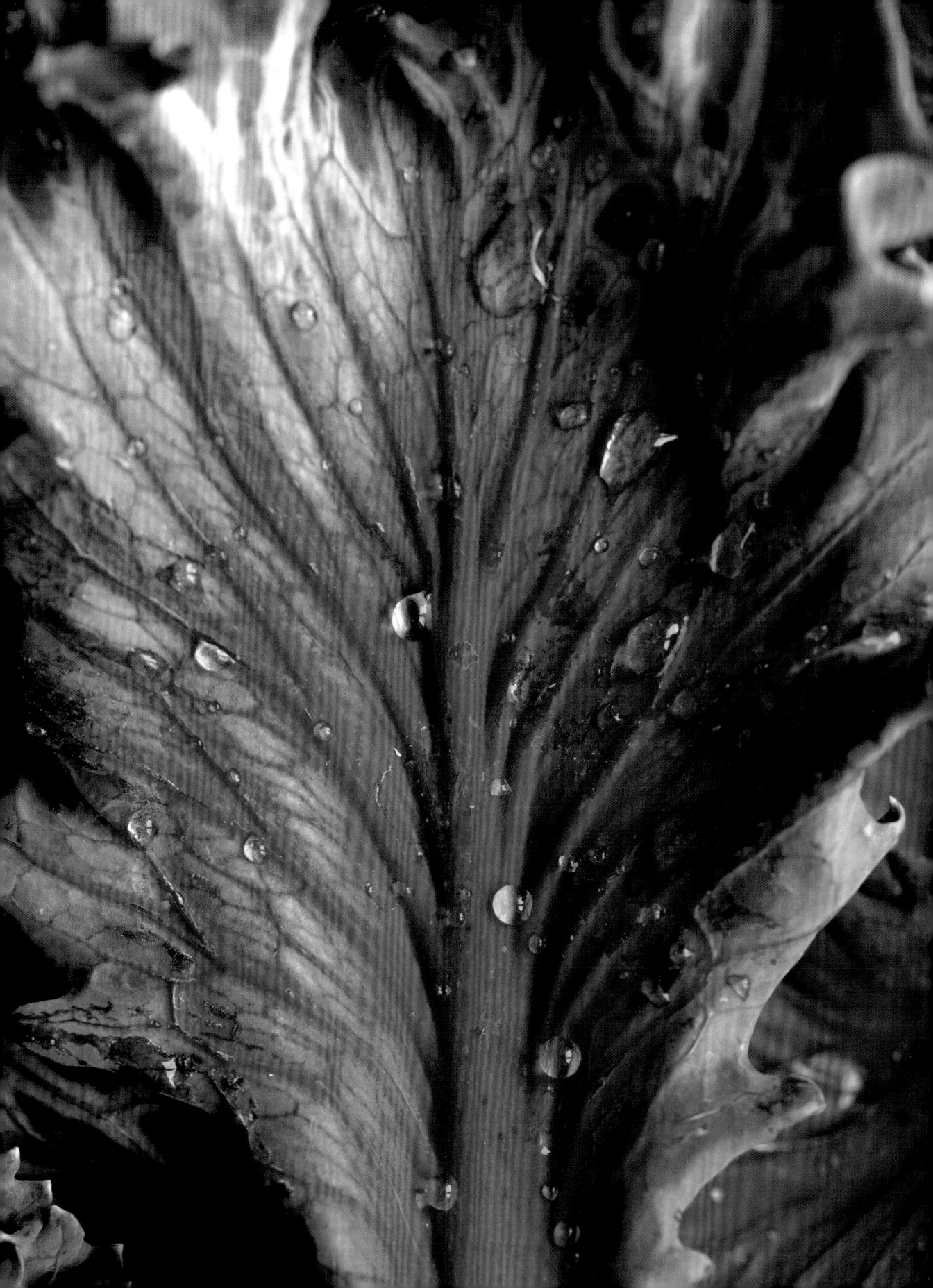

Dress to impress

It's all in the details. Without the final touches, food looks unfinished. We use garnish to add harmony, to unite the different elements in a dish, and to elevate its visual impact. It's this last layer that really tempts the eye.

"How can I make the dish look better?" is a question that always springs to mind when I'm styling food, because everything can be improved upon. Could the cake benefit from a layer of powdered sugar? Would a little pop of garnish in a complementary color to the main ingredient bring the photo together? Sometimes, something as simple as a generous drizzle of maple syrup on the plate can be the final touch that brings a dish to life. When it comes to savoury dishes, a

sprinkle of sea salt flakes and a pinch of cracked black pepper can complete the look.

When you think of how to dress your tasty dish, always take into account that it can't only *look* good; the flavor combination has to make sense too.

When you have to follow a recipe strictly, focus extra attention on how you place each element, ensuring it adds interest and helps make the dish as eye-catching as possible. Compositional techniques apply as much to what's on the plate as they do to the wider scene.

Below left & right: With something as simple as some golden flaxseeds, black pepper, olive oil and micro cilantro leaves, this grain salad bowl is boasting endless potential.

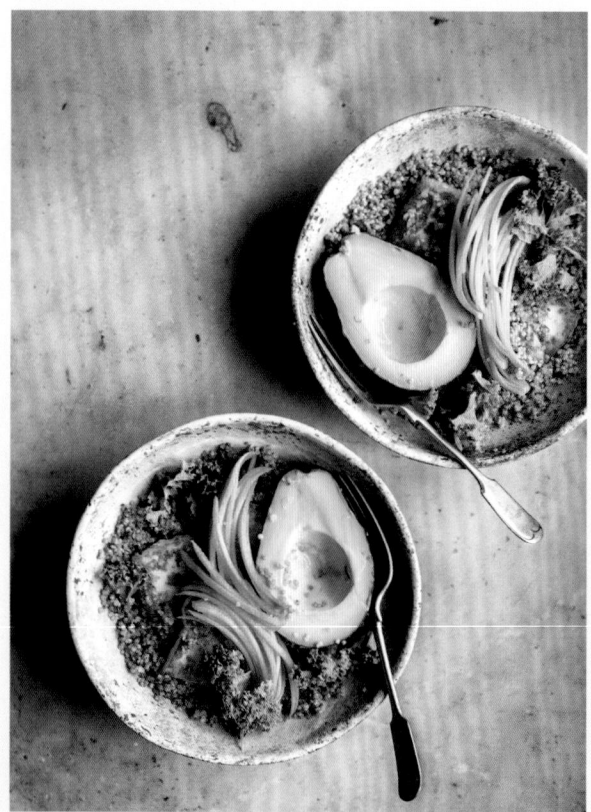
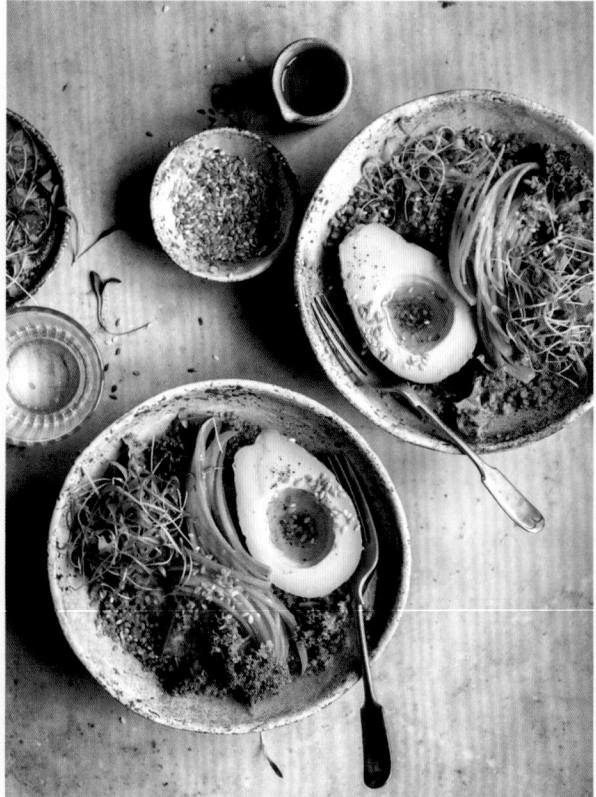

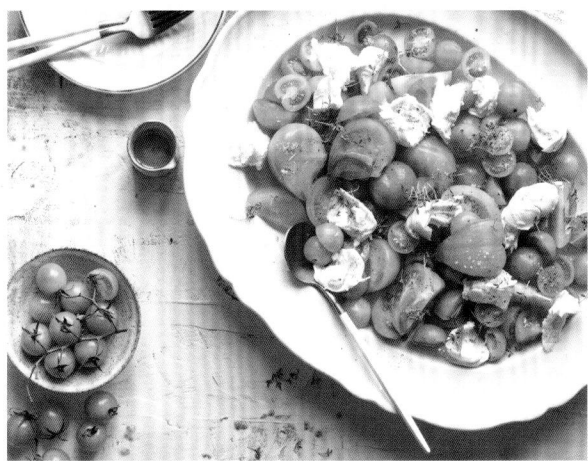 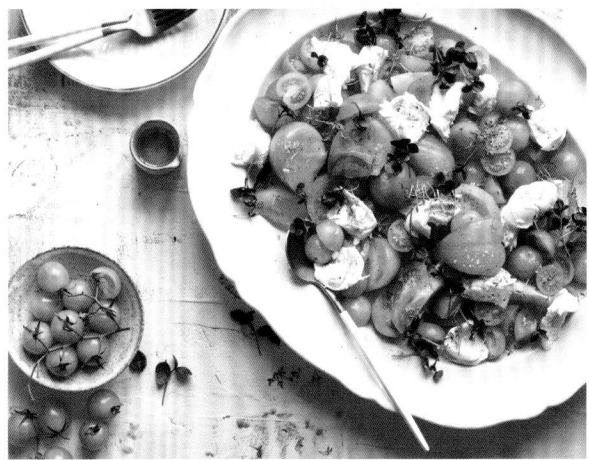

Below: Sometimes you can garnish a dish before it's baked or roasted. I decorated the crusts of these pizzas with seeds and topped them with tomatoes still on the vine before they went into the oven. In the same way, you can sprinkle coarse sugar on pie pastry before baking, or rub meat with spices or herbs before roasting.

Above left & right: Natural-looking clusters of purple basil add a pop of complementary color to this tomato salad. It was also dressed up with a little bit of olive oil, Greek cress, and a generous scattering of black pepper and sea salt flakes.

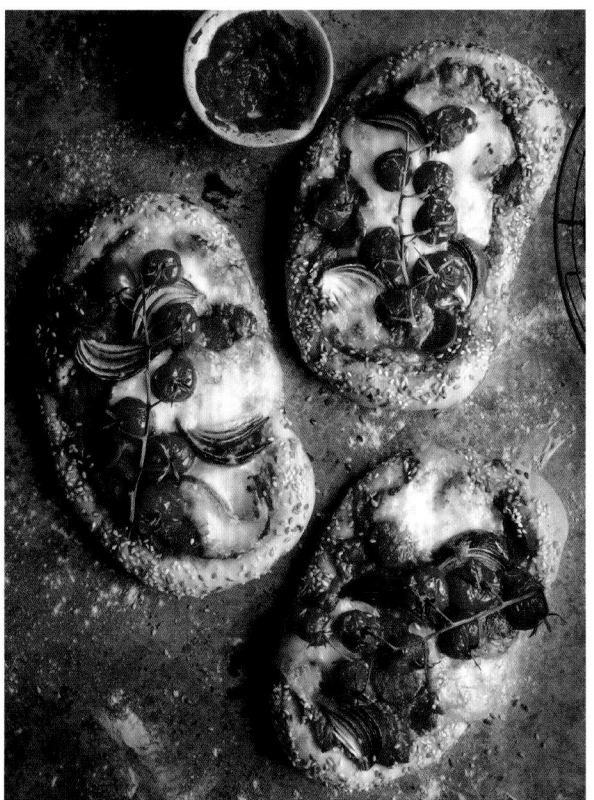

Tips

* Always look for interesting new garnish ideas.
* Use a garnish to hide imperfections.
* Place your garnish as naturally as possible, clustering it in small groups, positioning it at various planes and angles. Remember to turn some ingredients towards the light to catch the highlights in different ways.
* When you work with herbs, use the freshest and prettiest leaves out of the bunch. I like mine slightly curved for extra movement.
* A Pasteur pipette is a helpful tool for adding olive oil or dressing with precision. Apply to the spots that will catch the light.
* I always make sure my light, composition, and settings are spot on before finishing off the dish to avoid ingredients wilting or discoloring the other components.

Garnish ideas

Build your own library of garnish ideas as you go along. Here is mine.

For savory dishes
* A drizzle of olive oil or chile oil
* Chunky sea salt flakes (traditional or black)
* Freshly ground/cracked black pepper
* Spices and spice blends
* Herb leaves—fresh, roasted, or fried. Crispy sage, leaves go beautifully with carbonara, while roasted thyme is a great match for roasted meat. Some herbs look great on the branch too
* Herb flowers (chive flowers are my favorites)
* A swirl of cream or yogurt
* Nuts and seeds (toasted or not)
* Lemon and lime (wedges, slices, zest, or grilled wedges/halves)
* Sauces, dressings, and vinaigrettes (a little on the dish with the rest in a small bowl on the side)
* Cheese (shaved, finely grated, or crumbled)
* Onions (fresh or pickled, sliced or finely chopped)
* Garlic (roasted whole or thin slices fried)
* Crispy ginger
* Chile (whole, sliced, or finely chopped)
* Spring onion (curled or chopped: curl it by finely slicing lengthwise then dipping in ice water)
* Asparagus ribbons
* Arugula or lettuce leaves

Microgreens & microherbs
The baby shoots of vegetables and herbs are an excellent all-round garnish choice. Here are some of my favorites.

* Amaranth
* Cilantro
* Pea shoots
* Garlic chives
* Purple basil
* Greek cress
* Lemon balm
* Purple sisho
* Red vein sorrel
* Radish (purple or green)

For sweet dishes
* Sugar (powdered sugar, coarse, or pearl)
* Icing and frosting
* Cocoa powder
* Coconut flakes
* Almond flakes
* Nuts (chopped or whole)
* Seeds
* Spices (ground/whole cinnamon, nutmeg, vanilla beans/pods, and star anise)
* Praline
* Honeycomb
* Berries/fruit (whole, halved, or sliced, cooked or raw)
* Dehydrated fruit or powder (lemon/orange slices and raspberries are my favorites)
* Edible flowers
* Chunky sea salt flakes (traditional or black)
* Maple syrup or honey
* Caramel
* Chocolate (melted, chopped, or curls)
* Crushed cookie/crumble
* Granola
* A swirl of yogurt or cream

Drinks
* Edible flowers
* Herbs and spices
* Citrus slices, twists, or wedges
* Dehydrated citrus slices
* Cucumber ribbons
* Maraschino cherries
* Cocktail olives
* A sugar or salt rim
* Ice cubes in different shapes and sizes

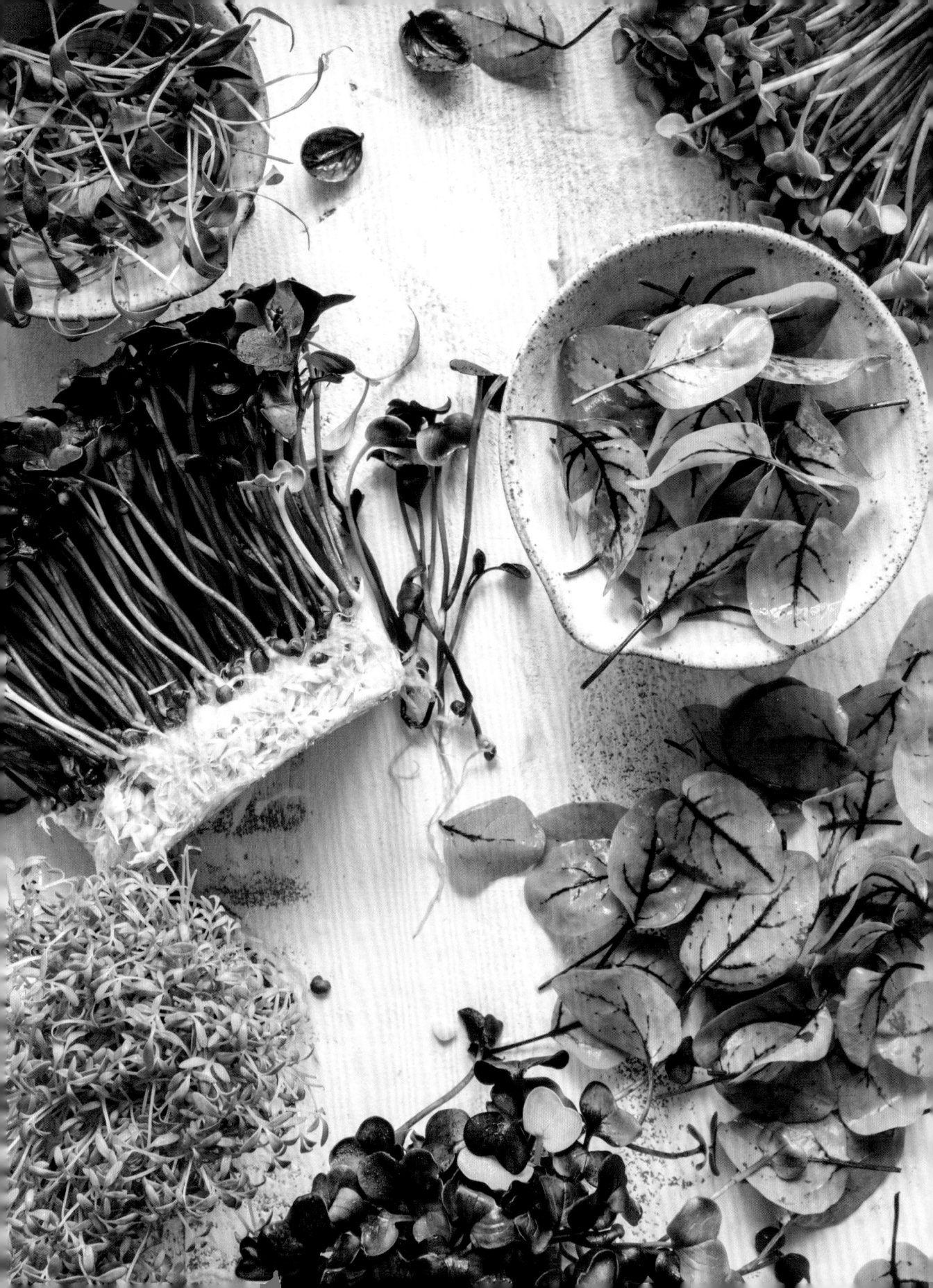

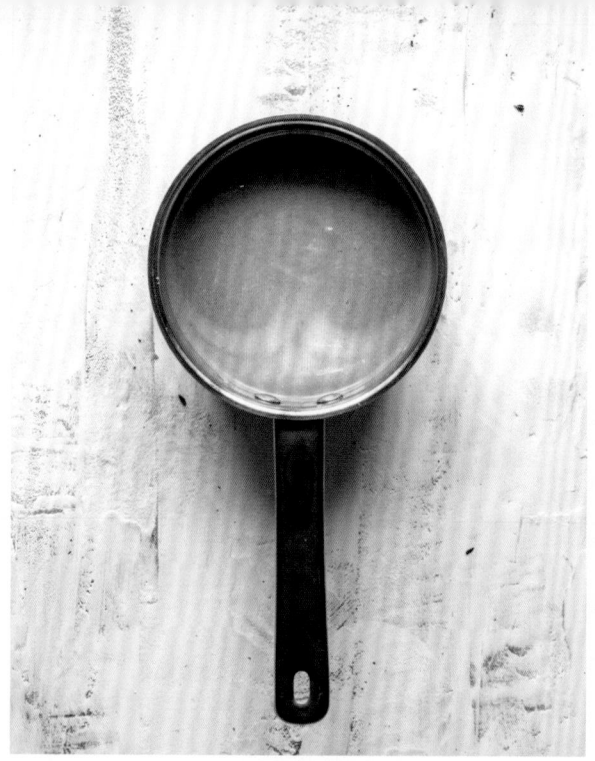
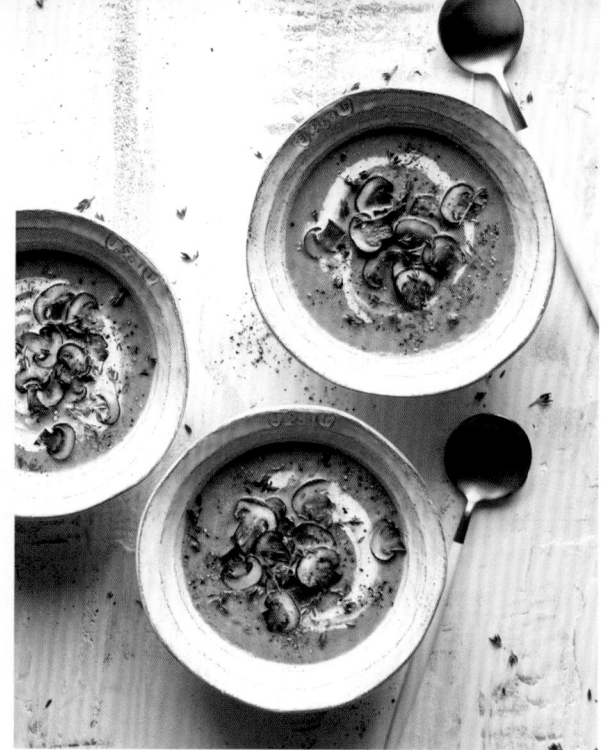

Troubleshooting

When people ask me "What job do you do?" I often joke that I make people hungry for a living, but it's so true! We food photographers are constantly looking for new ways to delight the senses and tempt our lovely viewers. But it's not always easy. What to do when the food simply doesn't look as good as it tastes?

If you know you will be photographing something tricky, do your research. Try to learn as much about the dish as you can and come up with a few ideas for how to get the best out of it.

Mushroom soup (above)

Brown, shapeless food is known for giving food stylists and food photographers a hard time. But we won't always be able to avoid it. When food just doesn't look appetizing, you have to think outside the box to make it more interesting. This mushroom soup smelled and tasted delicious, but if you only looked at the first picture, you wouldn't be convinced at all, would you? The flavor would be hard to guess as there are no clues that would indicate what it's made of.

A little clever decoration helps the viewer to visualize the taste, as well as adding texture and volume to an otherwise flat food. A swirl of cream, some thyme leaves, and browned mushroom slices do the job perfectly. If it hadn't been possible to include these mushrooms on top, I might have shown some fresh ones around the scene instead.

Finally, the carefully chosen textured background and props are essential to elevate this image. Echoing colors found in a dish in the props adds to the harmony and visual appeal of a photograph.

Keep in mind that if there is a recipe for the dish you're shooting, the color of the food can be enhanced but should not be changed completely during editing. People would be disappointed if what they make looks nothing like what they were expecting. Here, adding dry porcinis to the stock and a perfect mushroom-cream ratio made the color picture-perfect at the recipe-development stage.

Curry (below)

The biggest strength of this curry is the smooth, shiny sauce. Since you can't make out the ingredients hidden underneath, their shapes become crucial visual clues. When slicing the potatoes, I left out their ends as they would be less recognizable under the sauce. I bought twice as many chicken thighs as needed so that after frying I could choose the pieces with the most attractive shape and texture—the leftovers landed in the freezer.

The dish followed the recipe exactly, but I waited for it to cool before styling it—making sure that the sauce didn't dry out too much and it still had that smooth and shiny texture. Curry can look a bit messy when plated, so I decided to pile the ingredients loosely in the middle of the bowls so that they would be "framed" by the sauce. Additionally, each ingredient is carefully placed to best catch the highlights. The blue props and background help make the complementary golden-orange color of the dish pop even more. The red chilli slices and green coriander make a perfect complementary pair, too, although this is used only as an accent.

Think about...

* Using an attractive background and props—your dish will rely on them.
* Adding a pop of color—either in your props or something your dish can be served with.
* Choosing a strong garnish to bring your dish to life—something with a great shape, texture and/or color.
* Including recognizable shapes in your dish for the eye to focus on.
* When the flavor of your dish is not obvious in the photo, consider either styling the dish to show that ingredient, or include it somewhere in the scene if you can.
* Creating repetition by including a few plates or bowls of the same thing. Repetition is a foolproof method to distract from any imperfections your dish might have, by focusing the attention on the beauty of shapes, patterns, and visual flow.

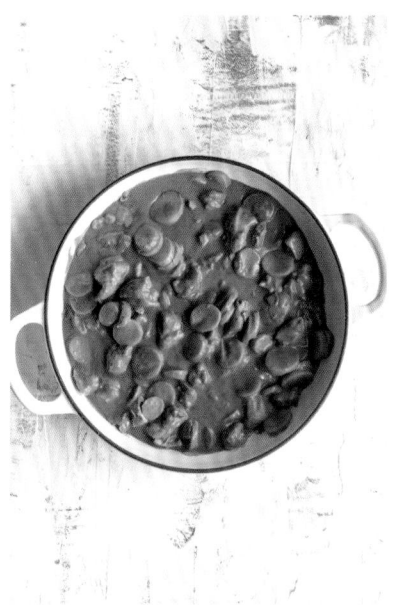
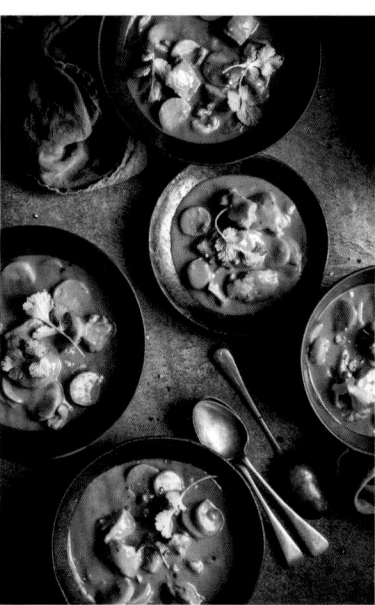
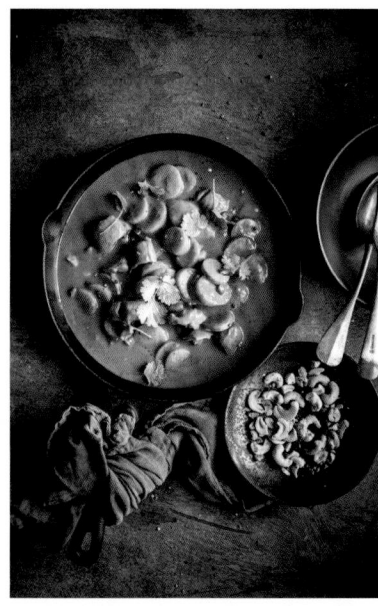

Working with a food stylist

There is nothing better than two (or more) creative minds coming together to work on a project that they are passionate about. The great thing about working with others is that everyone brings their own ideas and expertise to the shoot, which means you can create something truly special together. Working with a food stylist has a lot of advantages: they have an incredible wealth of knowledge and will make your job as a photographer much easier. At the same time, it will allow you to develop your creative confidence, explore diverse styles, work with different food and props, and keep your work fresh. Not to mention you will be able to do more in less time, which will allow you to take on more projects if you want to as well.

It's a good idea to make a list of studios in your area, as well as prop houses and food and prop stylists you can work with, so that when the time to organize a big shoot comes, you can make arrangements more easily.

Who does what?
A photographer is responsible for arranging the studio (unless the client takes care of that), bringing and setting up all the necessary equipment, shaping the light, working out the composition (although a stylist helps with that too), post-processing, and delivering the final images. Cleaning the shooting area and packing up the equipment are the least exciting things to do, but this is also our job.

A food stylist does the food shopping, prepares and plates the food, and makes sure every dish looks its best for the camera. They work with the photographer on set, to make sure every detail looks perfect.

You may also work with a prop stylist, who will arrange all the props to be delivered and label each setup so the team can see for which image the props are intended, and then take them away or arrange for a courier to pick them up at the end of the shooting day.

The order of the day
The food stylist will start getting the food ready while you are setting up the space. Often, a lot of the preparation (such as baking a tart shell) will already have been done the night before to make work easier and smoother on the shooting day.

Before we start photographing, I like to run through the brief with the stylist and check that we are on the same page regarding the schedule.

Great communication=great collaboration
You are working on this project together, so great communication is essential. It's key that each person knows what the other person is doing. The setup and camera should be ready at the same time the food is, so that the food stylist can finish the dish on set, and you can photograph it while it's still fresh and vibrant.

Check that the food stylist is happy with how the dishes look in the photograph. Take another shot if they want to tweak something; and if you move anything or turn a plate, let the stylist know too. After the shoot, the food stylist should receive copies of the photos (with the agreement of the client), in case they would like to show their work on their website or social media.

When you work as part of a team, it's also really important to have confidence in your own skills and trust your own instincts. If something doesn't look quite right to you, or if you feel that something could have been changed or improved upon, speak to your team about it. The confidence will come with experience.

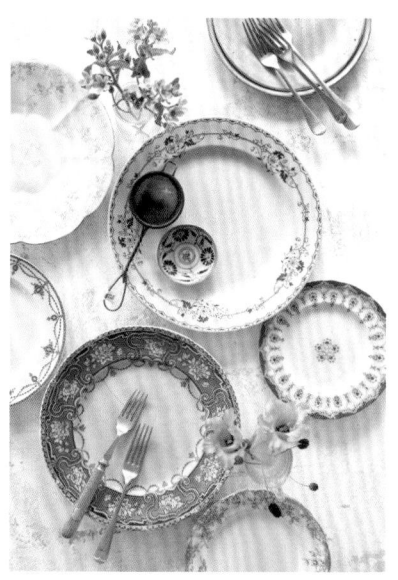

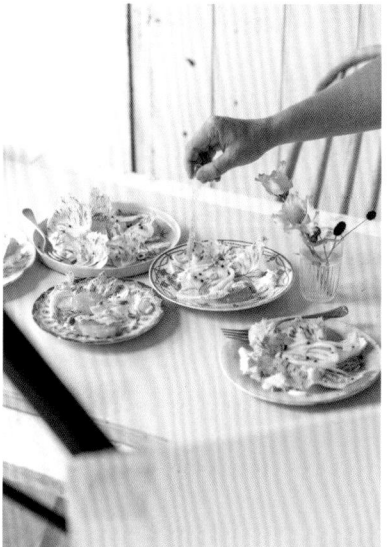

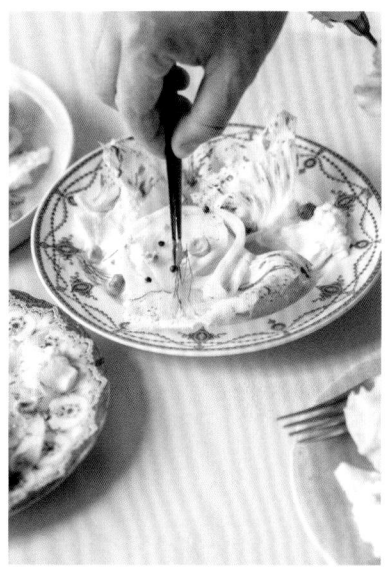

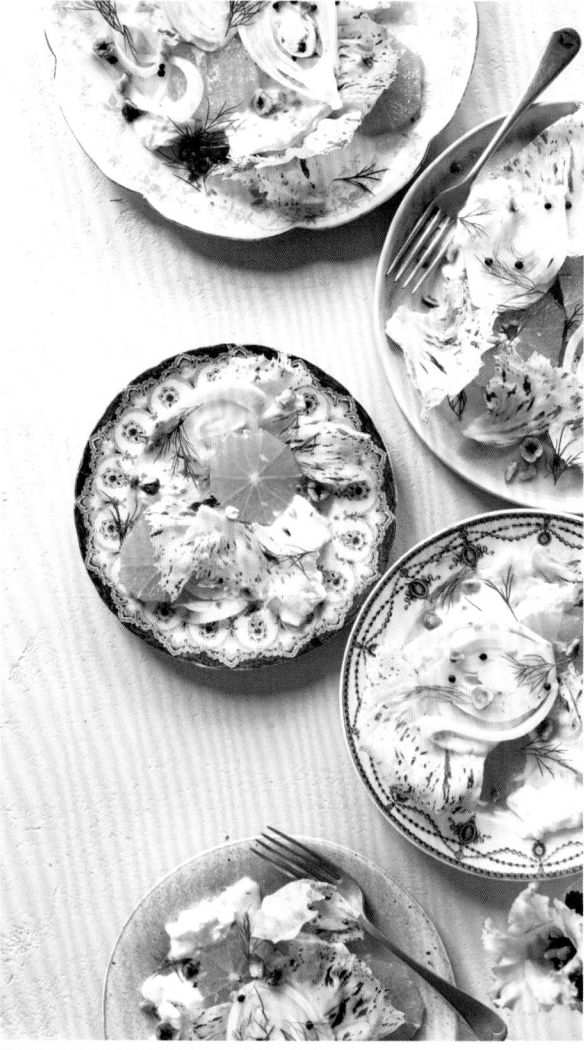

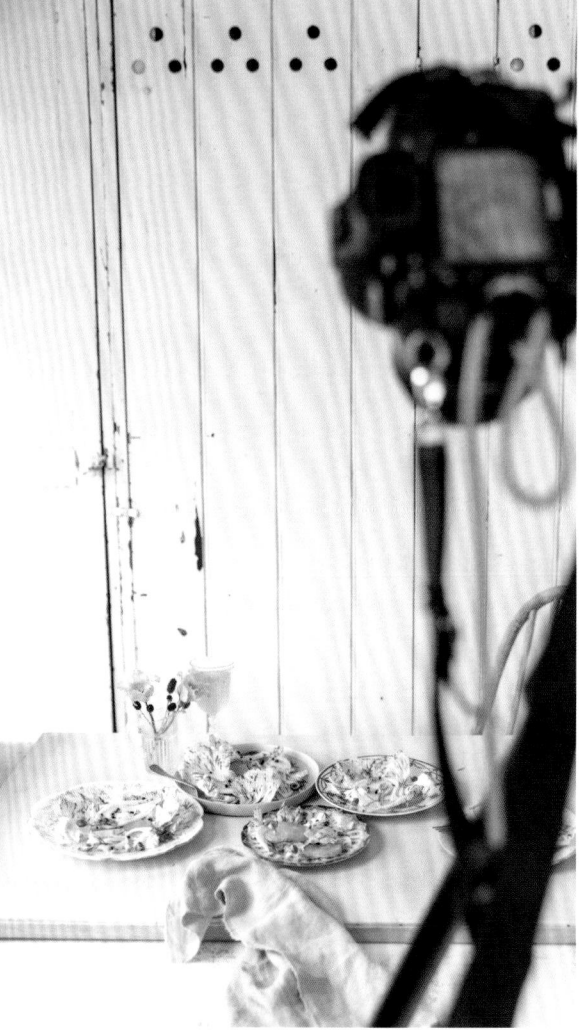

Food and prop styling by Amy Kinnear

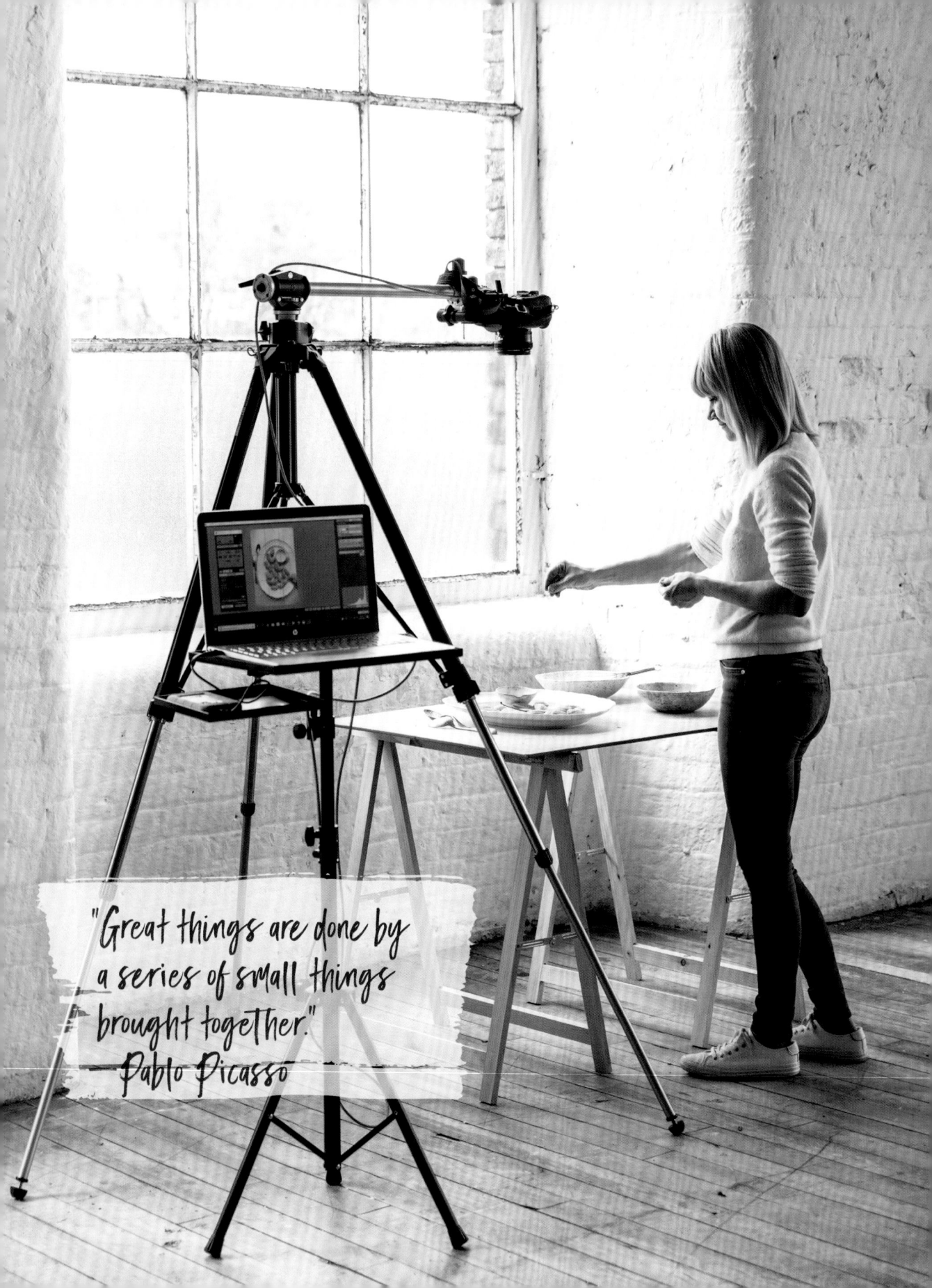

"Great things are done by a series of small things brought together."
— Pablo Picasso

Creative Process

Sometimes ideas jump out of nowhere; at other times they seem to hide away. Sometimes a shoot goes so perfectly that it almost seems to take care of itself, and at other times everything goes wrong! Having a creative process isn't about developing a way of working that you stick to rigidly. It's about having a smart, flexible plan and a few tested tactics in place that will help you be more productive and ready for the unexpected.

It all starts with the idea

As food photographers, we need to be coming up with creative ideas every day. It's not always easy, and it's even harder to come up with ideas that are both brilliant and unique. But when we see similar things over and over again, they don't spark the same excitement, so in today's world, where millions of images are shared every day, it's important to stand out. Images that catch the attention are those that are able to surprise us, show us less common perspectives, and different interpretations. This is why it's so useful to develop a method not only for finding but also for filtering and transforming inspiration, so that you can keep on having fresh ideas and creating images that reflect your unique way of seeing.

Turn your ideas into stories

The other thing that will elevate your photos is learning to how to tell stories with them. To do this, you need to know what moves you about your subject, what it is about your dish, your recipe, your ingredient that caught your attention and that you want to share with your viewer. Creating engaging stories every day takes awareness and attention to detail but with a few simple storytelling methods and a little bit of practice, it does become easier.

Photography is a work in progress

Creating a photograph is a work in progress: you try things, move elements around, add some items, and take others away. You need to be patient and work step by step to improve your frame. Having a good plan before the photoshoot will help you to be more effective and prepared, but it's also important to let yourself be spontaneous and let instinct take over while you create.

Ideas & inspiration

When your job is to come up with ideas and images on a daily basis, you have to find ways to feed your imagination and keep the creative juices flowing. There are times when inspiration strikes like a lightning bolt, sending a rush of excitement through your mind, motivating you to get to work immediately. But we all know we can't always sit still waiting for those moments to happen. To be able to keep working, we have to learn what encourages our creativity to show up. It will be something different for everyone—and it's important to recognize what makes it happen for you.

Finding your inspiration

Finding interesting ideas in everyday life takes a special awareness and a rested mind. You need to train yourself to notice things that other people don't see, as well as find ways to arm yourself against the daily distractions that steal your focus and get in the way of looking properly. If you practice being present, look closely, and try to find something extraordinary in ordinary things, you will be able to find inspiration everywhere.

One thing that I like doing is to schedule regular "days for the soul" in my calendar, when I get out of my usual routine by taking a trip to a city I've never been to before, to a gallery or exhibition I've never visited, or even just to a favorite bookstore. Looking for inspiration in less familiar places always sharpens my senses and sparks interesting ideas that I can try in my food photos. I feel that if we all hang out in the same place for inspiration and ideas (on social media for example), it's harder to create surprising and distinctive work. It can be so refreshing to find new inspiration off the beaten track.

But of course, surrounding yourself with beautiful imagery can help to trigger new ideas too. And it doesn't just have to be food photography—looking at what creatives are doing in other fields can be so eye-opening! For example, I am always inspired by the atmosphere wedding and travel photographers create in their work; and I often look at interior and graphic design for color palette and color proportion ideas.

Food for thought

Bringing ideas from outside your own field can help to breathe something fresh and different into your work, but at the same time you can't (and shouldn't) ignore what's going on in your own field. It's inevitable that you will be inspired by other food photographers too.

You just have to be mindful as what you don't want to happen is to negatively compare yourself to the people you admire, or be so influenced by someone else's work that you start to lose what's so special and unique about your own style. It's important to learn to filter through the ideas, and find the way to transform them into something truly yours.

The next time you are looking a photo that you wish you'd made, study the image, think about what you can learn from it and identify the one thing that you like most about it: it might be the lighting, the angle, the color scheme, the props, etc. If you take just one element while changing the rest and adding your own personal spin to the image, you will have a great repertoire of ideas to try, without your work ever looking like someone else's.

Rules of borrowing creatively

* Study
* Transform
* Always put your own spin on it
* Take inspiration from more than one place
* Take inspiration from outside of food photography

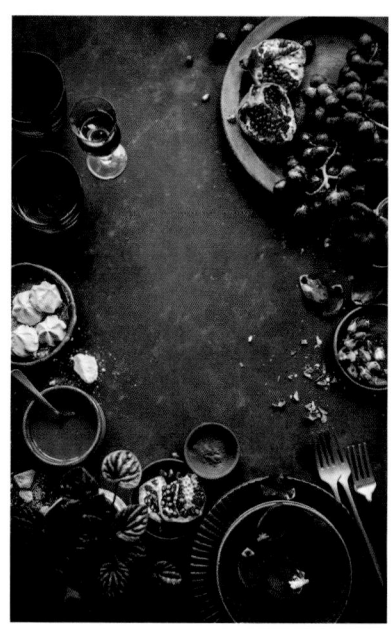
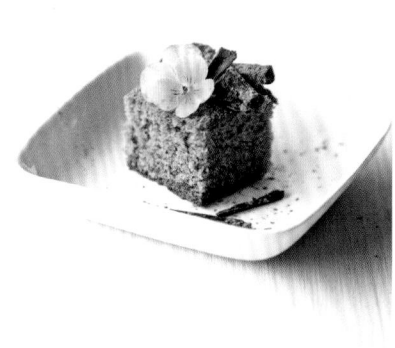
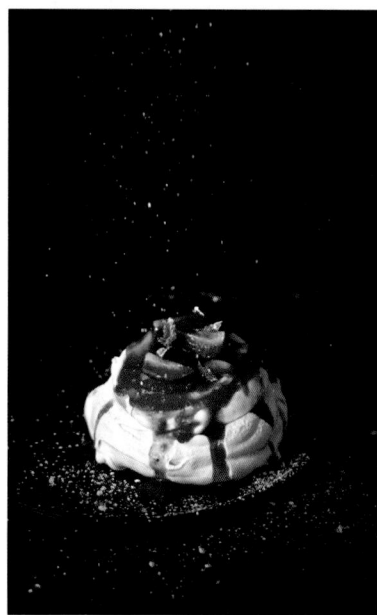

Creative borrowing (above)

Here's an example of how we can borrow ideas from others and transform them into something different. I remember when I saw this photo (left) by Claudia Goedke for the first time and thought "Why have I never considered pairing red/pink and black together?" It's such a gorgeous color combination and I have since tried using this palette in my own work.

Then, when I saw this image (center) by Rachel Korinek, I couldn't get over how powerful negative space can be in creating a harmonious image. It's something I started looking at and incorporating a bit more into some of my images.

My photo (right) borrows from both of these ideas, but it also reflects my own style.

Dare to be different

* Put your ideas before anyone else's. Before you start gathering inspiration, sit down and bring your own thoughts together about a subject you are about to photograph. What's so special about it? What do you want to draw attention to?
* Don't only study the photographs; also study the creator's mind. What do they pay attention to? What are they good at? What are their strengths? What can you learn from them?
* Be a rebel and take the unpopular path. What is everyone doing? What's currently popular? And then, what's missing? What is no one else paying attention to?
* Train your mind to think differently: if a certain subject is always served or shown in a particular way, think of ways to change it up.
* Put extra effort into everything you do, pay attention to the smallest details, and your work will always stand out.

Creative process structure

Creating a photograph is a process of trial, error, and improvement. What I have learned over the years is that a photographer needs to be a good problem-solver, always ready for the unexpected. Having a creative structure that works for you will help to keep things under control. Spontaneity is an important part of the creative process, but at the same time, I always get more out of a shoot when I have a plan in mind.

Inspiration

The creative process often begins with the client's brief (if there is one). A brief tells you exactly what the client's expectations are: what images they need and what they will be used for. I always read this carefully, make sure I am on the same page with the client and ask questions if something is not clear. If there is no creative brief in place, I usually create one myself.

What a typical brief includes
* Images for inspiration
* Colors and mood
* Angles and the number of shots
* Whether negative space for text is necessary
* Specific props
* Details about styling
* The recipe and reference image(s) of the final dish
* Any comments, things you should be aware of, and what elements are the most important

Mood board
This is where I gather all my ideas and research, as well as practical notes from the brief, in one place. Pinterest is a great place to create a mood board because you can make it private and share it with the client so that they can pin their own inspiration there, too. I like to include color palettes, angles and, often, non-food-related images that capture the atmosphere I am after.

Planning

The next step is to plan the shoot in more detail. I always start by thinking what I will need to execute it, what the timeline is and how I can make things easier and quicker for myself. Usually, at this stage, I consider whether there will be time to explore the subject in different color palettes and experiment with lighting, or whether I need to be strict with my shot list.

Story & atmosphere
"What story and feeling do I want to create in my image?" is the first thing I consider, and this shapes everything, from the lighting setup to the color palette and the props I choose.

Styling & composition
I always think about what I want to draw attention to and what I want the viewer to notice first, and then I consider how the food and the scene could be styled to show this off in the best way. What will be the best lens, angle, and orientation to use? What items can I bring to the scene to make it more interesting? Or should I keep it minimal? How can I give my image depth, movement, balance, and visual interest?

Preparation

Preparing for a food photoshoot requires far more than just planning your photographs. I always note down anything I want to make sure I remember, and take time to think about what could possibly go wrong and how I can prevent it from happening.

Ingredients & dishes
When it comes to the recipes, the first thing I do is read the instructions and the ingredient list. I think about when I should buy what I need—does something need to be bought fresh, ideally the day before? If it's something rare or not in season, I make sure I know in advance where I am going to get it from, and that I can definitely get it when I need it.

I will prepare anything I can on the day before the shoot. For anything that needs to be made on the day, I measure out and organize the ingredients I need for each recipe ahead of time.

Props
I gather all the props and backgrounds I want to use and experiment to see how they will work together.

Shooting order
You will come up with your own favorite workflow, but I find that starting from the easiest dish takes the pressure off my shoulders and is a great warm-up.

Execution

When it comes to the photoshoot, presence of mind, concentration, and intuition are extremely important. Also try to keep in mind that creativity doesn't like too much pressure. Try to force it and it will hide; let it play and it will reward you.

I will set up my space with my camera and equipment, and then get everything in place to shape the light. I take some test shots to warm up my creative eye— I like to try out different backgrounds and test the light.

If I know I won't have much time to photograph the food before it starts to look unappetizing, first I will style the scene, getting everything in place to shoot as quickly as possible. I prepare the food, style it, and then shoot, checking back to my plan to make sure I'm not missing any details I wanted to capture. And as I shoot, I slow down and take a moment to study my scene from every angle and keep an eye on what is working, what is not working, and what changes I can make.

After the shoot is finished, I clean up my space, pack everything away and get ready to start editing—a process we'll come to in the next chapter.

Planning

Research

Story & atmosphere

Shot list

Initial ideas

Mood board

Styling & composition

Client's brief

Inspiration

Supply

Preparation

Edit

Ingredients & dishes

Shoot

Test shots

Props

Set up

Shooting order

Execution

Troubleshooting

Always be ready for the unexpected. Things will go wrong all the time—that's normal, and it's your ability to deal with problems, stay calm, and troubleshoot that will set you apart. When things don't work out, fix them as you go. Photography is all about solving problems. What's not working? How can you make it better? Rethink and start again. If you can't come up with a solution the same day, go back tomorrow, and always give yourself a pat in the back for trying.

A great shot often starts as a bad shot. You've got to work at it, step by step, to make it better. Patience is what elevates average into extraordinary.

Be ready to change your mind (below)

In my head, I had a vision of photographing this noodle salad from overhead—possibly a bigger spread with two or three hero dishes and some additional ingredients around. I knew a blue background would beautifully highlight the green, so I tested three different shades and felt that a mid-blue worked best. However, something still wasn't quite right and I couldn't figure out what it was. Then it hit me—the color of the bowl wasn't working. I changed the bowl and this was when I realized I was too fixed on the overhead shot—that maybe I should try a different angle. That was it! Although it looked nothing like what I had envisioned in my head, it's good to sometimes let go of a vision that doesn't work to create something else that does.

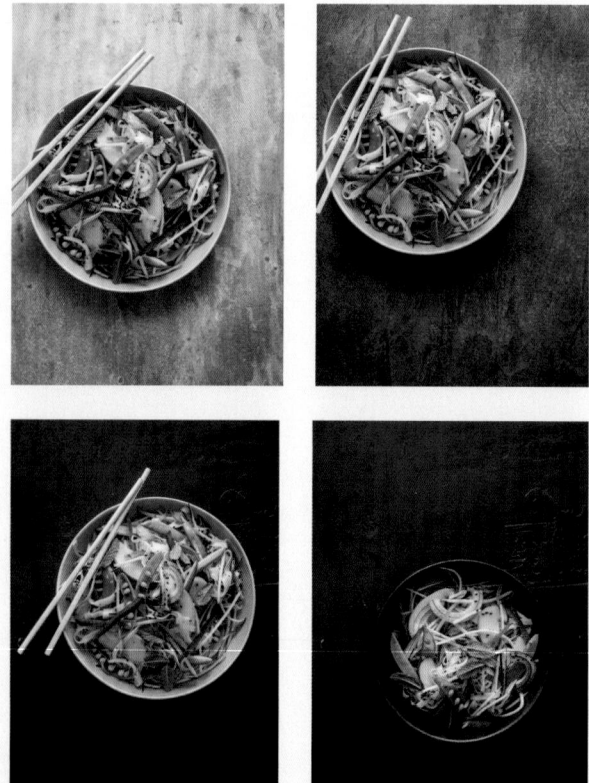

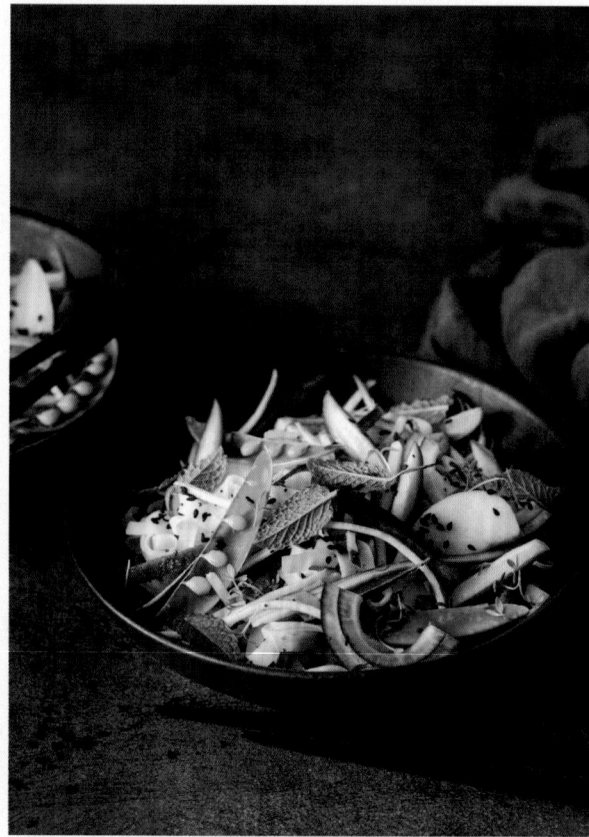

Look out for distractions (below)

Using a white surface didn't work here at all. The dish blended in with the background and there wasn't enough contrast to show off its beautiful shape. The second choice didn't do the trifle any favors either—its texture turned out to be too distracting. The scene also felt empty so I decided to add another element. Including a bowl of cream on the side proved to be a bad idea, however! Not only was the color too bright, so it competed with the hero, it also didn't make sense to have a small bowl of cream beside a huge trifle. I wasn't going to give up though.

It turned out that swapping a 50mm lens for a 100mm lens—which gave a tighter frame—was what the shot was missing. Choosing a different supporting element and shaping the light to darken the scene and add contrast were the final touches it needed.

Tip

Don't be afraid of making mistakes—analyze them and let them lead you to new discoveries. Photography isn't about hitting the winner every time. Some images might not feel like masterpieces to you, but they're all part of the creative process.

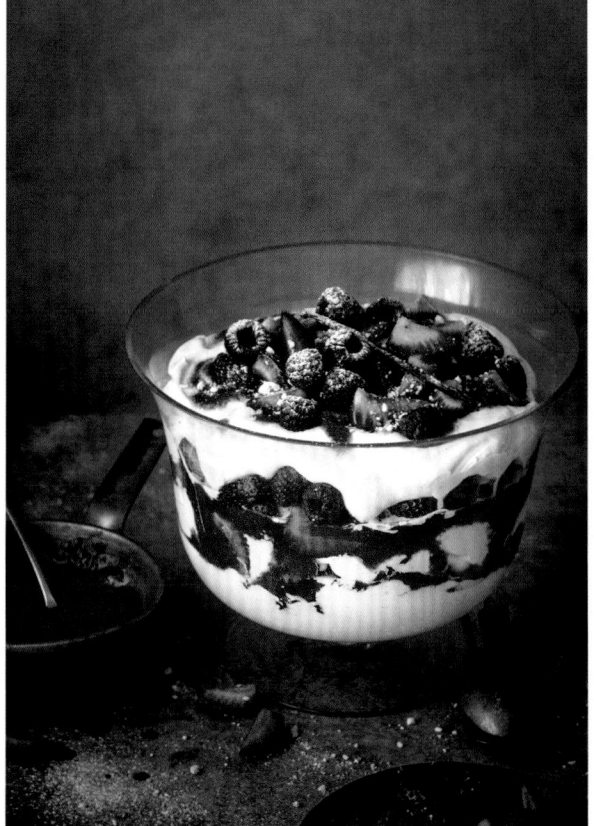

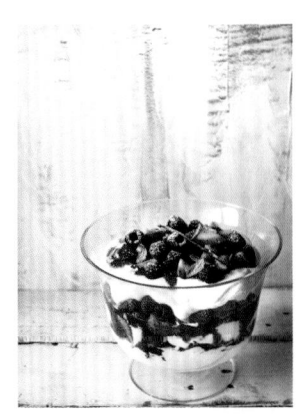

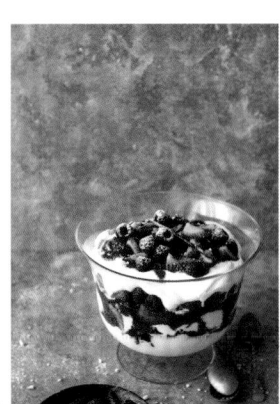

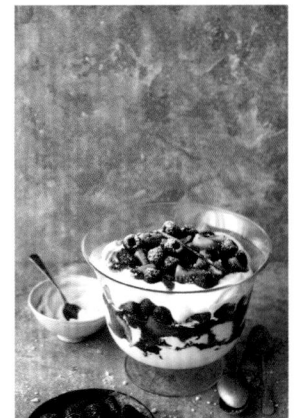

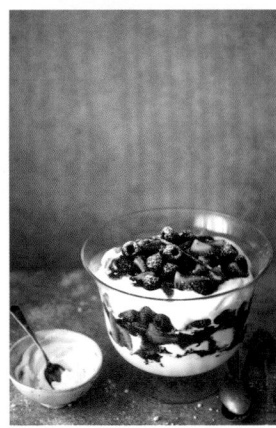

How to photograph different food groups

As a food photographer, you will often be challenged to photograph a new and unfamiliar dish, which can be a tricky thing. Don't get stressed out though: dealing with challenges is part of the job.

Be as prepared as possible. If you know you will be photographing something you never have before, try to learn as much about the dish as you can. A great way to do this is to create a mood board for this specific dish and add ten of the most inspiring images you can find. Then study them, note the things that stand out the most for you, and learn from them.

Fresh produce (below)

* Get the most beautiful produce available—local and seasonal is always a winner—and then keep it as fresh as possible.
* Use a mixture of varieties, shapes, and sizes, if you can.
* Focus on the beauty and shape of your subject.
* Try cutting some of your ingredients while leaving others whole for textural contrast.
* Face ingredients in different directions to create visual flow, and to reflect the light in an interesting way.
* Mist your produce with water (if appropriate) to add extra freshness.

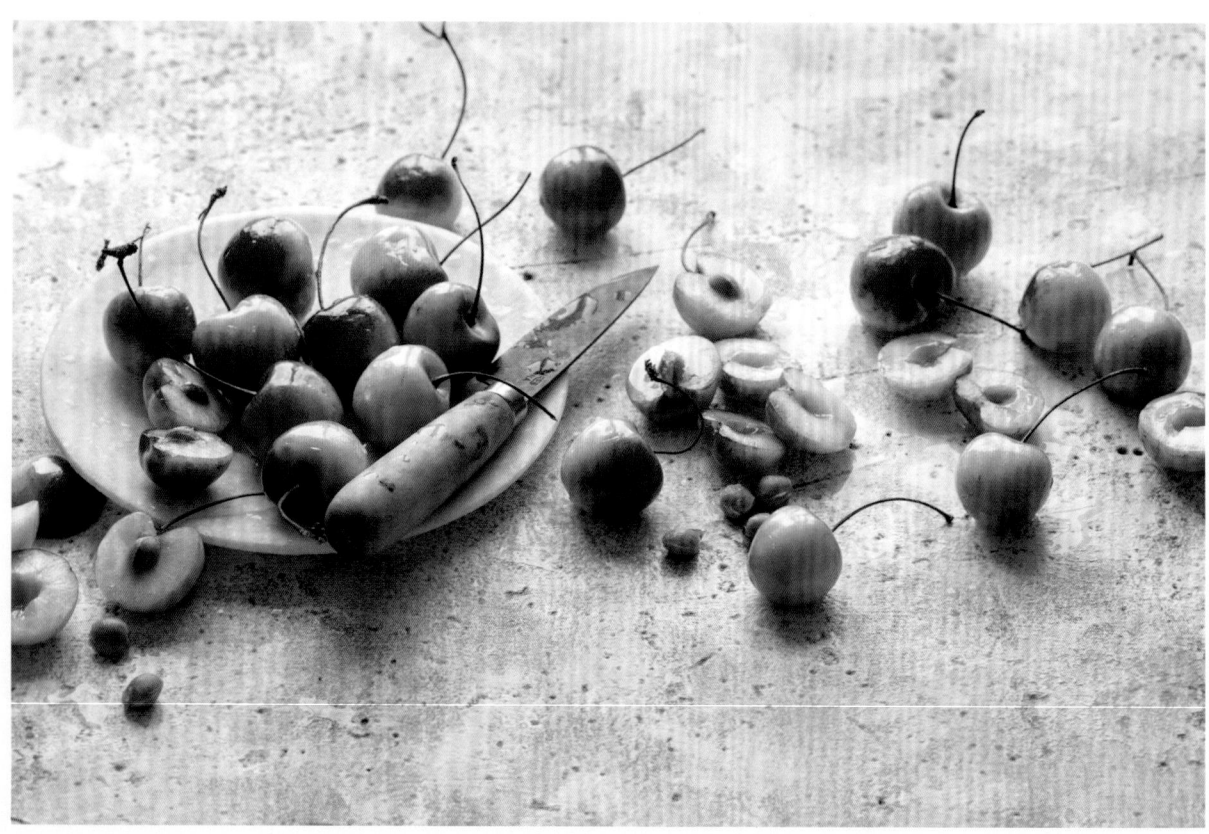

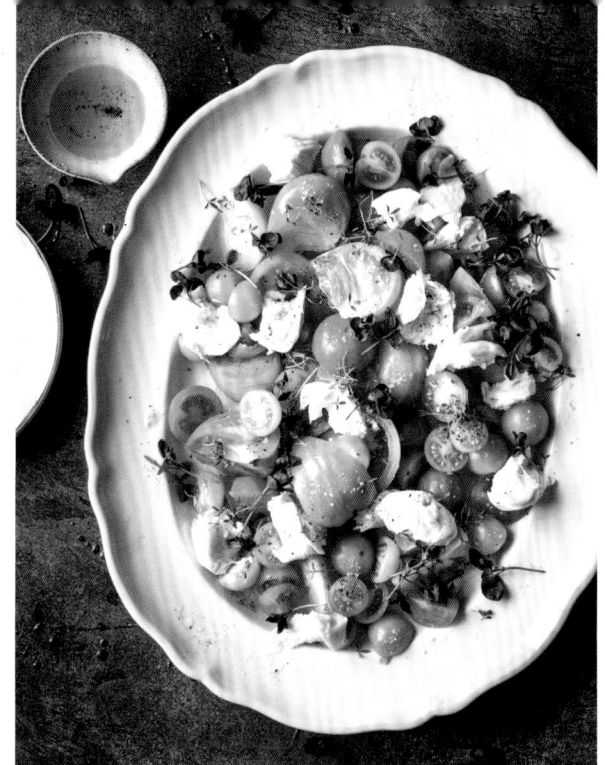
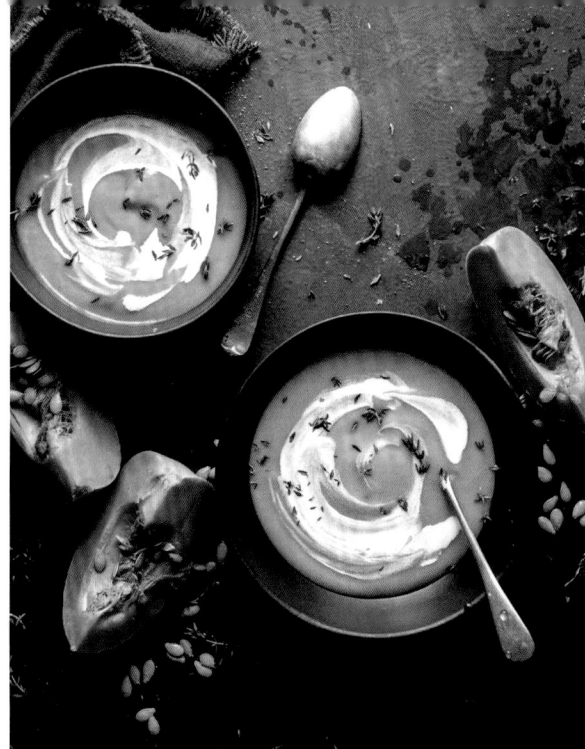

Salads (above)

* Shallow bowls, plates, or trays will be best for showing off all the ingredients.
* When choosing ingredients, try to keep the palette to three or four colors.
* Colorful salads will often appreciate plain props and backgrounds.
* Set up the scene with empty dishes, and once you are happy with the composition and light, fill them with your salad.
* Think about a superstar ingredient that you could include to give your salad extra interest.
* Keep your styling relaxed and make sure your salad has a lot of volume.
* Keep an eye on each ingredient and replace anything that doesn't look fresh anymore.
* Put only a little dressing on your salad so that you don't weigh it down or make it wilt. You can include more of the dressing in a pot next to the main dish.

Soups (above)

* Invest in beautiful, shallow bowls that will work with many soup recipes.
* Don't fill the bowls too much—let the rim be a natural frame for the food.
* To show off any vegetables or other chunkier ingredients in your recipe, try using shallow bowls and adding less liquid.
* Test a few interesting cutlery and napkin placements. I personally like to have my napkins flowing into the frame from a corner. When it comes to cutlery, I try to face the pieces in different directions for visual flow, or group them on the side.
* Consider letting the mood and colors reflect the season in which the soup would be served.
* Adding some ingredients that have gone into the soup around the frame or on top as a garnish can help visualize a flavor that's not obvious.
* For plain recipes, strengthen your subject through repetition by including several bowls in the frame.
* Watch out for the liquid rim that might appear around your bowl.

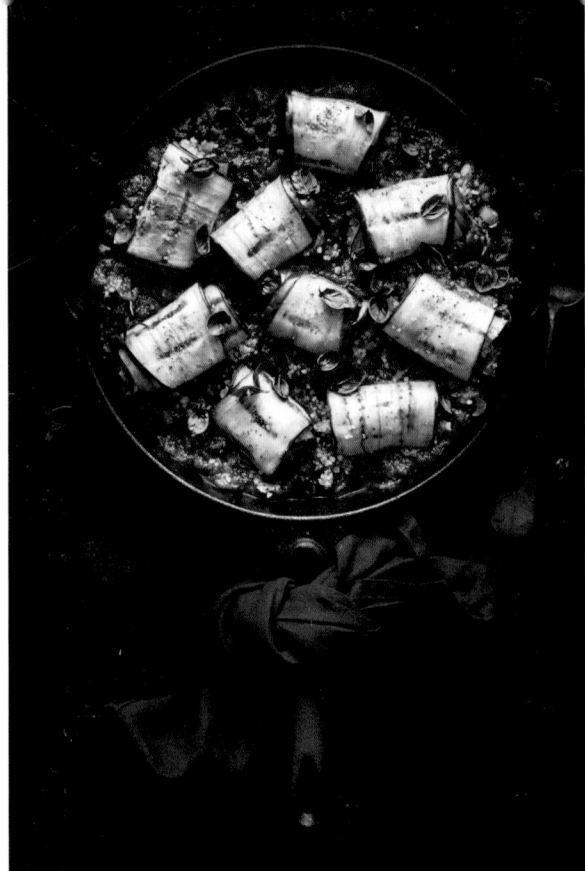

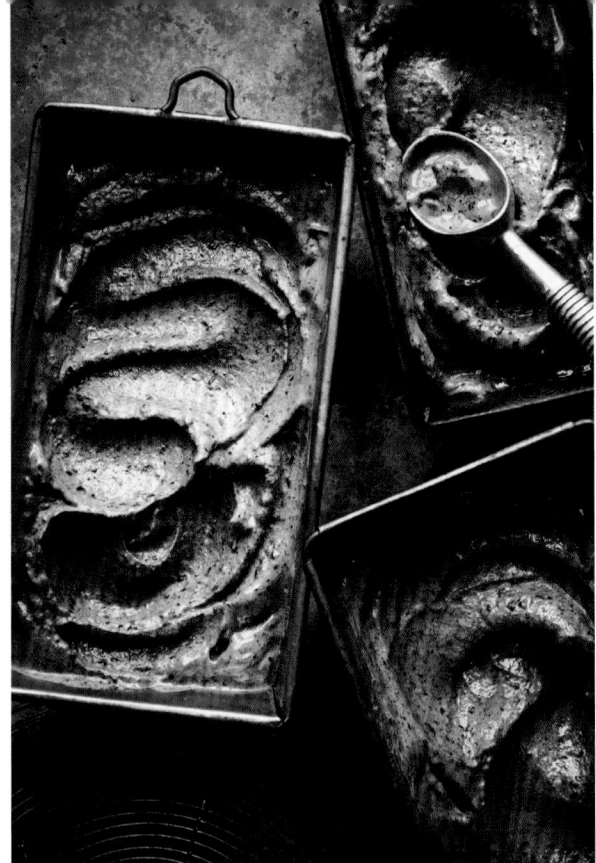

One pan (above)

* When preparing your dish, take care that it doesn't lose its vigor, color, shape, or texture.
* When necessary, prepare ingredients separately for extra control and put them together afterwards to avoid a messy jumble.
* Always make sure there are recognizable ingredients for the eye to focus on, and ensure that some ingredients that show the flavor are visible.
* Present it in a beautiful pan or dish—pay attention to its color and shape; it should add to the story but not distract from the food.
* You don't have to keep it in one dish; you could show it in a few smaller dishes.
* For "busy" recipes, I usually use plain props, while for plain dishes, I might try to enliven them with a more charismatic prop.
* Get creative with garnishes to bring the recipe to life.
* Set the scene up beforehand and photograph fast.

Frozen foods (above)

* Set up the scene, camera, and props in advance.
* Make beautiful shapes: get interesting molds and a good-quality scoop.
* Visualize the shapes in your composition while you're setting up. A scrunched-up piece of paper can be a good stand-in for a scoop of ice cream, and for popsicles, you can use their molds.
* When working with many subjects, prescoop ice cream/take popsicles out of their molds and return them to the freezer on a tray lined with baking/parchment paper.
* If the flavor isn't obvious, consider showing the viewer what it is.
* Show off the texture—frosty and crisp or softly melting: both are irresistible!
* Show drips to make your image even more tempting.
* Shoot fast and have more of your frozen subject, in case you need to replace things or start again.

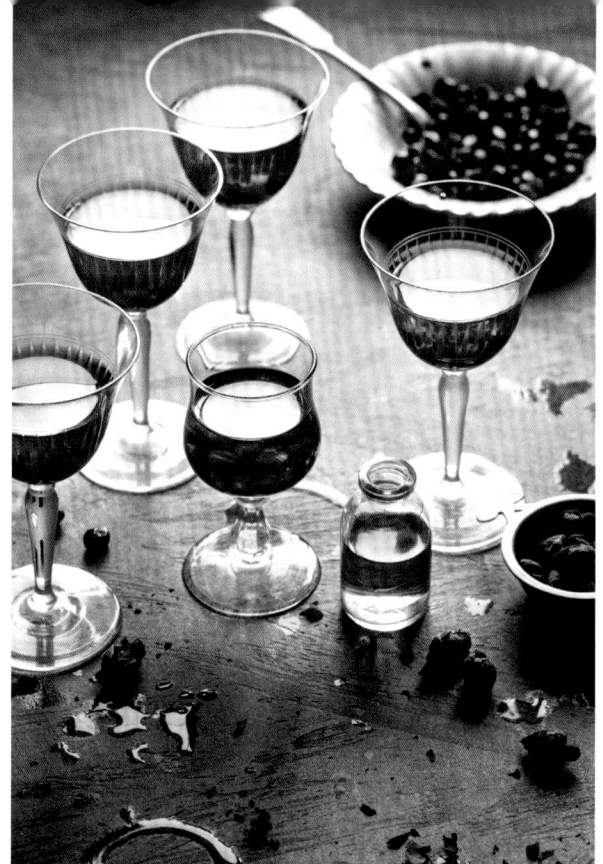

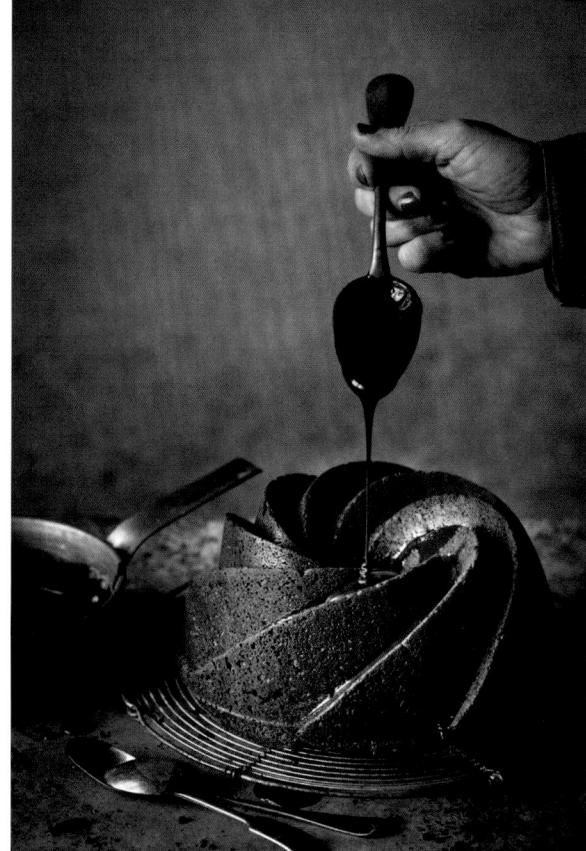

Drinks (above)

* Make sure the glass is perfectly clean (wear cotton gloves to avoid any fingerprints).
* Find unique and impressive glassware.
* When including several drinks in the frame, mix different styles of glassware for more visual interest.
* Capture steam from hot drinks and condensation on cold ones.
* Add interesting garnishes and accessories to better tell the story.
* Always watch the behaviour of the reflections on the glassware—play with the angle or move things around if you need to.
* Remember: drink shots love hard light and the backlighting technique.
* Drinks give you a great opportunity to capture an action shot—either frozen movement or a motion blur.

Sweets (above)

* The decoration possibilities are endless when it comes to sweet stuff: make it interesting!
* Think about how you can shape the food, before or after baking, to add more visual impact.
* Consider cutting it up or removing a slice.
* Show in-progress shots.
* With multiple subjects, think about decorating some of them and leaving others undecorated for a little variety.
* Add delicious drips and spills if appropriate.
* Use interesting props to add charm to your story.
* Consider photographing the same subject in different lights or with different color palettes.
* Try capturing movement, whether it's a chocolate pour, a honey drizzle, or a powdered sugar shake.

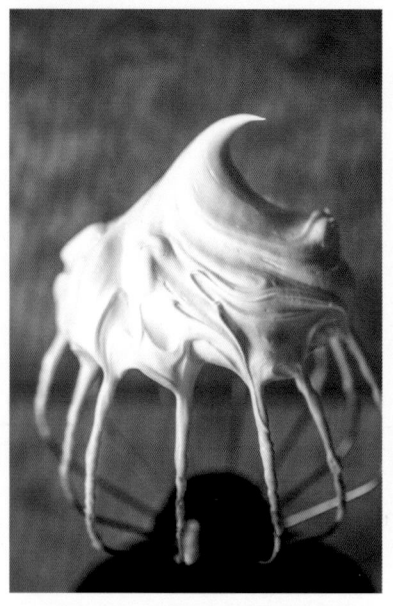
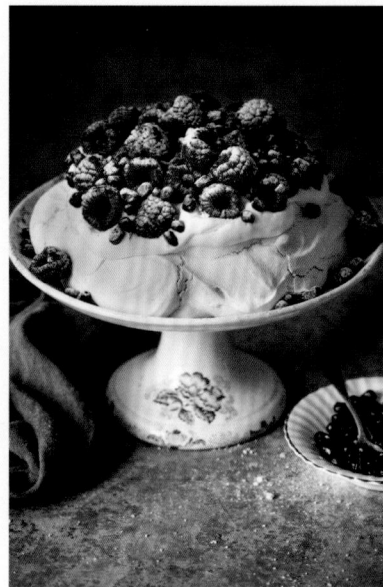
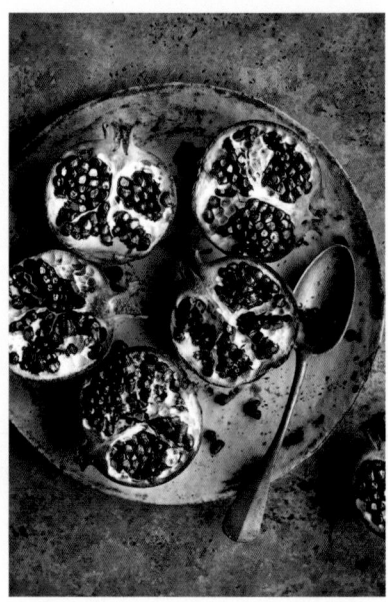

Crafting a story

A story is a message that you want to share with your audience. It's what you want your viewer to know about the ingredient or the recipe. They are not there with you during the preparation and shooting process—they can't smell or taste the food—so it's your job to give them as much detail as possible.

Ways to tell a story

To get to your viewer's heart, you've got to have them in mind when you create your image. What would you like them to know about the dish and recipe you are photographing? What is the most important part? The story you want to tell impacts all of your photography decisions, from the choice of light, props, composition, and styling to the final tweaks in post-production.

A story doesn't have to be complicated—in fact, it's best to start simple. Start by deciding whether you want your story to focus on a special quality of the recipe or dish, a mood or feeling associated with the food, or a holiday or event connected to it.

What's so special?

Is it a flavor? Or the aroma of a specific ingredient? You can help to visualize both by making sure that the important component is included and visible somewhere in the scene. If the star of your photo is vanilla cheesecake, for example, then including vanilla pods somewhere in the frame will subconsciously bring the vanilla taste and scent to your viewer's mind. Our senses are connected, and what we see can transport us back to even our favorite childhood dishes.

Perhaps it's a texture, color, or a shape? Or maybe something about the preparation of a dish that is interesting? Maybe it's a combination of several things? As a photographer you need to be curious, study your subject carefully, and then show your viewer what caught your attention.

How do I want my viewer to feel?

Another way to approach the story is to ask yourself, "How do I want my viewer to feel?" If you are having a hard time deciding, write a few words about how the recipe makes *you* feel. Then think about how you can trigger these emotions when crafting your image.

If the food you are about to photograph is comforting, try to create that cosy feeling in your photograph. You could choose a warm white balance and/or warm colors, include long shadows in the composition, place a soft napkin by the plate or even capture some steam. As another example, when I am photographing for a wellness magazine, I keep in mind that my client's audience is looking for uncomplicated, healthy recipes. To give the reader this impression just by looking at the image, I keep my composition simple and my lighting bright and airy, and I make sure the colors look extra fresh and vibrant.

Seasons & events

Seasons, special occasions, and where the dish comes from are also great themes to build your narrative around, because they tend to elicit specific emotional responses. Think about light, colors, and unique props that could help you craft your story and capture the atmosphere of the occasion or place.

On the next page we will explore some ways that you can approach seasonal storytelling, but there is no single way to portray a season. Think about what feelings each one evokes in you, what you love the most about them, and try to translate that into your food stories.

The elements of a story

As you start to shape your food story, these are the things you need to think about:

* Subject
* Setting
* What is so special?
* What is happening?
* What emotions are you evoking?

Make it evocative

* Consider how you can use highlights and shadows to help you imbue your image with atmosphere. Would it be well suited by a light, airy treatment or should it be heavily shadowed and dramatic, with high contrast? Should you add more energy to your image by shooting with hard light or using backlighting?
* Remember that color and white balance are powerful tools you can use to evoke emotion.
* Showing the process and visual details to indicate flavor stimulates the senses and adds depth to the story.
* Capturing movement—whether beautifully blurred or sharply frozen—can surprise and excite the eye.
* Show your dish from a unique perspective by using different focal lengths and distances. Think about whether you want to focus on a detail or show context in a wider scene.
* If you can, create a series of photos to better illustrate your story.
* Try out different orientations—portrait and landscape—and angles that show the dish from different sides.
* Choose props that enhance the story. Vintage or modern? What color or pattern? What size and shape? Is there something unique you can bring to the image?
* Add a human element, whether it's a hand holding a bowl, pouring honey, or pulling out a chair, to make the scene more lived-in and inviting.

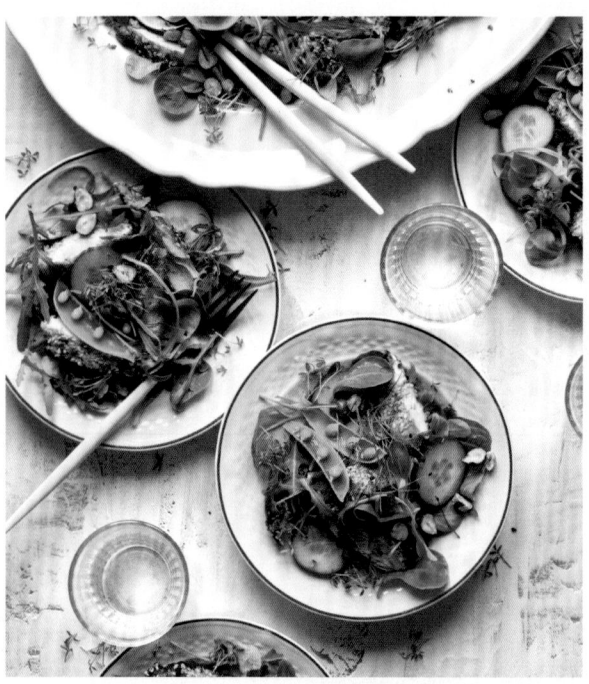

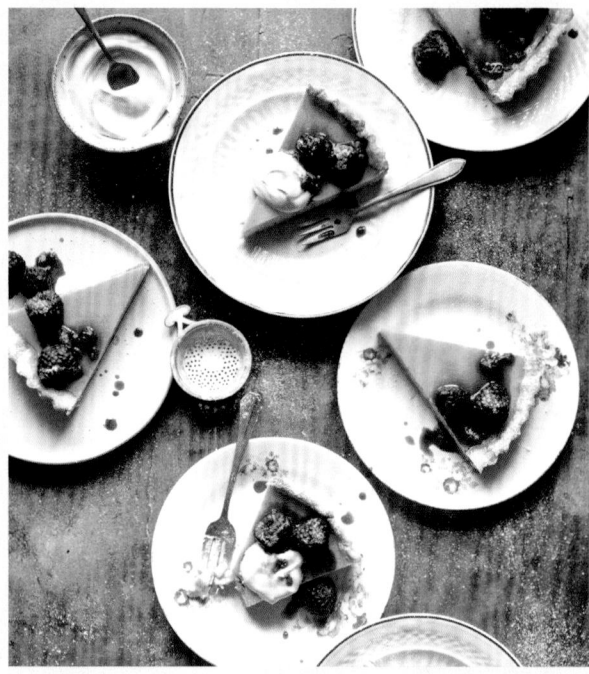

Seasonal storytelling

I love the contrast between seasons. Each one brings new light, colors, and ingredients with it. Each one tells a different story.

Spring (above)

To me, spring is green, lush, refreshing, delicate, gentle, light, spacious, and airy. After a long winter filled with rich food, we can't wait to dive into a world of lighter recipes and fresh green produce—that's what spring has to offer.

Using simple compositions with only a few things in a frame and leaving some negative space can be a great recipe for conjuring spring's light atmosphere. Lightweight ceramics and fabrics, as well as thin glassware, will also add to that feeling. To capture the season's character, I like to keep my shadows minimal and my white balance on the slightly cooler side for a fresh feel. Greens provide a perfect color palette for spring, but pastels and gentle tones also work beautifully. Spring food doesn't require too much saturation, but it does need to be fresh!

Summer (above)

Vibrant, energetic and colorful—that's summer in a nutshell. To recreate the cheerful mood of the season, I like to add dynamism to my images by using vivid, eye-popping color combinations. Stimulating pinks and yellows are a perfect choice to express the lively atmosphere; but summer can also bring blue skies to mind—I find that using blue as a background color can enhance almost every summer recipe.

Using colorful and/or patterned props and soft linens, adding flowers to your food scene, and shooting outdoors are a few ways to inject some summery vibes into your food stories. This is also a great time to experiment with high contrast and hard light, since a bold look can really help to portray the playful and charismatic spirit of the season.

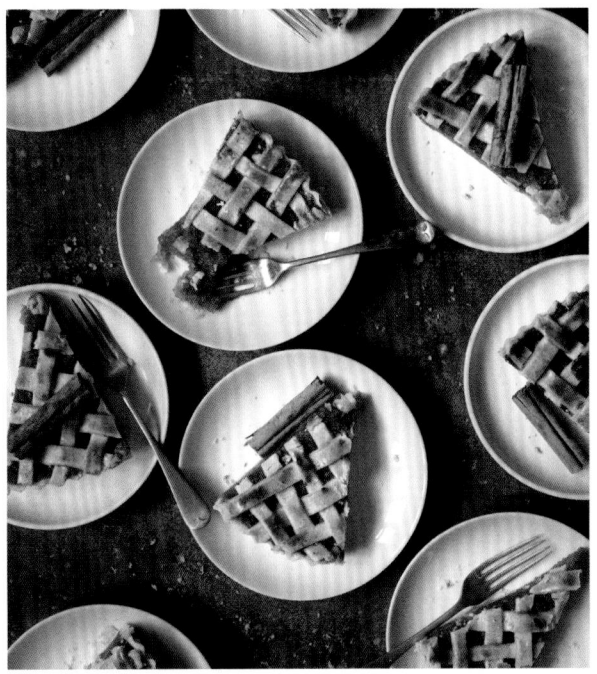

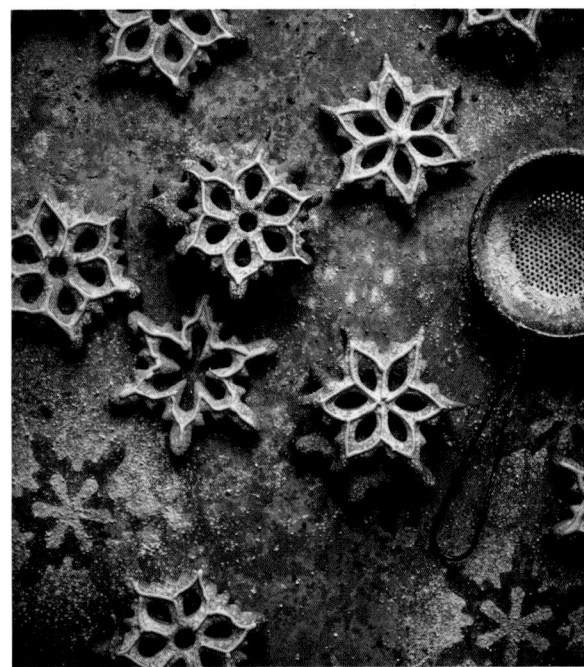

Autumn (above)

For me, autumn is all about the cosy and inviting atmosphere it brings. The fiery hues of the changing season can be so inspiring when it comes to our color choices, too. To achieve the comfy feeling that autumn brings, I like to keep my white balance on the warmer side and play with rich, warm, and saturated colors.

Filling the frame with layers and elements, as well as creating deeper shadows, will make your image feel cosier. Chunky props such as wooden boards, iron pans, hand-made ceramics, and thick fabrics will be a perfect match for the heart-warming recipes this season has to offer, and will also help you better illustrate an autumnal story.

Hot and cosy foods often have strong flavor or smell associations. I like to think of the flavors and scents the season brings to mind, and add them somewhere in the composition as a clue for the senses.

Winter (above)

Without a doubt, winter has something exciting to offer too. Its atmospheric light, deep shadows, and neutral and earthy tones can be extremely evocative.

Winter reminds me of crisp, frosty mornings and long, dark evenings. But it also brings warm fires, cosy blankets, and delicious, pungent scents to mind. To illustrate the contrasts this season conjures, I like to use a mixture of light and dark or cool and warm colors in my food stories.

This is a season that inspires nostalgia, so including scene-setting props such as vintage accessories, old photos, faded music sheets, handwritten recipes, or candles in the frame is a good way to strengthen this narrative.

Interview:
Linda Lomelino

Linda has been photographing food and running her award-winning food blog, Call Me Cupcake, for over ten years now; as well as writing her own cookbooks that are sold all over the world. She may have been doing it for many years, but her work never becomes stale and she manages to surprise and enchant with every new work she creates.

You have been a huge inspiration for food photographers over the years. Could you please share where you get your inspiration from?
My inspiration comes from all different places, but a running theme has always been old houses and antiques. There's just something special about things with a long history, like they almost have a soul. I don't go looking for inspiration for every shoot, as I used to do a lot in the first few years. I do, however, love browsing Pinterest to get myself inspired and excited. What I love the most is actually looking at interior photography. Just looking at beautiful places and rooms does something to me!

Do you ever feel uninspired? What do you do when this happens?
I'd say it happens every year, usually during the summer months. Maybe it's the sun and the beautiful weather that makes me feel like I should be on the beach or something, you know? The light is usually quite harsh if it's sunny, and our apartment gets insanely hot, so I just don't feel like baking or photographing. Come August and September, and I can feel the inspiration coming back to me slowly. There's something about autumn that fills me with excitement.

Sometimes it works to just power through, but I think it's important when you go through a period of not feeling inspired to recognize that maybe you need a break. But if you're anything like me, it is hard to take a break when you so desperately want to create!

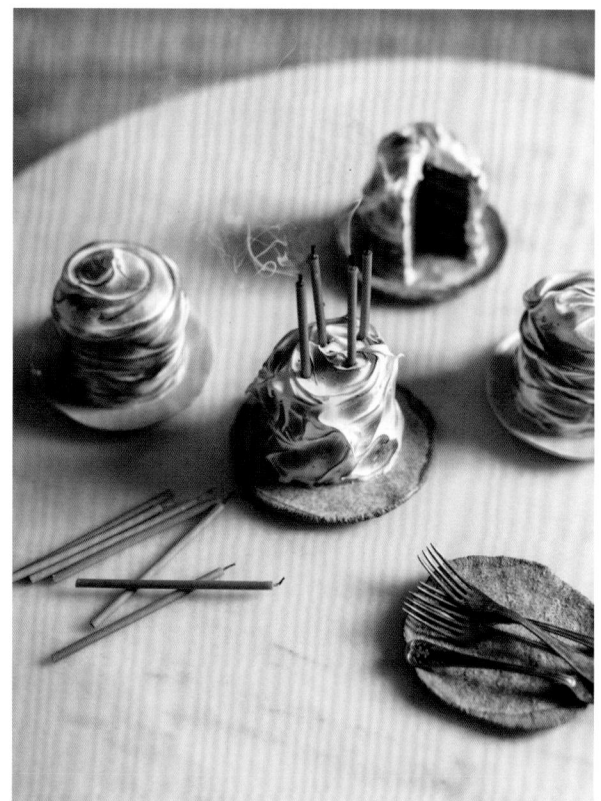

In your opinion, what makes a successful photograph, and what are the things that you pay attention to when you create?
I think it's sometimes hard to say what makes a photograph good, but certainly using light and shadows to create incredible depth, and making sure your food looks as beautiful as it possibly can will always add something special to your photographs. What I'm looking for in my photos is an overall balance, and making sure the eye flows through the composition. I don't follow any photography rules; I think the best thing to do is to trust your eye and not overthink it. I do pay attention to lines in photos, though; so if I'm shooting a flat lay with cutlery and utensils, I make sure they all don't point in the exact same direction. Personally, I also like the strong contrast that complementary colors create—there's something so satisfying about that.

Could you walk us through the creative process behind your photos, from when the idea is born to the final photograph?

I am quite a spontaneous photographer, and it usually starts with the inspiration. For my last shoot, it was seeing some wild strawberries growing in the garden outside our apartment building. I also had this beautiful antique serving platter that I had never used. From there, I had to think of something I could bake in a rectangular/oval shape, so I decided on a pavlova. Usually, I pull out props while something is baking in the oven and start taking some photos of them on the surface I choose. I usually try a few different surfaces to see what works best. If I'm shooting for my blog, I'll also consider what props and backgrounds I've used in the last few posts to make sure I mix it up—the same when I'm shooting for a book. If I'm using something I've used recently, I'll try to achieve a different atmosphere in the photo through different props, maybe another angle and different light.

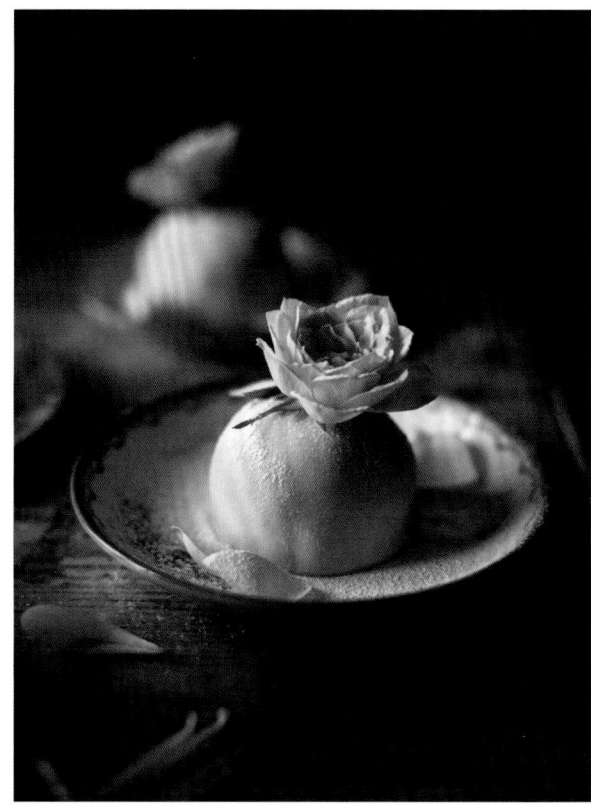

When I plate the dish, I just start taking pictures and see where this takes me. Sometimes I have to move to a different window if the light has changed too much, sometimes I switch out some props, sometimes ALL the props. I always take a lot of pictures to make sure I've got every single angle. You've put time and effort into preparation and your setup, so you might as well make the most out of it. Too many photos is better than too few—you can always delete the ones you're not using. This has paid off for me when I've been photographing for books, when after a shoot I think, "I wish I had that angle or a close up of that," and usually I do have something. I do get a little carried away when something is beautiful. If I were shooting portraits, it would be a different story, but cakes have so much patience. Until they melt.

I usually edit the photos on the same day unless it's really late. The shoot usually takes me around one to four hours depending on how happy I am with the styling from the beginning. Sometimes I nail it immediately, but usually not. If you count writing the recipe, baking, test baking, styling, shooting, and editing, it can even take a couple of days.

How do you decide on light, colors, and atmosphere for your images?

I tend to favor darker images—it comes more naturally to me and it's so much easier to edit those too, in my opinion. Also the autumn and winter in Sweden are so long and dark that it's hard to shoot bright images anyway.

I prefer to use only a couple of colors in my styled food images, and different shades within those colors, because I feel that fewer colors make images calmer as there is not too much going on to distract. But there are always exceptions of course! Usually I use complementary colors. I didn't even realize I was doing this in the beginning, but when I learned about color theory, it completely made sense why some colors just looked so good together and created strong contrast in the photo.

Let's say I'm shooting something with purple icing, I'll want to use something yellow in the photo such as beeswax candles or perhaps some yellow flowers. I used to have my kitchen wall painted a dark grey-blue tone, and almost everything looked good in front of it because a lot of baked goods are an orange shade.

Do things ever not go to plan? What do you do when something turns out to be more challenging than you thought?
Oh, absolutely. A month ago, I made a pavlova for a shoot and the bottom was completely black! It didn't show in the photos, though, so I decided to shoot it anyway and just eat the top.

Ever since we moved to the new apartment a few years ago, I have to put a little extra work in when it comes to the light in my photos. That can be challenging compared to my old place, where the light was constantly perfect. Now it's more difficult, mostly because we live across from a bright brick building so when the sun is out, the wall reflects a bright and orange cast into my office/studio! When this happens, I just move to the kitchen. Or I will try to photograph early in the morning or a couple of hours before the sun sets, if I can. I just have to move around a bit more here, and I find that photography takes me longer.

A photoshoot is always all about trial and error. If something isn't working, I take a little break, swap some props out, move things around, and just try to get a new perspective. Of course, sometimes I get frustrated when something isn't working out as I imagined it! But I've learned by now that I just need to take a break, so I go lie down and close eyes. Literally within two minutes of silence, I am ready and it always gets so much better after that!

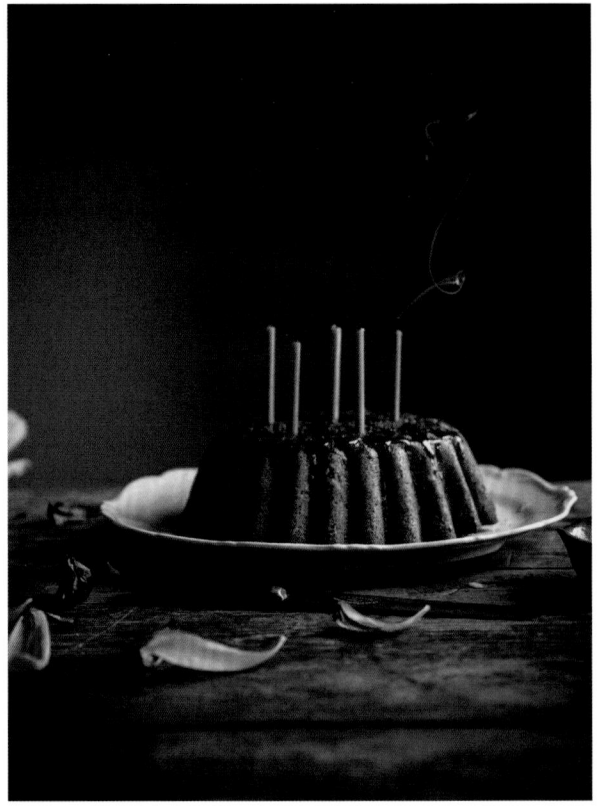

What would your advice be to someone who would like to improve the storytelling in their images?
I like to add small details around the main subject so that the eye wanders around the photograph, and that helps to tell the story about the main subject. For example, apple peels and cinnamon sticks around an apple pie. I also shoot the same scene from many different angles, including wide shots, action shots, maybe some macro shots, and some flat lays. Maybe I'll go outside to pick some apples and bring my camera with me, and then take some photos of the process of making the apple pie—that way I get a variety in the whole series, which is especially important for food stories for my blog. Also, be selective when choosing your images for a photo story. I often remove several before publishing a post—either they're not adding to the story or they're too similar to one another.

Finally, remember that we're all unique and have an individual story to tell. I've seen this so many times at the photography and styling workshops I host. Even if we're all taking photos of basically the same things, each person's photos come out so differently in the end. It's amazing, really!

How do you always keep things fresh and exciting in your photography, even after years of working in the industry?

After working for so long on my own, I've been craving collaboration with others. I've gained new perspectives from collaborations and so much inspiration from other creative people. So many friends have inspired me to think in new ways! I think it's also because I get bored so easily myself that I try to always have a fresh perspective. I'd get tired doing the same thing every time. Incorporating something new and simple such as an antique spoon I haven't used before, a new backdrop, or just shooting in a different location can be so inspiring.

What has been one of your biggest challenges, and what have you learned from it?

When I got the contract for my first cookbook, I was SO scared! I had three months to finish it, while working thirty hours a week at my old "regular" job, so I really spent all my free time working on the book. I knew I could do it all—for some reason I never doubted it, even though I hadn't been baking that long—but I was terrified going to all these important meetings in Stockholm and trying to convince everyone that my book was awesome. It was just a completely new and scary world for me. After a while, I realized, okay, they are all just regular people, too! And they're all just doing their job. That took the edge off for me and it wasn't as scary anymore. But I'm definitely still most comfortable at home in my little town, doing what I love.

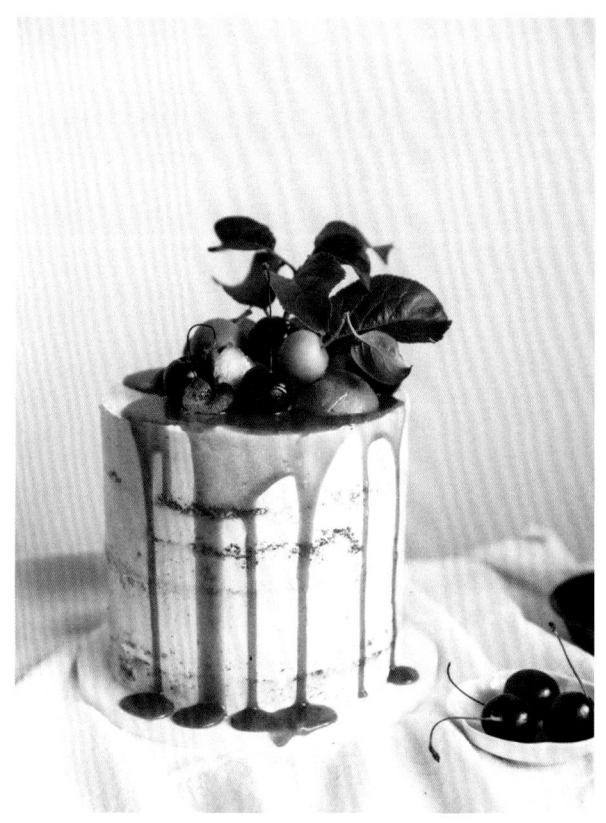

Get more inspired by Linda's work at:

www.callmecupcake.se
www.lindalomelino.se
@linda_lomelino

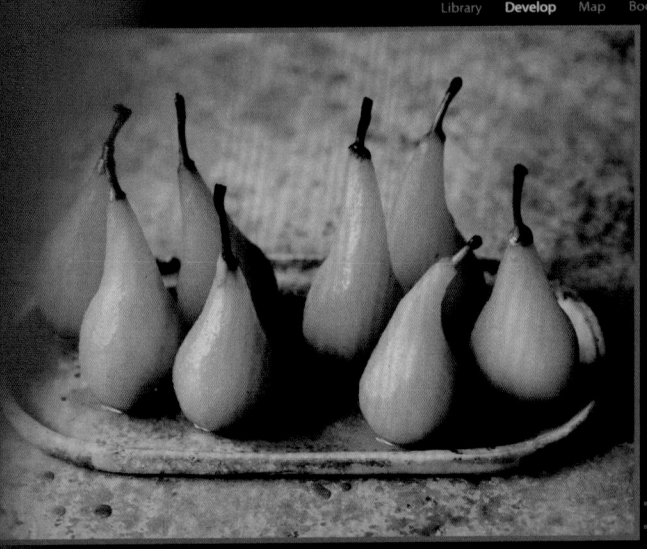

"You don't take an image, you make it."

— Ansel Adams

Library **Develop** Map Book Slideshow Print Web

Histogram ▼

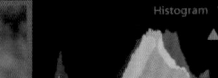

ISO 100   100 mm   f / 5.0   1/10 sec

☐ Original Photo

Profile   Adobe Color

	WB :	Custom
Temp		6000
Tint		+ 10
	Tone	Auto
Exposure		− 0.20
Contrast		+ 5
Highlights		0
Shadows		− 20
Whites		0
Blacks		0
	Presence	
Texture		0
Clarity		+ 5
Dehaze		0
Vibrance		0
Saturation		+ 11

Tone Curve
HSL

★ ★ ★ ★ ★   ▪ ▪ ▪ ▪   ← → ▶   Zoom   Fit   Show Grid: Auto

Previous   Reset

∧ ▭ ⓘ 🔊 ENG

hp

The Art of the Edit

I ignored editing for a long time. Partly because I was overwhelmed by the huge number of settings to learn about, and partly because I believed that to be a great photographer, a photo should be perfect straight out of the camera. I also thought that being stuck in front of a computer would take creative time away from me—time I could spend behind the camera. The truth is, this thinking only limited my work's full potential.

Eventually, I realized that editing my images well was the last piece of the puzzle that my creative style was missing, and I decided to devote more time every day to learn about the tools available in post-production software. What I discovered was that editing not only gave me more control over the look and feel of my images, it also added a professional quality that made my work stand out. Surprisingly (to me), editing turned out to be a super-creative and fun process too, and it is now one of my favorite parts of making an image. I learned once again that you can improve anything if only you open your mind and put some time into it.

Editing is not used just to fix problems; it should be the finishing touch to every single photo. It's the tool that will add that polished quality to your work. Taking a strong image in the first place will of course always give you the best results in post-production, but that doesn't mean you should beat yourself up if your photograph is not perfect straight out of the camera. On many occasions, knowing how to salvage an image in Lightroom or Photoshop has saved me hours of reshooting.

Editing is not faking it either. The purpose of great food portraiture is creating a new reality— a captivating food scene that will evoke positive emotions. It's showing your audience how you see things and what's inside your creative soul. If it inspires someone, that's real!

The essentials of editing

File formats

Raw

A Raw file is the unprocessed file that contains all the data your camera sensor records at the time of taking the photo. Raw files are huge, but because they have so much data, it means they have enormous potential in what you can achieve with them during the post production process. Since the Raw file is unprocessed, it is not ready for display and you wouldn't share it until you have applied a series of edits and saved it as a different format: JPEG, for example. This means you need software to view and process it. When first loading up a Raw image in your software, it will look underwhelming, flat, with low contrast and dull colors. But all the information about the light and color is still available, ready to be transformed into something extraordinary. It takes a little bit of time, patience, and technical know-how, but if you put the effort in, you will be rewarded with images that reflect your vision.

* Large file size
* Needs to be processed
* Takes more time to craft the final image
* Huge control over what your final image looks like

JPEG

A JPEG file is the final product. Setting your camera to take JPEGs means that your camera will make the final decisions of how the image is processed. Out of all the information from the scene, your camera will pick what it thinks is best and discard the rest, and you can never get back what's thrown away. You can still tweak your image in post-production, but your options are limited. However, it is still worth using at times, for example when you need to quickly send a test shot to a client.

* Small file size
* Processed
* Instantly ready for display
* Less control over what your final image looks like

Organization

Think of your collection as a library of images: you need to organize this library into groups and folders that make it easy to navigate. Every photographer will have a different method, but it all comes down to this question: How will I find my images a few months/years from now? You could, for example, divide your photos to each year and/or specific file names; for example "Client work," "Personal projects," or "Travel."

How you name your photoshoots is the most important consideration; it should be something that will bring the shoot to your mind. For my personal work I use this naming convention: [FOOD GROUP]_[SPECIFICS]. A food group could be "salad," "drink," "cookies," "produce," etc.—the category where your dish belongs. Specifics could be, for example, the flavor or something that will remind you about the shoot. For instance, last year I photographed a lot of soups and I used names such as:
Soup_coriander and carrot
Soup_ramen_on cream background
Soup_ramen_with purple radish

You could also add "_raw" and "_final" at the end to keep a Raw folder separate from the final JPEG selection.

For client work, I use this naming convention: [CLIENT NAME]_[DATE–YYMMDD]_[DESCRIPTION]. When I send final JPEGs to a client, I always add my name to the file name.

If you use Lightroom, try color-coding or use collections to organize specific photo groups: for example, landscape-format images. Then when you are looking for a landscape photograph for a website header, for example, you can just click on that collection or the color you chose to tag all your landscape images with, and you will find them all in one place.

Backing up & hard drives

3-2-1 backup strategy
This is a process for backing up your images that I highly recommend. Keep three copies of your files: one working copy and two backup copies, each on its own hard drive. Store one of the backup copies in a remote location (e.g. a deposit safe or a friend's house).

This means you have one file to work with, one backup copy that is always accessible at your studio in case something happens to the working file, and one copy that will be safe at a different location.

My backing-up workflow
When tethering, I always save my files straight onto my working hard drive. Then as soon as the shoot is finished, I will back it up right away (both the Raw and .xmp files—.xmp files essentially record the edits you have made). Once a month I will copy my jobs over to the second backup copy. Every December, I put all the file names from that year into a document that I keep on my computer, and which I label with the hard drive the files are on. Then when I'm looking for a specific photoshoot, I can simply scan through the documents and see which hard drive or folder it's in.

Hard drives
To take good care of the hard drives storing your precious images, be sure to keep them in a cool place (away from direct sunlight), and plug them in from time to time to let the fan work. Don't fill them up completely; it's recommended that you only fill them to 80 or 90 percent.

Editing programs

Choosing an editing program is like picking a camera: we all like to work with different tools. I will be showing you how I like to edit my images in Lightroom Classic, but in other software, many of the same or similar tools will be available. The most common editing programs are Lightroom, Photoshop, and Capture One.

Get familiar with your software of choice, going through each setting with curiosity, checking out what it does. You can always undo what you've done! Your editing software is like a toolbox with different tools available to you. Sometimes you might use just a couple of tools, other times you will use more, depending on the task. You will need to learn to analyze what your specific photograph needs and pick the best tools for it.

Tips

* Find your favorite editing light. I personally prefer to edit in the daylight, and even if I have to edit in the evening, I won't send images to the client until I review them again in the daylight.
* Have a break from the screen. Before I send my images to the client, I also like to have a 30-minute break before a final edit review.
* Always question your workflow. Can the adjustments be applied quicker next time? Can some editing tasks be automated? Are there any adjustments you've never used or always avoid?
* I usually don't delete images unless I have duplicates of the same shot or if they are blurry. How you feel about an image can change over time.
* Keep up with technology. Post-production software is constantly evolving and frequently updated, and in my opinion it's important to stay interested and up to date.

Lightroom library

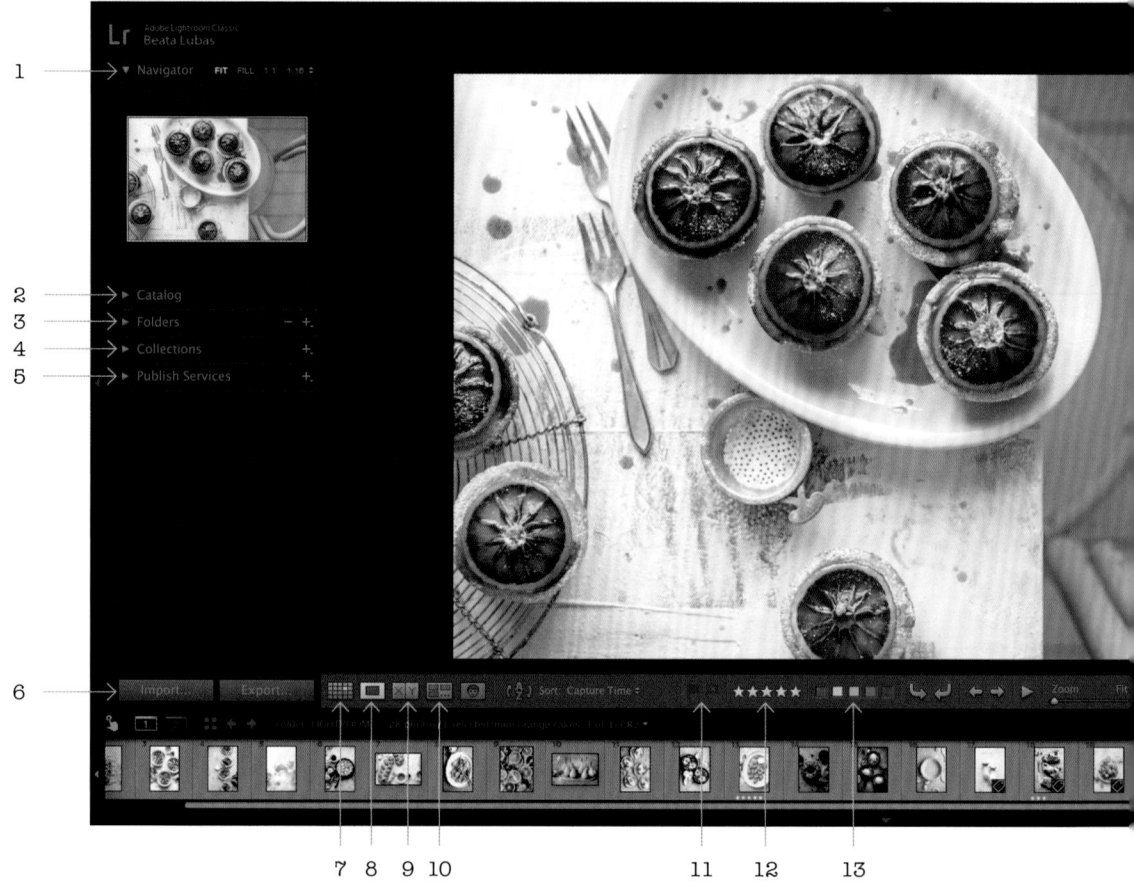

1. Navigator—Used to set the zoom and ratio at which the image you are working on is displayed.

2. Catalog—Lets you navigate through all your photos, quick collections, or just your latest import.

3. Folders—Browse and organize the folders of photos saved on your hard drive.

4. Collections—These are virtual folders (they don't exist physically on your hard drive) which you can create to organize and navigate specific groups of images.

5. Publish Services—Lets you export to your hard drive or to various social media platforms.

6. Import & Export—Import photos from your camera, memory card, or hard drive to Lightroom, and export from Lightroom with various options to control file size, naming conventions, metadata and so on.

7. Grid View—View your images as a grid of thumbnails. A tool

called Painter within Grid view allows you to "spray over" the photos you want with keywords, ratings, metadata, rotation, target collection, and more. Click the spray can icon in the tool bar to use it. The Library Filter bar will help you filter through images if you are looking for a specific photo.

8. Loupe View.

9. Compare two images.

10. Survey view—if you want to compare or view, several images together, highlight the images you want to view and click here to see them all at once.

11, 12, 13. Flag system, star rating, and color labelling: use these to sort and rate your images.

14. Click this triangle to customize your toolbar (Loupe and Grid View will have slightly different options available).

15. Sync Settings—if you want to apply the same settings (e.g., exposure, white balance) over a number of photos, select the

16

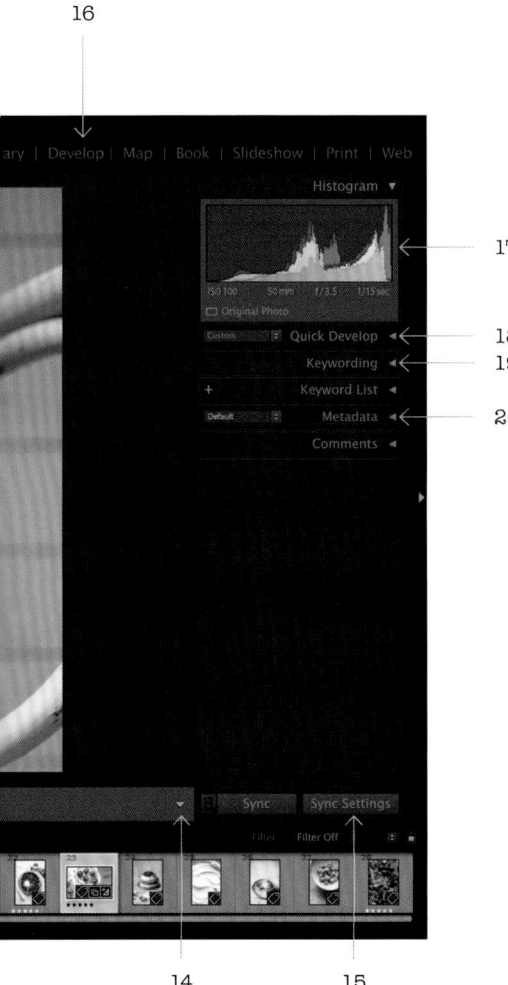

17

18
19
20

14   15

photos you want to sync from and to, and click this.

16. Library / Develop / Map / Book / Slideshow / Print / Web—
the modules you can work within in Lightroom.

17. A histogram of the image you're viewing.

18. Quick Develop—Quickly applies various settings across
one or a number of photos. You won't have the same control
as you do when working in the Develop module.

19. Keywording & Keyword List—add keywords to your
photos to help you sort and find them. The Keyword List
contains all the keywords you have already used, so you
don't end up with lots of slightly different ones.

20. Metadata is the information written into the image
file. This can include your camera and shooting data (such
as lens focal length, aperture settings, etc.), as well as
copyright information and captions.

Tips

* Lightroom itself doesn't store your images, so to use
  this software, first you need to import your images to
  work on. Once the images are edited and ready, export
  them and save in a dedicated space.
* Consider having .xpm files automatically saved with
  your Raw files. (These contain your editing information.)
* Right-click (CTRL-click on Mac) on the background to
  change its color.
* Click the dropdown triangle to see more options for
  each function.
* To create a virtual copy, right-click (CTRL-click on Mac)
  on the image and choose "create virtual copy."
* To highlight two or more images, click on the first
  image, hold CTRL (Windows) or CMD (Mac), and select
  the other image(s).
* To highlight a row of images, click on the first image,
  hold SHIFT, and click on the last image in the row.

Essential Lightroom Library shortcuts

Use CTRL on Windows and CMD on Mac.

* Grid view—G
* Survey view—N
* Loupe view—E
* Show/hide toolbar—T
* Show/hide side panels—TAB
* Full screen preview—F
* Lights out mode—L
* Information about photo (only in Loop view)—I
* Flag system—Picked: P; Rejected: X
* Star rating—1, 2, 3, 4, 5
* Color rating—6, 7, 8, 9
* Rotate left—CTRL/CMD [
* Rotate right—CTRL/CMD]
* Zoom in—CTRL/CMD +
* Zoom out—CTRL/CMD -
* Develop module—D
* To see the full list of shortcuts—CTRL/CMD /

Global adjustments

We've had a brief look at Lightroom Classic's Library module, where you organize and view your images. Now we're moving into the Develop module, where the post-production wizardry happens.

Edits made to images can be thought of as either "global" or "local"; first, we'll discuss the global variety. Global adjustment are edits that are applied throughout the whole image. So, if you add brightness, for example, the entire photo will be brightened. Or if you adjust the orange hues, all the orange hues in the frame will be affected. Global adjustments are the foundation of your image and are a great starting point for stylizing your photo.

Panels

Lightroom's Develop module is simple to navigate. The image you're working on appears in the center, and on the left- and right-hand side are panels, under which you can find your tools. On the right-hand side, you will see the following panels:

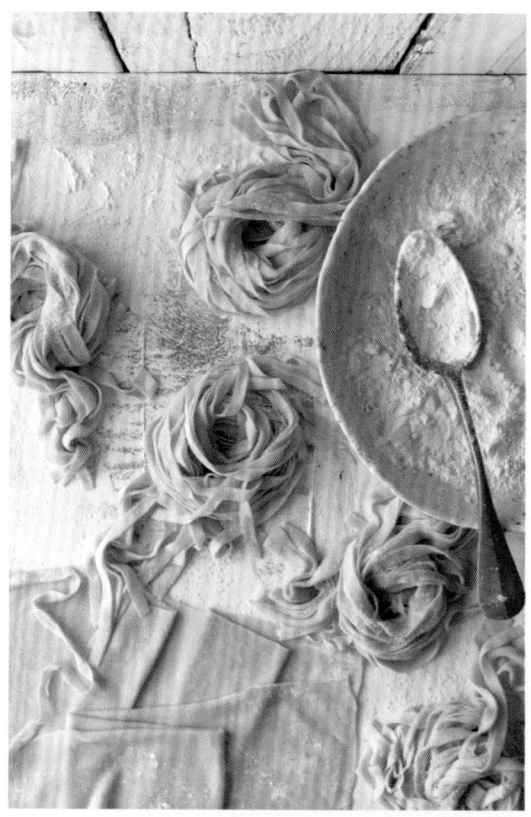

* **Basic**—Includes all the basic adjustments, such as white balance, exposure, and contrast.
* **Tone Curve**—Either brighten or darken each tone individually or add color to a specific tone.
* **HSL/Color**—Adjust the hue, saturation, and luminance of individual colors in your images.
* **Split Toning**—Add and adjust color of your highlights and/or shadows.
* **Detail**—Contains powerful tools for sharpening and noise reduction.
* **Lens Correction**—If your lens distorts an image or adds a vignette, you can correct it here.
* **Transform**—Straighten the perspective if your angle is slightly off. If you use this tool, check "constrain crop" to remove any white lines that might appear on the edges of the frame.
* **Effects**—Allows you to apply vignettes and grain.
* **Calibration**—Adjust the camera's Raw color interpretation for a particular camera or image.

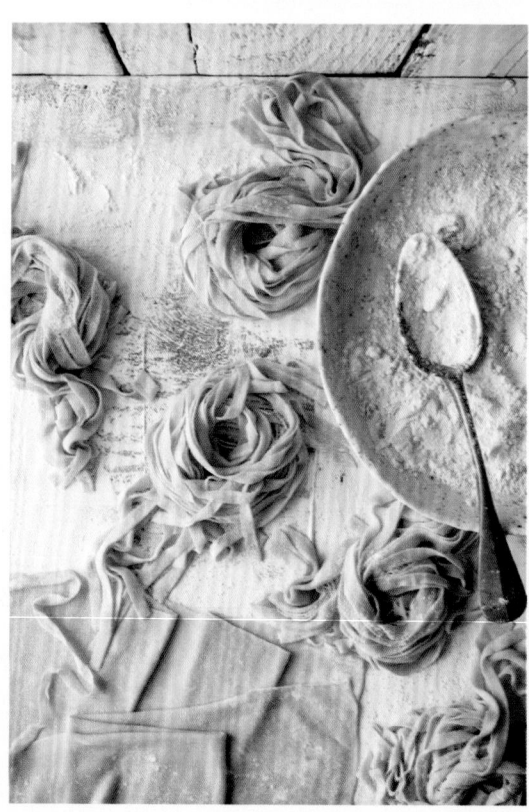

Sometimes it only takes few sliders to make an image pop (left)

I made the following adjustments in the **Basic panel**: Highlights +8, Shadows +13, Whites +20, Blacks +20 and Clarity +15. And in the **HSL/Color panel**, I adjusted the following on the Yellow slider: Hue -10 and Luminance +10. Job done!

Other times, it takes a little more (right)

First I rotated the image slightly in the **Transform panel** to ensure the horizontal lines were running straight. Then to fix the white balance, I clicked on **White balance selector** in the **Basic panel** and dragged it over on my image to look for a spot with a neutral grey color where R, G, B have roughly the same value (see the bottom of the square in the middle picture). Once I found something close enough, I clicked again and the software automatically corrected the white balance. This is a good starting point, but always remember that sometimes you might want it a little bit cooler or warmer than what Lightroom calls "neutral." Here though, Lightroom did a good enough job, moving the white balance from 4800K (as shot) to 5800K, but I moved the tint from +5 to +10 as it looked slightly too green to me.

Additionally, I made the following adjustments in the **Basic panel**: Contrast +10, Highlights +15, Whites +20, Shadows +15, Blacks +10 and Clarity +10. And in the **HSL/Color panel**: Orange Hue -5, Saturation 5 and Luminance +20.

Tip

Every setting has a little icon like this on the left-hand side of the panel: you can toggle it on and off to see your image with and without an effect applied.

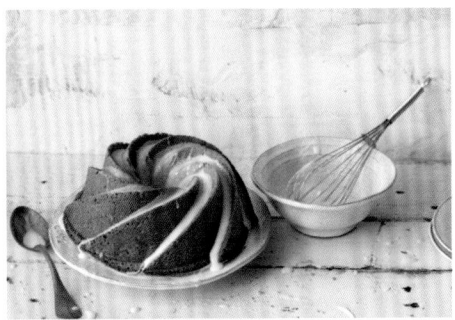
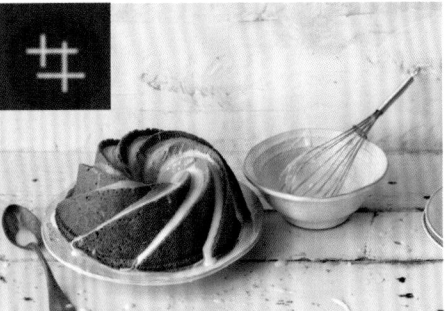
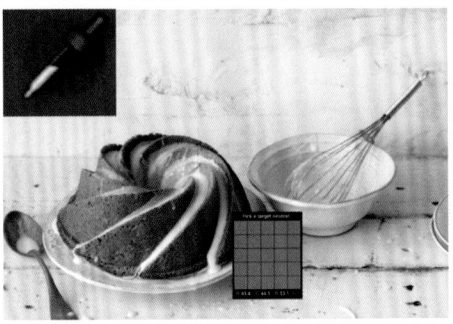
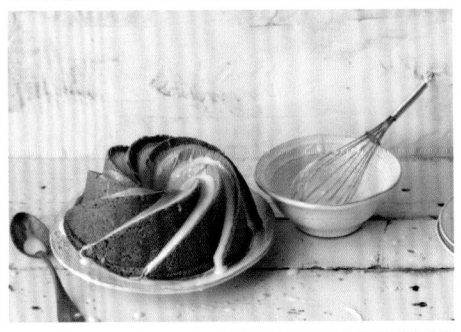
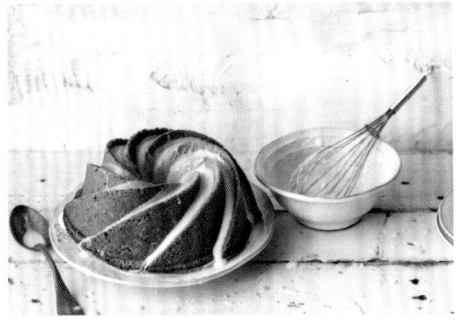

Point curve vs region curve

Tone curve is such a powerful and important function in your editing toolbox: it allows you to tweak each tone to your liking to create a stronger image. You can brighten and darken each tone (highlights, lights, darks, shadows) individually with little more than one click of a button. Lightroom offers two different kinds of curve under this tool: **Region curve** and **Point curve**. There is a small box with a curve symbol, found in the bottom-right corner, which you can click on to swap between the curves.

To adjust a **Region curve**, move the sliders to the right to brighten or to the left to darken a specific tone. As you do this, you'll see how the tone curve bends automatically too. To adjust a **Point curve**, click on the white line in the specific tone you'd like to adjust and you'll see a dot appearing in that exact spot. Drag the dot up or down to brighten or darken any specific tone.

If you're only just beginning to use curves, **Region curve** is an easier place to start than **Point curve**. However, once you feel more confident, **Point curve** will give you much more control.

Tip

Click on this icon in the top left corner of the **Tone curve** and drag it anywhere on your picture to see which tone this particular part of the image is. If you drag it onto a deep shadow for example, a little dot will appear in the Shadows region of the curve. Using this tool, on the picture click and hold on the tone you want to adjust, and then scroll up or down with your other finger slightly to make this tone lighter or darker. **Tone curve** is very sensitive so the tiniest movement will make quite a difference.

Region curve

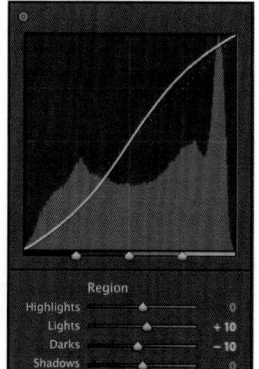

Point curve

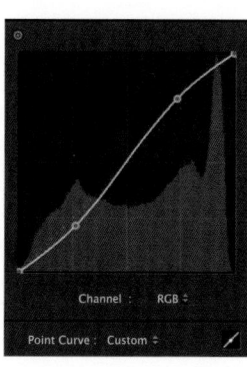

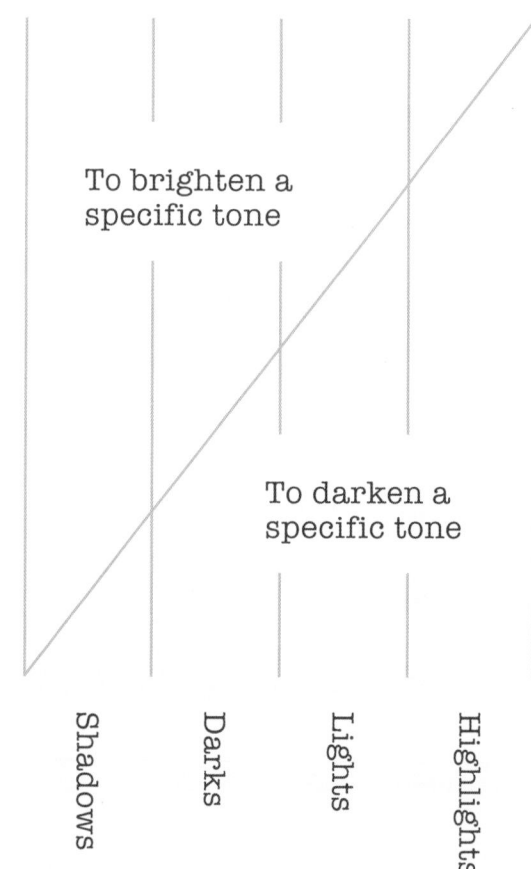

To brighten a specific tone

To darken a specific tone

Shadows

Darks

Lights

Highlights

Playing with tones

I wanted to bring this image to life by adding a little contrast. I did so by making my light tones brighter and dark tones a touch darker, creating a subtle S-curve (first example). It's worth remembering that as you boost contrast in your images, the saturation also goes up, so in this example I made sure to go back to the **Basic panel** to set my Saturation to -5.

An interesting thing happens when you lift the end of your **Point curve** on the left (shadow) side. It makes the blacks less black and more "milky," which gives your image a "filmic" and faded look (second example).

Within **Point curve**, you can also add or remove color from a specific tone. When you select **Channel: RGB**, you'll see that you can choose **Red**, **Green**, or **Blue** from a dropdown menu. By selecting any of them and dragging your curve up or down, you can add color to any tone in your photo to create a unique mood. In the **Red tone curve**, you can add red by dragging it up and cyan by dragging it down. In **Green**, up to add green, down for magenta. And in **Blue**, up to add blue and down for yellow. It's also an effective tool to balance out any color cast in your image. If your photo, for example, has a yellow color cast, you can neutralize it by adding an opposite color (in this case, blue) to the tones.

In the third example, I locked my tone curve in the middle by adding a point there, and then added blue to the darks and shadows, which made this image appear much cooler. When you do this, the upper part of the curve will bend automatically in the other direction— here, adding just a touch of yellow to the lights and highlights. If I didn't want this effect, I would need to lift that side back up a bit. To delete a point, right-click on it and press delete.

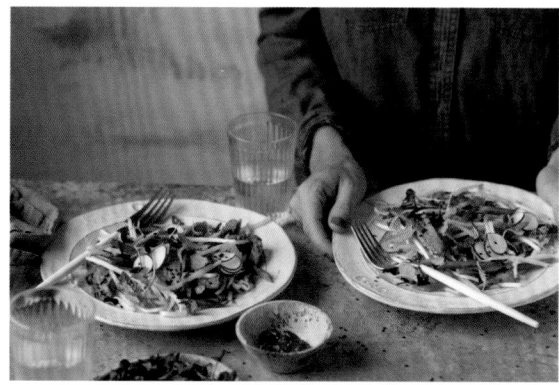

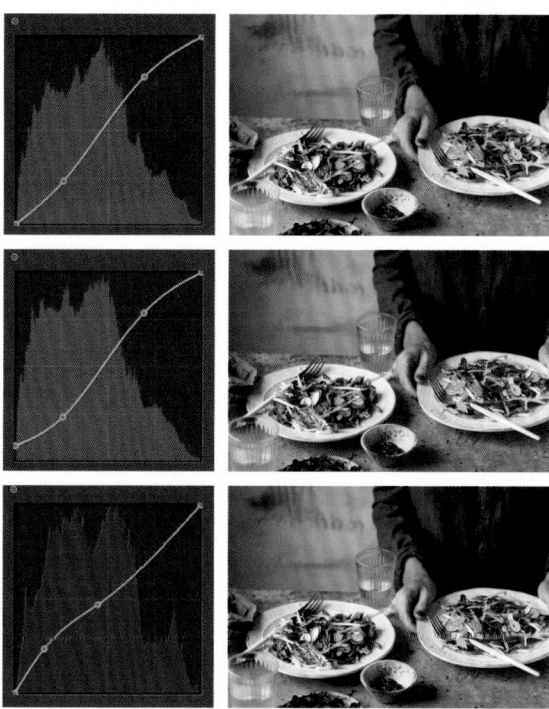

Tip

If you find a tone curve that you use often, consider saving it as a preset. All you have to do is press the dropdown box by "Custom," and select save. The separate box will show up, where you will need to name your new tone curve and hit save again.

Enhancing colors (top)

The **HSL/Color panel** gives you incredible control over how your colors look. Lightroom divides images into eight basic colors: red, orange, yellow, green, aqua, blue, purple, and magenta. Under each color you will see three settings to adjust. **Hue** is the precise shade you see; **Saturation** is how intense that color is; and **Luminance** is how bright that color is.

How much color enhancement is needed will vary from scene to scene. Beautiful colors are crucial in food photography, but they can be easily overdone: stand back and ensure the colors are pleasant to look at.

In this example I made the following changes on the Red slider: Hue -23, Saturation 19, Luminance +10. On the Orange slider, Hue -4, Saturation 36, Luminance +25. I also made the image pop a little more by adding a little color to the Highlights in **Split toning**: Hue 340, Saturation 5; and to the Shadow settings: Hue 2, Saturation 5.

Changing colors (bottom)

Color can be distracting too. If the background or a secondary element is pulling the eye more than the hero subject, you can desaturate it or change its color to bring your hero subject forward.

By making changes on the Blue slider to Hue -40, Saturation -25 and Luminance +30, I created a gorgeous teal background, which also made this a more balanced photo. In the second example I desaturated the blue completely, and I was pleasantly surprised by what a great effect it had.

Tip

Click on this icon in the top-left corner of the **HSL/Color panel** and drag it anywhere on your picture to see what Hue Lightroom "reads" it as (it will appear highlighted in your **HSL/Color panel**). On the picture, click and hold on the color you want to adjust, then change the hue by scrolling up or down with your finger. You can do the same with saturation and luminance too.

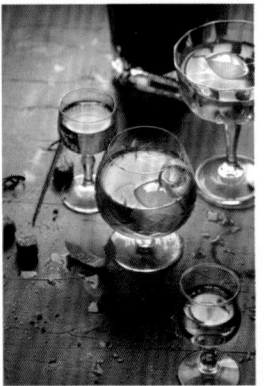 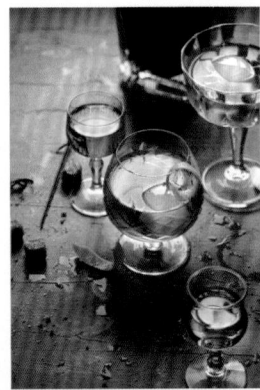

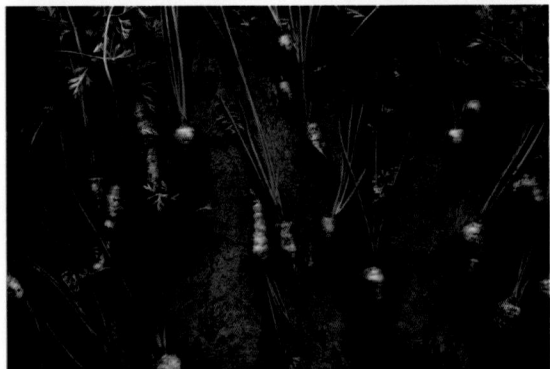

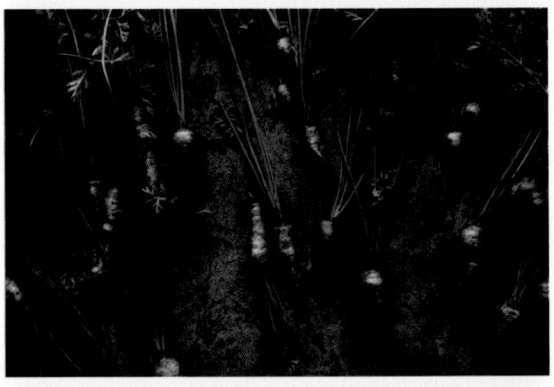

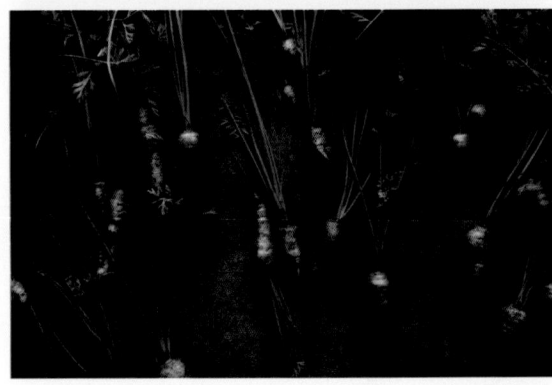

Noise reduction (top)

You will find the **Noise reduction** function within the **Detail panel**. I highly recommend clicking the **Zoom** icon and dragging it over your photo to scan and recognize the level and type of grain you're dealing with. Color grain can be recognized by multicolored pixels in an area of the photo that should be a solid color; luminance grain is less colorful and shows up as a fine texture. In this image, I am tackling luminance grain.

The **Luminance slider** reduces the grain in the image (there is an equivalent slider for color grain), but since noise reduction is a process of smoothing the pixels, it does mean losing some fine detail along the way—moderation is your friend here. Very often, if you move the slider all the way, your photo will look unrealistically smooth. The **Detail slider** allows you to recover some of the lost detail, but when you use this slider too much, you will be adding grain back into your image.

Last is the **Contrast slider**, which allows you to recover some of the contrast you lose during noise reduction—again, you have to be careful not to add too much noise back in.

Changes: Luminance +55, Detail +30, Contrast +10.

Creative cropping (bottom)

The **Cropping tool** is a great tool to use if you want to crop something out of the frame, but it also gives you an opportunity to find "new" photos within the photos you already have! This is the first tool in the toolbar right under the histogram.

In this example the scene is the subject of the photograph, but that also means that some details are lost, because there is so much to look at. Cropping heavily into one specific area of the scene helps the viewer pay attention to the details. You can crop freehand or on a fixed ratio (e.g., 1:1 if you wanted a square crop for Instagram). Clicking the **Padlock** icon locks the ratio, and selecting **Tools**; **Crop guide overlay** lets you crop your composition to certain guides.

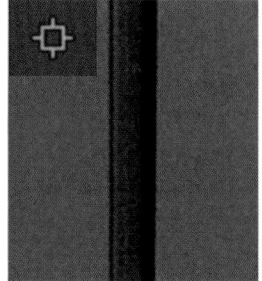

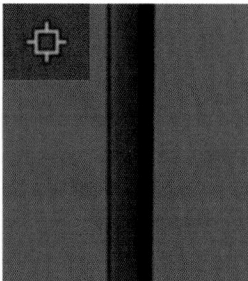

Original   After noise reduction

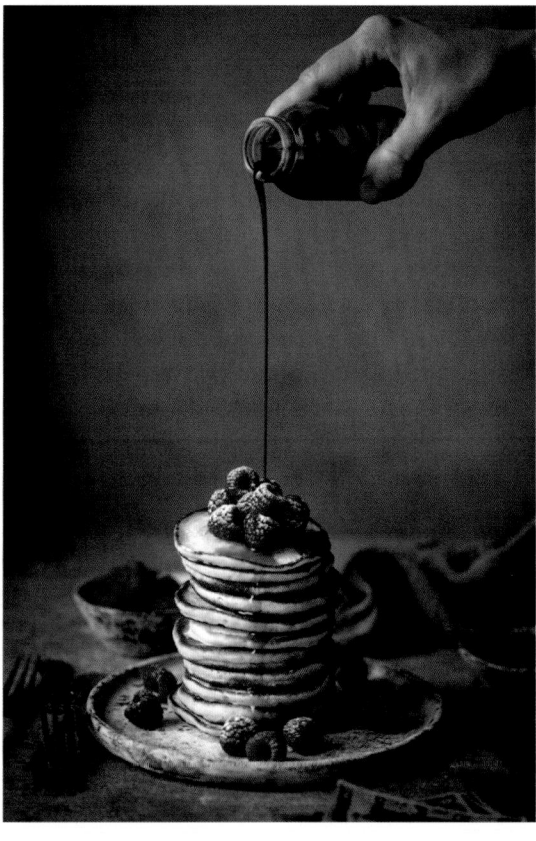

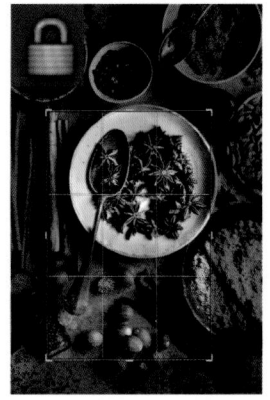
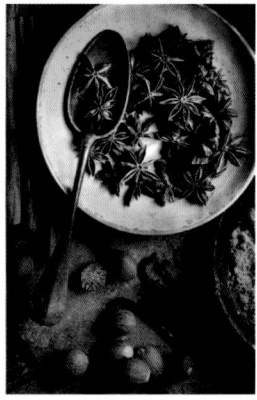

Local adjustments

Local adjustments affect only a selected part of your image. For example, if you want to brighten only your hero subject, leaving the rest of the photo untouched, you can do that.

Tools available:
* **Spot removal**—Lets you remove imperfections by **Cloning** or **Healing**.
* **Red eye correction**—Probably not very useful for food photography, but allows you to fix any red eyes appearing in your photos.
* **Graduated filter**—Allows you to apply effects on a gradient. You can also control how sharply the gradient will be applied (i.e., with a hard transition or a smooth one). Click, hold, and drag to apply.
* **Radial filter**—Applies an elliptical mask to a size and area of your choice. You can make selective adjustments within or outside that area. If you want to apply edits within the radius, you need to have Invert selected. Click, hold, and drag to apply.
* **Adjustment brush (+/-)**—Allows you to apply adjustments freehand by "brushing" over the area you want to work on. You can subtract areas from your selection by clicking Erase. You can change the size, feathering, flow, and density of this tool.
* **Range mask**—Allows you to apply local adjustments to a selected range of either tones (e.g., just to highlights) or colors (e.g., just to oranges). To activate this tool, you need to apply **Adjustment brush**, **Radial filter**, or **Graduated filter** first.

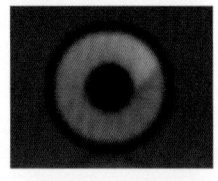

Spot removal

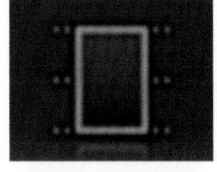

Red eye correction

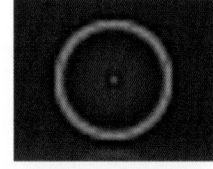

Graduated filter

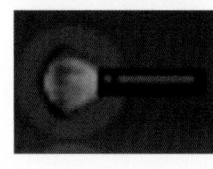

Radial filter

Adjustment brush

Tip

The **Graduated filter** and **Radial filter** adjustments have a Brush feature that allows you to extend the area of the mask or remove the adjustment from a certain area within the mask: not to be confused with the **Adjustment brush**.

Above: The local adjustments available in Lightroom Classic. You can find these adjustments in the toolbar under the histogram.

Even exposure (top)

One of my favorite ways to use the **Graduated filter** is to even out the exposure. In this example, the right-hand side of the frame has a strong shadow, which I wanted to reduce to create a softer look. I placed a **Graduated filter** vertically and increased the overall Exposure by +0.41 and the Shadows by +50. This made the image look more balanced right away, but there was another shadow to tackle by the small prop. To reduce that shadow and remove its blue hue, I zoomed in on the photograph, then used the **Adjustment brush** to brush over the shadow with precision, and moved the Shadows slider to +80 and the Temperature slider to +12.

Making your subject stand out (bottom)

When you apply a **Radial filter**, you can choose to make changes to either what's outside or what's inside of the radius. In this example, I applied a first **Radial filter** (feathering +15) over my dish to adjust Clarity +25, Shadows -11 and Exposure -0.26 in the scene, but without affecting the curry. To remove these adjustments from the bowl of cashews, I clicked on the mask's Brush tool (on the top of the panel) with Erase (on the bottom of the panel) selected, and brushed this part out.

I then applied second **Radial filter** (feathering +100), selecting Invert to make changes only to the inside of the radius, then gave the curry a little extra pop by adding Brightness +0.67 and Warmth +5.

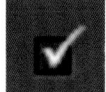

Tip

Check and uncheck the box beside Show Selected Mask Overlay or press O to view where the mask is applied. By pressing Shift and O you can change the color of the mask too.

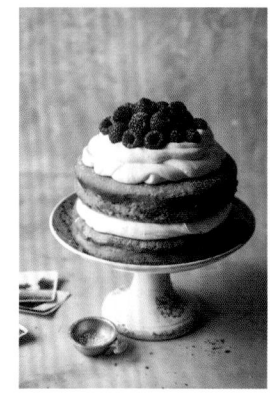
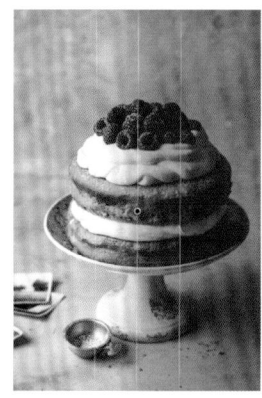
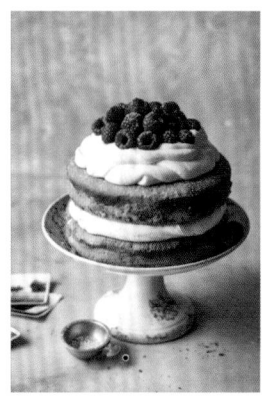
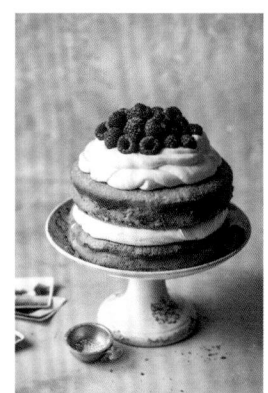
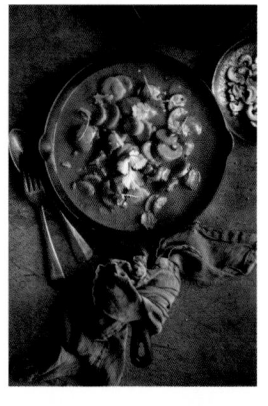
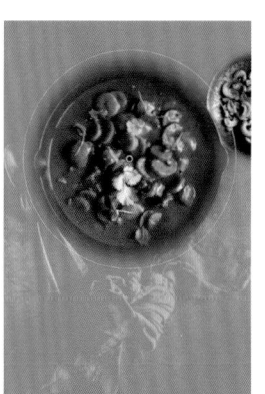
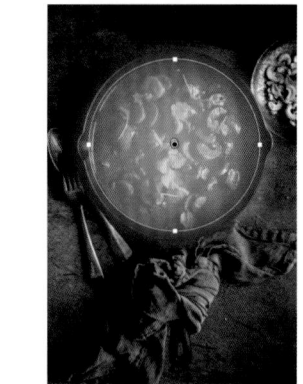
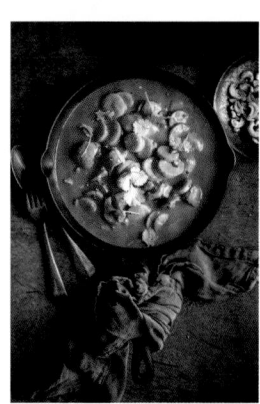

Mix & match your adjustments

You can apply as many global and local adjustments as you like, mixing and matching them to achieve the desired effect.

1. Global Adjustments

I began by moving Exposure to -0.26 to make the image slightly darker. I then made the following changes, also in the **Basic panel**: Shadows -30, Blacks -20, Clarity +10. I made a subtle S-curve in the **Tone curve panel** to add contrast. In the **Effects panel**, I added a delicate **Vignette**.

2. Radial filter + Adjustment brush

I then applied an inverted **Radial filter** to the plate to brighten it up with Exposure +0.46, Highlights +5 and Whites +5. I selected the **Adjustment brush** and brushed over the honey to add Clarity +10, then I clicked onto the white rectangle with an X by Color and chose Hue 39 and Saturation 46% to enhance the color of the honey without affecting the skin tones.

3. Range mask with Brush

To change the color of the dress I applied a **Graduated filter** over the whole frame and switched on a **Range mask**. Holding down the Shift key with **Color range selector** selected, I clicked on a few areas of the dress to let Lightroom know I wanted to make changes only to the area of the photo that was this specific color. Even though I moved the Amount (range) slider to 0, Lightroom was getting confused, reading the side of the plate and the tattoos as being the same hue as the dress—this happens sometimes! I picked the Brush, then Erase, and brushed out those areas, then I applied Hue 238, Saturation 62% for some complementary color magic. To make the most out of the color change, you might have to play with the saturation, temperature, and tint sliders in the mask's panel. Here, the dress was fairly neutral so the color change was applied easily.

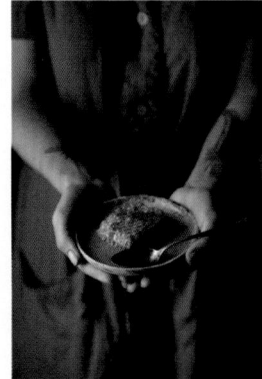
Original

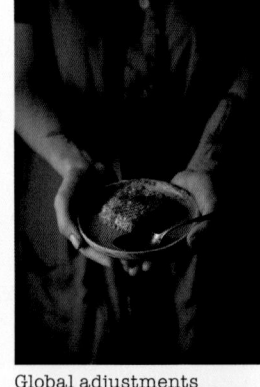
Global adjustments

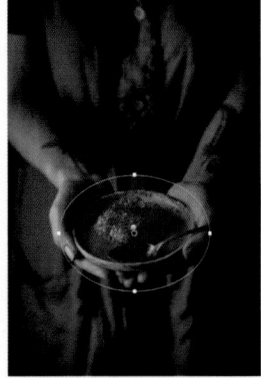
Radial filter

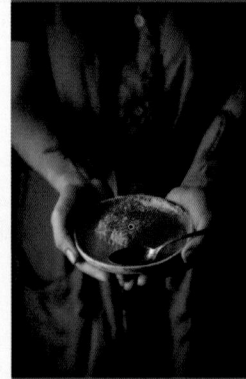
Adjustment brush

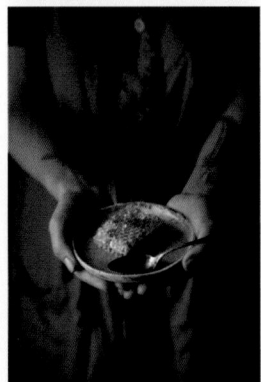
Effects applied to honey

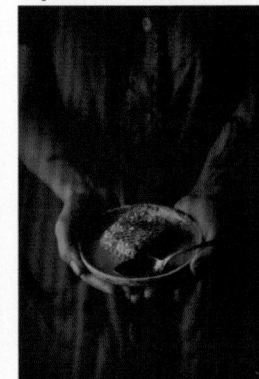
Graduated filter

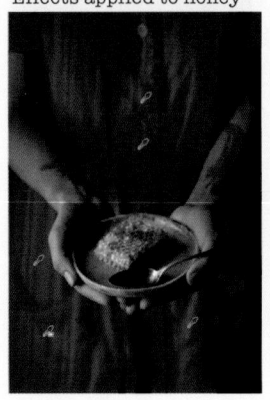
Range mask

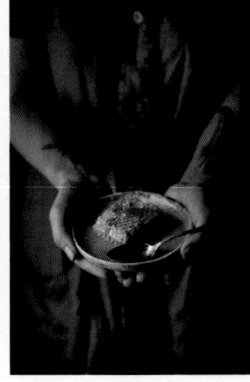
Final image

Editing for mood

Sometimes when you edit, it's just about fixing a particular problem in the image. Other times, you're looking to create or enhance a mood or atmosphere. When I begin to edit, I always consider whether I am editing for a bright look, a dark look, or somewhere in the middle. This then gives me the first step of my editing workflow, as illustrated by the diagram on the right: am I adding light (for bright images) or am I taking light away (for dark images)? Then I will decide on the white balance: warmer for a more comforting and cosier image; cooler for a fresh, crisp, or moody look; or perhaps I want to keep it neutral. The final choice to make is whether I am going for something soft (softer shadows, less saturated colors, and a gentler contrast) or something more dramatic (darker and longer shadows, more vivid colors with more obvious contrast).

It all goes back to these questions: How do you want your viewer to feel? What kind of atmosphere do you want to create?

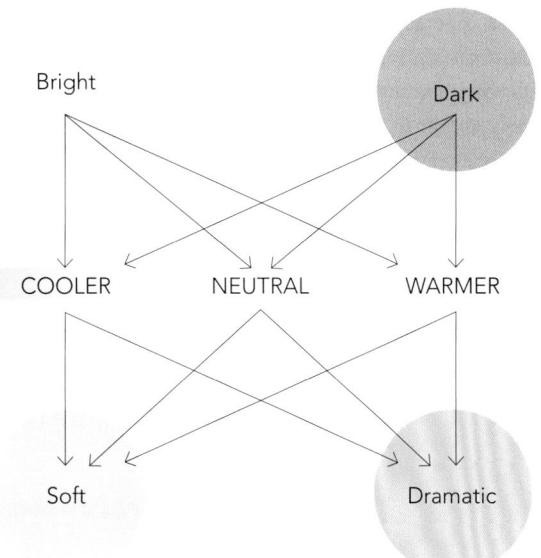

All eyes on the hero

Earlier in the book we looked at how you can draw more attention to your subject. This applies to post-production too, so when I edit I always think about how I can enhance my hero to make it more prominent. Here are few tricks I like to use local adjustments for:

* **Make it brighter**—The lightest area of an image is where the eye naturally travels, and darker areas help to direct it there. For that reason I often make the whole image slightly darker, and then add some brightness to my hero only. This technique works really well for overall darker images such as the honey image on the opposite page. A subtle vignette can help to emphasize this effect too.

* **Enhance its color**—Rich colors catch our attention first, so I like to make sure that colors found in my dish are beautiful (but look natural!). If a background or a supporting element has a distracting hue or is too saturated or too vibrant, I will change its color or desaturate it slightly in post-production.

* **Make it pop with contrast**—Add a touch more clarity (midtone contrast) or contrast to the hero than to the rest of the frame to make it stand out more. I find this trick works best for three-quarter-angle or straight-on images with a soft and blurry background. Always make sure the subject doesn't start looking dry.

* **Keep it balanced**—The key is to draw the eye without making your techniques too obvious, so always keep the word balance in mind.

Dark, dramatic waffles

I (almost) never underexpose my dark images in camera, so that I have more details to work with. For those more dark and dramatic photos, I like to play with enhancing the shadows and contrast, making my scene slightly darker to than brighten the most important elements in the frame for more visual interest.

Graduated filter

The first thing I did was even the exposure by applying a **Graduated filter** to the top part of the frame and moving the Exposure slider to -0.50. I used the mask's **Brush** with Erase selected to brush out the areas that I didn't want to be affected (such as the plate).

Global adjustments

Next, I moved the **White balance** from 5500K to 4700K, I darkened the **Exposure** by -0.24 and then I added a little contrast with a **Tone curve**, but I lifted its end slightly. I then moved these sliders in the **Basic panel**: Highlights +10, Whites +20, Shadows -21, Blacks -15, Clarity +10, Saturation -5. In the **HSL/Color panel**, I used the Orange and Red sliders to enhance the colors of the food. On the Orange slider: Hue -10, Saturation 5, Luminance +15; on the Red slider, Hue -9, Saturation 2.

Radial filters

I applied a first **Radial filter** (inverted) on the top plate with Exposure +0.13 and Saturation 6, then right-clicked (CTRL-click on Mac), duplicated the filter and applied it to the other plate; here I adjusted only Exposure +0.44.

Graduated filter with brush

I applied a final **Graduated filter** to the entire frame but brushed out every element to apply changes only to the background (I could also have done this with a **Range mask** if the background was a different color), where I adjusted Clarity +20. In this example, adding clarity to the whole image made the waffles look a bit dry.

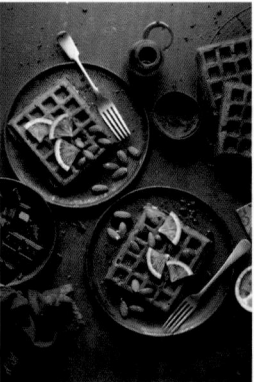
Original

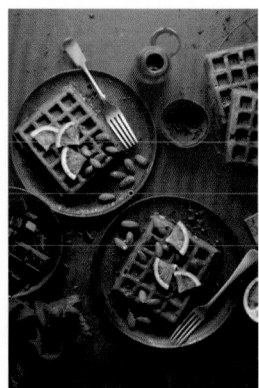
Graduated filter

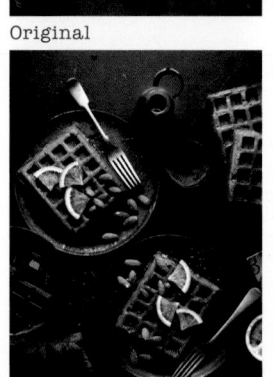
Global adjustments

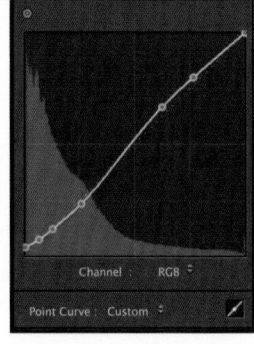
Tone curve

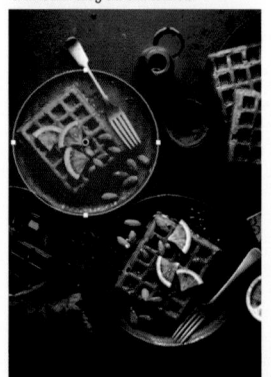
First Radial filter

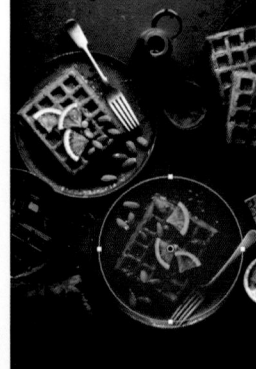
Second Radial filter

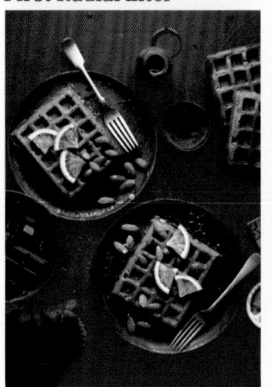
Graduated filter with brush

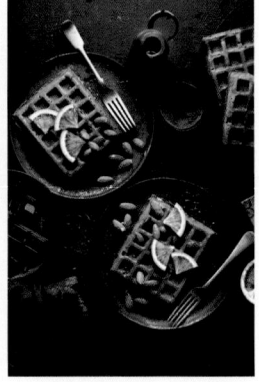
Final image

Bright, airy pavlova

My vision was to create a bright and soft image, but as the weather and the small window I had to work with had other ideas, I achieved it in Lightroom instead. For bright and soft photographs, I like to have an even exposure throughout the frame, and I focus on softening the shadows and enhancing the whites and highlights. Here, I kept the image on the cooler side for that crisp feel, and added a touch of contrast to the strawberries to make them pop a little more.

Graduated filters
I used a **Graduated filter** to lighten the shadow, with the following settings applied: Warmth -4, Exposure +0.44, Whites +5, Shadows +62. As the shadow darkened towards the top of the frame, I had to apply a second **Graduated filter** and target that part with Exposure +0.73 to make it bright throughout.

Global adjustments
I lifted the **Tone curve** to add brightness to selected tones, then I made the following changes on the **Basic panel**: Highlights +15, Whites +10, Shadows +20, Clarity +10, Blacks +10. And on the **HSL/Color panel**: Red slider, Hue -20, Saturation 20, Luminance +15; **Split toning**: Hue 229 and Saturation 15% in the shadows.

Radial filter
I then applied an inverted **Radial filter**, targeting the strawberries with the following settings: Highlights +15, Whites +15, Shadows -20.

Adjustment brushes
I used an **Adjustment brush** on the right-hand side of the meringue to reduce the shadow with Exposure +0.10 Shadows +17 and Temperature -5, then restored some textural details on the left-hand side of the meringue by applying another **Adjustment brush** there (not shown) with Exposure -0.35, Highlights -21, Whites -5. If my original image had been overexposed, I would not have been able to get these details back.

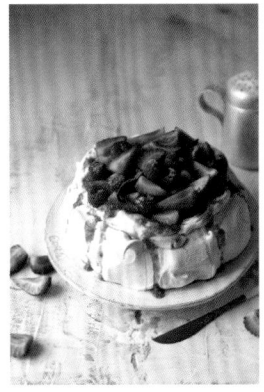

Original

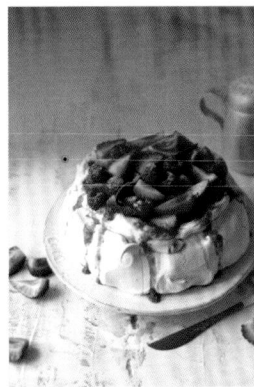

First Graduated filter

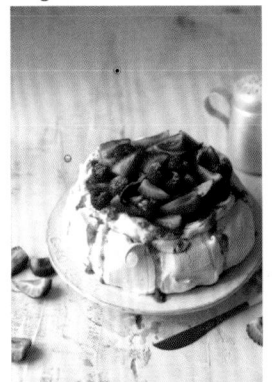

Second graduated filter

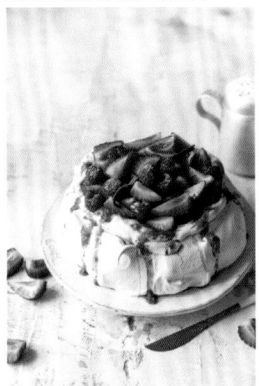

Global adjustments

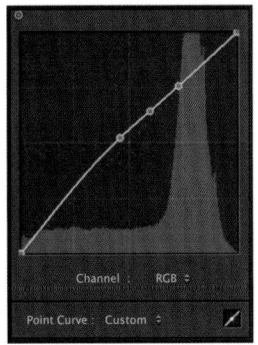

Tone curve

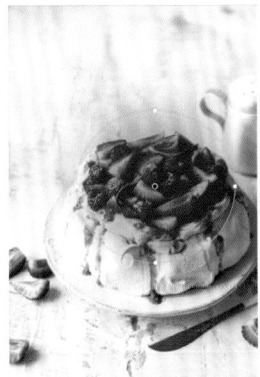

Radial filter

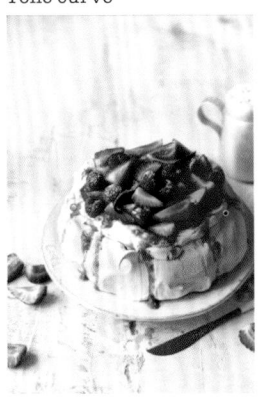

Adjustment brush

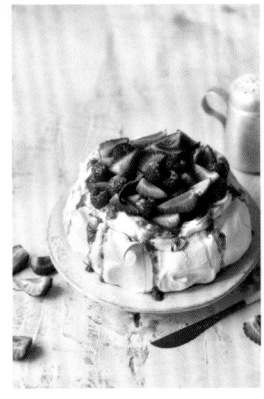

Final image

Retouching for details

Things are not always as perfect as we would like them to be, and that's when a few simple retouching tools can come handy. These tools give you the ability to clean up and make tweaks to your image, often saving hours of preparing and reshooting the dish.

The tools we'll explore include **Clone** and **Heal** in Lightroom, **Spot healing brush**, and **Clone stamp** in Photoshop.

Cloning works by copying pixels from another area of the image, allowing you to cover imperfections as well as replicating parts of your image. Healing tools blend pixels from around the selected area or from another source point, making it a good tool to use for fixing textural imperfections in your food.

Drips & pimples

The caramel poured perfectly over the cake… except for one drip. Attempting to fix it with a drip bottle might have ruined the whole cake, so instead I decided to clone one of the more successful drips. I used Photoshop's **Clone stamp** tool, with which you first select the "source" or area to clone from by pressing Alt (Windows) or Option (Mac) and clicking, and then you stamp it onto the destination or area you want to fix. Here, I didn't just clone another drip—I copied right side of one drip and left side from another drip for a more natural result.

You can choose the perfect sized brush, the edges (i.e., feathered or hard), and opacity of the brush, too. It's worth using the zoom and working slowly, taking care to building up to a result that looks authentic.

Because I wanted to use backlight, a few pimples were showing up on the surface of the caramel. Here, it was the **Spot healing brush** that saved the day. This is such a simple and effective tool to use for small textural imperfections; all you've got to do is select the size of the brush to perfectly cover your spot and click on it. Photoshop will automatically blend it in.

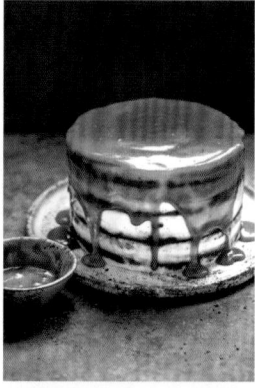

Original

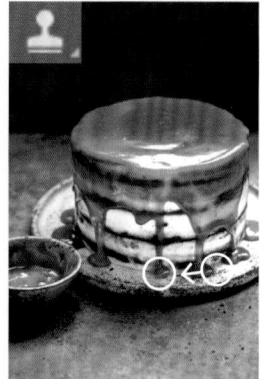

Clone 1

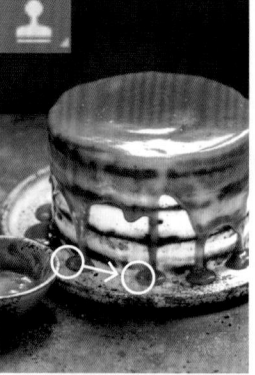

Clone 2

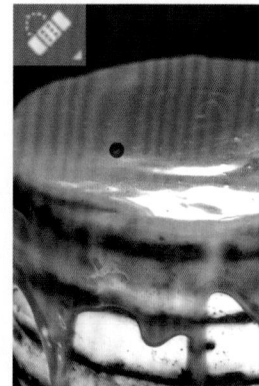

Spot heal

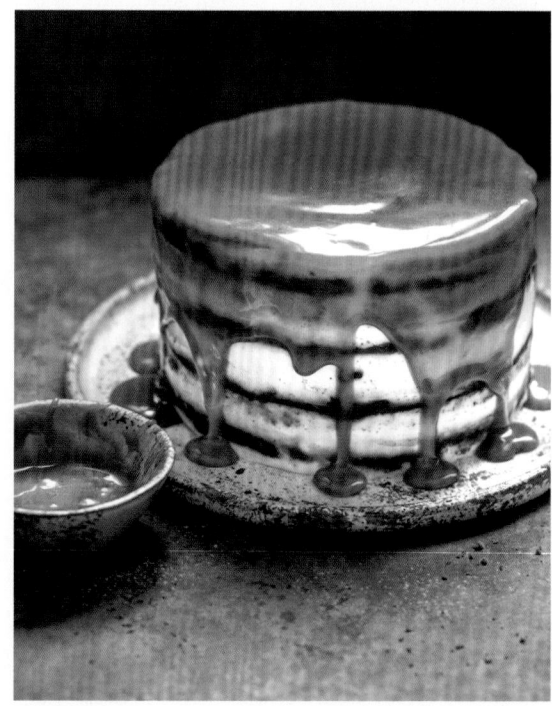

Final image

Surface distractions

Sometimes our surfaces are not as big as we need them to be for a certain shot. I never stress over it too much, because I know that as long as I leave a little negative space, I can clone another part of the surface onto the missing part. For this image, I used Lightroom's **Clone** tool. I started by selecting the area where the background was missing, after which Lightroom suggests the area to copy from, and then it automatically replaces and covers the respective area. If Lightroom doesn't choose a good source point, you can change the area to clone from by dragging it with your mouse.

For seamless retouching when using the **Clone** tool, make sure that the areas you're cloning from and to have the same exposure and depth of field.

I also decided to fix the line on the background, which was a little distracting. I retouched this using Lightroom's **Heal** tool, which works in a very similar way to Photoshop's **Spot healing brush**.

Sometimes, you can miss things when you're looking at the photograph at a size where it fills the computer screen. It's a good idea to zoom in on your image and scan it inch by inch to check that there aren't any distracting imperfections that could be removed.

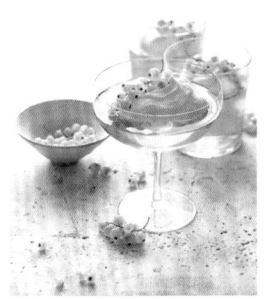
Original

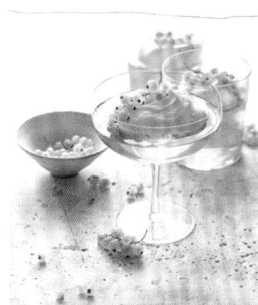
Cloning the background

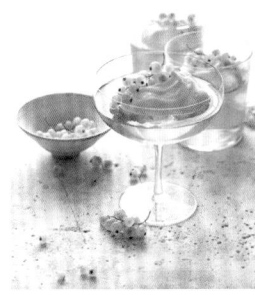
After cloning

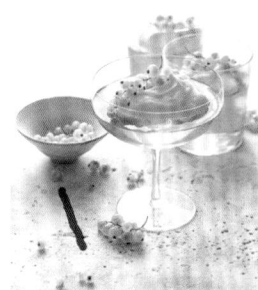
Heal

Tip

In Lightroom's Develop module, press Y to see the photograph before and after the editing.

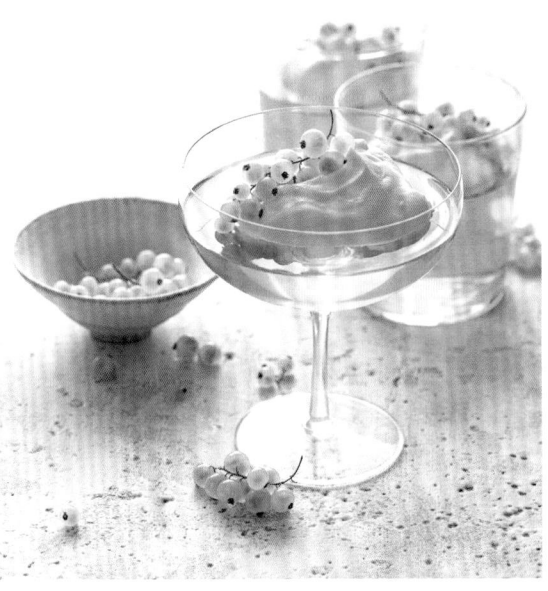
Final image

Interview:
Rachel Korinek

I am delighted to share a conversation with one of my favorite photographers on the planet! Rachel pushes food photography forwards; she digs into every area of photography and generously shares her knowledge on her blog, Two Loves Studio. She has an incredible eye for details and although we have known each other for years, her approach to photography never ceases to amaze me.

I am always fascinated by how you bring the best out of every picture. I'd love you to tell us about your approach to post-production and what you pay attention to when you edit. Could you please walk us through what goes on in your head when you sit down with your images in Lightroom?
When I first sit down to edit or when I am tethering during a shoot, I start by thinking about the light I am shooting. Based on that, I think about the workflow I will use to start shaping the image. I don't use presets for reasons you'll discover below. I make my base global edits, then I start tweaking and perfecting with local adjustments.

When I'm on a shoot, I compare the images as I go; seeing how they feel together as a set, and make any adjustments as needed. After the shoot, I just look at the images on screen for a while. I might go away and make a cup of tea or clean up, but keep popping back to feel the images. Sometimes having that break can allow us to see new things.

When it comes to finding a photography style I feel like post-production is one of the most important components. What helped you find your signature editing style?
When I first started out in photography, I didn't really edit much at all. I first tried out VSCO presets—they are nice, but they weren't me. I realized that pretty quickly. It wasn't until I read a quote by Ansel Adams, "We don't take a photograph—we make one" that

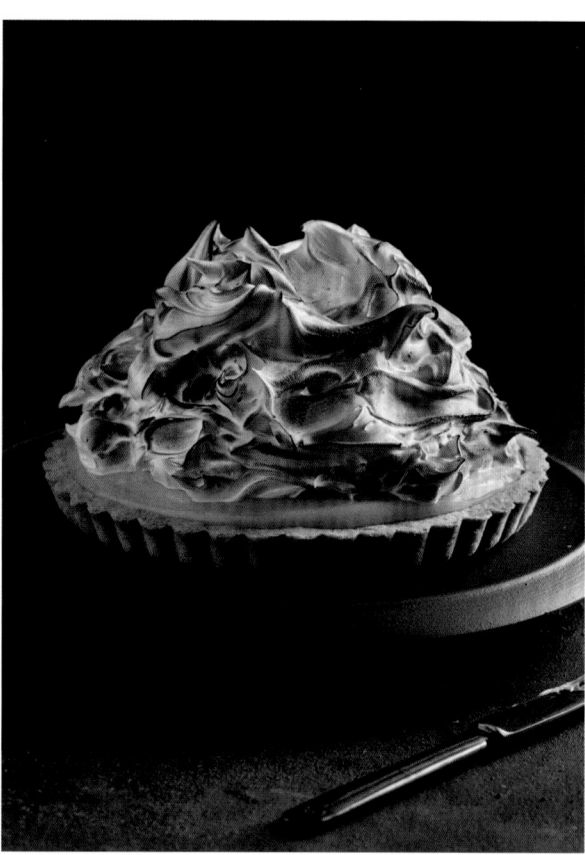

I realized that part of making an image was to edit the way I would edit.

In my opinion, using presets is applying another photographer's vision, and I wanted my own vision. Going beyond "click and go" empowered me to find my own style. Making hideous editing mistakes so I could learn helped me find my style, also asking myself what the most important elements in my image were, and how could I make them stand out, gave me the focus to define my vision.

Did it take you long before you started feeling satisfied with your final edits?
I honestly don't remember how long it took to find my style, perhaps because I enjoyed playing, testing, and discovering. But like anything in photography, things take time. Taking an editing course can open the doors to finding the right way to edit from the get-go. This is one of the reasons I created my online editing course,

Lightroom Magic, to show food photographers how to use the tools to best match their style. Satisfaction, for me, comes from making all the mistakes you can make, then solving them one by one. Until finally you end up with a style that you can be really proud of.

Your images always stop me in my tracks. What do you pay attention to the most in post-production to make your images stand out?
When it comes to food photography editing, there are three key areas I pay attention to: exposure, color, and contrast. How I edit for each of these areas changes based on my subject, the brief, and the mood of the photograph. Most people don't realize that there are over six ways to adjust exposure, color, and contrast in Lightroom, even up to eight ways! Knowing each different way to adjust exposure means that I can have a lot of control over fine-tuning this key area.

How do you find that balance between too much editing and not enough?
Not too much, not too little: just right! My husband sometimes jokes that I am Goldilocks, and not because of my hair color, but because I always strive for the "just right" zone.

Finding my "just right" will be different for each image. Sometimes a concept requires a little more post-production for a whimsical look, or the scene could be more realistic and require very little. In food photography, I think the story and the food are always the most important elements. The editing should be just right so that the viewer focuses on the food. Under-editing can risk your image not being noticed. In a world where billions of images are shared every day, standing out is crucial.

Over-editing can come from a limited understanding of what editing tools actually do. There is a tendency to use just a few adjustments with a heavy hand. This leads to images feeling unnatural. For me, the just right spot comes from using a large number of small adjustments. Think of it like cooking. The best dishes are made from

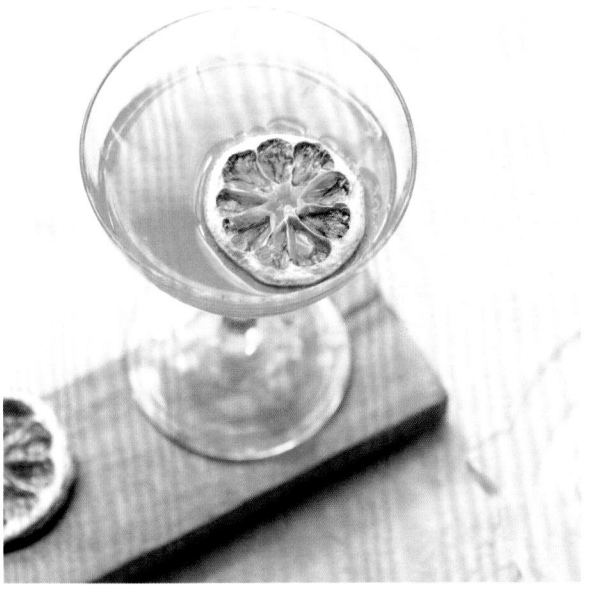

a balance of subtle flavors; like a dish that uses a small amount of ten different spices. You can imagine how interesting and complex that would taste compared to a dish that uses a large quantity of just two spices. The perfect amount of editing is just like that.

Which Lightroom settings could you not live without?
Rather than thinking about what we use in editing as settings, I like to think about them as tools. Settings vary depending on the light you use and the mood you're trying to capture. What is consistent, though, are the tools we use.

My personal must-have tool is Local Adjustments. They are essentially masks that we use to make edits in an image, localized to the specific area we want to target. Local Adjustments help me tweak and perfect every part of my image independently. This gives me a lot of control over the final look.

Do you have any top tips for staying organized in Lightroom?

How you set up your catalogue is crucial for staying organized, being able to locate images quickly, and for speed. There are many ways to set up a catalogue: based on each new year, or by clients, even by the genre of photography, for example. I also recommend not keeping all of your files on your computer. I use two hard drives simultaneously: one that I work from and one that is a backup. I organize images on my hard drives by year, client, and food. This is then reflected in my Lightroom catalogue. Using keywords and starring or color-coding methods can help you filter your images and find the hero selects quickly.

And how do you speed things up when you have a ton of images to process?

I go through my images and make selections using the rating system in Lightroom. Then I narrow it down to 10 or fewer selects. I edit my hero image, then sync my global settings across the set of images. I will make any final local adjustments to each image individually, then compare the set to ensure they match for white balance and exposure. Syncing base edits across a set will save you time, but you need to give a little TLC to each individual image in order for it to look its best. It's worth taking the extra time to finish each image separately.

You have been educating food photographers about editing for few years now. What do you think is the most common mistake people make? And what's the solution?

The most common mistake I see is photographers not understanding that the light we shoot changes how we edit. We will always use the same tools, but the settings and approach will differ. Presets are great and they save time, but the idea of a one-size-fits-all preset is a myth. If you're always shooting the exact same light, they can be helpful, but as professional photographers, we are required to capture different light.

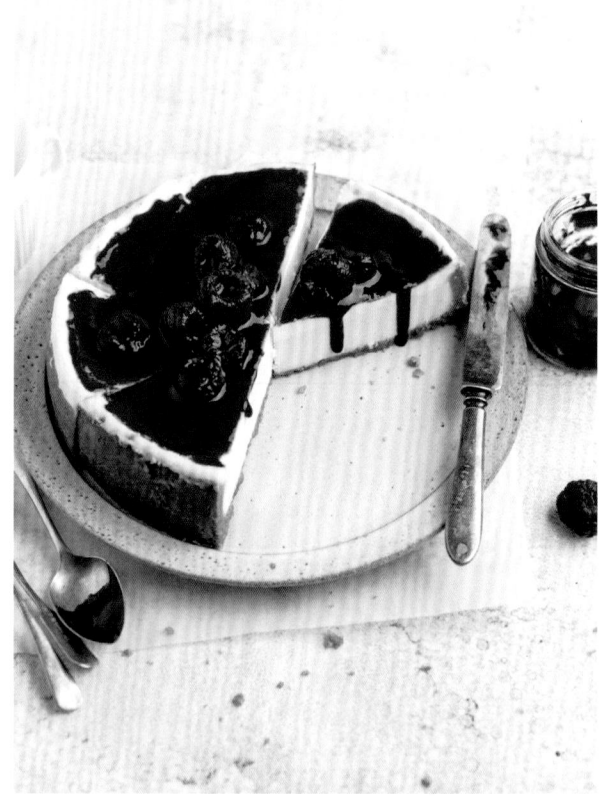

If you're not happy with your editing or you feel held captive to your presets, it's time to find the magic that's waiting for you. The solution is to edit from scratch for your next three shoots. Change how you use the tools to match the lighting and mood. Then you might also discover something truly great: your own personal style.

What are some of the most important lessons you've learned about editing from the years of working as a professional photographer?

The biggest influence on my work is light: it's always light. So the biggest influence on my editing is also the light. I spend a small amount of time each day observing the light around me. How it dances, how it sculpts dimension and enhances texture. When I am shooting, I am thinking about how I can use my camera to capture light in a way that I know will match how I want to edit an image. For me, they go together hand in hand. Sometimes having that break can allow you to see new things. I also love contrast, so I first create it in my images by shaping the light, then I enhance it through the editing process.

My most important editing lesson is that your approach changes depending on what the content of the image is, what the client needs/wants, and what is popular with current trends. As a professional photographer, it's part of my job to keep up with trends for client work. When it comes to editorial work, editing needs to look super realistic. There are certain edits that are popular on Instagram, but you wouldn't see in an editorial magazine. Clients expect the photographer to understand that and adapt.

Discover more about Rachel's work at:

www.twolovesstudio.com
www.rachelkorinek.com
@twolovesstudio

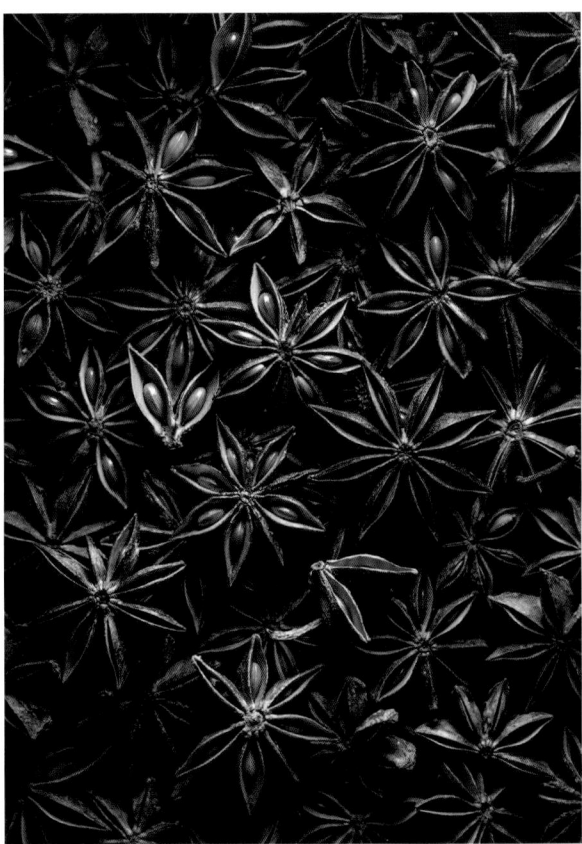

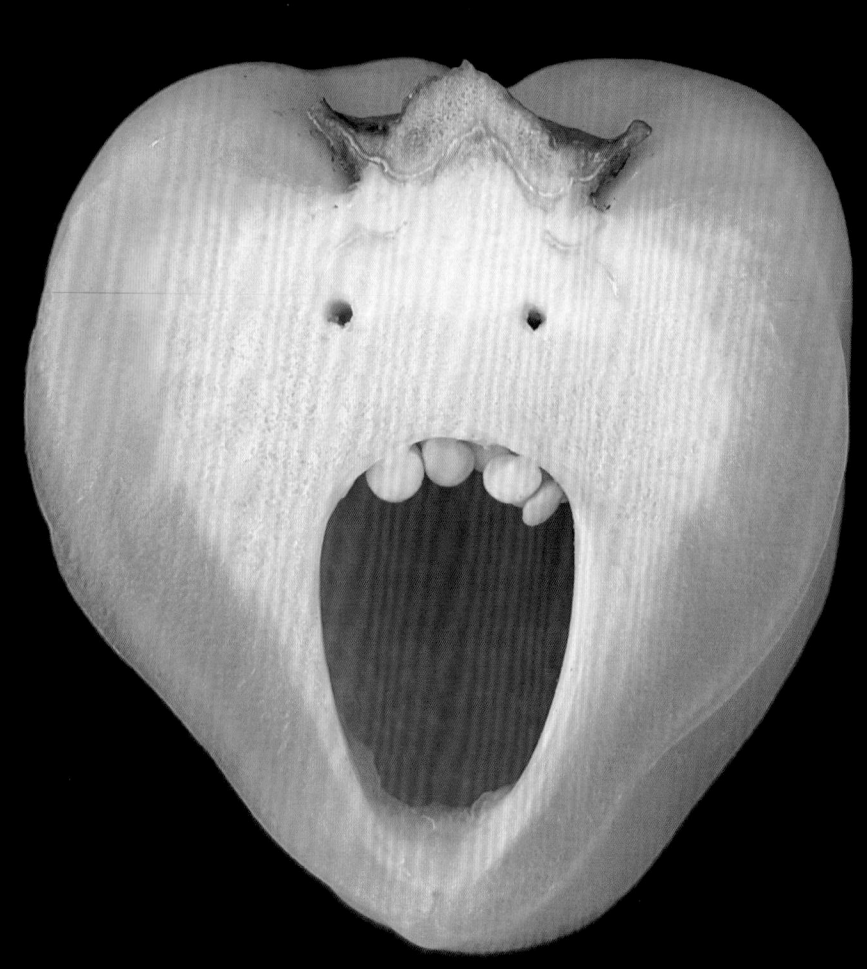

Mindset & Growth

What no one told me when I first started photography is that I would get disheartened. That even if I jumped into it with a heart full of big dreams and deep passion, I wouldn't be able to avoid disappointment. That a lot of my creative projects wouldn't work out the way I envisioned them. That the people I wanted to work with wouldn't reply to my emails. That my work would feel invisible. And that I would often feel lonely.

But I loved my craft so much that I had no other option but to keep going and keep creating. And now I'm glad that I refused to give up.

The truth is, when you dive into the world of photography, it's inevitable that you will come across challenging situations and somewhere along the way feel discouraged, but don't ever lose your enthusiasm. Being stubborn is the only way to make it.

What makes a successful creative? Excellent technical skills? Sure, that helps. A creative vision that stands out from the crowd? Absolutely! But there is one more thing that we need to equip ourselves with: a strong mindset.

When I was growing as a photographer, I soon realized that getting my work seen was about so much more than just expanding my photography skills. Sure, creating outstanding images is important, but sharing my work with the world and trying to get noticed brought a whole new level of challenges and lessons. I knew that if I wanted food photography to become my career, the quality of my mind mattered as much as the quality of my work.

I wish I could say that your self-doubt, negative comparisons, and struggles will evaporate with time, but that wouldn't be true. The trick is to never let them stop you.

Lessons learned

My favorite part about this journey is the lessons it brings along the way. Every challenge, every struggle, every mistake can become a learning experience, if you are willing to stop and listen. Here are some of the lessons I've learned:

To do big things, you've got to do little things every day

To write a book, you write a page a day; to build a portfolio, you start by turning on your camera every morning; to create a meaningful personal project, you start by working on it for an hour every day.

Growth happens outside the comfort zone

If you want to stretch yourself as a photographer, you will have to schedule some time for doing things that make you uncomfortable, whether it's working in a new studio, trying a new technique, or photographing a dish you've never shot before.

Working with others opens new ways of thinking

It's fascinating to see how other people work and it's what always sparks new ideas and "aha" moments for me. Collaborate often, learn from others and do things together that wouldn't be possible just on your own.

Build your creative confidence

Often, it's not our photography skills but our lack of confidence that stands in the way of wonderful job opportunities. As you grow your skill set, it's essential to work on your creative confidence too. It all starts with learning to trust your own taste and respecting yourself for showing up and doing the work. At the same time, keep your feet on the ground and stay humble.

Be stubborn in reaching your goals.

Whether it's learning something new, improving your skills or getting your name out there, be brave enough to keep trying.

Grow at your own pace

As artists, we need to evolve and regularly introduce new ideas and techniques into our work and our business. However, the constant need to get better can be overwhelming. Progress at your own pace, even if that means tiptoeing sometimes. Being still and actually just stopping from time to time is a hugely important part of the process of growing, too.

Carefully consider advice

Listen to people who have been in the industry for longer than you and be grateful when they share their experience, but at the same time, think about any advice you're given through the filters of who you are and who you want to be. Does this advice work for you?

It's okay not to know everything

As professionals, we can feel that we have to know everything about our industry—but is that even possible? I personally hope I never reach a place where there is nothing more to learn. It's not your mistakes or what you don't know that defines you; it's the way you solve problems and deal with new challenges that matters.

Don't take yourself too seriously

Fill your creative process with joy, let go of perfection, and don't take the outcome or yourself too seriously. The ability to laugh at yourself and your mistakes is an amazing skill to have.

Put yourself on your to-do list

There are always lots of exciting things to do and work on, but you can't do your best if you are exhausted. Be kind to yourself, eat well, move, rest: it's the best investment you can make in your creativity.

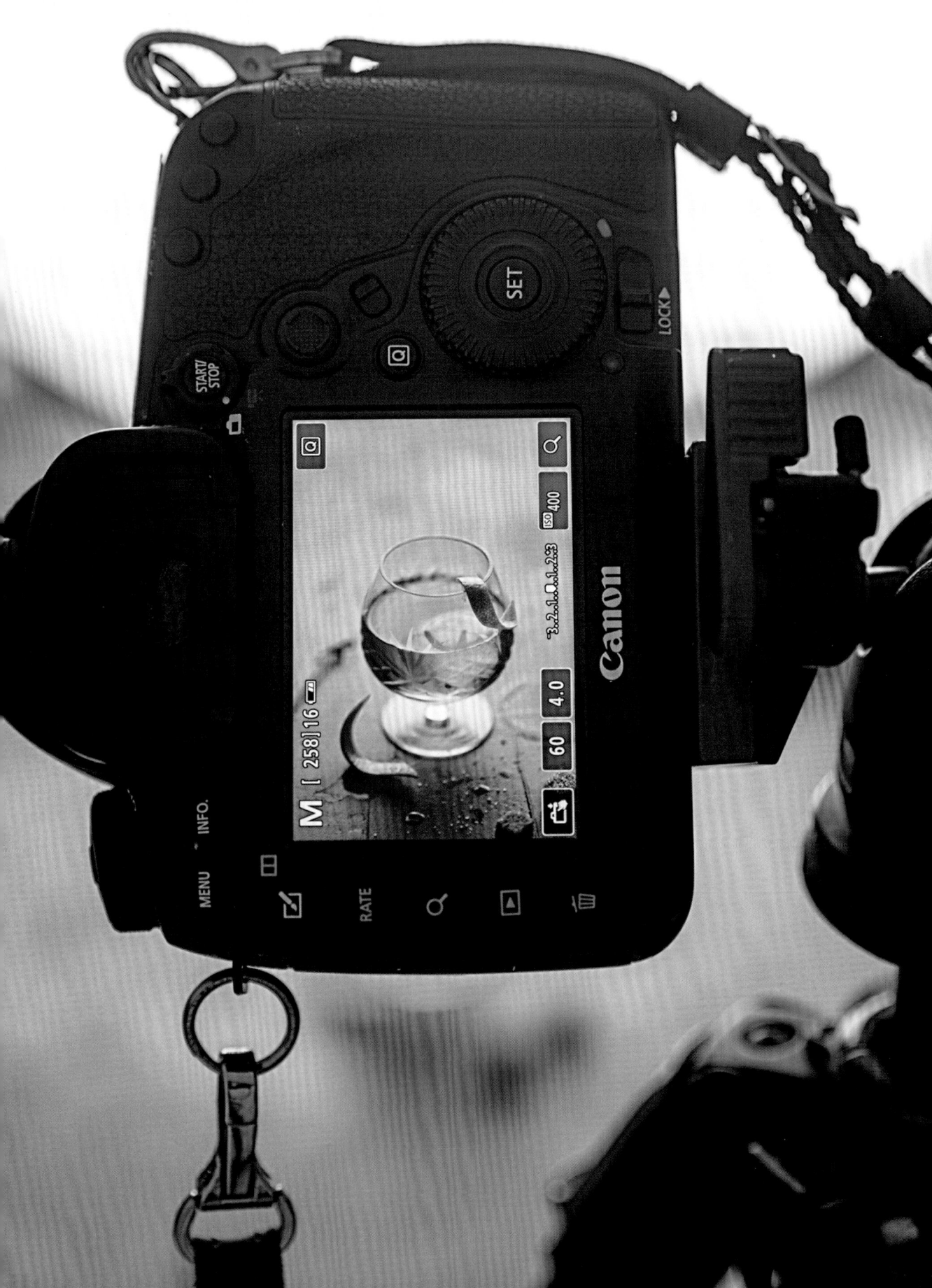

Your style is your currency

Photography is all about making decisions. Blur part of the image or keep everything in focus? What props and backgrounds to pick? Where in the frame to put the hero subject? Where to move the supporting elements? The decisions and preferences that show up in your work repeatedly over time will become your style. When something feels right, pay attention: the key to your style is there. Your visual instincts will dictate what works for you, and what doesn't. Don't underestimate that instinctive gut feeling, because your style is crafted through intuition.

In the first few years of your photography journey, things can feel a little confusing. You don't have a lot of experience under your belt to help you make these decisions. You are still discovering which approaches you prefer and which ones you don't like at all.

That's where personal projects come in. When you experiment and try something you've never done before, you find new ways of shooting to add to your repertoire. You will learn what shutter speed to use to perfectly catch powdered sugar falling on a cake, how to make the world's ugliest food look irresistible in seven different ways, and how to shape the light to create various moods in your images. You will also get to know that some things don't work for you and your style, and that you like some techniques, placements, and details more than others.

Pay attention to the choices you make

To do this exercise, gather the images that you are the most proud of. You could also bring together images that inspire you the most and analyze them to help you answer these questions and find a common thread.

* What type of food do you enjoy photographing or looking at the most?
* Do you focus on food only or do you include the scene around too?
* What lens is your favorite to photograph with? Do you like to shoot close up or farther away?
* Do you enjoy building a scene from scratch or is documentary, journalistic style your jam?
* Do you like to photograph with a shallow depth of field to keep your images soft or do you prefer to show more details around your frame in focus?
* What angle feels the most natural to you?
* What type of light inspires you? Do you keep your photos on a brighter or darker side? Do you like long or minimal shadows? Or maybe both?
* What are the colors you are most attracted to? Do you like vibrant, saturated hues or maybe softer and more gentle color palettes?
* Do you prefer a warmer or cooler white balance?
* What props speak to you? Modern and clean, vintage or rustic? Do you keep them to a minimum or do you like them to have a bigger role in the story?
* What do you focus on when you edit? What editing tools do you always use in your work?
* What details and decisions show up repeatedly in your work? Or in the photographs that inspire you?

Tip

The most skilled photographers shoot more than others. But it's not about pressing the shutter unconsciously though, just to hit the mileage. It's about taking the time to reflect and study the results. What went well? What didn't go well? What could be improved next time? I've always kept "discoveries" notebook that I would fill in with my thoughts and conclusions after each photoshoot. I can't even tell you how much it helped me grow.

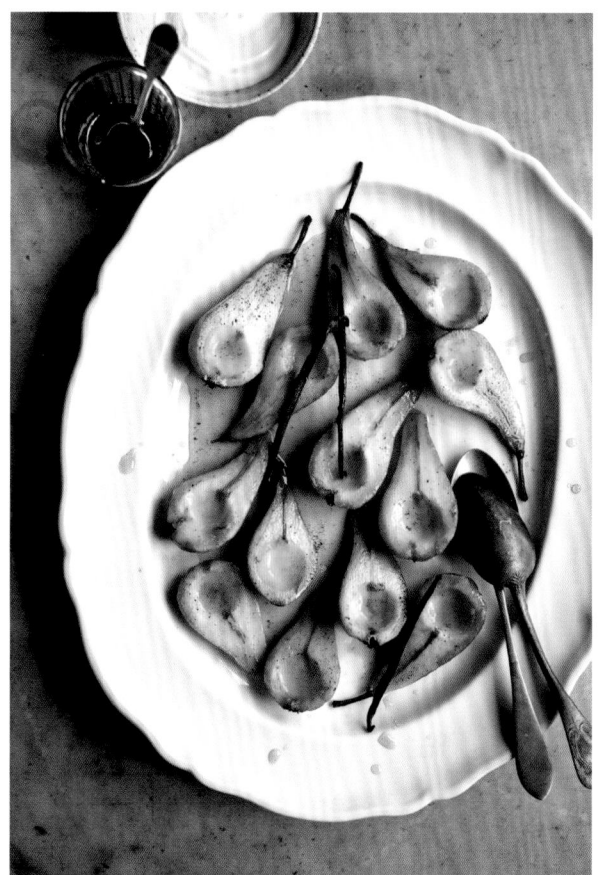

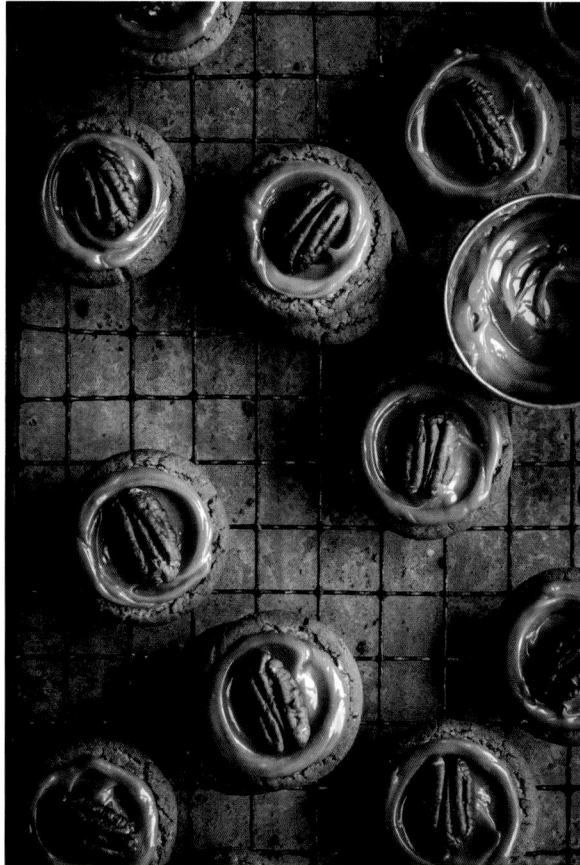

The evolution of style (above, left & right)

Although my style has evolved a lot over the years, the choices I favour the most are more and more prominent in each and every food story I create. 50mm and 100mm have remained my favorite lenses and they have influenced the way I compose my images immensely. Playing with contrasts and focussing on "light catchers" are decisions that show up in my work repeatedly, too. As is hopefully demonstrated in the photographs above, I always pay a lot of attention to how light is catching the textures, and the angle of food and the camera plays a hugely important part in capturing those mesmerizing highlights. Other things that I feel contribute to my style include constantly trying out different color combinations and being picky about my props—always going an extra mile to find unique items.

Embrace the journey

Discovering your style isn't something that you will "nail down" one day, so leave plenty of room for little discoveries. Try out different styles, experiment and pay attention to what feels good. It's not something you have to stick with for the rest of your life. Actually, that would be a dangerous thing to do, because your style should always be evolving. Style is a constant change.

Your style DNA

There is one more crucial ingredient to your style: you. If you want to be a better photographer, you've got to learn more about yourself first. A photograph is like a mirror: it's a reflection of a photographer. Of you. Of how you see and feel. Of your taste. Of your influences. Great images don't just tell us something about the photographed subject: they tell us about the person behind the camera too. To add personality to your work, you've got to dig deep and think about what makes you YOU—what sets you apart and makes you different from everyone else. Then infuse that special spark into your work to make it truly unique.

More than anything, style is knowing who you are, what you like and value, and celebrating it all with confidence in your work. Be honest with yourself about what you enjoy and what you are good at. The better you understand yourself, the stronger your work will be.

Be you, bravely

Not everyone will like your style and that's okay. It's fantastic, even! If we all loved the same thing, the world would be a boring place. What's important is that you learn to like and respect your own work, and don't let anyone else's opinion knock your confidence or make you lose your enthusiasm. Show the world the way you see food and make your audience see something they might not have seen before—something only you see!

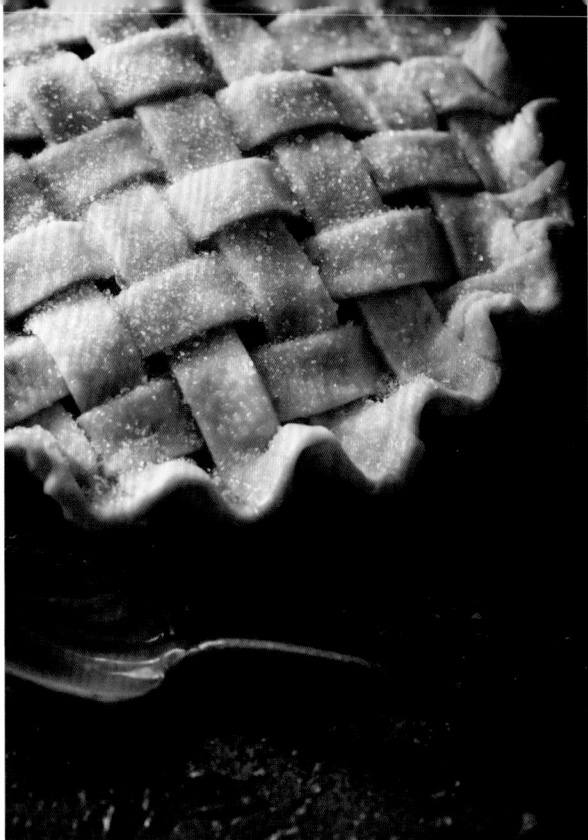

Above: When I finally understood that it's ME who makes my work unique and I decided to show more of myself in my images, I started to feel more at home with the work I created. The foundations of my style are built on my love for making food look beautiful and my eye for noticing the smallest details. But you can also see how growing up in Poland influenced my color awareness, as well as how living close to nature impacted my passion for seasonal storytelling.

Tip

When you work for a client, it's no longer only your vision. Listen to what others want to bring to the table, even if your creative ego wants to rebel sometimes. Of course your clients hire you because they love your style, but projects are often very specific and have to please a number of different people, each with their own tastes and concerns. You have to find balance; always staying true to yourself, but also respecting and taking into account those you work with.

Close the gap

"Your first 10,000 pictures are the worst."
—Henri Cartier-Bresson

When you are searching to define your own unique style, you should know that feeling dissatisfied with your own work is totally normal. You will feel that the photos you create are nothing like what you had envisioned. Everyone goes through this. Your skills are trying to live up to your expectations, but they are not quite there yet. To bridge that gap and get to the other side of your ambition, you have to go through a volume of work. The more you photograph, the quicker you will get there.

So how to get through that volume of work and stay sane?

* Get comfortable with your gear: that's how you will free up more creativity.
* Be honest about your weaker points and work towards improving them.
* Commit yourself to learning instead of focusing always on the end result. Read books and blogs, join online communities, take courses, and attend photography events.
* Experiment and photograph as much as you can.
* Shadow someone or get a mentor.

Never stop learning

In my opinion you can bridge the gap, but you can't close it completely, because as your skills and knowledge evolve, so does your taste and ambition. Even after years of working as a professional photographer, I have days when I don't like my own work. When this happens, I take a deep breath and say to myself, "Okay Bea, it looks like your taste is getting better again, and that means it's time to shake things up a little bit and learn something new."

Now give yourself a huge pat on the back. You are doing great!

The gap

A few years ago, my dear friend and a wonderful photographer Kym Grimshaw quoted these words by Ira Glass to me. It felt like one of those big "aha" moments.

For the first couple years you make stuff, it's just not that good. It's trying to be good, it has potential, but it's not. But your taste, the thing that got you into the game, is still killer. And your taste is why your work disappoints you. A lot of people never get past this phase, they quit. Most people I know who do interesting, creative work went through years of this. We know our work doesn't have this special thing that we want it to have. We all go through this. And if you are just starting out or you are still in this phase, you gotta know it's normal and the most important thing you can do is to do a lot of work. Put yourself on a deadline so that every week you will finish one story. It is only by going through a volume of work that you will close that gap, and your work will be as good as your ambitions.

—From The Gap by Ira Glass

Grow your skills

Challenge yourself to learn something new from time to time and dig deep into the topic—that's how you will stretch your creative muscles and grow into a better photographer. Don't wait for motivation to show up—make it part of your routine.

Personal projects

One of the best ways to learn something new and to keep excited about your craft is to create a personal project. There is no right or wrong here, as we all work differently, so make sure you find a structure that works for you. I usually have one or two long-term projects running in the background, that I don't think much about on a daily basis, but when the right opportunity shows up I make sure to capture the shot and add it to this "project collection."

At the same time, a few times every year I will come up with a more specific personal project, and for these I like to focus on one at a time to give it all my attention and energy. I will make a plan, set a timeline, do the research, follow my curiosity, and go as far as I can with it. I don't take it too seriously though: I allow myself to play, make mistakes, and let the mistakes teach me something I should pay attention to the next time. Then I take time to reflect and study the results.

Ideas to explore

* **A gap**—Something you feel is your weak point that you avoid, but that your work would benefit from.
* **An unfamiliar subject**—Something you have never photographed before.
* **Your favorite subject**—Explore it to the maximum and make it your signature thing.
* **Light**—Backlight, hard light, chiaroscuro—make light the subject of your photograph.
* **Color**—Choose a specific color palette and create a story around it.
* **Texture**—Focus on details that often go unnoticed.
* **Shape**—Pay attention to shape only.
* **Movement**—Delve into the beauty of frozen details, capture creative motion blur, and add more visual flow into your compositions.
* **A human element**—Try to capture images with human element in a few different and unique ways.
* **Story**—Is there a story of a certain ingredient, dish, or cuisine that you'd like to explore in more depth?
* **Your dream job**—Which project do you wish you would be hired for? Hire yourself for it!

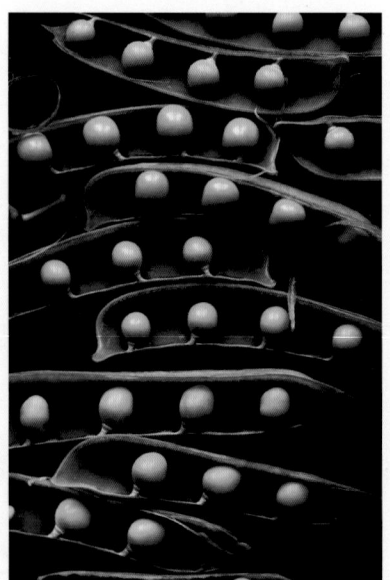
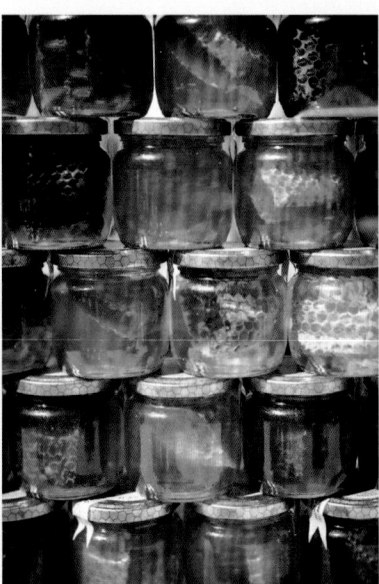
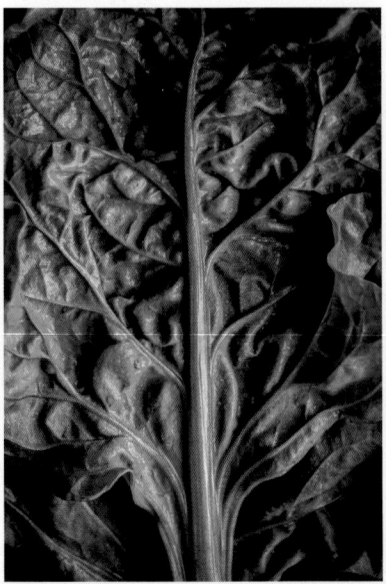

Stretch your creative muscles

* Allow yourself to be a beginner at any new skill: don't be afraid to be bad at something at first.
* Shoot at different locations.
* Photograph a dark version and a bright version of the same subject.
* Try doing the opposite to what you always do.
* Experiment with compositional "rules."
* Explore Lightroom settings you've not used before.
* When something doesn't work out, try again.
* Take the time to rest and reflect—it's a crucial part of growth

When we want to become better photographers, it's normal for us to focus on nailing our photography skills. But there's a huge amount of value in stretching other muscles. For example, taking up gardening unexpectedly improved my photography skills by teaching me to see food from a totally different perspective. Think about what other, non-photography-related skills might help you grow as an artist.

And how about staying consistent?

Over the years I have totally ignored "be consistent with your work" advice, and explored different lighting, from super bright to very dark, played with different colors, tried various compositions and angles, and experimented with editing. Yet a funny thing happened—my work still looked consistent. Our style is made up of many different, often unconscious decisions and it's rooted in us deeper than you think. From the choice of lens, how you crop your frame, what details you pay attention to, the way you tell the story, and what you see to how you craft the final image in post-production.

Don't worry about consistency too much. Just photograph what makes you happy, because what connects all your images is the person who created them: you.

Below: Twelve months ago I set myself a project focussing on the beauty of raw produce. Most of the time, my job involves a perfect shot of a final dish—that's what clients commission me for—so concentrating on the texture, color, and shape of ingredients with no or minimal propping felt really refreshing. In the long run, it turned out to be a great lesson, and it made me pay attention to notice what made each produce so special, details that I would otherwise miss.

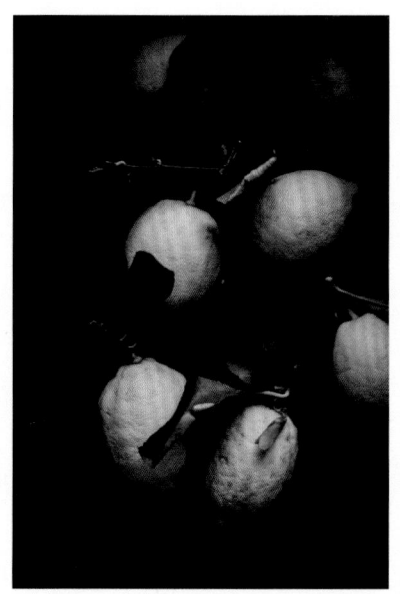 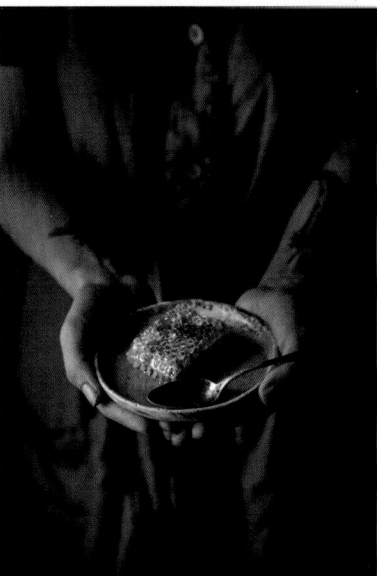 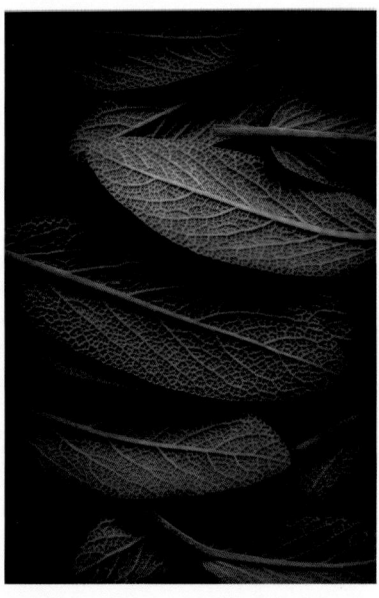

Artist vs businessperson

"Do not measure success by today's harvest. Measure success by the seeds you plant today."
—Robert Louis Stevenson

I got into the world of photography because I loved creating, and although making it my full-time job meant running a business, all I cared about was taking great pictures. I believed what everyone kept on saying: create outstanding work and clients will find you. However, I soon learned that although my photography had to be exceptional, it was not everything. I would be invited for interviews with publishing houses that loved my work, but they also wanted to know whether I could manage a team and work with assistants and food stylists, how organized I was, and how I dealt with problems on set.

Suddenly I went from working on my own to working with others. From working with only my own ideas, I moved to executing someone else's vision. I couldn't just create, I had to learn how to get my work out there, how to work with clients, and how to price my work. The moment I realized I needed to equip myself with a new set of skills was the moment I started to grow as an artist and as a small business owner.

Artist

It can seem like the artist and the businessperson have contradicting personalities and tasks to do, but it's possible to be both and stay sane. I make sure to keep my artistic soul happy with personal projects, time for experimentation, trips to book stores and libraries, and studying art. My creativity is at the heart of my business and it's also what brings me the most joy, so there is no other option but to keep my artistic soul well nurtured.

Businessperson

When it comes to turning your passion into a full-time job, it's not only about creating anymore. For me, it meant that I had to get business savvy and learn how to navigate in the areas I wasn't familiar or comfortable with.

Time management

Organizing your space, your equipment, files, and yourself might be time-consuming at first, but it will save you tons of time in a long run.

Time yourself to learn how much time different tasks take you. Always question yourself if things can be done quicker or better. Keep lists of useful things, such as studios in your area, people who can help you on bigger shoots, places to buy or rent props, as well as an equipment checklist to take with you on a photoshoot. I spend time making templates of emails I send out often: for example, with questions I send out to clients about the shoot, or for when I can't take on a job but I want to recommend others. I also have templates for tasks that I repeat often, such as creating a brief. By saving time on the business side, you will have more time to spend on creative things.

Branding

Branding is the message we send out to the world about who we are and what we do. It's showing what you are good at and what people can expect when working with you.

What impression you give people when they land on your portfolio page, when they read an email from you, or meet you in person is an incredibly important part of branding, and what will ultimately win—or lose—you a job. What would you like people to know about you and your photography business? How can you communicate it more clearly? How can you show your personality more?

Working with clients

Clients first fall in love with your work, but that's not everything—show them that you are also a pleasure to work with. Positivity, honesty, and clear communication is the simplest and most successful formula when working with others. Underpromising and overdelivering, and giving your client something extra and unexpected will always leave a long-lasting good impression.

Negotiate

One thing that my artistic side really struggled with was learning to negotiate, but the more I practiced, the easier it became. It really is a skill that can be learned. Often, the biggest fear is that we will lose the opportunity if we ask for more money, but in a lot of cases, when a client can't afford the fee you've quoted, they will let you know what their budget is, hoping for a compromise. If it's lower than what you'd accept, you could offer to create fewer images for that price, or offer a different solution. But it's also important to be ready to walk away.

Getting your work out there

Getting your work out there is a test of character. It can be challenging. The way I like to look at it is that it's like sowing seeds. It takes time and effort, some seeds might never germinate, but if you're patient enough, others will blossom into wonderful opportunities.

So where to start? Open your email or social media inbox and reach out. The internet has given artists the opportunity to connect with others like never before. Take advantage of it! Don't assume that people you've never spoken to are inaccessible. Reaching out landed me my first interview with one of the biggest magazines in the UK—and I didn't even think my work was good enough back then.

When you reach out, just remember that the people you are contacting likely get dozens of pitch emails like yours every day. They don't know you or your story, and to make things even harder, they are extremely busy people. Write your pitch email and read it out loud. Be honest with yourself: if you didn't know the person who sent it and you were overloaded with work and tight deadlines, would this email catch your attention? Think about how you could make yourself a little bit more memorable. And most importantly, do your homework and make sure that each email is specifically tailored to the person you are pitching to.

And don't be afraid to follow up. If you are kind and polite, and leave time in between emails, the chances are that if you send several emails, they will remember you more than the person who only sent one.

Don't take things personally

If you've never put yourself out there before, it will almost certainly feel weird and uncomfortable at first. This is normal. The best way to start is not to have expectations, get used to rejection and don't take things personally. I always say that, before I became a photographer, I was a professional pitch-email sender. I was rejected so many times that I honestly lost count! But the more rejections I got, the more determined I was to sit down and to send out more. Then, somewhere among those rejections, opportunities started showing up. Only because I persevered.

Established photographers still have to look for work

No matter how many followers you have or how long you've been in the photography business, it's important to show your face, remind people that you exist, and introduce yourself here and there—even if you have work lined up for a few months. People often don't hire you, not because you are not good enough, but because they don't know, or have forgotten, that you exist!

Tip

It's important that your business skills are as creative as your photography.

Create a portfolio

A portfolio is an important investment and something to consider even if it seems like everyone looks at your social media to see your work these days. It shows that you are serious about what you do.

What to include? (Opposite)

Diversity, most of all! Make sure to include a great variety of dishes and drinks, moods, colors, angles, and focal lengths, as well as examples of both portrait and landscape images. Don't only include polished images of finished dishes; keep it interesting by adding some in-progress shots and portraits of the ingredients. Try to make it even more engaging and show off different techniques, creative use of various types of light, and examples of frozen and blurred movement captures, as well as some images with a human element. Adding some clever stop-motion or cinemagraphs in between the still shots is a sure-fire way of making your portfolio look original and keeping your potential client on your page.

Your portfolio is a place to exhibit your best work, so make sure it is strong from start to finish. It's better to have a few great pictures than a lot of average ones. Show the work you'd like to be hired for. Always start and end with a WOW image and remember that your best work doesn't always mean your favorite work. Ask a few fellow photographers or close friends what they think your strongest images are—I am sure you'll be surprised by what they say.

In today's fast-paced world, the first impression is more important than ever before. You usually have only three seconds to grab someone's attention from the moment they click onto your page before they decide whether to stay or to leave, so make sure to include something that will pleasantly surprise your viewer and make you more memorable.

Let your personality shine through

People will often hire you not only because of your skill set, but because of your enthusiasm, your personality, and your positive attitude. That's why your "About" page is so important—it's easier to connect with a photographer when you feel like you know something about them.

Website, email & print

These days, you can easily create a website using an online platform like Squarespace or Wix, which provide beautiful templates for you to customize. Choose one that puts your photography front and center, is easy to navigate, and make sure you include contact details and where you're based, and link to your professional social media. If you can afford to purchase your own domain name, it always looks more professional than the free domain name that usually includes the platform in its URL. Make sure you help people to find you too—this is where a little SEO (search engine optimization) know-how will be useful.

If you can't afford a website yet, create a beautiful presentation that you can attach to your pitching emails instead. PDF is the standard format and it should be small enough (below 20MB) to attach to an email, but of good enough quality that your work still shines.

Print your work too. Clients' eyes will light up when they see you come into a meeting with printed work. I think it's especially important if you are meeting with a magazine or book publisher—of course they want to see what your images look like in print! That's what they will be buying from you, after all.

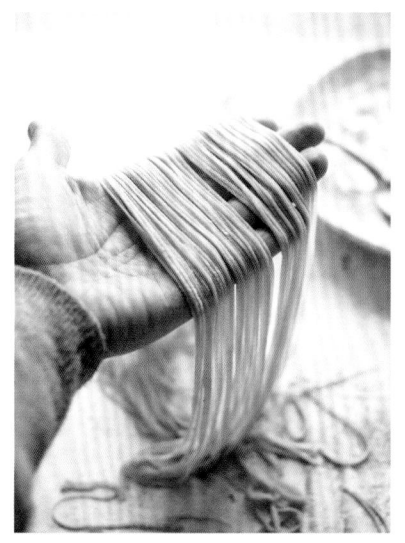
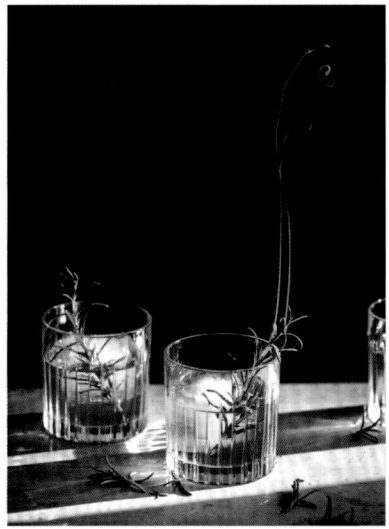
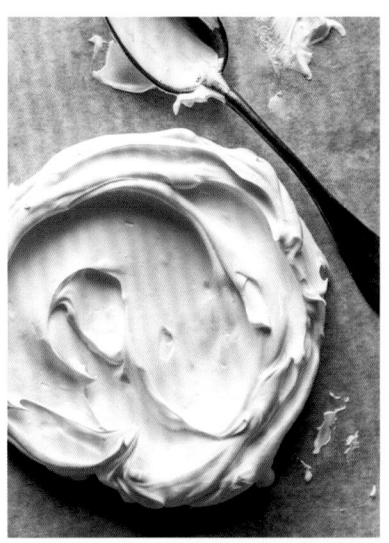
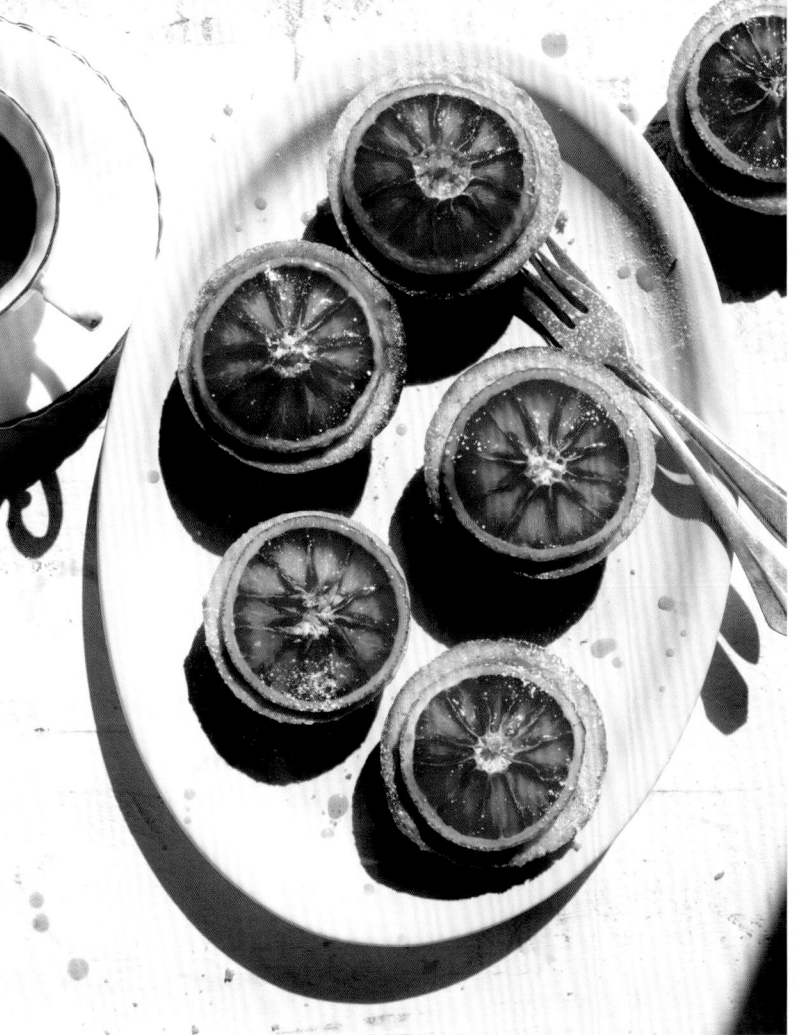
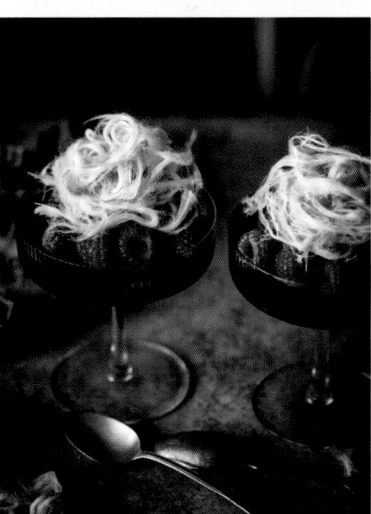
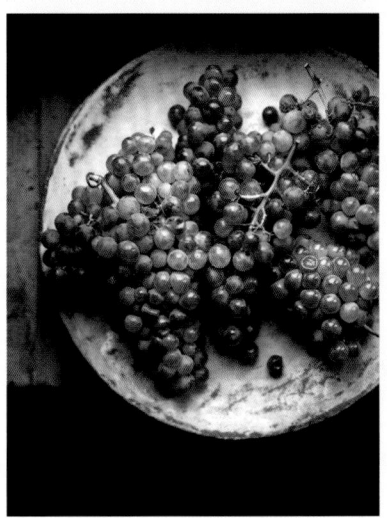

Instagram

Instagram is great for building relationships and getting your work discovered. But if you spend a lot of time on social media, it's important to build healthy boundaries too.

Build honest relationships & connections

A lot of my Instagram friendships grew into real-life collaborations, as well as work opportunities, and it blows my mind that it often all starts from one single message saying, "Hey, your work really inspires me." Social media is an enormous part of our lives and work these days. I see being part of this online world as a huge responsibility to always be honest and transparent, as well as kind and respectful. It's also how you will get the most out of it as a professional.

* Don't forget that there is a person on the other side with feelings and emotions just like you.
* Support people in your industry and recommend others without expecting anything in return.
* Encourage inspiring conversations.
* Think of fun ways to collaborate with others.
* Be interested in what other creatives have to say.
* Use people's names when you reply to them—it's so much more polite and personal!

What to share

Of course you want to share the work you are most excited about, but don't overthink it too much and don't put too much weight on the response. Overthinking slows you down, triggers self-doubt, and creates problems that don't even exist. When it comes to Instagram, there is no logic. Some of my images that I think are terrific don't get much love, while others I think aren't that special get people super excited. "Final" shots are not the only thing you can share; here are some ideas to help you keep things interesting:

* Take people behind the scenes, share your process, and show how much energy and focus go into everything you do.
* Share ideas. These could be quick tutorials, inspiring words, food for thought, solutions to problems, or what you are currently learning.
* Post how-tos and case studies.
* Share what inspires you and celebrate others.
* Give a sneak peek into your personal projects.
* Share things that didn't work out as planned—we are all human and people will be able to relate.

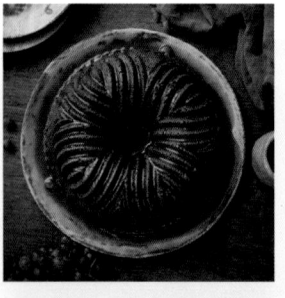
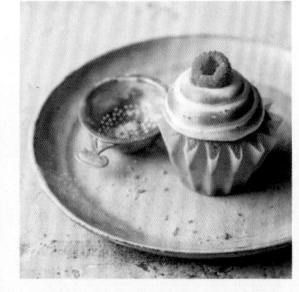
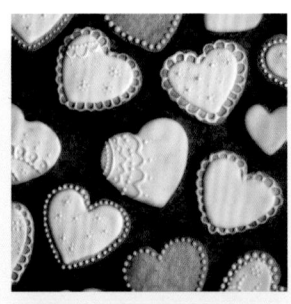
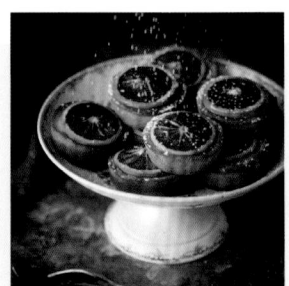
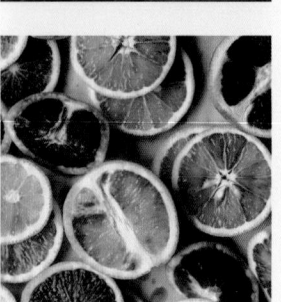
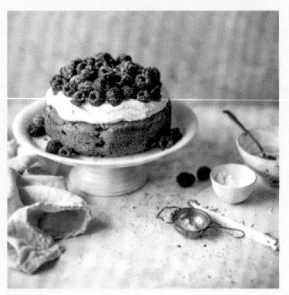
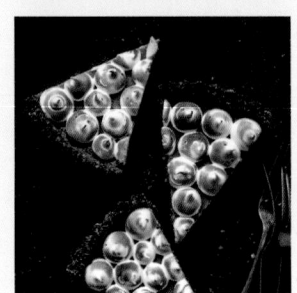
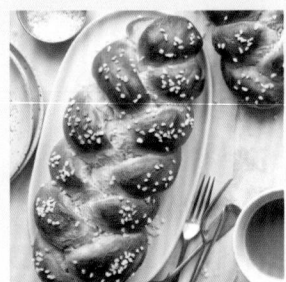

How to get the most out of Instagram

* Be sure to include your name, country where you are based (but never your personal address), email address, and website in your profile information.
* Be yourself and share what you love creating—the work you share is the work you'll be hired for.
* Commit to regular posting and engaging, but that doesn't mean you've got to be active every day.
* Give credit to the people who have inspired you, ideas you've read somewhere, the restaurant you went to, or recipe you tried.
* Consider tagging brands that you love and whose products you use on a regular basis, or used in a certain photo. Learn more about people you would like to collaborate and work with by following them and genuinely engaging with their posts.
* Use hashtags of brands and communities that inspire you—if they reshare your photo, you could gain more visibility.
* Show raw enthusiasm. It is so contagious!
* Keep your account safe. Read Instagram security tips and consider switching on two-factor authentication. Always use a different email address in your profile than the one your account is registered with.

Healthy boundaries

* Don't let social media numbers get into your head: these numbers don't define whether your photos are good or bad, they are based mainly on how active you are on the app.
* If you are not realistic about your time on social media, it might soon get out of control and leave you very little time for meaningful photography projects. Dedicate time slots that work for you, be strict with them, and have breaks regularly.
* If you ever feel like you are behind everyone else or that you are not good enough, no matter how much you work, don't forget that Instagram never shows the full story of someone's life. Define what success means to you, stick to your own values, and don't get distracted by what everyone else is doing.
* Never compromise your creativity or style for social media likes. If you are only posting "safe" images because you are worried about people not liking your work and ignoring what you want to do for yourself, there is a huge risk that sooner or later you will starve your creativity.

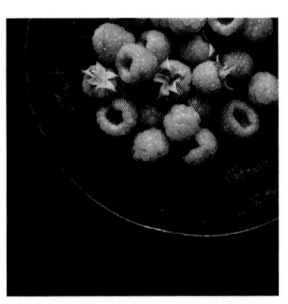
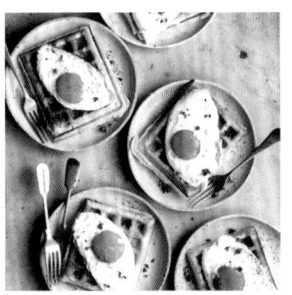
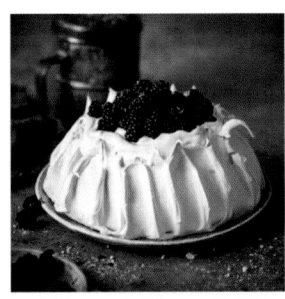
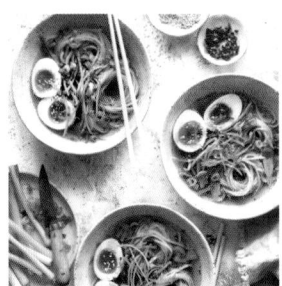

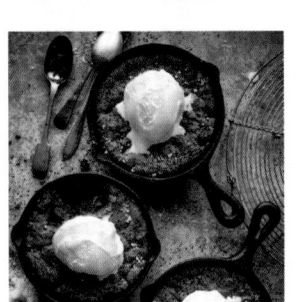
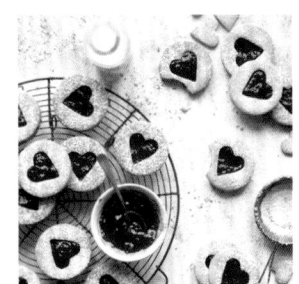
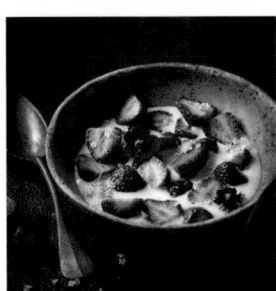

Interview:
Eva Kosmas Flores

Eva Kosmas Flores makes impossible things possible. Whatever she sets her mind to, she makes happen. She hosts creative workshops all over the world through her company First We Eat, has bought and is restoring a clear-cut forest, and reaches thousands of students through her online courses, all while successfully writing, styling, and photographing two cookbooks, running Adventures in Cooking, her beautiful and inspiring blog, and constantly supporting the community.

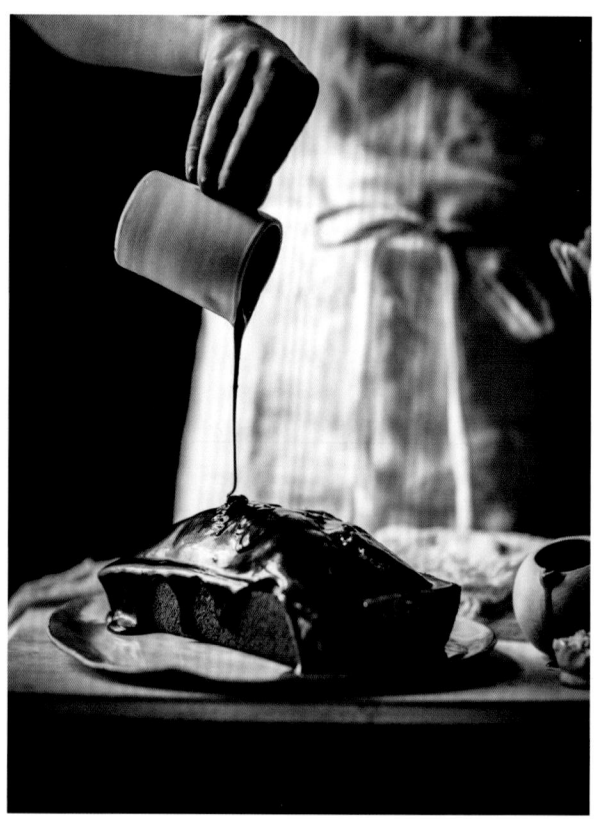

Being a food photographer is so much more than just perfect photography skills. What qualities have you learned to cultivate over the years to build a strong business?

I totally agree, being a successful food photographer requires a lot more than just taking great pictures. One of the most important qualities is organization, because being a successful food photographer also means being a successful small business owner, and owning a small business comes with a lot of moving parts and responsibilities. There are so many projects to keep track of, with different timelines and communications with clients to stay on top of, plus everything in the social media realm—it's a lot of stuff to keep in your brain. So for me, having an organized system for keeping track of my projects and staying on top of client communication has been a huge part of making my business successful. I'm obsessed with Asana task management software, and I have all my tasks outlined in my Google calendar so that I know what to tackle each day. It helps make sure I only commit to projects that I can follow through on and keeps me from feeling stressed because I have a structure in place to make sure nothing falls through the cracks. I talk a lot about this in my online courses, but I can't emphasize enough how important it is to stay organized and get a project management system in place that works for you.

Getting yourself out there and winning clients is one of the toughest parts of being a photographer. What was your breakthrough? And what advice would you give to other photographers?

I started through Instagram and that's still how I get the vast majority of my clients. The breakthrough came when I was included in one of Instagram's old "weekend hashtag" projects and was featured on the @instagram account, through which I gained around 30k followers in just a couple of days. It was insane! After that, I started getting emails from brands and companies that wanted to have images taken, and the business just grew from there.

As for advice, I'd recommend trying to get as good at photography as you possibly can. If you want to attract attention and grow an audience, the most efficient way to do it is to take beautiful photos. And the best way to do that is to always be learning. Take classes. Read books. Go to workshops. Whatever you can do to increase your skill level, do it. You'll also learn so much from collaborating with other artists and seeing how they shoot and approach situations. It's such an eye-opener and will really take your work to a new level.

What's the secret to managing your time to fit in everything you do?

I am a really efficient user of time and I also use time-blocking to help increase my productivity. So that basically means that I set aside X number of hours on X day to do one particular task. For example, I could set aside two hours to edit photos for a client project, and during those two hours I will do nothing else but that task. No getting up for tea. No phone nearby. Everything is on do-not-disturb mode. It really helps me get in the zone mentally for that task, and eliminating any other distractions helps me be much more prolific in terms of the quality and quantity of my work for the task at hand. I also try to do the most important work stuff when I have my own personal energy peak, which is the morning because I'm definitely a morning person. So when I'm scheduling all my tasks, I know that the most important ones should be done earliest in the day when I'm most effective and focused.

Do you ever feel scared of chasing your dreams or of the problems that may arise along the way? How do you not let the fear stop you?

I definitely do. I have a bit of a knack for setting insanely high expectations for myself, but not really realizing how absurd they are until much later on. Then, when I really think about it, I get scared because of the possibility of failure, or all the things that could go wrong. But then I think about what spurred me to set those goals and dream so big in the first place. It always comes back to passion. I truly believe that if you make your passion a part of your life, even in a small, part-time way, you will be better for it. So when I get nervous about my ambitions, I just focus on the light at the end of the tunnel, and summoning the confidence to know that I'll be able to tackle and solve the problems that come up.

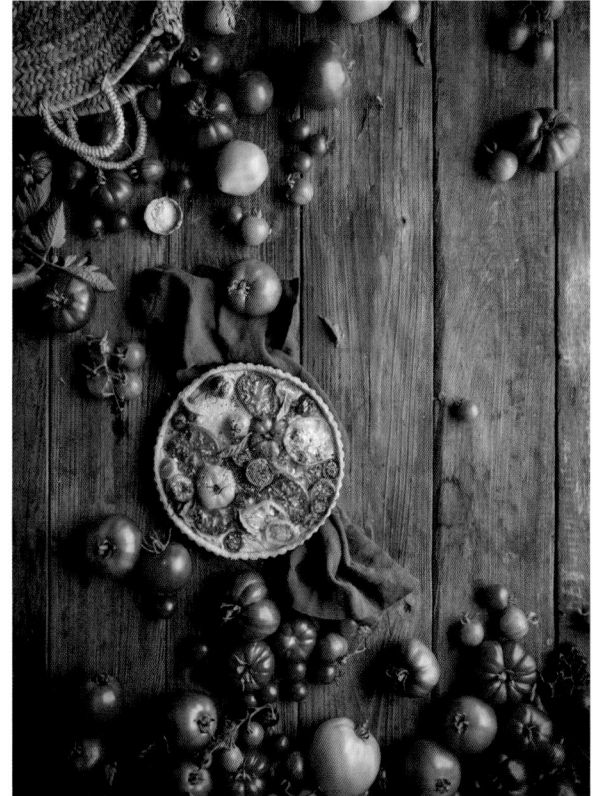

What are some of the lessons you've learned from years of running a photography business?

The biggest lesson I've learned has been to listen to my gut. Whenever I've felt hesitation in situations and haven't spoken up, the thing I was worried about ended up happening later on, every time. Your intuition exists for a reason and the sooner you learn to listen to it, the better. Part of being able to act on your gut instinct is having the courage to do so, and it's taken me a while to gain that. I do think that there's something to be said about knowing what you don't know in the beginning, and deferring to others who are more experienced and seriously considering their perspective. That being said, you need to really develop your confidence as you work so that you're able to honestly communicate what you want and need. There's a lot of balancing between being firm in your beliefs and limitations, and also being pleasant and easy to work with. I think a lot of that has to do with the way you communicate.

You've worked with many different creatives over the years and I have seen how good and considerate you are with other people. Why do you think it's important to work with others and how can you stay assertive and true to yourself at the same time?

Being respectful of other people's time and also just being nice in general is a moral standard for me. I can't stand it when people are mean or rude to others, whether in social or professional settings. It says a lot about a person's character, and I don't work with people who I've seen or heard to be unkind or disrespectful. It takes so much more energy to be mean or selfish—I just don't understand it. Kindness is free, and it feels good to be kind! Let's all just be nice to each other as the standard, shall we?

When you're working with a client, it's so important to be polite, timely, and respectful. It's easier to continue working with existing clients than it is to find new ones, and if you're a pain to email with, rude, or demanding, chances are your repeat clients are going to dwindle. On the flip side, it's incredibly important to be honest about any hesitations you have about a project, or anything that seems like it could be a problem down the line. So much of client communication is not as much about what you say, but how you say it. If you phrase your concerns in a way that shows the client that you want the project to be the best it can be, and these are just some things that you'd love to solve so that it will flourish, they'll be much more receptive than if you just say X, Y and Z aren't going to work and that's that. Don't save your concerns for until you're right in the midst of the issue you were worried about—it's much better to bring them up while there is still time to make a plan B.

As more and more food photography is being shared, what do you think it takes to stand out?

There's a really amazing book called *Steal Like an Artist* by Austin Kleon. In it, he talks about how all art is a form of theft, since we're all borrowing ideas and styles from each other all the time. But he talks about how

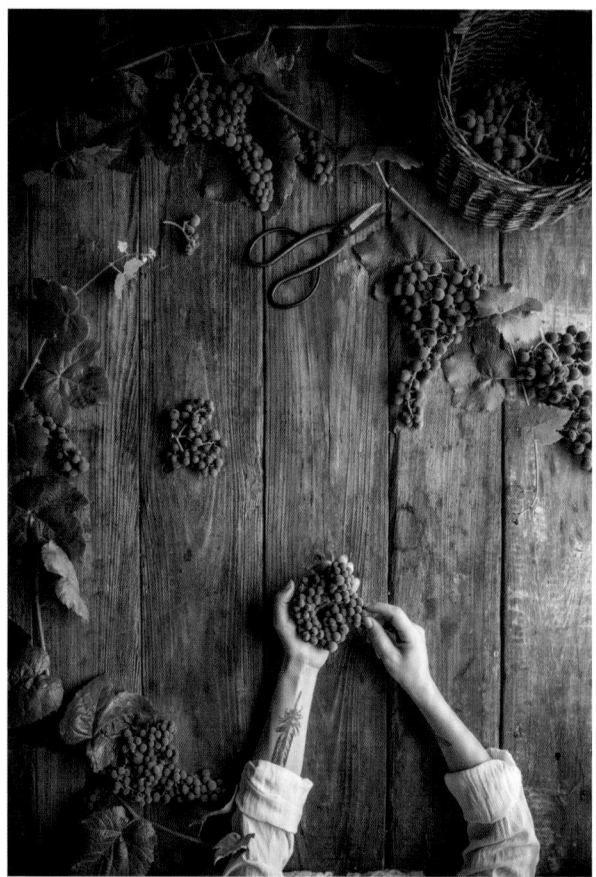

a bad artist borrows the work of one artist and copies it exactly. A good artist, on the other hand, borrows the work of many different people and uses it for inspiration to create something completely new. And I think that applies so accurately to standing out today. Open yourself up to all sources of inspiration, be they food, architecture, portraits, or fashion. See what you like and what you don't like, and combine all the things you're ecstatic about to create your very own style.

Have you got any tips about how to not let social media get inside your head?

Algorithms are the reason why some photos are liked or commented on more than others; it has nothing to do with your value as an artist or the quality of your work. If you are satisfied with your image, that is all that matters. What's important is that you're creating something beautiful and putting it out there to share with the world, whether it's 10 or 10,000 people who see it. Yes, of course it is frustrating when you're unable to reach everyone who has chosen to follow you. But at the same time, it can be liberating to realize that it is entirely out of your hands and all that you really have control over is what you create.

That knowledge makes me dive even more passionately into creating, because at that point, it's just for me and I don't have to worry about how people will engage with it. I just get to create what I think is captivating and what makes me happy to look at. And you know what? That imagery really resonates with people, because what *you* like is what *so many other people* like—it's the magic of the human condition. I also think that having healthy relationships outside of social media is really important, too. While socializing on the internet is fun and wonderful, and I've made so many incredible friends through it, there's no replacement for a warm real-life hug or a drink with a friend. It helps put the digital world in perspective when you're getting too in-your-head about it.

Also, don't play the comparison game. Everyone is showing the best side of their life on social media and not all of it is real. Nobody really has their stuff all together, and that's okay! We're all just chugging along in life, doing our best.

What is the best piece of advice you've received?
KISS: Keep It Simple, Stupid. It was a big piece of advice they told us in film school, back in the day—it's an oldie but it is so true on so many levels! The more complicated things become, the greater the chance of things going wrong and the more stressed you'll be. When it comes to work projects, your personal life, hobbies, travel plans, everything. As someone who is in my own head a lot, having too many moving parts going on really makes me anxious. But if I simplify everything and eliminate the unnecessary aspects of my life, it helps take all that anxiety away and makes me feel lighter and more free to create and live my life to the fullest. I can't recommend it highly enough.

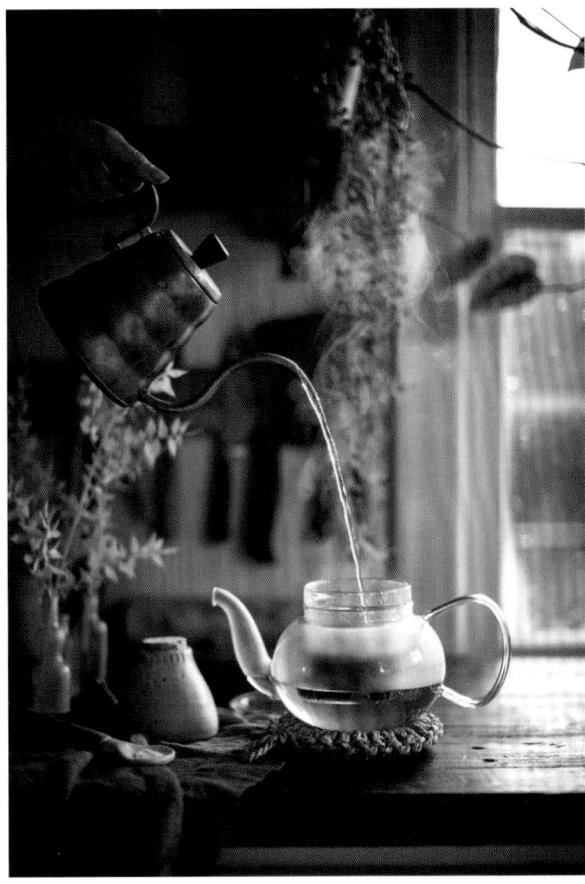

Be inspired by more of Eva's work at:
www.adventuresincooking.com
www.firstweeat.co
@evakosmasflores

Final words

February 2013

Sitting on the floor in the living room, with my back warming on the radiator and a laptop on my lap, I typed the words "food photography" into Google. I had got my first DSLR camera couple of months before, and I was still figuring out what to do with it, but the fact that the kitchen was my favorite place to photograph and that the camera was always covered
in flour gave me a good idea of the kind of work I wanted to create.

The second website that came up in that search was the Pink Lady Food Photographer of the Year competition. I said to my husband, "I am going to enter … next year." Darek looked at me with curiosity and asked, "And why not this year?" The answer was simple: I needed to get better; the deadline for entering the images was the next day, and I didn't have any good pictures. The competition was judged by the most influential people in the industry and I knew it was very unlikely that my work would catch anyone's eye, but I couldn't stop thinking about it. At the end of the day what did I have to lose? I looked through the handful of images that I had and entered one of a chocolate bar that I had taken a couple of days before.

Two months later, that photo was hanging on the wall in The Mall Galleries in London as one of the finalists. What's more, it came second.

We can't control luck—but we can help it

I often think about the experiences and opportunities that have come my way. Sometimes they've been due to the follow-up email I sent, the coffee I invited someone to, or the photography event I showed up at. At other times, it's been thanks to a conversation on social media or just by posting a photo that someone felt inspired by. Ambition, hard work, being eager to learn and improve your skills, and cultivating a strong mindset are what will make you a better photographer, but you also need a little bit of that magic luck for the right opportunities to show up at your door.

It's true that there are times when we bravely put ourselves out there, enter the photography contest or try to start a conversation—and nothing happens. But if you are patient enough though, if you stay open-minded, have no expectations, keep putting yourself out there, and take chances, you will be giving yourself more opportunities for that elusive luck to come along—and eventually, it will. Often when you least expect it.

Bea x

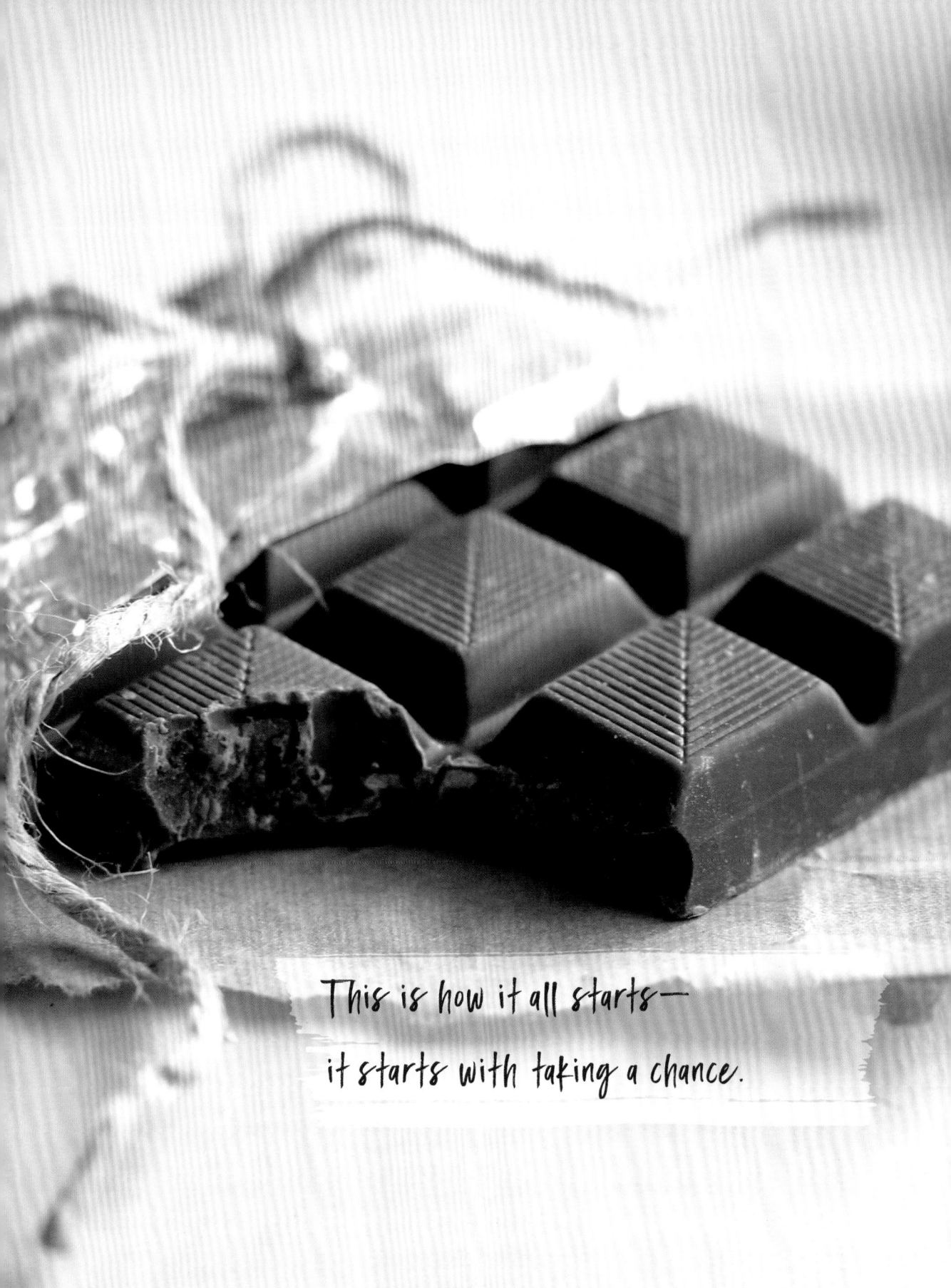

This is how it all starts—
it starts with taking a chance.

Index

A huge, heartfelt thank you

To you dear reader
Thank you for reading my thoughts about food photography and letting me share my experience with you. More than anything, I hope this book will encourage you to learn more. Take the ideas that you found inspiring and useful, put them into practice, reinvent them through your own lens, and go and inspire others.

To my wonderful family
Darek: I feel so lucky to have you in my life. Thank you for always being there for me, for supporting my dreams, and for signing up for this wild writing ride with me—even though it meant seeing your wife in joggers, with hair bun, no makeup, and with either a camera or laptop in front of her face for 14 months. Thank you for brewing endless cups of tea, for breakfasts in bed (every morning!), and for making sure I take vitamins. Thank you for believing in me before I believed in myself, for motivating me on the days when I was tired, for making me laugh on days I was being too serious, and for all needed hugs on days when nothing was going as planned. I love you.

Mum and dad: Thank you for always encouraging my creativity, for filling my life with delicious food, and teaching me the magic and power of stories and storytelling. Thank you for giving me the freedom to be who I wanted to be. I love you.

Daisy: For keeping me fit on our walks, greeting me with a wagging tail, and daily cuddles: you deserve a big treat.

To my lovely friends:
Claudia, Linda, Rachel and Eva: THANK YOU so much for saying a BIG YES to contributing to this book and sharing your genius creative minds with others. I am so grateful to know you: your incredible skills, talent, kind spirit, and generosity never stop inspiring me.

Amy: It was such a pleasure to work with you to create the gorgeous food scenes for the "Working with a food stylist" section. You are amazing at what you do.

To Ilex & Octopus:
Adam Juniper: Thank you for sending that first email, and for planting the seed in my mind that this book could actually be possible.

Alison Starling: Thank you for believing in this book, for listening, for supporting, and for your professionalism at every step of the way.

Stephanie Hetherington: Thank you for organizing my hefty first draft into a beautiful, reader-friendly structure.

Ben Gardiner and Leonardo Collina: I am so honoured and grateful to have you design this book. I could not be happier with the way it looks. Thank you for making it so incredibly special.

Rachel: This book wouldn't be possible without you. Thank you for caring about it as much as I do. For putting all your passion and smart ideas into this project. Thank you for patiently listening and for always speaking your honest opinion. I could not have asked for a better editor. I have learned so much from you. THANK YOU for helping me create a book that I am so proud of.

To my fellow food photographers:
You guys rock! Thank you for inspiring creative conversations around food photography and helping each other stay positive. Food photographers need to stick together, that's how we'll all grow!